BEHAVIOR AND ENVIRONMENT
The Use of Space by Animals and Men

BEHAVIOR AND ENVIRONMENT
The Use of Space by Animals and Men

Proceedings of an International Symposium held at the
1968 meeting of the American Association for the Advancement of Science
in Dallas, Texas

Edited by Aristide H. Esser

Letchworth Village
Thiells, New York

Ⓟ PLENUM PRESS • NEW YORK-LONDON • 1971

First Printing – January 1971
Second Printing – February 1972

Library of Congress Catalog Card Number 73-142038
SBN 306-30521-6

© 1971 Plenum Press, New York
A Division of Plenum Publishing Corporation
227 West 17th Street, New York, N. Y. 10011

United Kingdom edition published by Plenum Press, London
A Division of Plenum Publishing Company, Ltd.
Donington House, 30 Norfolk Street, London W.C. 2, England

Preface

The International Symposium on "The Use of Space by Animals and Men," sponsored by the Animal Behavior Society, took place at the 135th Annual Meeting of the AAAS in Dallas, Texas, on December 29-31, 1968. This book presents the text of all papers and edited discussions, as well as the contributions made by several individuals who were unable to attend the Symposium.

The idea of holding the Symposium evolved following my presentation of a paper to the Animal Behavior Society in 1965 [2] on the use of space by psychiatric patients. Members in attendance at that session, chaired by G. Gottlieb, shared his interest in my compilation of human data presented in a measurable spatial context. This pleasant experience persuaded me that a discussion of space might be shared as a frame of reference which could open avenues of communication between behavioral scientists, the design community, and the decision makers in our society.

Conceptual dichotomies in the study of behavior give rise to many interpretational difficulties and misunderstandings between biological, psychological and sociological disciplines. The science and technology of human life is not enhanced by narrow conceptualizations such as animal vs. human behavior, naturalistic observation vs. laboratory experiment, or innate mechanism vs. learned adaptation. Attempts are made regularly to reconcile these dichotomies with comprehensive theories intended to provide generally acceptable frameworks for productive communication. I tried to bypass discussion of dichotomies by establishing a setting that would encourage a mutual willingness among the investigators to listen to each other. The Symposium would be a "neutral" ground with appeal to representatives of factions who ordinarily would have little opportunity to meet for an open exchange of ideas. The use we make of the space we live in provides us with an as yet uncontested ground full of common, implicitly recognized but ill-defined problems in which scientists of all disciplines feel a keen involvement.

This proved to be the case. With very few exceptions, the scientists who had been invited were in agreement with the format and expressed a willingness to participate. The participants selected were chosen primarily for their firsthand research experience with projects involving spatial behavioral parameters. Other bases of

v

selection were: study objectives, scientific disciplines and geographical background. It was stipulated that formal presentations
would have to deal preponderantly with data derived from observations
on natural behavior. Subsequent discussions would stress experimental
and cultural influences [3].

It was fully recognized that the Symposium would be merely an
initial chapter in the discussions on the myriad aspects of the use
of space. It was believed impossible to include topics such as the
nature of the experience of space or its relation with time; the human transaction involved in the symbolic representations of space;
the occupation of space by species other than birds and mammals; and
a host of various other considerations.

Some inroads have been made into the study of the use of space
and certain directions of research are now visible. In the first
place, the meetings have emphasized the multidisciplinary character
of this investigation and the necessity for consciously choosing
this approach. The contributions by J.B. Calhoun and A.H. Esser
plead for an integration of findings from many scientific areas. It
is becoming clear that we are witnessing the emergence of a social
biology which has, in effect, a behavioral systems approach. Its
growth is spurred predominantly by data which, in past decades, were
within the domain of either ethology, ecology, or social psychology.
Social biology can now be said to deal with the evolutionary processes
of group-living animals. J.B. Calhoun stresses the role that space
plays in determining the manners of group-living individuals: a particularly striking and mysterious example of this process is demonstrated in his experiments in which the initial number of animals
inhabiting a place determines the final number of animals living when
the population reaches equilibrium. The test postulating a group
toxicity effect (differing reactions noted when a drug is administered
to an animal living alone or in a group [1]) illustrates another mysterious property of group living. These seemingly unrelated facts
may become organized into a concept which is able to explain why living in groups is advantageous to the evolution of many species, including man. In his lecture in the Frontiers of Science series, J.B.
Calhoun illuminated the important ancillary roles of many disciplines
in constructing this concept, a major strategy of Life. In point of
fact, the multidisciplinary discussions during the Symposium proved
that many previous restrictive uses of such concepts as territoriality
and dominance are obsolete. For instance, the contributions of P. Leyhausen, G. McBride and V.C. Wynne-Edwards lead from these immediately
visible components to an ultimate system structuring our life.

In the second place, an important contribution to the meeting
centered around the derailments in the quality of life subjected to
the constraints of the environment. K. Myers et al. offer much
new experimental information on the biological effects resulting from
different population densities. Supplementary reports and the dis-

cussions presented during Sessions 3 and 5 added further material and
highlighted again the need of an interdisciplinary interpretation of
such social factors as density and crowding. Although man's cultural
history has dealt, in some manner, with the various aspects of these
problems, it must be emphasized that the technical solutions at our
disposal to date are completely unsatisfactory; man must find radically different ways of relating to physical and conceptual space.

In the third place, much time was spent discussing the manner
in which animals and man overcome spatial constraints or use the environment itself in communication. E.T. Hall and I. Eibl-Eibesfeldt
provided, in their discussions, new insights into the heritage of human understanding, at the group level as well as at the individual
level. It is important to know how man can use available information
in seeking new avenues toward the compassionate understanding of his
fellow man. Methodological prejudice in this specific area not only
acts to the detriment of the scientific disciplines involved, but directly affects <u>man's relation to man</u>.

It may be said, in conclusion, that the Symposium increased our
interest in methodology; stress was placed on the importance of applying newly available techniques for data collection and analysis,
and in adopting approaches recently introduced in other disciplines.
Investigators, such as J.R. Tester, D.B. Siniff and C.R. Jensen discussed electronic data processing applied to the animal's use of
space. Other important innovations, particularly techniques for the
notoriously difficult observations of man, were represented in the
photographic techniques of R.E. Herron, E.T. Hall and I. Eibl-Eibesfeldt; and the observation methods discussed by I. Altman and R. Sommer.

The ultimate importance of the Symposium is achieved in the
<u>actual</u> meeting of the minds on this important issue and the realiza-
tion that a parochial approach no longer satisfies the requirements
for an understanding of behavior. An immediate outcome of the mutual
interactions which entered into play at the Symposium is to be found
in the correspondence between K.R. Barbehenn and P. Leyhausen, which
began immediately after the meetings and is published here. We look
forward to more of these dialogues, since so many participants discovered, to their amazement and pleasure, that they got along well
with each other. This was beyond expectation and it augurs well for
future multidisciplinary meetings.

The travel and maintenance of the foreign participants of the
Symposium was made possible by the generous contributions of my
friend Dr. M. Thorner, the Schering Corporation of Bloomfield, New
Jersey, the Population Council and the Psychiatric Research Foundation, both of New York. Miss Ellen Samson has been of great help
throughout all the phases of this Symposium. The administrative assistance of the Animal Behavior Society and the American Association

for the Advancement of Science, especially Dr. W.G. Berl and Mr. D. Thornhill, was deeply appreciated. Mrs. Harriet Goldstein was invaluable in the final preparation of this book. Dr. Virginia Hannon and Mrs. Lois Cohan offered important assistance in preparing the bibliographies and proofreading. Mr. N. Lambert prepared the illustrations, Miss S. Florentine helped in editorial research and Mrs. L. Bodnar assisted with typing.

I thank all the Symposium participants for their fine cooperation and the generosity of their contributions. I thank my wife, Ada, for the constancy of her assistance to the Symposium and to the preparation of this book.

Aristide Henri Esser
Symposium Organizer

New City, New York
April 69–August 70

REFERENCES

1. Chance, M.R.A.: Aggregation as a factor influencing the toxicity of sympathomimetic amines in mice. J. Pharmacol. Exp. Therap., 87:214–219, 1946.
2. Esser, A.H.: Social contact and the use of space in psychiatric patients. 132nd AAAS Meeting, Berkeley, 1965.
3. _____ : The use of space by animals and man. Science, 162:700–702, 1968.

Contents

SESSION II: SPACE AND CONTACT BEHAVIOR

AAAS FRONTIERS OF SCIENCE LECTURE III

Contributors

Irwin Altman, Naval Medical Research Institute, Bethesda,
    Maryland 20014*

Stuart A. Altmann, Yerkes Regional Primate Research Center,
    Emory University, Atlanta, Georgia 30322

J. Ralph Audy, The G.W. Hooper Foundation, San Francisco Medical
    Center, University of California, San Francisco,
    California 94122

Robert Ardrey, Piazza dei Mercanti 25, 00153 Roma, Italia

Edwin M. Banks, Department of Zoology, University of Illinois,
    Urbana, Illinois 61801

Kyle R. Barbehenn, Center for the Biology of Natural Systems,
    Washington University, St. Louis, Missouri 63130

J. LeGay Brereton, Department of Zoology, The University of New
    England, Armidale, N.S.W. Australia

John B. Calhoun, Unit for Research on Behavioral Systems, NIMH,
    9000 Rockville Pike, Bethesda, Maryland 20014

Charles C. Carpenter, Department of Zoology, The University of
    Oklahoma, Norman, Oklahoma 73069

Daniel Carson, College of Human Development, The Pennsylvania
    State University, University Park, Pennsylvania 16802

Kenneth K. Craik, Institute of Personality Assessment and Research,
    University of California, Berkeley, California 94720

Mario von Cranach, Max-Planck-Institut fur Psychiatrie,
    Kraepelinstrasse 2 und 10, 8 Munchen 23, Germany

David E. Davis, Department of Zoology, North Carolina State
    University, Raleigh, North Carolina 27607

Ireneaus Eibl-Eibesfeldt, Max-Planck-Institut fur
    Verhaltensphysiologie, Seewiesen, Germany

---

* Present address: Department of Psychology, University of Utah,
    Salt Lake City, Utah 84112

Henri F. Ellenberger, Faculte des Sciences Sociales, Universite de
          Montreal, Case Postale 6128, Montreal 26, Canada

Aristide H. Esser, Rockland State Hospital, Orangeburg, New York
          10962 and Letchworth Village, Thiells, New York 10984

Fred Fischer, Untere Zaune 9, 8001 Zurich, Switzerland

James M. Fitch, School of Architecture, Columbia University,
          New York, New York 10027

Frederick Gehlbach, Department of Biology, Baylor University,
          Waco, Texas 76703

C. S. Hale, CSIRO, Division of Wildlife Research, P.O. Box 109
          Canberra, Australia

Edward Hall, Department of Anthropology, Northwestern University,
          Evanston, Illinois 60201

R. E. Herron, Baylor College of Medicine, Texas Medical Center,
          Houston, Texas 77025

R. L. Hughes, Department of Zoology, University of New South
          Wales, Sydney, Australia

C. R. Jessen, Department of Ecology and Behavioral Biology,
          University of Minnesota, Minneapolis, Minnesota 55455

John R. Kaufmann, Department of Zoology, University of Florida,
          Gainesville, Florida 32603

Kenneth P. Kinsey, Department of Biology, Bowling Green State
          University, Bowling Green, Ohio 43402

Paul Leyhausen, Max-Planck-Institut fur Verhaltensphysiologie,
          56 Wuppertal-Elberfeld, Germany

James A. Lloyd, Division of Endocrinology and Reproduction,
          Albert Einstein Medical Center, York and Tabor Roads,
          Philadelphia, Pennsylvania

David Lowenthal, American Geographical Society, Broadway at 156th
          Street, New York, New York 10032

Halsey M. Marsden, Primate Ecology, Box 363, Lajas,
          Puerto Rico 00667*

_____

* Present address: Unit for Research on Behavioral Systems, NIMH,
          9000 Rockville Pike, Bethesda, Maryland 20014

William A. Mason, Delta Regional Primate Research Center, Tulane
          University, Covington, Louisiana 70433

Glen McBride, Animal Behavior Unit, University of Queensland,
          St. Lucia, Brisbane 4067, Queensland, Australia

Emil W. Menzel, Delta Regional Primate Research Center, Tulane
          University, Covington, Louisiana 70433

Griscom Morgan, Community Services, Inc., Yellow Springs,
          Ohio 45387

R. Moss, The Nature Conservancy, Banchory, AB33PS, Scotland

Kenneth Myers, CSIRO, Division of Wildlife Research, P.O. Box 109,
          Canberra City, Australia

R. Mykytowycz, CSIRO, Division of Wildlife Research, P.O.Box 109,
          Canberra City, Australia

Ulla Olin, United Nations Development Program, Private Address:
          230 Jay Street, Apt. 3C, Brooklyn, New York 11201

*Richard S. Peterson, University of California, Division of
          Natural Sciences, Santa Cruz, California 95060

Walter Sheppe, Department of Biology, The University of Akron,
          Ohio 44304

D. B. Siniff, Department of Ecology and Behavioral Biology,
          University of Minnesota, Minneapolis, Minnesota 55455

Robert Sommer, Department of Psychology, University of California,
          Davis, California 95616

Charles H. Southwick, Department of Pathobiology, The Johns
          Hopkins University, Baltimore, Maryland 21205

Raymond G. Studer, College of Human Development, Pennsylvania
          State University, University Park, Pennsylvania 16802

J. R. Tester, Department of Ecology and Behavioral Biology,
          University of Minnesota, Minneapolis, Minnesota 55455

Delbert D. Thiessen, Department of Psychology, University of
          Texas, Austin, Texas 78712

John G. Vandenbergh, Research Division, Dorothea Dix Hospital,
          Raleigh, North Carolina 27602

----

* Deceased, contact Burney J. LeBoeuf at same address

Adam Watson, The Nature Conservancy, Banchory AB33PS, Scotland

Bruce L. Welch, Memorial Research Center, University of
            Tennessee, Knoxville, Tennessee 37920 *

Vero C. Wynne-Edwards, Natural History Department, Marischal
            College, University of Aberdeen, Aberdeen, Scotland

* Present address: Maryland Psychiatric Research Center,
            Baltimore, Maryland 21228

Front row, left to right: J.L. Brereton, A. Watson, K. Myers, G.
                           R. Sommer, H. Ellenberger, I. Eibl-Eib
                           F. Fischer, M. von Cranach, P. Leyhaus

Second row, "   "   "   K. Barbehenn, J. Kaufman, E. Banks, C.
                           G. Gottlieb, E. Menzel, C. Southwick,
                           A.H. Esser, D. Lowenthal, K. Craik, J.

Third row, "   "   "   J.B. Calhoun, G. Morgan, U. Olin, R.G.

International Symposium on the Use of Space by Animals

December 31, 1968, Rose Room, Adolphus Hotel, Dallas T

The Importance of Defining Spatial Behavioral Parameters

Aristide H. Esser

ABSTRACT. *Viewed in the contexts of space and time, all animal behavior is inconspicuous; for only the young or diseased specimens of a species exhibit less than perfect adaptation to their physical environment. Our growing awareness of complex spatial relationships among objects, together with our perception of these relationships, enables us to determine the role they play in our lives.*

Most complex relationships are unconsciously determined patterns of action. But the emergence of Mind manifests itself in that precise moment when the structure of these relationships is recognized and primary reality is transformed into experienced reality. In the beginning of man's evolution, this transformation was accomplished exclusively through real movements. Later with the vertebrate stage of development, imagined or "virtual" movements were able to replace the actual acts. Of course, movement, as an objective given of our world, can only exist in perceptible space. It must be understood that perceptible space differs from species to species, from individual to individual.

If we were to study the experience of space in humans only, we would have no hope of arriving at essentials; for with Mind, all actions stem from mental images (either images of feelings [qualities] or of space-time relationships). More crucially, our mental images are indirect expressions of the realities which gave rise to them. In addition, mental images are altered; they become stereotyped during maturation. The essentials of spatial experience can only be understood by studying their antecedent history. This Symposium is to put into perspective our present knowledge of the evolution of <u>animal</u> perception of and reaction to space, in the hope of gaining access to those processes essential to our imagery.

1

All manifestations of life are determined by their locale. When this relationship is not apparent in their present forms, it should become apparent in their development. Implicitly, Man has always known this manner of Nature; but it took a Darwin to interpret that the inter-island differences of the individual Galapagos finches was due to natural selection, thereby creating one of the cornerstones of the theory of evolution [3].

We now also understand that the evolution of social behavior in different locales contributes to the chances of survival of groups. In 1922, Carr-Saunders described the principle of the optimum number in relation to habitat resources in the case of human populations [2]. Wynne-Edwards has made a general case for this principle in Animal Dispersion in Relation to Social Behavior, compellingly summarizing evidence that strict localization and adherence to conventional so- cial behavior patterns is advantageous to group selection [11]. We can therefore say that space as environment molds life. But, it is equally true that life influences the place in which it develops. Space, here, becomes place. This quality of life is just beginning to be discerned; i.e., that for the living being, space is not the abstract vacuum, separating objects, as it is considered in much of our scientific and technical thinking. Rather space, as place, is part of the manifestation of life (as an internalized action in man). As such, space becomes part of man's tacit knowledge.

A perfect harmony exists between the animal and his environment; therefore, its local evolution and its use of space is inconspicuous in nature. With man, however, the use of space has become conspicu- ous, and, in the comparatively short time of his evolution, he has irrevocably altered his original natural environment. The human pro- cess of incorporating space and the objects therein has helped to make man's domination of the earth possible. (The implications of this continuing process will be discussed by Calhoun in his Frontiers of Science Lecture [1]).

In human evolution, the collective memory of the incorporated, and thus imagined spatial relations, with the additional dimension of language, is responsible for most of our behavior. The first systematic studies of territory and peck-order, reflections of order in imagined object and space relations, date from the 1920's [5,9]. These basic ordering principles of behavior are endangered by the far- reaching and irrevocable changes which culture is causing in our bio- physical context. This awareness has come only recently and none too soon, as will be discussed in the other sessions of this Symposium.

When I tried to trace the first steps by which man was able to break the bonds of locale and its resources, my attention was drawn to the peculiar development of the mental images which allow us the conscious experience of space. According to Rothschild, imagined movements replaced actual acts only in vertebrates [8]; only these animals can experience space without actually doing something in it, (e.g., traversing it).

Lorenz tells a remarkable story about the so-called path-habit in King Solomon's Ring [6]. He watched young shrews explore their caged environment, dashing back to their familiar "home" periodically to make sure they knew how to get there when necessary. They did this not by going straight into the door but by jumping on the roof, falling over and scurrying up through the opening; just as they had done the first time they ran "home." And they contrived to do so even after each animal knew its surroundings perfectly well. Only the shrew's memory of the spatial relations experienced at the time it made its first successful retreat can be responsible for this behavior. This memory is the recognition of the structure of reality through exact reproduction of the sequential movement patterns which in the past had dealt successfully with this reality. In psychoanalytic terms, we can attribute this early memory to what is called reality-testing, appearing for the first time when the infant recognizes the changes in his environment caused by his motor actions.

Human memory has grown millennia beyond this stage of reliance on direct motor images. Mind emerged when the rigidity of sequential instinctive motor actions was broken up, bit by bit, in the process of experiencing. Experience remains a mysterious faculty, because so much of it relies on unconscious perception. Polanyi recently summarized why the particulars of much of our perception, and hence our knowledge, are as yet inaccessible to analysis. Polanyi calls this knowledge, which cannot be reduced to specifics, tacit knowledge, and he doubts that man will ever be able to particularize it [7]. This scientifically unfortunate fact may be the essence of our being: if our mind uses the substrate of our brain to experience, how are we to perceive and analyze this particular substrate function?

Piaget has remarked that, in the development of the human infant, the concept of unitary space begins as an active manipulation of objects in near space. Only after near space has become a perceptual part of the self - has been incorporated - can the infant construct objective, spatial relations among objects [4]. The theory that ontogeny recapitulates phylogeny applies to the mind as well as to the brain. Rothschild has underlined the importance of our capacity to influence the experience of real movements with that of virtual movements by pointing out the structural counterparts of this capacity in our central nervous system [8]. The evolution of our brain reflects the evolution of our mental images and their connections, especially in the visual sphere so important to our perception of space. And this capacity for imagery enabled the higher animals and man to represent, mentally, object relations in the immediately perceptible space. More importantly, man evolved in the experiencing of time the capacity to control his reactions to the immediate

environment. Finally, the combined space-time imagery enables man
to conceptualize abstractly and to shed the environmental control of
his actions by sequential ordering of their images.

One might be tempted to think that, by the processes that helped
unshackle us from the bonds of our immediate physical space, our
mind has achieved independence from the environment. If we integrate
with our social matrix in new ways, such as the one Calhoun suggests
[1], this may come about in our future evolution. But it is not the
case at present, and two reasons which prevent our optimal conceptualization of man-environment relations can be identified.

In the first place, there is no generally accepted theory of the
phylogeny of the human space-time perception. This is due, in part,
to the difficulty of the subject matter, since the many scientific
disciplines, with their detailed knowledge of its aspects, can still
not find enough common ground to come to integration. This cannot
be helped, but what can be helped is the other part responsible for
this lack of perspective. The behavioral sciences, whose data will
have to form the framework for the panorama, seem to impede their
own progress with obsolete discussions on the particulars of this
broad behavioral scene. The continuing controversy concerning the
relative importance of innate or learned behavior factors obscures
the importance of specific behavior in the formation of our mental
images. For instance, as a research psychiatrist, I would prefer to
draw analogies between animal territorial defense and what are called
defense mechanisms of the ego in psychoanalytic terminology, rather
than quibble over the question whether man is territorial by nature.

This brings us to the other factor preventing clear thinking on
man-environment relations. Not only do our individual mental images
recapitulate their phylogeny, but they have become almost the only
means of our contact with reality. We, therefore, partake only indirectly in each others' scene, and we must begin to realize that we do
not share vast areas of the perceived environment. In this respect,
each of us lives in his own world.

At this point, I should refer briefly to some formulations regarding the formation of mental images, derived from psychopathology,
which unfortunately extended beyond the limit of this Symposium. In
the beginning of this century, Freud made the first crude formulations
about the role of our unconscious in daily life. Since then, we have
increased our understanding of the relationships of different parts
of our mind, which, by whatever name they may be labelled, always refer back to the images of our early childhood. These images are extremely malleable during certain critical periods in our life, e.g.,
the pre-school years and puberty. But they tend to become stereotyped in the course of reaching adulthood. Anybody who has tried to
influence their shapes and relationships (and that is what teaching,
psychotherapy, advertising, etc. is all about) knows that it is very

hard to change someone else's mind at this stage. In mental illness,
it proves sometimes impossible to change the faulty interplay of
images without first interfering with the brain function itself, e.g.,
by the use of drugs and brain surgery. If we understand from this
perspective how aberrant, deformed and rigid our mental images may
be, then we can begin to see why these very building blocks of our
mind prevent us from reflecting our psycho-sociophysical environment
clearly.

To emphasize the crucial and as yet not precisely definable role
which individual spatial mental images play in our life, may I tell
you something of my growing-up.

I am part Asian, born in the native surroundings of Indonesia,
a beautiful land of grandiose proportions and with a multitude of
quiet, gentle people. On the island of Java where I lived, plains,
ravines and mountains are fully cultivated without a loss of their
natural contours. With a population of more than 1000 per square
mile, it belongs to the most densely populated areas in the world.
Yet, the beauty of its landscape and the relaxed, open mind of its
people produced in me images of freedom in an unlimited beautiful
world.

Where as a child I experienced this large-scale environment, as
an adolescent I breathed in a small-scale European milieu. Holland,
the country which gave me my schooling, looked ridiculously petite
when I arrived by boat. The flat land with its obviously man-made,
neatly spaced, small areas in which people were constantly on the
move has, in an oppressive manner, superimposed on my naive feelings
of freedom a preoccupation with being "right" morally as well as
technically. Psychologically, these developmental images cannot
blend entirely without harming each other. It is fortunate that my
images from these contrasting environments came about in their order,
since it is easier to clear the mind of adolescent rather than of
childhood impressions. I had to relegate the imprint of life in Holland to its proper place in order to allow the optimism of my Indone-
sian images to blend with the prevalent American spatial image: wide
horizons offer unlimited opportunities. Even if it is, unfortunately,
an infantile view of the largesse that Nature displays toward Man, I
am happy to share the stereotyped American image: "The sky is the
limit."

The above represents one part of my tacit knowledge, the experience that space molds life. The other part is formed by my experience of how life influences the space it inhabits. In Indonesia,
culture blended with nature. The changes which humans brought about
in their environment seemed in accord with a pre-conceived harmony
in our universe, as many Eastern philosophers have it. The process
of my growing up took place within that natural surrounding; I remember the sea, mountains, a lake, a village with rice terraces and

garden plots. In this warm and friendly childhood climate, where
little work was needed to guarantee a living from the extraordinarily
fertile soil, only my Holland-directed primary school education prepared me for the cold, hard-working and reserved attitude of the spatially limited Dutch. Holland, in its history, exemplifies the hard-
headed determination with which man literally creates his place under
the sun using the most advanced technology to wrest more and more
acres of living space from the sea. Again, there is no doubt that
this perpetual quest of the Dutch has led to a stereotyped image of
what man can achieve against Nature. Some say: "God may have created the world, but the Dutch certainly made Holland." This self-
sufficient attitude of the Hollanders has been sustained by their
adoption of regimented societal life styles with strong cultural
sanctions against those who look for a more universal frame of reference. My personal concern with the adverse effects of such rigid
stereotyped self-images has been reflected recently when Lynn White
wrote: "In their epic combat with Neptune, have the Netherlands
overlooked ecological values in such a way that the quality of human
life in the Netherlands has suffered? I cannot discover that the
questions have ever been asked, much less answered." [10]

I would like us all to think of such questions and their answers.
Reflecting from my present day position and style of life, I can only
hope that the images brought about by the singular freedom of mind in
the U.S.A. will not become disfigured by our increased reliance on
technology. If we want to know the shape of our future life, we will
have to conceptualize without the pressure of present-day commitments
and regardless of the limitations of present-day techniques, as we
will try to do in the last session of this Symposium.

Now that I have tried to particularize the framework of tacit
knowledge responsible for my own concern with the topic of this Symposium, I can return to its substance. The participants in this
meeting, and I include the members of the audience under this rubric,
will try to piece together the outline of what can be seen as a jigsaw puzzle representing our common understanding of the space around
us. In so doing we realize that we reduce the dimensions and that
many of our formulations are not only tentative but will also, of necessity, be incomplete, because our language cannot adequately convey
the rich variations in our spatial and temporal experience. This
Symposium hopes to provide the basis for the development of a scientific terminology for spatial behavioral research.

There are some aspects of spatial behavior which can presently
be defined reasonably well, and the Symposium has sessions devoted
to conflict resolution, crowding and communication. The methodology
evolved for the study of these topics has been much strengthened by
recent technical progress in data acquisition and processing. It is
to be hoped that these established techniques will allow observation
and experiment, and will thus define additional parameters which may

illuminate the evolution of our spatial behavior. There are many
instances in which such knowledge would have immediate practical consequences. For instance, it might answer the question whether the
theory that our social behavior goes back to the spatial organization
of groups of 12 of small rodents can be linked to the fact that rats
and mice have been a successful model for the human in biochemical
and pharmaceutical research. If we look at the brain as a social organ, the analogy in the backgrounds of human and rat social behavior
would justify extrapolations from the reactions of neurohormones to
psychotropic drugs in the rat to identical processes in the human.
A further consequence: If the evolution of the biochemistry of our
brain follows the evolution of our social behavior, we would then
have a new parameter in determining which of the non-human primates
is the appropriate animal for psychopharmacological research.

Our many areas of theoretical interest are to lead directly to
the concern for practical human problems. The _kind_ of growing, present-day, popular concern about man-environment relations reflects
our society's helpless awareness of its loss of perspective. Our
culture and our individual behaviors reflect the images we have of
this world and of ourselves. We, here, should use our multidisciplinary knowledge of the evolutionary perspective to understand the increasing magnitude of the effects our mental images have on our universe. Our recent success in completing the first orbiting of the
moon has changed nothing in our present conceptualization of space.
But the fact that men have actually moved around another planet will
undoubtedly influence our future spatial concepts. I am convinced
that the progress of our exploration of outer space is a complement
to the progress of our exploration of inner space - the Mind.

REFERENCES

1. Calhoun, J.B.: Space and the Strategy of Life, Frontiers of Sci-
        ence Lecture, AAAS 135th Meeting, Dallas, 1968, in this
        volume.
2. Carr-Saunders, A.M.: The Population Problem: A Study in Human
        Evolution. Oxford, 1922.
3. de Beer, G.: Atlas of Evolution. Nelson, London, 1964.
4. Flavell, J.H.: The Developmental Psychology of Jean Piaget.
        Van Nostrand, Princeton, 1963.
5. Howard, E.: Territory in Bird Life. Murray, London, 1920.
6. Lorenz, K.: King Solomon's Ring. Thomas Crowell, New York, 1952.
7. Polanyi, M.: The Tacit Dimension. Doubleday, Garden City, 1966.
8. Rothschild, F.S.: Das Zentral Nerven System als Symbol des
        Erlebnis. Karger, Basel, 1957.
9. Schjelderup-Ebbe, T.: Beiträge zur Biologie und Sozial- und
        Individual Psychologie bei Gallus Domesticus. Greifs-
        wald, 1921.
10. White, Jr., L.: The historical roots of our ecological crisis.
        Science, 155:1203-1207, 1967.

11. Wynne-Edwards, V.C.: Animal Dispersion in Relation to Social
       Behavior. Hafner, New York, 1962.

Ten Phases of the Animal Path: Behavior in Familiar Situations

Fred Fischer

INTRODUCTION

Spatial relationships govern animal life to a degree scarcely comprehensible to man. However, even the most tangible aspects of such relationships remain fleeting and are radically altered by the slightest movement or change of position. For the purpose of our discussion, unarticulated space is essentially irrelevant. We shall confine our remarks to spatial change induced by movement, juxtaposing unfamiliar and familiar space.

All changes in the animal's distance relationships develop along paths. Under certain sets of conditions, the animal's change of position leaves traces or tracks which may be marked or signposted by the animal. The paths, "established" in this manner, have concrete spatial delineation. They may be delineated on four sides (e.g., a corridor), on three sides (e.g., a hollow path or gallery), on two sides (e.g., a traverse) or on one side (e.g., an animal run in the snow). The paths may be visible or, as in the case of an air corridor, invisible. Each path, even if used frequently, remains unique and is strictly determined by a variety of factors. When first created, it is called a virgin path. The "run" is a particular form of the habitual or familiar path. Hediger [9, p.44] has defined the run as the regularly used path of communication between fixed points in the animal's living space.

The first position, prior to the path proper, is the point of departure. From here on, all the points along the path are ordered within a specific hierarchy - the path hierarchy - and may be fixed by subjective markers [18, p.90]. Thus we see a strictly determined

and irreversible relationship between the subject and its environment. In this respect, the animal path may be compared to the course
of a river. In any event, it is important to realize that the animal path, irrespective of its dimensions, is a part of the animal's
life pattern. And the path hierarchy is, in effect, a mirror of the
animal's space-time experience.

The first distinction we must make is between the home and the
destination or goal. Between these twin aspects, the animal path
may be broken down into individual component parts such as the single
step, the movement of a wing or a fin, in short, any single action
within the development of the path between one point and the next or
between one hazard and the next. In English, the word "away" takes
the home as its orientation, the home being taken as a starting-point.
In Greek, on the other hand, "hodos" implies movement towards a goal.
This twin orientation is present at every single point along the animal path, since each step is a movement away from a "home" towards a
"goal". The home is left when unrealized individual desires need to
be fulfilled. The goal becomes "desirable" because it is the point
where certain desires and needs can be fulfilled.

The path itself may be broken down into a number of phases with
corresponding characteristic (objective) behavior and characteristic
(subjective) moods. These phases vary with motivation and with the
animal's relation to conspecifics. It is vital to realize that each
individual phase must be seen both as a component part of the path
and as a separate entity.

The phases may be designated as follows:

The need for change of location: *Das Bedurfnis zum Ortswechsel*
The start integration   : *Die Integration zum Start*
The first step   : *Das Einpendeln des Weges*
The outward stretch   : *Der Streckenhinweg*
Before the goal   : *Der Zielbann*
At the goal   : *Am Ziel*
The turnabout   : *Die Umkehr*
The return stretch   : *Der Streckenruckweg*
The approach to the home   : *Die Annaherung ans Heim*
Entering the home   : *Die Einheimung*

PHASE 1: THE NEED FOR CHANGE OF LOCATION

The animal's initial impulse to move is induced by a need for
a change of location. The path thus takes on something of a "personal" aspect. The reasons may be endogenic or exogenic in origin –
the appearance of an enemy, a threat to the home, climatic change,
instinctive compulsions, hunger, thirst or pathological states. On
the other hand, the animal may be motivated by the simple need to explore, to be "on the move". This drive, in its relation to the ani-

mal's environment, is the antithesis of sleep, which manifests itself
as a withdrawal from the environment. The impulse to be on the move
springs from the diffuse state of awakening and leads to appetitive
behavior which, in turn, prompts the animal to move from one location
to another, either to establish contact or to avoid contact.

One special aspect of this impulse is the need for movement pure
and simple. Both man and a great number of animals are obliged to
live in a border zone between earth and air. These two aggregate
conditions result in an incomplete mechanical adaptation of the body.
In the marine world of primeval history, the situation was quite different. Modern movement therapy, which includes hydrotherapy, thus
corresponds to a natural necessity. In cases of pathological restriction of movement, as in forced bedrest, serious decubitus, or bedsores,
will develop. Indeed, with the need for movement on the one hand and
the energy output required by man's phylogenetically upright position
on the other, we are, biologically speaking, "between the devil and
the deep blue sea". In the case of many marine creatures, movement
is essentially a means of combatting the current and remaining in contact with their original environment. By dint of a negative rheotaxis,
the creature's environment has come to be decisive for its locomotion.
Rheotropism, the phenomenon of roots growing against the pull of the
current, is an indication of how the plant attempts to strive towards
its goal. Paradoxically, plant life is far more effective in "secur-
ing" its "path" than animal life. The source of vegetative growth
in space is perhaps analogous to the animal need to explore space.

PHASE 2:   THE START INTEGRATION

If the original need to be on the move is not superseded or is
canceled (e.g., when a threat of danger has passed), the animal pre-
pares to move off. This preparation is characterized by a series of
locomotor actions which precede actual movement away from the point
of departure. The position of the body is induced by the movements
of the individual organs. To express this more simply: in order to
pluck an apple from a tree I may have to do no more than stretch out
a hand, or, I may have to take a few steps. In other words, the
phases of the animal path may be seen as a "pattern of behavior which
is governed by a variety of compulsions" [13, p. 133]. There is a
definite distinction between body movement with and body movement
without a change of location, as Leonardo da Vinci noted some centuries ago: "The simple movement may be divided into two parts. The
body may move about its own axis without changing position...or the
whole may move from its original position." [12, p.451] The path becomes a consumptive process, when an economic balancing of the desirability of the goal and the effort required to reach it occurs.

The phenomenology of the path may be seen as a system of waves
and wave patterns which are of different sizes and which overlap.
Each small undulation corresponds to the overall pattern, and the

overall pattern is mirrored in the smallest undulation. The "integration" or "preparatory" phase before the first step is actually taken is like the drive to the airport before take-off. Or: "The alpha male in a group of primates will move off first, in his typically stiff-legged gait, and will thereby create a general pattern of movement for the others to follow." [11, p.80]

The entire process of integration before moving off is highly diverse, either varying with a change in locomotion or with an extension of a movement or position already present. Thus, for example, the grazing animal does not have to rise to its feet before taking flight. The process of orientation is also part of this integration phase, whether it be a movement of the head or a "false start".

The concept of "beginning" is etymologically related to the word "yawn" (originally in the sense of "open", "encompass") and is, in effect, indicative of an oral function. The environment is encompassed by the mouth, the hands and feet - by swallowing, by processing and movement. In the case of "swallowing" the situation is slightly different inasmuch as the body organs come to represent the environment and the paths through it. In the case of movement there is, in vertebrates, a phylogenetic development from caudal (the fish's tail) to cranial: the process of movement becomes "plurilocal". The process of movement, i.e., the drive and the direction, forms a functional entity in the animal organism.

The first two phases can be seen as preliminary phases which, when interrupted or disturbed in some way, will demonstrate their connection with the entire development of the path. Thus, the absence of a need to flee from danger (Phase 1) can be as dangerous to man or animal as would be a broken leg (Phase 2).

PHASE 3:   THE FIRST STEP

In the third phase, the inner need to make a move is complemented by the external possibilities provided by the path. Openings and obstacles in the environment determine the development the path will follow. The subject is influenced by matter and forces (i.e., terra firma, water, air, gravity, friction, the rotation of the earth). Under terrestrial conditions at least the space through which the path leads is never a total vacuum. Leonardo da Vinci pointed out that change in the body position is a dislocation: "That which moves gains as much space as it loses." [12, p.22] The sense organs (in humans, also artificial aids) make it possible to establish immediate contact over a distance and to avoid collisions by taking evasive action. Pushing and restraining (as externals) correspond to compulsion and hesitation (as internals).

The transition from the stationary position has not only loco-

motor aspects but also aspects specific to the path itself. The subtlety of the first change of place or dislocation with the first step
springs from the fact that, in walking, each foot comes down on a different and specific point. (Stumbling can be, quite literally, a
Freudian slip!)

Provided there are no pathological barriers, every living creature - given its appropriate environment and depending on its physiological make-up - can commence moving with those organs best adapted
to the path to be followed. Even minute deviations from the anatomi-
cal norm - minor aches and pains - will lead to an individual difference in the first step. In man, right-handedness is known to be pre-
dominant. On the march, however, the step is called on the left foot.
The statistical analysis carried out by Braus [2, p.18] reveals that
in humans the upper right extremity and the lower left extremity are
more strongly developed. Similarly, observations relating to cross-
gaited animals - these have to be fully confirmed - show that, all
things being equal, the first step is more frequently taken with the
front right extremity. With equal reservations, one may also remark
that in many species of fish the first movement of the tail is more
frequently to the left.

Apart from an individual difference, one may also assume a genetic difference which can perhaps be traced back to the pressures
of natural selection, the geo-physical causes of which are the rotation of the earth and the Coriolis forces.

The path commences with the pendulous movement of the first step,
just as the course of a mountain stream is dictated by accumulated
water, the incline, the bed of the stream, and geo-physical forces.
Many ritualized start patterns may, in fact, spring from the conflict
between the home and the goal. The circling of the philanthus trian-
gulum, a species of wasp, is an impressive example of this conflict
[19, p.17].

Acceleration of movement results in a locomotor "straightening"
or "stretching" of the path. Haste - which causes a fleeting assessment of environmental factors, leads to a sensorially determined
"straightening". As the path is stretched, contact with the environment is reduced. A meandering of the path leads to an increase in
contact with the environment. In following a path, the animal continually requires impulses which will overcome the opposition of its
environment. In other words, the animal path is experienced as a
struggle against forces which act against movement. (The psychological concept of "aggression" derives thus quite logically from the
Latin "ag + gredi", "to move forward".)

The straightness of the path is relative. It is vital, however,
to avoid the mistake of confusing the "eye-path" with the "foot-path".
In these days, when many means of transportation enable us to reach

our destination by the most direct routes and irrespective of obstacles, the subtlety of the animal organism in finding a path is
often overlooked. The path between the point of departure and the
destination can be thought of in terms of periodic, a-periodic, sub-
ject-determined or environment-determined wave structures within and
around the axis of orientation. The desire to spend as little time
as possible in "foreign" space leads, spatially speaking, to the
bridge between the two points being made as short as possible. Caution also dictates the choice of gait and its wave pattern. The constant tendency to turn around for reassurance is particularly noticeable on the outward stretch and must be taken into account in the
wave patterns. Hediger's maxim [10, p.10] that "animal paths are
never straight over longer stretches, but tend to meander" is, biologically speaking, by no means a contradiction of one of Leonardo
da Vinci's most celebrated observations [1, p.11]: "Every process
in nature is completed along the shortest way possible."

PHASE 4:   THE OUTWARD STRETCH

The outward stretch continues from the pendulous starting movement and stops at the point before the goal. It is dominated both
spatially and temporally by the obstacle of "distance". In fish,
we find that the further away they are from home the less prepared
they are to engage in fighting and the more ready they are to flee
[14, p.13]. The animal divides the outward stretch (and also the
return stretch) into two sections - the stretch behind him and the
stretch which is still to come. This relationship has engendered
the concept of "the half-way point" which has associations with
time, supply, obstacles and danger. At the half-way point one can
turn back. (The airline pilot knows this as the point-of-no-return.)

The new and unfamiliar is determined by the old and the familiar,
as illustrated by the process of birth. Environment and goal are subject to a metamorphosis of apperception due to the change in distance
relationships. Every outward stretch carries the stigmata of self-
control and self-denial: it marks a renunciation of the home in favor of a risky undertaking. On this outward stretch, the behavior
of both man and animal is particularly circumspect. When they move
together in a group, the closed formation and its implied rigid hierarchy can be seen as fulfilling a protective function [11, p.79]. The
outward stretch passes through the foreign space and no-man's land,
engendering insecurity and loneliness. Distance and time are in the
foreground.

Every outward stretch is a difficult experience. When a patient
visits his doctor and leaves in a better frame of mind, the improvement in his spirits is, at least in part, due to the fact that he has
mastered the outward stretch. The same is true of every undertaking
which has a specific goal. Human disinclination to return by the
same way may well be related to the memory of the spiritual stresses

of the outward stretch.

PHASE 5:   BEFORE THE GOAL

The subject enters the final stretch from the moment he per-
ceives the goal. The successive integration of sensory impressions
which comes with the approach to the goal may make the goal more appealing or may lead to disinterest. The goal as imagined need not
be identical with the goal in reality. Man is often disappointed in
his great expectations. In man, this final stretch before the goal
can begin with a pre-conceived notion. Optical, acoustic, olfactory
and tactile impressions superimpose themselves on this "image" and
supply correctives to it. The sequence of sensory perceptions involved in the integration of the final stretch may vary with the species. The relationship between the appearance of a final stretch
component and the distance involved is important in order to trans-
mit the sensory impression into a motor impulse. Thus, the final
spurt must not start too early, lest the subject exhaust himself too
soon. The orientation hierarchy can be dangerously disturbed if the
sensory impressions of the goal emerge in an unfamiliar sequence. A
mother's call from across a busy street will disrupt her child's pru-
dence. Where the sequence of movements is instinctive, a change in
environmental relationships will lead to meaningless activity. "Ducks
which are fed grain on land still act as if they were looking for food
in the water." [13: ch. 4, p.60] It is most likely that there exists
a critical distance between the subject and the goal. This emerges
as a caesura in the subject's forward motion. Depending on circumstances, the ensuing movement will be either accelerated or deceler-
ated. Fear of the goal ("Our difficulties grow as we approach our
goal" [13]) and intoxication with the goal ("He who approaches his
goal begins to dance with joy" [15]) lead to various modes of behavior before the goal.

Different sets of relationships arise when the goal is mobile,
when it is missed, when it has to be avoided or when it suddenly disappears from sight. If the primary goal cannot be reached, the outward stretch is continued in the pursuit of a secondary goal. In
case the goal is forgotten or renounced, the outward stretch will be
followed by a turn and the immediate commencement of the homeward
stretch. If the goal can be neither attained nor postponed, there
will be either a physiological substitute for the goal or death of
the subject.

PHASE 6:   THE GOAL

The subject is driven towards the goal by the need for contact
with it. In the case of ungulates, F. Walther [10, p.43] sees the
need for contact as the antithesis of territoriality. Hunger and
thirst, rivalry, sexual drives specifically characterize behavior
during the outward stretch.

Motor activity subserves the goal as an object which is spatially separated from the subject. That which cannot be reached via
simple organ movement must be attained by means of locomotion. Thus
there are measures which act at and over a distance. These are: the
actual physical movement along the way; (*Greifsprache*) the active language of touch which sends out voice, gesture, sight and scent (as opposed to the *Tastsprache* which is the passive language of touch which
hears, sees and smells); and the distance weapon, such as a bolas, a
boomerang, a bullet or even spittle. It is no coincidence that the
German *"Ziel"* (= goal) derives from the Gothic *"tila-rids"* (literally = aiming at a goal), the expression used for "spear".

The path appears as a developing tool which, as an intermediary
member, connects the subject's arm with the object to be grasped.
This motor connection becomes evident in the case of transportation
via a funicular, a tow-ferry, a conveyor belt, or a moving staircase.
In all these constructions, the substratum of the path becomes a path
machine.

The goal or destination is reached when contact between the subject and the object has been established, either directly or indirectly (for example, via a weapon). The goal is consummated at the moment of contact. In all, three different types of contact can be
distinguished:

1. Reversible contact between object and subject. Among the
inanimate objects are the location of the goal itself, light conditions, temperature conditions; among animate objects are various
forms of partnership.

2. Irreversible contact with the object: stripping of the
goal, capturing prey, killing an enemy.

3. Irreversible contact for the subject as in fertilization
or death of the subject, e.g., in battle.

The presumptive goal and the actual goal are not one and the same
thing. At the goal, the distance between the point of departure and
the point of arrival has been covered and the outward stretch is at
a close. The change of location has ended and the consummation of
the goal begins, ending when the potential of the goal has been fully
exploited. When the goal has been reached and has been exploited, a
process of re-assessment begins. The subject's relation to its environment is revised. The goal, as such, has disappeared. It has
disappeared like a piece of meat which a dog has eaten and around
the traces of which it continues to sniff. The goal continues to
exist only in the memory of the individual or of the species (where
it emerges like a Phoenix from the biological ashes). The goal
phase marks the burial of the goal: "a consummation devoutly to be
wish'd". [17]

There are goals whose attainment marks the end of the path, such as in the case of the new-born kangaroo, which moves only once, from the genital aperture of the mother into the mother's pouch. The adult human frequently leaves the parental territory, never to return except in his imagination; there the outward stretch is completed in reality, the return stretch in the imagination. For some, the life process itself is an outward stretch with no return; for others, death is the return.

PHASE 7: THE TURNABOUT

The turnabout is the beginning of the return stretch. In primates, "the point of turn is often a significant point in the landscape, e.g., a thick wood or a hill" [11, p.79]. We should like to distinguish the physiological turning of the body from the turnabout point as a phase of the animal path. They are related to each other in three ways: the turn may precede the turnabout, the two may coincide or the turn may follow the turnabout. The turnabout can be made via a circling turn or by a figure-eight turn. In the latter case, there may then be a false or a genuine crossing of return stretch and outward stretch. On level ground, the turnabout can be with an actual turn to right or left or without a turn (extended turnabout), forwards or backwards. The most genuine example of an extended turnabout forwards is the circumnavigation of the earth; an extended pseudo-turnabout forwards is found in the search for an ad hoc home. Spatially speaking, we can also distinguish an upwards and a downwards turn. Here, the turn mechanisms deserve attention not only as technical but also as psychological phenomena. The turnabout is an undertaking which has grave consequences inasmuch as it radically changes the aspect of the path. The turn itself is not without its share of difficulties. The animal body is rotated 180° and consequently exposed to a totally new picture of the environment. Each turn has its turning crisis, at the high point of which the body bends in an attempt to become less conspicuous. At the turnabout crisis there is a decision made as regards the path, one which determines movement away from the goal and a return to the home. This moment of doubt or indecision at the turnabout can be extremely dangerous for the subject. The turn can be "too early", "properly-timed" or "too late". In addition, the "attacking turn" (familiar to us from the turn reaction), must be distinguished from the "flight turn". It is interesting that the Swedish word *"kesan"*, etymologically linked with German *"kehren"* (= turn) means "to flee". Perhaps we may one day succeed in specifying the psychological meanings of the various forms of turning.

For the human psyche, the turnabout very often means a return to society. Martin Buber [3, p.69] wrote: "The one thing which can be fateful to man is his belief in fate. This suppressed the thought of turning back." (In this connection, the turn is upwards.)

PHASE 8:   THE RETURN STRETCH

The return stretch differs from the outward stretch, even though they share the distance factor. Both phases are within the same circulus, whether as "single or return" or as a "round trip". As opposed to the outward stretch, which is embedded between home and goal, home and goal are identical on the return stretch; the point of departure lies within an infinite foreign space. There is no home to offer the subject protection from behind, which may result in the return stretch being covered backwards. This constellation also entails, among other things, a particular haste and a "straightening" of the path. In the case of Myrmica ruginodis Nyl., a species of ant, the outward stretch meanders whereas the return stretch is in a straight line [10, p.234]. Kurt and Kummer made the following observations among primates: On moving off, the whole herd remains close together and moves at great speed. It then becomes more and more loose in formation and slows down. At the turning point, it comes to a stop and resolves into separate groups which return to the rock at increasing speed [11, p.79]. Thus, the return is marked by a reduction of the rigid social hierarchy of the outward stretch, which was an attempt to compensate for the loss of territorial security. The drop in vigilance on the return stretch may lead to the "accident on the way home"; the familiarity of the way home can be deceptive. In his book "The Early Swiss and His Wars", W. Schaufelberger tells of "retreats from the field which were indescribably disordered". [16, p.205] The return stretch has in common with flight orientation towards the home; but the flight path, in contrast to the return stretch, is seldom straight. The outward stretch has orientation towards the goal in common with the attack. In the case of the attacking subject, the home is present in the rear and the "radial effect" of the home must be taken into account.

The relationship between foreign space and enemy thus contributes to a differentiation between anxiety and fear, (Angst und Furcht). Anxiety, as an expression of enclosure, of being "hemmed in", is spatially delineated. As opposed to this, fear calls our attention to the object [6, p.410]. The concept of "pain" or "smarting" goes back to the Indo-Germanic root "smerd" which means "to sting or bite". The concepts of anxiety and fear and of pain or "smarting" emerge as a spatially and distance-determined alarm sequence. Anxiety signifies the lack of a way out (claustrophobia), fear refers to an object (the enemy) and pain to pressure (contact). To over-simplify, fear governs the outward stretch and anxiety the return stretch. Anxiety and fear anticipate pain just as seeing anticipates touching and aiming anticipates grasping.

Particular paths emerge from the tendency to return to homes of a temporally earlier order. A geriatric phenomenon, caused by the deterioration of memory with approaching senility, emerges when patients, in their confusion, seek to return to their parent's home

which they have not seen for many years. Bird and fish migration
also correspond phylogenetically to a search for earlier homes. "They
celebrate marriage where their cradle once stood" [8, p.12]. It is
also feasible that the sexual drive is marked by a tendency to return
to "homes" or states (environments). Finally, the Freudian death instinct (*Todestrieb*) might be considered in this light. When a person
dies, he is often said to have "gone home". "An instinct is", according to Freud, "an urge inherent in organic life to restore an earlier
state of things which the living entity has been obliged to abandon
under the pressure of external disturbing forces..." [5, p.213]. An
accidental form of the loss of home is represented by displacement
or kidnapping. The return via memory is an imaginary form of the
return stretch towards an earlier home. That which was forgotten on
leaving home is replaced by imagined recollection. In such earlier
"homes", the subject looks for his physical and psychic balance, a
balance which developments have upset. It looks in space for that
which it has lost in time.

PHASE 9: THE APPROACH TO THE HOME

The approach to the home is related to the approach to the goal.
In the approach to the goal, the goal itself dominates the place;
in the approach to the home it is the place which dominates. It
should be mentioned that the goal can be a place and that the home
can be non-stationary. The goal is not the subject's property until
it has been appropriated and consummated, even if this process is
only optical ("It's mine, I saw it first" is a phrase common to children and to adults.) In contrast, the home is something which the
subject considers to be his from the very start. It is only the approach to the home which may pose a possible confrontation, inasmuch
as the home takes on the properties of an object just as the child,
in being born, becomes the partner of the mother. In those cases
where objectivization leads to a total eclipse of spiritual rapport
with the home, the home no longer exists and the subject loses all
desire to return to it. In man, anything can then take the place of
home.

The confrontation with the home leads to a caesura during the
approach to it. A pull towards home may result in or create a new
departure from home, depending on the circumstances which encourage
or prevent entering the home. Caution, slowing down and an increase
in meandering are most frequently due to a change of locomotion prior
to landing, camouflage of the home (by camouflaging the entry to it)
and occupation of the home.

As the home is approached, the readiness for aggression increases, just the opposite of what happens during the outward stretch.
An interesting historic example: "When the Bundner and the Tiroleans
had been reconciled after the putsch of Munstertal in 1499, the confederates who had hurried to the scene of conflict could not content

themselves with returning peaceably towards home. Once they were in
the field they were not to be contained. Although the fighting urge
was probably equally strong on both sides, it is to be assumed that
the Swiss were the first to strike. Not only because their later ex-
cuses seemed less than convincing, but also because the people of Uri,
on the way home from Coire suddenly broke loose in Ragaz and, in spite
of warnings to the contrary, moved *in to the attack*. Before anything
was noticed, the confederates had slipped across the Rhine in two or
three small boats and had set fire to a couple of houses. This was
the beginning of the Swabian war." [16, p.159] (my italics). This
increase in aggressiveness in the vicinity of the home is particularly dangerous in the age of ICBM's.

PHASE 10:   ENTERING THE HOME

The first major occurrence on the path was the movement over the
threshold from the home environment into a foreign environment. The
last great occurrence is the actual return into the home environment.
Time has elapsed and developments have occurred both inside and outside the home since the departure. The subject has changed due to
its experiences; the home has changed, among other reasons, due to
the absence of the subject. The subject has become acquainted with
a portion of the foreign environment and, at the same time, a portion
of the home environment has become foreign to him.

The parable of the prodigal son and his very accommodating father illustrates the subjective difficulties encountered when entering the home once more. Perhaps the very impossibility of doing this
may lead to a nomadic life, with the subject recognizing the various
reasons involved. If the home was left originally because it did not
meet certain needs such as protection, nourishment or sexual needs,
it would be supplemented on return by those places where satisfaction
was obtained. Here perhaps we may glimpse the genesis of territoriality as an extension of the home. The various goals along the path
have become "home stations", the tracks have become bridges to the
home which, the substratum of the path permitting, are fixed by markers and acquire home characteristics. If the paths become a network,
the intervals between them are absorbed as territory. Excluded from
this process are only certain biological one-way streets, "false"
streets and those which, due to displacement of the substratum of the
path, have become inaccessible. The engrams of territory which have
settled in the animal psyche cannot be erased. In man, they are subject to psychic re-working but, in the form of prejudices, may hamper
his ability to perceive and correctly assess the future.

A particular form of "non-entry" is found in the case of disorientation due to a false assessment of the foreign environment, the
path environment or the home environment. Such disorientation can
occur at any one of the ten phases of the path and is specific to
each phase. It can, in itself, lead to a nomadic existence. In in-

stances where disorientation cannot be conquered by the establishment of a new home, it leads – for exogenic reasons – to confusion
and panic which probably relate – for endogenic reasons – to confusion due to false assessment of the environment.

After the home has been entered, the process of the path gives
way to rest and sleep.

A study of the relationships between several paths should follow
each extensive analysis of the individual path. Such a study should
concentrate on the animal encounter and the ensuing accompaniment.

REFERENCES

1. Blaschke, W.: Leonardo und die Naturwissenschaften. Hamb.Math.
         Einzelschriften, Heft 4. B.G. Teubner, Leipzig, 1928.
2. Braus, H.: Anatomie des Menschen, Band I. J. Springer, Berlin,
         1929.
3. Buber, M.: Ich und Du. Insel Verlag, 1923.
4. Eibl-Eibesfeldt, I.: Grundriss der vergleichenden Verhaltens-
         forschung. Piper, Munchen, 1967.
5. Freud, S.: Jenseits des Lustprinzips. Theoretische Schriften.
         1931.
6. _____: Vorlesungen zur Einfuhrung in die Psychoanalyse.
         Gesammelte Werke, Band XI. London, 1940.
7. Goethe, J.W.: Die Wahlverwandtschaften (Teil II. Kap. 5. Aus
         Ottiliens Tagebuch).
8. Hediger, H.: Bemerkungen zum Raum-Zeit-System der Tiere; ein
         kleiner Beitrag zur vergleichenden Psychologie. Schweiz.
         Z. Psychol. Anwend., 5:241-269, 1946.
9. _____: Tierpsychologie im Zoo und im Zirkus. F. Reinhardt,
         Basel, 1961.
10. _____: Die Strassen der Tiere. Vieweg Verlag, Braunschweig,
         1967.
11. Kummer, H. and Kurt, F.: Social units of a free-living population
         of Hamadrayas baboons. Folia Primat., 1:1-19, 1963.
12. Leonardo da Vinci: Tagebucher und Aufzeichnungen. P. List,
         Leipzig, 1940.
13. Lorenz, K.: Das Sogenannte Bose. Zur Naturgeschichte der Aggres-
         sion. G. Borotha-Schoeler, Wien, 1963.
14. _____: Darwin hat recht gesehen. Opuscula 20. G. Neske,
         Pfullingen, 1965.
15. Nietzsche, F.: Also sprach Zarathustra. (e. Teil, vom hoheren
         Menschen, 17). G. Hauser, Munchen, 1955.
16. Schaufelberger, W.: Der alte Schweizer und sein Krieg. Europa
         Verlag AG, Zurich, 1952.
17. Shakespeare, W.: Hamlet. III:1.
18. Tinbergen, N.: Instinktlehre, Vergleichende Erforschung ange-
         borenen Verhaltens. Paul Parey, Berlin-Hamburg, 1956.
19. _____: Tierbeobachtungen zwischen Arktis und Afrika.
         Paul Parey, Berlin-Hamburg, 1967.

Dominance and Territoriality as Complemented in Mammalian Social Structure

Paul Leyhausen

INTRODUCTION

"One very cold night a group of porcupines were huddled together for warmth. However, their spines made proximity uncomfortable, so they moved apart again and got cold. After shuffling repeatedly in and out, they eventually found a distance at which they could still be comfortably warm without getting pricked. This distance they henceforth called decency and good manners."

I chose this old fable for an opening because it sums up nicely four points I want to make. First, that individual distance as a phenomenon does not in itself mean mutual hostility; second, that even in non-aggressive animals a too close proximity can become very prickly; third, that individual distance means a balance between dispersive (not necessarily violent) and cohesive forces; and fourth, that, through individual distance, space itself becomes the vehicle of social meaning.

I apologize for introducing my subject from a theoretical angle, which is certainly not the way we ourselves started out; because our observations and investigations were primarily not aimed at finding out anything about social behavior. But I hope that, by making our way backwards in a sense, the broader meaning of the facts to be presented may become more apparent.

FROM INDIVIDUAL DISTANCE TO RANKING ORDER

There are innumerable organisms which often keep individual distance without hostility (for instance, lower marine organisms), literally as a kind of breathing space. They may struggle to obtain and keep it, but rather as if wriggling free from an obstacle and not as if fighting an adversary. However, where evolution has equipped the organism with structural and behavioral prerequisites for fighting, we shall almost invariably find that fighting is also, and often mainly, employed to keep conspecifics at a suitable distance. For this to be effective, two more sets of factors are necessary: a defeated animal, or one not ready to fight, must be able, must have the behavioral differentiation, to flee; at the same time it must have some reason to approach and keep close to the other animal, or there would be no fight in the first place; and afterwards the animals would, at least in theory, disperse so as never to meet again. All these behavioral differentiations are so universally present in vertebrates that, in those rare cases where one or the other is absent, we are compelled to conclude that it is a secondary loss. Since I am to talk about mammals, we may start from the assumption that the behaviors outlined above are as a rule at the disposal of all the species in question.

Anger and fear (terms I use here to describe the motivational states underlying certain behaviors, without any reference to subjective feelings which may or may not accompany them) command the behavior patterns of aggression and flight and, when flight is blocked by external or internal factors, of defensive fighting and submission.

Whether the fighting originally starts because one animal approaches another too closely or because of something else, the outcome will eventually show that stronger or more aggressive animals keep a greater distance in relation to other animals, or are kept at a greater distance because of the avoidance action of others. Thus develops what I might call an "individual distance differential." Space becomes a status symbol: the size of the area around an animal which it can keep free of others and how far it dares to penetrate into the "free sphere" of others, is, among other things, a very precise indicator of the social status of an individual within a group.

THE TIME FACTOR IN DOMINANCE

The overall motivational state of an animal varies with circadian, seasonal and other rhythms and also because of interference by non-rhythmic factors. The kind of halo which surrounds an animal as a result of keeping individual distance and of ranking is, therefore, not rigid but pulsates, as it were, more or less regularly and rhythmically. Remembering that this pulsating halo of rank-determined individual distance is individual with respect not only to the owner but also to its relationships with each individual member of the group, and that in this respect the halo resembles somewhat the common field of gravity of two celestial bodies, it becomes obvious that the function of space in shaping the social interactions within the group is far from being straightforward and easy to understand, and that the extension into the fourth dimension is partly rhythmically repetitive and partly not.

To demonstrate this, I shall give you a short report on an investigation which my student Ingeborg Heinemann and I made on a small,
free-grazing herd of cows (8). The original supposition to be investigated was very simple. Animals with an almond-shaped pupil (which
in the head-low grazing position is practically horizontal) have, without much movement of the head, an almost fully circular field of
vision. The idea was that the leader of a herd therefore need not be
in front but could, at least to some extent, direct the movements of
the herd, while grazing for instance, from a position farther back.

To begin with, in order to get an idea which animal might be the
leader of the herd, which animals might be more dominant and which inferior, we first had to assess the ranking order among the ten or
eleven animals by other means - behavior at the water well, at the entrance to the stable, and so on - and then indeed it could later be
found that an animal approaching from behind could "push" the one in
front of it and get it to move on with the same ease as a leading
animal could "pull" another along behind it. But the correlation of
this capacity to lead was not a straightforward one with ranking order.
It was found that the "pushing" capacity of an animal was more closely
linked with rank, whereas "pulling" was to a certain extent, and in
many cases to a great extent, caused by something we could not help
calling a kind of personal attraction of one animal to another. In
this way, the determination of the direction which the whole herd took
when grazing was a more or less statistical affair resulting from the
differential of the overall directing capacity (leading and pushing) of
the individuals. By plotting these facts - how often an animal was
pulled or could pull another one, how often it pushed other animals
and was pushed by them - we could obtain a fair measure of both these
capacities; and by adding them together we found a measure of the
overall leading capacity of an animal. In this way, incidentally,
the animal which was most effective in directing the grazing movement
of the whole herd was not the one which ranked $n^o 1$ but $n^o 2$ because it
was more attractive and could pull more animals. We see that even such
an apparently simple thing as the slow movement of a grazing herd of
cows is by no means determined in a simple way, that there is no one
animal which could be designated as The Leader, but that the direction
the entire herd takes is more or less a result of the interaction of
all the individual animals and their differential capacity for changing the direction of others. There is one more point which I think
is very significant, although it may seem only a small fact in itself;
whereas a high-ranking animal cannot normally be pushed by a low-
ranking one coming from behind, if two or three low-ranking animals
form a compact group and approach from behind in this formation, they
can push the high-ranking animal. So there is also a kind of majority
rule involved.

These rules are valid only for the grazing situation. Other activities, as they occur in the course of the day, show an entirely different picture. For instance, if the herd is panicking from a sudden
startling stimulus, there is absolutely no leadership at all; the one
which moves first pulls all the others behind it. When they march at

a brisk pace from one place to another, the marching order is again
different: as a rule the low-ranking animals are in front, the high-
ranking animals in the middle and the others bring up the rear.   When
they go to rest, or chew the cud in the shade over mid-day, again the
picture is entirely different and depends far more than in the other
situations on mutual attraction or what one might call friendship between the animals. So the whole picture of the spatial relationships
between individuals in the herd, when observed over the course of the
day, becomes very complicated and very variable, and from assessing
only one of these situations you would never discover anything about
the social structure of the herd. This extends as much in time as it
does in space, and so it is a time-space structure, a fabric made up
of both. We cannot, therefore usually hope to achieve anything in
determining the social relationships of a group without taking the
time factor into account, even with respect to what is traditionally
called the ranking order or what I call the <u>absolute social hierarchy</u>.
For instance, the animals which keep together on the move are not
necessarily those which keep together while resting, because in every
situation the mutual attractions are different, just as the people I
like to have with me for a spree on the Reeperbahn in Hamburg may be
different from those with whom I like to have an earnest scientific
discussion. Thus the social value of the individual differs widely
in accordance with the situation; already on this - the cow - level
this is quite clearly noticeable and must be taken into account, even
when forming concepts like social hierarchy. But apart from all these
variations in time and space, one can still say that if there is a
ranking order in such a group, it is, within the situation and taking
into account all the other implications of the situation, invariable.
It is observed by the individuals under all circumstances, at all
times and in all places. This is why I call it an absolute social
hierarchy.

FROM INDIVIDUAL DISTANCE TO TERRITORY

This kind of ranking order was for a long time thought to be the
only ranking principle and almost the only principle shaping animal
communities, especially with such mammals as live in groups, herds,
prides or whatever they may be called. As opposed to this principle,
a concept of territory and territory ownership was usually adduced in
so-called "solitary" mammals. What makes an animal territorial? I
think one way to approach this question is to imagine what would happen to individual distance and the relationship between ranking order
and individual distance if the individuals were locally fixed. If an
individual becomes home-conscious, if it attaches itself to one place
or district, the fact of individual distance will result in an area, a
fixed area, a geographically definable area, instead of a moveable
halo around the animal; and this is called territory. Then, of course,
evolution and natural selection get hold of this phenomenon and put
it to a great number of various uses in different species. If we look
at territories as they occur in practice in different species, it is
hard to find a common denominator of the phenomena as they are now.

But I think if we go back in evolution the common denominator can be
found in an animal which keeps an individual distance - which may incidentally become a considerable individual distance - to other animals, thereby becoming locally fixed, becoming, so to speak, a settler.

From the outline of mammalian territory as given by Fischer just
before, it might have seemed to many of you that, by forming such a
network of pathways and places to live in and a time-schedule by which
this network is used, the animal would put itself into a kind of time-
space fabricated strait-jacket. But we must bear in mind that by
parcelling space and activity we turn both into manageable units, and
that in this way the expanses of space and time become organized and
are at our disposal. By becoming partially enslaved by schedules, we
emerge as the masters of both, and there is no reason to assume that
in this respect the higher mammals are basically different from man.

Territory was once compared by Julian Huxley to a kind of elastic disc which surrounds the animal (3). Neighbors can push the
boundary and indent the elastic disc, so that the resultant shapes
may be very varied. The elasticity persists, however, and if any of
the neighbors become extinct or move away or become weaker so that the
animal can push them off again, this bend is mended and the animal has
a tendency, so to speak, to restore the integrity of its elastic disc.
In practice, we see from the start that animals are rather more sensible and do not insist on a theoretical circular-shaped elastic disc.
Instead they orient themselves along natural lines in the shape of the
environment - ditches, ridges, streams and so on - which are easily
accepted as natural boundaries. Apart from this, in most mammalian
territories one must realize that the real territory is the network of
paths and places to visit and use as Hediger said (2), on which the
animal moves around and where it has its activity, and not an area inside a fixed boundary. In many cases such a boundary simply does not
exist. This mainly results from a mammal not being able, like a song-
bird perched high in a tree, to survey the whole of its territory all
the time, and so territories mostly overlap considerably. In the areas
of overlap we can often observe that a kind of traffic regulation is
installed, that animals making communal use, for instance, of the border pathways do not do so at the same time, but that one animal coming
there may have the right of way and the other is compelled to wait. If
you have an opportunity to wander round the countryside where there are
free-moving domestic cats, you can observe this quite easily. You will
very often see a cat somewhere in the surroundings sitting and observing fixedly an object some distance away. If you investigate without
disturbing, you will find that in most cases the object is another cat
moving along a ditch or path or something you could describe as a "cat
road." As soon as this cat has disappeared from there, you will mostly
see that the observing cat gets up and moves off to use the same path-
way. It works very like the section block signals on a railway, and my
suspicion is that in many animals which are guided more by their sense
of smell than cats, whose social relationships are mostly guided by

visual perception, the odor marks may play a great role in setting
the block section signals rather than warning off other animals completely, as they are traditionally supposed to do. A fresh mark
means "section closed," an older mark means "You may proceed with
caution," and a very old mark means "Go on, but before you use this
please put your own mark so that the next one knows what to do."
This is the origin of signposts of this kind being used by many individuals in the neighborhood (9).

THE RELATIVE NATURE OF TERRITORIALITY

This kind of behavior and the question, when two meet at the same
place, who has the right of way and who must wait, is decided in territorial border fights, and by such fights it is decided, as in ranking order fights, who is superior and who inferior. But if you observe more closely, you will find that the resultant ranking is more
or less rigidly fixed to the place where the fight occurred. This
can perhaps in part be explained by the fact that the territorial
animal feels stronger the nearer it is to its first-order home, as
Hediger called it (2), and that its fighting elan diminishes with increasing distance from its home, so that the relative distance from
their first-order home at which the two contestants meet might from
the start already determine the outcome of the fight. This, of
course, would explain why a fight which took place closer to the home
of A would be decided in A's favor, and at this place A would establish its dominance, and vice versa. Thus we observe in free-ranging
cats - and there is a great deal of data on this, it is not supposition - that the ranking order between neighbors differs according to
place. When neighbors become better acquainted they learn each other's
schedules, and then secondarily the ranking is also fixed to time,
so that if an animal, in principle dominant in place X, approaches
place X at the wrong time of the day, it may lose its superiority.
So ranking based on territoriality is relative to locality and time,
and I call this relative social hierarchy (7).

When observing cats in laboratory groups, a number of investigators, including myself (6), have found that they are apparently unable
to establish a firm ranking order. When I first published this fact,
I tried to explain it by assuming that solitary animals are simply
incapable of establishing a stable ranking order. This, however, is
wrong. For instance, within the litter the siblings establish a well-
working absolute social hierarchy, ranking order in the traditional
sense. If you observe free-ranging cat populations you will find that
the male cats of an area are also able to establish an absolute hierarchy among themselves by rival fighting. However, this hierarchy is
valid only as long as they meet on, so to speak, neutral grounds. I
must explain that male cats do not confine themselves as rigidly to
their territories proper as the females do, and that their defense of
territory is weaker than that of females. Frequently, mostly during

the reproductive season but also outside it, they move beyond their
territorial boundaries and meet in this way on neutral ground. It is
on these wanderings that the rival fights take place, which may be
enhanced somewhat by the season of the females, but is not exclusively
dependent on it. I might mention in passing that territorial fighting
and rival fighting of the male cat are not identical in internal causation. It is the same kind of fighting, no doubt, taking fighting as
a kind of tool to do something with, but the internal causation is
different. Rival fighting is clearly dependent on male hormone supply.
If you castrate a male it will more or less give up rival fighting,
but at the same time it will become more territorial. I have friends
who breed pedigree cats; in order to be able to give them a little
more freedom without the females being bred by stray males from the
neighborhood, they also keep a huge neutered male. Because of its
body size it is superior to any intact male and at the same time it
is territorial, which intact males in this situation are not. As
soon as he hears or sees a strange male around, he makes straight for
it and gives chase, thus being a very effective means of keeping the
back garden clear of strange male cats. So one must view simplified
models of male fighting with caution. Fighting can be triggered off
by not one but a number of different releasing mechanisms geared to
different external situations. What the hormone seems to do is to
alter, not the readiness to fight, but the relative balance between
the thresholds of these releasing mechanisms. With male hormone,
the threshold for the rival situation is lowered; without male hormone
this threshold is raised and the one for the territorial defense situation is lowered.

I have said that in the laboratory set-up we could not observe
such ranking at first, but when the existence of relative social hierarchy dawned on me and I re-examined the laboratory situation, I
found that the cats could very well form a stable ranking order in
some respects, for instance at the food-bowl, but that in others there
were still reserves of relative social hierarchy, e.g., with respect
to resting places. Very rarely indeed will you see a high-ranking
animal drive even the lowest pariah, as I call them, from its traditional resting place. Even this vestigial home is respected and here
the prerogatives of the other animal stop.

In free-ranging males, even after heavy fights, the defeated
male will not normally be driven out of its home; once returned there
it has a place where it can heal its wounds and where, as a territory
owner, it is again superior to all others in the neighborhood. So we
see that in this social set-up there is a combination of these two
mutually complementary kinds of ranking order, and this works very
well indeed. After fighting it out among themselves, the male cats
of such an area know after a while who is stronger and who is not
quite so strong. They settle for a stable ranking order, then become
accustomed to move around together in troops of two or three or more
and form what I call, for want of a better term, a brotherhood. They

also become <u>positively</u> attracted to each other, not merely through
the fact of fighting and establishing a ranking order. Within such
a brotherhood you will very rarely observe open fighting. There may
be a little display now and then, but this is more of a formality.
The cases of hard fighting in such cat communities originate when a
young male in the area starts on the road to maturity. This animal
will not accept defeat - it goes out for a fight, it looks for a
fight. If at some time it should become a little reluctant to come
out and fight, the others of the "Establishment" walk up to its home
and call it out to fight. After a while the young male will come out
and fight and will be beaten up severely every so often, but unlike
the adult male which accepts defeat and finds its grade in the ranking
order, the ascendant, the young male, does not. This goes on for a
year or so, and very often the young animals are severely wounded.
But they retreat to their homes, heal their wounds, and then out they
go again. So much for there not being a specific drive for fighting.
There <u>is</u>, even in animals which have had no relevant childhood experience. In fact, such animals lust after a good fight more than the
others. A single male kitten of a female cat is, when mature, usually
more aggressive than one raised with siblings.

The two principles working toward a balance establish a coherent
community. The cats of such an area are not strictly solitary but
also have their social gatherings. You can usually observe this at
night, as I have done for years at intervals in various places. The
cats leave their territories at times, gather round in certain places,
and there they sit close together and look at each other; there is no
fighting, no reproductive activity going on, it is just a social
gathering. After one or two hours it dissolves and the cats go to
their homes again to sleep - and this among animals which at other
times you can see engaged in serious territorial fighting. So again,
"being territorial" is something which is also governed by circadian
and other rhythms within the motivational system of the animal. It
is not an absolute fact, not a rigid order: "this is my territory."
Consider a comparison: you invite guests to your home, it is enjoy-
able, and after a while your guests depart again; but if you wake up
in the middle of the night and find one of your guests prowling in
your sitting-room, I think your superciliary corrugator muscle will
be innervated somewhat. In such a situation a slight frown would
cross your forehead, if no more. This is the same man you greeted
very warmly into your home some hours ago, but now you show at least
some sign of territory defense. He is not expected and it is an
improper time for him to be there. So you see that the concept of
territorial behavior also has to be understood in relation to time.

And, now, after we had realized the existence of both these
principles, we saw how they worked together. For instance, in free-
ranging cat communities there are at least two social spheres, maybe
more, where there is absolute ranking - within a litter and within a
brotherhood of adult males - and relative hierarchy in almost all
others. There are many indications that both types of social

hierarchy are also present in animals which are traditionally regarded as governed exclusively by absolute hierarchy. For instance, Krott insists that the brown bear is non-territorial (he actually says the animal is "socially neutral," by which he means "indifferent") (5), whereas other investigators have shown that, at least at times, brown bears - for instance grizzly bears in this country (10) - are territorial. So there is a certain flexibility as to where the extremes lie, and both ways of life may be realized in the same species. The investigations of Altmann on the elk show that these animals have group territories in one habitat and apparently none in others (1). In other words, the balance between absolute and relative social hierarchy is species-specific according to the communal life of that species, and within the species-specific limits this balance may shift more towards one or the other.

The effect of crowding on this species-specific balance of the two hierarchies is a growing preponderance of absolute hierarchy, which eventually becomes despotism, tyranny. The rights, the indisputable rights of the individual grow less and less, until all relative social hierarchy is completely suppressed. This is why in the laboratory cat community under crowded conditions you usually do not see much of the relative social hierarchy, because under such conditions absolute hierarchy has a tendency to grow, to prevail and to repress the other order.

It can easily be understood how and why, in primarily nomadic species like the higher primates, this aspect of territoriality becomes obscured or is not easily observed. But because of this inherent capacity for both hierarchical orders in I should think almost all mammals, the relative hierarchy element starts to become more prominent when the members of such a nomadic species establish permanent residence and thus become territorial. This has probably happened in the evolution of our own species when we evolved the tendency to establish homes. The evidence for absolute social hierarchy in humans is so abundant that I need not produce examples, but the tendency to establish oneself as a kind of territory-owner is equally obvious if one only looks for it. I would remind you only of the studies of Klimpfinger on kindergarten children and their tendency to show signs of hospitalism when crowded together in kindergartens, as was usual (4). This hospitalism could be prevented from developing if the children were given an opportunity at times during the day to withdraw from the others and to build a kind of blind around themselves to shield the others off - they were allowed to move the furniture and their toys and to build little areas, homes, castles, for themselves, and nobody else was allowed to enter these areas without permission. This is exactly the way in which, for instance, the Andaman hut originated (11). The Andaman people built communal huts, but these are not erected in the way we would plan and erect such a building. In order to understand the process, one has to know that other primitive, nomadic hunters and food-gatherers, like

the bushmen of the South-west African Kalahari, wander around their
territories in family groups. At nightfall the family erects a windshield made of branches and shrubbery, behind which they seek shelter
from the cold night winds of the desert. They erect a different
shelter every night, just as the chimpanzees build a new sleeping
nest nightly. The permanent hut of the Andaman people is essentially
a number of windshields encircling a common central area and touching
each other at the edges. Thus, each family builds its own "windshield" part only and is responsible exclusively for the maintenance
of that part of the hut. Also, starting from the "windshield" edges,
each family marks out an area of the hut floor with stones, shells,
etc., which only the family members may enter without being formally
invited to do so.

Animals which are basically equipped with the same kind of "raw
materials," like innate behavior patterns, will, when the ecological
need arises, come up with very much the same answers to it. Whether
you call this homology or analogy is not particularly relevant, but
the basic behavioral conditions and mechanisms within a mammal simply
leave only one of two possible solutions to a new problem, or maybe
two of three, and this is, I think, an undeniable fact in our own
society also.

Some people say the claim that such biological structures un-
derlie even the most sophisticated, most institutionalized and most
conventional structures in our own societies is socially naive biolo-
gism. I think such an accusation derives mainly from the fact that
it is these people who are socio-biologically naive. If one would
investigate, one would soon find that conventions and all those additional institutions have a basis for existence simply because they
are founded on such very old evolution-determined behavior structures.
Because of this, it is not possible for an indefinite stretch of time
to sin with impunity against these, our species-specific properties,
and if we want to prosper and flourish as a species for a long time
ahead we must see that we reharmonize our social conventions with the
biological foundations of our social behavior.

This also involves a balance of numbers and density, because the
capacity of the individual to take part in undertakings requiring
authority and the willingness to respect authority (this is absolute
ranking order) and at the same time to preserve his personal independence, and as such to become an independently co-operating, a
self-supporting and self-reliant citizen, is density-dependent.
These two functions of a citizen in a democratic social structure depend on a proper balance of the two hierarchical orders. Also, to a
certain extent, it is not irrelevant which function is governed by
the one or by the other. I think some of our present social trouble
and unrest is caused by the fact that, with growing numbers and increasing crowding, relative social hierarchy is disappearing rapidly
from the public scene. Majority rule and what we generally call

democratic procedure depend for their efficiency on the capacity of the citizens for independent thinking, informed judgment and resistance to undue pressures. This free participation of equal citizens and their majority decisions become farther and farther removed from the actual issues, eventually being confined to formalized voting on abstract party programs of which the majority of the voters are unable to realize the full and practical consequences if they were carried out to the letter. Thus we are subjected more and more to the tyranny of despots, whether they be personal, in the form of dictators, or impersonal, in the form of the "common good," which becomes more and more of a tyrant, taking more than it gives. At the same time, as a reaction against this, we see the attempt to introduce relative hierarchy into social areas where it has no place, such as family life, schools and so on. It is ludicrous that a pupil should tell the teacher how to do his job and what he wants to learn. This does not exclude sensible discussion, but it does imply that in some fields, for instance the family, decisions have in the end to be made by authority and be accepted from authority, and this is as much a <u>need</u> of the human individual, and especially of the growing child, as is freedom. Freedom can be had only under and because of these conditions. By trying to transfer relative hierarchy to the areas of authority as a kind of compensation for lost independence and "territorial rights" in the public sphere, we are actually undermining the very basis of democracy in the real sense of the word.

Thus, if we do not implement means to control ourselves - not only individually, not only on the level of communities, societies, states and nations, but on the species level - we may as well stop trying to control or manage anything, such as food production, natural resources, wildlife, or the moon. There is no doubt about this. I confess that I am sick of hearing and reading continually of this-control and that-management while there is almost complete neglect, in practice if not in theory, of the fact that the main question - virtually the all-important question - of management and control at the moment is management and control of the human species. Everything else will then solve itself, or at least be much easier to tackle.

REFERENCES

1. Altmann, M.: Social behavior of elk (Cervus canadensis Nelsoni) in the Jackson Hole area of Wyoming. <u>Behaviour</u>, 4:116-143, 1952.
2. Hediger, H.: Säugetier-Territorien und ihre Markierung. <u>Bijd. Dierk.</u>, 28:172-184, 1949.
3. Huxley, J.: A natural experiment on the territorial instinct. <u>Brit. Birds</u>, 27:270-277, 1934.
4. Klimpfinger, S.: Kindergartenstudien I und II. Film der Bundes-staatlichen Hauptstelle für den Unterrichtsfilm. Wien, 1952.

5. Krott, P. and Krott, G.: Zum Verhalten des Braunbaren (Ursus
            arctos L. 1758) in den Alpen. Z. Tierpsychol., 20:160–
            206, 1963.
6. Leyhausen, P.: Verhaltensstudien an Katzen. Z. Tierpsychol.,
            Beiheft 2, 1956.
7. _____: The communal organization of solitary mammals.
            Sym. Zool. Soc. London, 14:249–263, 1965.
8. _____ and Heinemann, I.: Kriterien der "Leitfunktion"
            in einer Kuhherde. In press.
9. _____ and Wolff, R.: Das Revier einer Hauskatze. Z.
            Tierpsychol., 16:666–670, 1959.
10. Meehan, W.R.: Observations on feeding habits and behavior of
            grizzly bears. Amer. Midland Natur., 65:409–412, 1961.
11. Schmidt, W.: Das Eigentum auf den altesten Stufen der Mensch-
            heit I. Munster/Westphalia, 1937.

Prepared Contributions for Discussion of Session I: Territoriality and Dominance

SOCIAL ORGANIZATION AND COMMUNITY COMPOSITION

K. Barbehenn

and ANSWER TO BARBEHENN *by P. Leyhausen*

Barbehenn:

Most of the detailed studies on the way animals use space are concerned with relatively conspicuous diurnal species or with animals in captivity. Typically, these studies focus in depth on intraspecific behavioral interactions and their diverse consequences to the individuals and hence to the population. I would like here to introduce a relevant and common biological variable that otherwise will not be considered in this Symposium - that is, the way in which the presence of some species modifies the behavior of other species in the same community.

It is perhaps to be expected that significant interactions will take place between predator and prey and that closely related competitors may influence each other; but it is now apparent, at least among certain small mammals, that very dissimilar species, such as shrews, voles, and mice may interact significantly. This fundamental fact was first recognized by Calhoun [1]. The subjects in nature, of course, are hardly suitable for direct observation and their interactions have been recorded by very indirect means - i.e., by removal trapping.

If an area of several acres is trapped for several days, one frequently observes that the species that seems to be most abundant initially is caught at a rapid rate. As its numbers are depleted, a second species makes up the bulk of the catch and may, in fact, prove to be more abundant than the first species. A third or fourth species may not be trapped at all during the first few days, yet prove to be common with continued trapping. Recognizing the true structure of the community thus is hampered by the nature of its organization.

The interpretation of such observations is that the presence of a "psychologically dominant" species in a community inhibits the use of space by more subordinate or behaviorally cryptic forms. When the dominants are removed, the other species expand their use of space, possibly alter their response to strange objects and are thus trapped. This interpretation has been confirmed in the laboratory.

Cryptic withdrawal is typical of shrews (Soricidae), and my recent work with Suncus murinus on Guam suggests that local variations in the size of the home range in this introduced species depends on its behavioral interactions with the rats (R. rattus and R. exulans). Population structure and reproductive status in the shrew vary with home range size, and all seem to be relatively independent of population density, season and preceding patterns of rainfall.

This all implies that community composition and organization may have profound effects on, at least, the subordinate species; and, if we are to develop a comprehensive theory concerning the use of space by mammals, we must eventually include the presence of other species as a normal variable. Considering that most recent insectivores and primitive primates are relatively cryptic in their behavior, the nature of these interspecific behavioral relationships might well have had a bearing on human evolution.

In view of the preceding account, I would like to ask Leyhausen whether the differences in social organization and spatial behavior that have been observed in the same species in different geographical areas may not be a consequence of differences in the composition of the community?

REFERENCES

1. Calhoun, J.B.: The social use of space. In Mayer, W. and Van Gelder, R., eds., Physiological Mammalogy. Vol. I, pp 1-187, Academic Press, New York, 1964.

Leyhausen:

On my recent trip to East Africa, India and Ceylon, in the short time available, I naturally could get only glimpses of free-ranging leopards. Even so, the contrast in their habits in these different regions is striking. In the Serengeti, the leopard seems to be largely nocturnal and almost invariably takes his prey to the lower branches of a tree where he can be safe from the interference of both lions and hyaenas. In the Indian Gir Forest, the leopard seems likewise nocturnal, but, from what I could gather from the game wardens, rarely takes his prey up a tree. This may indicate that this latter habit is due rather more to hyaena than to lion competition: In the

Gir, there is a relatively high lion density, but there are none of
the spotted hyaenas so abundant in the Serengeti and only very few
striped hyaenas. In the National Parks of Ceylon, leopards can be
met out in the open at almost any time of the day, although much of
their predatory activity still takes place at dusk or during the
night. On Ceylon, the absence of both lion and tiger makes the
leopard "top predator."

However, I should like to point out that many such differences,
including those quoted by Barbehenn, may have to be interpreted in
terms of time schedule rather than actual differences in the use of
space. Some years ago Eibl-Eibesfeldt kept two stone-martens in an
outdoor enclosure of about 12 x 18 feet. When he had to go away for
several days, he put in a number of white rats in the hope that this
would keep the martens busy and alive until his return. The martens
certainly caught and ate some of the rats, but the rest of the rats
found a crevice to retreat into, which they soon enhanced by digging;
and they adjusted their own activity in the open so well to the resting periods in the activity cycle of the martens, that the resulting
equilibrium persisted for months even in such a restricted space.

Even where spatial behavior is directly affected by other species sharing the habitat, it does not mean that intraspecific factors
have ceased to regulate the use of space, individual motility and mobility therein, and individual claims to certain areas.

IS TERRITORIALITY DEFINABLE?

J. H. Kaufmann

The seemingly endless variety of territoriality in different
animals has so far defeated all attempts to present a single clear
and generally valid definition.

Noble [11] simplified Howard's [9] complex presentation by defining territory as "any defended area," Burt [3] applied this definition to mammals, and subsequent studies have generally concentrated
on this aspect. For example, Ardrey's [1] entire review and discussion is based on the concept of defense.

This purely behavioristic definition of territoriality is especially appealing when considering the psychological value of the
stimulation derived from territorial squabbles. Darling [4] introduced the idea, Fisher [7] enlarged on it, and others, including
Ardrey, have eagerly embraced it. This concept arose from a growing
awareness that purely economic explanations of territory did not fit
all of the examples coming to light.

Appealing as the "defended area" definition is in its simplicity,
it too, however, ignores numerous cases of spatially and socially

oriented behavior which clearly belong in a discussion of territoriality. Pitelka [12] emphasized that territory is primarily an ecological phenomenon, and defined it as "an exclusive area, not merely a defended one..." He was primarily concerned with the economic functions of territory, i.e., the exclusive use of resources and the dispersion and limitation of the population, and dismissed as irrelevant the mechanisms by which exclusiveness is maintained. Pitelka proposed this definition in a discussion of territoriality in pectoral sandpipers, which actually show classical territorial defense. I found in Panama, however, an example of a purely "functional" territory, maintained without overt aggressive displays.

Such a functional territory is the core area in the home range of a band of coatis, Nasua narica [10]. Each band of females and young males spent about 80% of the time in a core area which included only about 40% of the band's home range. Although the home ranges of neighboring bands overlap freely, even into the core areas, the core areas themselves do not overlap. Even when two bands meet in the core area of one band, there is, at most, fleeting hostility, primarily among the juveniles. After a brief greeting, the bands simply separate and amicably go their own ways, with no attempt on the part of either band to drive the other away. Thus we have substantial areas where each band has virtually exclusive use, maintained without defense.

Studies on the Australian quokka (Setonix brachyurus) have provided another example of apparently undefended areas of exclusive use [8]. Ten years of mark-recapture records of 709 animals revealed that the home ranges of groups of 25-125 individuals overlap to form group territories. Individuals rarely go beyond their natal territory. The boundaries of the group territories are stable, and permanent changes in group affiliation are rare, even after the population of adjacent territories has been greatly reduced. The quokkas are neither gregarious or overtly hostile within the group territory, and no territorial defense has been observed.

Recently I studied the social behavior of whiptail wallabies (Wallabia parryi) in New South Wales. They, too, have undefended group "territories" that are simply avoided for the most part by members of neighboring mobs. Each mob had 20-40 members, which generally ranged over most or all of the mob's home range. The home ranges of neighboring mobs overlapped at the edges, and frequently the members of the two mobs fed together, without overt hostility, in the overlap zones. Nor was there unusual hostility shown to the occasional strangers who invaded the heartland of a mob. Two males changed mobs during the study, and met no hostility beyond that exhibited within the normal male hierarchy of their new mob. The males in each mob have a linear dominance hierarchy, established by ritual fighting, which serves only to determine priority of access to estrous females. During the study forage conditions were good throughout the

area, but there is some evidence that in periods of drought the pattern of exclusive mob ranges breaks down at least partially and members of several mobs feed peacefully together wherever forage is
available. It would be instructive to know what the dominance relations are between the males at such times.

Emlen [6] attacked the "defended area" concept of territory by
emphasizing the aggressive aspects of the phenomenon. He defined
territory as a space "in which a particular bird is aggressive and
largely if not supremely dominant with respect to certain categories
of intruders." Thus territory was clearly linked with dominance.
Davis [5] went a step further, suggesting that territoriality and
dominance hierarchies may represent poles of a behavioral continuum.

Recent field studies by Brown [2] on Stellar jays and Willis
[13] on bicolored ant birds have shown clearly how territory and social dominance can be intimately linked. In their examples "territory", in the sense of defended or exclusive areas, does not exist.
Neither species excludes conspecifics from the nesting area, but both
show strong social dominance in feeding situations in their own nesting area and a corresponding submissiveness in the nesting areas of
neighboring pairs. Thus Brown expressed the territorial pattern of
Stellar jays as overlapping concentric circles of diminishing dominance outward from the nest sites, rather than as a mosaic of discrete territories. Willis made this spatially related dominance reversal more explicit in defining territory as "a space in which one
animal or group generally dominates others which become dominant
elsewhere." He also emphasized that aggression is only a part of
territoriality--submission is just as important.

There need be no conflict between the territorial concepts of
exclusive use and dominance reversal, if we will agree that what is
important in such cases is the priority of access to resources:
food, water, shelter, space, receptive females, etc. This, after
all, is what dominance hierarchies are all about--exclusive use is
not necessary if the intruders defer to the residents in economic
matters. The avoidance of other groups' ranges by coatis, quokkas
and whiptails can be interpreted as an extension of the submissiveness or respect for another's territory which Willis emphasized. In
these cases the need for aggressiveness by the resident owner is reduced to the vanishing point, so that even when incursions occur
there is no defense or guilty retreat.

Leyhausen and others have introduced the concept of time as a
territorial parameter. One application of this idea comes from recent work in Tasmania by B.C. Mollison (unpublished mss.) on two
macropods, Thylogale billardieri and Wallabia rufogrisea. These animals inhabit primarily forested areas, using well defined runs in
their travels from resting areas to feeding areas. Use of some
trails and feeding areas was heavy, but direct confrontations were

kept to a minimum by the different schedules used by the various animals. Exclusive use of the feeding areas is not necessarily of crucial importance to these nongregarious grazers and browsers, but freedom from disturbance while feeding in small areas may be. It is not necessary that each animal keep to the same schedule each night; rather, exclusive use for a short time can be achieved through avoidance behavior.

A somewhat similar situation exists among male coatis during the mating period. Adult males are normally solitary, occupying overlapping home ranges. In the mating period, one dominant male travels and mates with each band of females. He establishes scent posts by rubbing urine on trees and lianas and viciously drives off all other males which approach the band. The scent posts do not keep other males out of the area, but they do warn them of the presence of a dominant male in the immediate vicinity. The subordinate males avoid direct confrontations, thereby minimizing physical conflict. Thus dominance relationships serve the same purpose as spatial exclusion, but still provide for the presence of "spare" potential breeding males in the area. Exclusive use of the area exists only in a temporal sense, but this is enough to insure exclusive use of the resource (females).

No simplified definition or explanation of territory yet advanced can cover all of the related kinds of behavior known, and perhaps it is naive to look for one. Territory unquestionably has many economic and psychological functions and many manifestations, from conspicuous defense and exclusion, to dominance reversal, to mutual passive avoidance. The interdependence of territoriality and social dominance seems to fall mainly within the economic realm, where they act as related and by no means mutually exclusive mechanisms for allocating resources among the members of a population.

REFERENCES

1. Ardrey, R.: The Territorial Imperative. Atheneum, New York, 1966.
2. Brown, J.L.: Aggressiveness, dominance and social organization in the Stellar jay. Condor, 65:460-484, 1963.
3. Burt, W.H.: Territoriality and home range as applied to mammals. J. Mammalogy, 24:346-352, 1943.
4. Darling, F.F.: Social behavior and survival. Auk, 69:183-191, 1952.
5. Davis, D.E.: The role of density in aggressive behavior of house mice. Anim. Behav., 6:207-210, 1958.
6. Emlen, J.T. Jr.: Defended area? - a critique of the territory concept and of conventional thinking. Ibis, 99:352, 1958.
7. Fisher, J.: Evolution and bird sociality. In Huxley, J. et al., ed., Evolution as a Process. Allen & Unwin, London, 1954.

8. Holsworth, W.N.: Population dynamics of the quokka, (Setonix
          brachyurus), on the west end of Rottnest Island, Western
          Australia. Aust. J. Zool., 15:29-46, 1967.
9. Howard, H.E.: Territory in Bird Life. Atheneum, New York.
          (Reprinted). 1920.
10. Kaufmann, J.H.: Ecology and social behavior of the coati, (Nasua
          narica) on Barro Colorado Island, Panama. Zoology,
          60:95-222, 1962.
11. Noble, G.K.: Dominance in the life of birds. Auk, 56:263-273,
          1939.
12. Pitelka, F.A.: Numbers, breeding schedule and territoriality in
          pectoral sandpipers of Northern Alaska. Condor,
          61:233-264, 1959.
13. Willis, E.O.: The behavior of bicolored antbirds. Zoology,
          79:1-127, 1967.

SOCIAL ORGANIZATION IN A LABORATORY COLONY

OF WOOD RATS, *NEOTOMA FUSCIPES*.

K. P. Kinsey

A study was conducted to investigate the social organization of
wood rats, Neotoma fuscipes, in a large outdoor observation cage, designed to test the hypothesis that a shift from territoriality to social hierarchy behavior will result, due to artifically increased
densities in confined groups of rats [4].

In their natural habitat, wood rats are highly aggressive toward
members of their own species. According to Linsdale and Tevis, members of this species occupy and defend individual stick houses
throughout the year [5]. Only one rat is found in these houses, except when females have young and for short periods during the breeding season when males temporarily take up residence with the females.

Davis presented the hypothesis that territoriality and social
hierarchy are two poles on a continuum of behavior that is dependent
upon density [3]. At all densities, the individuals are territorial,
but at high densities they may associate into groups which have social rank. In this study, an attempt was made to determine if the
continuum hypothesis could be applied to the social behavior of wood
rats confined in groups in the laboratory. If such a continuum is
in operation, increasing population densities in the observation cage
should result in a shift from territorial to social hierarchy behavior.

A total of three experiments were conducted during the normal
breeding season of the species and a total of 25 adult rats were
used in the study. All rats were marked with a commercial hair-
lightener for identification and were isolated for at least one week

before being used in an experiment.

The observation cage was divided into three levels connected by
a ramp. Two shelves, in addition to the floor of the cage, provided
approximately 90 square feet of floor space. The cage was illuminated
by red outdoor flood lights and 25 watt red light bulbs situated within the cage so that the rats could be observed at night. Food and
water were available ad libitum throughout the study and one-gallon
cans and sticks were provided for nesting material. The floor and
shelves were covered with sand and rocks to provide a semi-natural
environment, and all these materials were replaced after each experiment.

Observations were made during a period which began shortly before sunset and lasted an average of 90 minutes. Preliminary observations indicated that the rats were most active during this period.
A mean of 2.5 observation days per week was maintained throughout
the study.

In each experiment, the rats were placed in the observation
cage at the same time to avoid the establishment of territorial ownership by any individual. Each aggressive or sexual interaction and
the time of its occurrence was recorded, using individual identification for each rat involved. Other forms of social behavior were
recorded as they occurred, and the time of emergence in the evening
and initial activities of each rat was studied.

In the first experiment, lasting 96 days, three male and three
female wood rats were placed in the observation cage and observed
for 48.5 hours on 34 observation nights. The second experiment involved six females and lasted 31 days, during which the rats were
observed for 23.25 hours on 12 observation nights. The last experiment, lasting 39 days, involved four male and four female rats, which
were observed for a total of 28.5 hours accumulated from 19 observation nights. Two additional rats were introduced into each experimental group to determine the effect of their introduction on the
social organization of each of the original groups.

The results of this study support the hypothesis that a shift
from territorial behavior to social hierarchy behavior results when
wood rats are removed from their natural habitat and placed in confined groups. A stable dominance hierarchy was established among
the original members of each of the three experimental groups within
the first week of observation. In each of the experiments, an initial high level of aggressive activity occurred following the introduction of the rats into the observation cage; after about one week,
the number of aggressive interactions decreased. The social rank
order of the rats in each group appeared to be determined by the sex,
size and experience of the individual rats. Large experienced males
were always the highest ranking or alpha rats. These alpha males

were often seen patrolling the cages in the early evening, displac-
ing the other rats from their hiding places and chasing them about
the cage. Such patrolling behavior, or "making the rounds," has
also been reported in studies of confined populations of mice [2,6].

Males were generally more dominant than females, although some
females ranked high in the dominance hierarchies. In the two experiments, which involved equal members of each sex, the alpha males initiated approximately 45% of all aggressive interactions and won more
than 98% of these interactions. In the second experiment, which involved six females, a stable dominance hierarchy was established, but
no individual rat exhibited the degree of dominance equivalent to
that of the alpha males in the other two experiments. The three
highest ranking females had nearly equal numbers of wins, but differed in the number of losses in aggressive interactions. Later in
the experiment, a large male rat was introduced. He immediately became dominant over the entire group, initiating 43% of all aggressive
interactions for the remainder of the experiment. He also won all
but one of 187 of these interactions.

In the third experiment, the highest ranking rats were removed
one by one at the end of the experimental period to determine the
effect of their absence upon the social organization of the remaining rats. In two cases, males which had previously shown little
aggressive activity, became highly aggressive when the dominant rats
were removed. In both of these cases, the individuals concerned
moved up the social hierarchy and became alpha males, despite the
fact that females who had previously ranked above them were still
present in the cage. It appears that the aggressive behavior of
these males had been suppressed by the presence of the alpha males
in the original group, so that they appeared to rank low in the hierarchy. When the alpha males were removed from the group, the other
males had an opportunity to express their dominance and were seen to
move up to a higher social rank. This elevation of rank occurred
only in the case of the two males mentioned and did not occur among
any of the females. These two males had previously suffered a number
of defeats from higher ranking females, but, when the alpha males
were removed, they became very aggressive and won all aggressive interactions with the other rats.

A total of 2,633 aggressive interactions were observed in the
study. Most of these interactions occurred during the initial portion of each experiment, before the formation of stable dominance
hierarchies. After stable dominance hierarchies were established,
there was a gradual decrease in the number and intensity of aggressive interactions, until eventually a point was reached when only
one or two interactions per rat were observed on a given observation
night. Accompanying this decrease in the level of aggression, there
was an increase in the number of nonaggressive social interactions.
The rats became more tolerant of each other and began grooming, eating

and sleeping together. Large stick houses were constructed, largely
through the efforts of the females. In the first two experiments,
all the rats of the original groups eventually slept together in one
"communal" house. In the last experiment this was not observed, although large groups of rats slept together in several nests in the
cage.

The six additional rats, introduced into the three experimental
groups after the dominance hierarchies had been established, were attacked vigorously by all members of the original groups. All except
one of these introduced rats were persecuted by the other rats and
relegated to the lowest social rank, similar to the findings of Barnett in studies of wild rats [1]. These newcomers were often seen
to be active in the daytime, eating and exploring the cage while the
other rats were inactive. At night, when the other rats were active,
these low ranking individuals were frequently observed clinging to
the screen on the side of the cage or hiding behind rocks or in the
nest cans, fleeing when they were approached. This avoidance behavior enabled submissive rats to survive introduction into the experimental groups. One large male, mentioned above, was able to dominate
the other rats when he was introduced into the second and third experiments and became the alpha individual in both cases. On the
other hand, another large male in the first experimental group was
promptly attacked and killed when he exhibited aggressive behavior.
In all the introductions, all the rats in the groups took part in
the conflict with the newcomers. It is interesting to note that introduced rats which were submissive were quickly ignored by the high
ranking males, but were persecuted by some of the lower ranking females of the original groups. In one case, the lowest ranking female in the group began a regular pattern of patrolling and became
highly aggressive when another female was introduced into the experimental group.

The emergence order of the rats after sunset appeared to be determined by individual differences in activity and social rank. The
introduced rats in each of the experiments were invariably first to
become active in the evening. They were often active long before
sunset, attempting to get food while the other rats were inactive.
During the initial part of each experiment, the alpha males were observed to become active before any of the other rats in the original
groups, in order to be able to perform their patrolling activities.
Following the establishment of stable hierarchies, the alpha males
ceased their patrolling activities and were less despotic than they
had previously been. They did not become active as early as they
had at the beginning of the experiments. It appears that, after the
dominance hierarchies had been established, the alpha males no longer
actively had to assert their dominance in order to maintain a stable
form of social organization. Little difference was observed between
the emergence times of males and females. The mean emergence time
for all the rats in the study was 6.7 minutes after sunset.

Only two copulatory attempts were recorded and no reproduction occurred during the entire study. This lack of sexual activity was attributed to the high population density among the confined groups of rats in the observation cage. The despotic rule of the alpha males during the early phase of each experiment discouraged the establishment of individual territories and houses, which may be essential to normal reproduction in this species. Later, when the rats became tolerant of each other and slept together in groups, they appeared to show no sexual interest in one another.

The increase in tolerance among members of each experimental group, especially the communal nesting behavior and the hostile reaction to newly introduced rats, gives cause for speculation as to the possible existence of a cohesive social "bond" among the members of each group. This bond probably was the result of the establishment of a dominance hierarchy type of social organization based upon mutual recognition of individuals and their social ranks within the groups. This individual recognition may have been dependent upon visual and olfactory cues and might have involved a specific group odor which enabled members of the group to distinguish strangers introduced into the groups. In each of the three experiments, introduced rats were immediately recognized and attacked by all of the rats, while very little renewed aggression occurred among the members of the original groups. The original group appeared to be defending a common group territory, represented by the entire observation cage. The possibility of a group odor is further supported by the fact that all of the rats urinated and defecated in certain group-dunging places to mark their territories.

In conclusion, wood rats, like many other animals, have the capacity to adapt themselves to confined situations through the formation of a dominance hierarchy type of social organization, despite the fact that they maintain separate territories and are quite aggressive toward members of their own species under natural conditions. This type of social organization has great survival value to a species; since it is a means by which the aggressive tendencies of each individual can be channeled into the establishment of dominance hierarchies, with the eventual decrease in aggressive interactions, enabling the individuals to coexist peacefully in close confinement. In a dominance hierarchy, the individual members are able to recognize each other's social rank and fighting is minimized. At the same time, newcomers are recognized and driven away if possible. Wynne-Edwards described the function of a dominance hierarchy as that of identifying the surplus individuals whenever population density reaches critical levels [7].

REFERENCES

1. Barnett, S.A.: An analysis of the social behavior in wild rats.
        Proc. Zool. Soc. (London), 130:107-152, 1958.
2. Brown, R.Z.: Social behavior, reproduction and population
        changes in the house mouse (Mus musculus L.).
        Ecol. Monogr., 23:217-240, 1953.
3. Davis, D.E.: The role of density in aggressive behavior of
        house mice. Anim. Behav., 6:207-210, 1958.
4. Kinsey, K.P.: Social Organization in a Laboratory Colony of
        Wood Rats. San Diego State College, Masters Thesis,
        1968.
5. Linsdale, J.M. and Tevis, L.P. Jr.: The Dusky-Footed Wood Rat.
        Univ. California Press, Berkeley and Los Angeles, 1951.
6. Lloyd, J.A. and Christian, J.J.: Relationship of activity and
        aggression to density in two confined populations of
        house mice (Mus musculus). J. Mammal., 48:262-269,
        1967.
7. Wynne-Edwards, V.C.: Animal Dispersion in Relation to Social
        Behavior. Hafner Publishing Company, New York, 1962.

Discussion of Session I:
Territoriality and Dominance

PANEL: C. C. Carpenter (Chairman), R. Ardrey,
        J. L. Brereton, K. P. Kinsey,
        P. Leyhausen, R. S. Peterson

Carpenter:

Iguanid lizards begin to lay claim to space and attempt to determine their own individual distance shortly after birth or hatching as evidenced by aggressive displays. Population structure in most species studied is based on territoriality in the male. The male maintains his territory by posturing and displaying, thus using these visual signals in declaring his defense of space. The aggressive displays are species-specific and are called display-action-patterns. They are used in species recognition and thus function as a species isolating mechanism.

These display-action-patterns (aggression) differ from behavior movements used in courtship by the males and by females and juveniles responding in males.

When such species are placed in enclosures in numbers exceeding natural density, territoriality gives way to despotism (as Leyhausen also described) with one male dominating all others, his subordinates. Hierarchies usually do not exist. When such a dominant is removed, there is an increase in activity of the other males with a new dominant arising. Such shifts of dominance can be repeated many times. There are certain postures assumed by dominant and subordinate individuals which appear to act as visual cues in social interactions. The dominant of territory holding males has access to more females. In most iguanid lizards, the females show little aggression and live in the territory of a particular male. There are often two or three females in a territory, giving rise to the concept of a lizard harem. If such lizards are crowded in a cage, such despotism may not be apparent.

46

Space demands may be seasonal as seen in the marine iguana (<u>Amblyrhynchus</u> <u>cristatus</u>) of the Galapagos Islands. The males set up and defend territories over a period of from two to three months, then leave their territories and form loose aggregations. Following this the females move to nesting beaches and exhibit aggression towards one another in regard to nesting sites.

Brereton:

I would like to address Dr. Leyhausen in his remark that territoriality develops from a hierarchical system. I find that rather implausible. From what I have seen, not working with mammals but with birds, I am inclined to think that, at least sometimes, territoriality is the basic phenomenon from which some other kind of social system (moving toward a gregarious, flocking type) is the more likely evolutionary sequence. With cats, as he has described them, it is a basically territorial system, and the evolutionary consequence of the need to adapt to a different distribution of resources, more widely scattered, would take us away from territoriality to a more flocking kind of system. I realize that this does not accord with what our chairman has said: if you take an animal that has a territorial system and constrict it, then you get a hierarchy.

Leyhausen might have considered a greater range of social systems. He mentioned ungulates and larger groupings, and seemed to suggest that we could look at them from a territorial kind of strategy. To me, this is not so. We move from territory to an interspersing kind of system which is hierarchical without geographical defense (there is population regulation in it, but it is not geographical) and then towards highly gregarious flocking species where there is little population regulation. In this conference, we extrapolate from rats to man, from cats to man, from mice to man. In this sense we should be able to extrapolate from the highly territorial gibbon, at one end of the spectrum in sociality and regulating exactly in the population sense, to the promiscuous chimpanzee and gorilla at the almost other end of the spectrum. I ask you, where does man fit in this spectrum of adaptations? It seems to me, he lies well towards the promiscuous gorilla end, and has, as a consequence, little capacity to regulate his population size.

Leyhausen:

As to the first question, I should say that, of course, we do not really know which was there first, the hen or the egg. Why evolution chooses one way for a given species and not the other, we certainly do not know in most cases. I should not commit myself exclusively to one way or the other, both types of adaptation must be considered. It is possible for a more or less vagrant species to establish greater individual distances, whereupon the individuals become, more or less, locally fixed, settled. It can also happen the

other way around, as Davis has shown in the Crotophaginae, and I have
also left out the more complicated cases where large populations
tend to establish subgroups, and where the individuals not only have
to cope with individual distance but with inter-group distance as
well. What I gave here was a very short review, and I had to leave
the embroideries out.

With regard to man, I must say that, from observations on human
groups and societies, we are certainly justified in saying that the
two principles (territoriality and dominance) are operating there
too. But their extent, the areas in which and the limits within
which they are operating are unknown. We must also take into account
the "under-cover", subversive, unobtrusive ways in which they often
operate. Before anyone notices that there is something going wrong
in society, one suddenly suffers from the symptoms. And, since we
do not see the underlying principle, the illness remains unknown,
and the symptoms are treated as if they were the illness itself.
Because of this symptomatic treatment, we will never effect a cure.
All these things have to be studied, and I want to instigate the
feeling that such studies are more urgently needed in our present
situation than anything else we could do in science.

Ardrey:

I wanted to step up in agreement with Leyhausen. Since my interest is associated so much with what I have called the territorial
imperative, I suppose I should be expected to disagree. I come more
and more to feel, however, that the underlying motivation is one of
dominance. Territory represents dominance over a piece of space
which may or may not be an expression of dominance over others. But
it looks to me - if we are talking about the cart and horse - that
the horse is probably dominance.

I stepped up, however, very briefly to lay not so much before
Leyhausen as really before the Animal Behavior Society the question
which has been bothering me for some years, and which I do not think
the behavioral scientists have come to a quite proper conclusion on
as yet. As we have come to know more and more and think more and
more about territory and its relation to dominance, we find our old
Noble definition of territory as a defended area more and more inadequate. I find that there are two distinctly different areas of
thought concerning territory which lead into numerous disputes, to
my mind quite unnecessary, particularly in primate reports. Is it
a territory because it is defended, or is it a territory because it
is exclusive? I think it was Pitelka, in 1959, who first brought
this up, and Struhsaker, in his vervet monkey work, repeated it last
year. We continually find primate students saying: "Oh, a certain
species isn't territorial because it doesn't defend...." Well, it
does not defend for the simple reason that no one intrudes. Territory is established by avoidance - this does not make the animal

non-territorial. I believe that the question is largely one between
the different interests of ecology and ethology. In terms of behavior one is interested in psychological processes of defense, in
terms of ecology one is interested in spatial divisions. Wynne-
Edwards, in his quite wonderful work, is obviously looking at territory in terms of its consequence on spatial division; whether it is
divided by avoidance or defense is not greatly material. From the
behavioral standpoints, however, in such questions as we are speaking of here concerning dominance, the problem of defense is greater.
I am not here to answer questions, I am just here to ask them; and
I think that everybody who is involved with animal behavior should
give more profound thought to the definition of territory as we are
using it these days.

Leyhausen:

I should like to make one more point. In the lecture I stated
specifically that I take it for granted that, on the evolutionary
level of mammals, the capacity for fighting is always present; and
if the species under consideration has this capacity, it is almost
invariably implemented, along with other behavioral mechanisms, for
keeping social distance. But it is possible to keep social distance,
individual distance, without fighting. I am, in principle, opposed
to a definition of territory as something which is kept free of conspecifics exclusively through fighting. I think that an animal,
keeping individual distance, can certainly dominate an area and be
territorial in that sense without defending it violently. For instance, Koala bears do not fight but disperse until a certain individual distance is achieved; they avoid proximity. On the other
hand, I would stress the following point: We know that at least
some higher mammals, such as deer, (from the work of Graf, Dasman,
and Taber), are capable of tradition and also of transferring social
status by tradition from parent to child. Territory in some mammals,
as I have demonstrated, has to be defined in time as well as in
space, and investigators must design their methods accordingly. If
we find, by observing animals for only a few hours per week, that one
week at 12 o'clock Rhino A was in the observation area, and that the
next week at 14 hours Rhino B was there, we simply must not conclude
that rhinos are not territorial. For all we know, the territorial
fight might have taken place fifty years ago. We will not be able
to say anything about the social structures of long-lived animals,
such as rhinos which live for thirty to forty years, before we have
a conclusive and complete study of at least one generation in one
given area. The grandparents of the study animals might have fought
over it God knows when; anybody who goes into an area for three months,
observes a few hours per week, may very well never be eye-witness to
a fight, since rights established two generations ago might still be
respected. He would certainly make some very interesting observations
- and please let no one make the mistake that I do not esteem my colleague Rudolf Schenkel, I do. On the issue of studying Rhinos however,

I think he is wrong. If we want to study the social structure of an
animal which lives almost as long as we do, then we have to plan our
study for a lifetime. For social structure exists in space <u>and</u> time
 - and very much in time.

Peterson:

     I am very intrigued by the idea that territoriality and dominance
systems complement each other. The concept that they have complemented each other evolutionarily is an idea that is particularly intriguing to me, because I have recently completed studies on closely related animals, pinnipeds, which demonstrate the two systems.

     Both patterns are illuminated with unusual clarity, territoriali-
ty (sight-fixed) in one species, and a dominance hierarchy system,
for which there is no sight-fixing, in the other. In the California
sea-lions and in the Northern fur-seal, spacing is accomplished by
sight-attachment, territories are dependent. In the Northern elephant seal and apparently in the grey seal, strict tendency to particular sites is replaced by a ranking system, in which individuals
restrict their activity in space and time relative to the position
of other familiar animals.

     Why do these two systems occur differently? This has been a
primary question in my mind; and I'd like to make just two points
about it, and tell you a little bit about my thinking about why the
two systems occur.

     First of all let's say we won't be able to adequately understand
behavioral systems (I use the word systems advisedly) as complex as
territoriality and dominance unless they're studied in their natural
environment at least at some state in their analysis. The causal factors which occur or did occur, structuring these systems, are present
only in the natural environment and I think that's the place where
the ecological or behavioral determinant input-factors can most readily be dissected. Laboratory analysis will yield description of the
system but not the kind of analysis we need.

     The second point I want to make is that, among the mammals, the
seals, sea lions (pinnipeds in other words) provide extremely good
and observable examples of these two systems in operation, perhaps
the most readily studied among mammals.

     What kinds of implications do our studies of these pinnipeds
have? In the first place, why do pinnipeds space themselves across
their breeding grounds rather than aggregate haphazardly? What kind
of ecological functions might this serve? Are they crowded into a
small area and therefore space-limited, holding territories? Or does
this behavior represent some kind of innate territorial imperative
which may instead be limiting population growth? I think we need

further observation to get an answer to that.

The second question is: why should territoriality and dominance occur in other species that live under apparently similar ecological conditions? Why do different species consistently exhibit two different patterns. And I might add that in our studies we don't see a transition from one system to another depending on crowding. As far as we know, in fur seals and sea lions territoriality is exhibited under all population densities. Similarly in elephant seals, apparently even when the population is very, very low, and a new area is being invaded, the dominance system continues to operate. It does not look as though we get the change from one to another.

Why do they occur then? Habitat requirements may be important. For example, one species holds out mostly on sandy beaches, the other on rocky ledges; and maybe different geographic requirements may affect the system. I must emphasize my major point, that further analysis of the natural environment is indispensable.

Kinsey:

In contrast to the behavior of fur seals discussed by the previous speaker, my work with wood rats (<u>Neotoma fuscipes</u>) has shown (see prepared discussion on page 40) that a shift from territoriality to a dominance hierarchy can be induced when groups of rats are confined in a large outdoor observation cage. It was observed that this shift resulted in a gradual decrease in aggressiveness, accompanied by an increase in tolerance among the members of three experimental groups observed in this study. This was especially evidenced by the fact that all the rats eventually began sleeping together in "communal" houses near the end of each experiment, despite the fact that they maintain and defend separate stick houses in the field.

Throughout the study each experimental group appeared to have established a group territory and there was evidence of a common group odor, which may have been the result of sleeping in groups and urinating and defecating in certain group "dunging" places. Newly introduced rats were quickly recognized and were vigorously attacked by all members of the groups, especially the alpha males. The stability of the hierarchy of a group could be disrupted by the removal of the alpha male. In one experiment, a large female ranked second and another female ranked fourth in the dominance order. Upon removal of the alpha male, the order was disrupted by the emergence of the third ranking male as the new alpha individual. This rat became highly aggressive and defeated all the other rats in the group, including the female who had previously ranked above him. When these two rats were in turn removed, another male, originally ranking fifth, became highly aggressive and became the alpha male. This suggests that certain individuals within the group may have been suppressed by the dominance of the original alpha male, as evidenced by

the fact that they were seldom seen active and suffered many defeats
in aggressive interactions with the higher ranking females, until
the alpha male was removed.

Carpenter:

I believe that this discussion has brought out some interesting
points which can be readily summarized:

Territoriality and dominance hierarchies often complement one
another, but present the question of which came first, if indeed one
had to be first. Both appear, perhaps in different ways for different species, to be related to space availability and space utilization for both individuals and groups. Differences in interpretation
may arise relative to a strictly ecological (space) approach or a
strictly ethological (defense) approach. It was pointed out that
time is often a very important parameter in this problem. We are
left with the question, "Is Man, as an animal species, regulated by
these phenomena of territoriality and dominance hierarchy in the
same way as other animals?"

Theories of Animal Spacing: the Role of Flight, Fight and Social Distance

Glen McBride

SPACING BEHAVIOR

The field of animal spacing is a difficult one, with little agreement on the interpretation of field data, and no single theoretical framework which is universally accepted. There is no lack of theory, and the contribution of any speaker is influenced by his own views on the whole subject. Because of this, it seems desirable to give a brief outline of my own interpretation of spacing phenomena, incorporating the specific topics at the appropriate points.

The tendency of animals to space relative to conspecifics is an extremely general feature of social behavior. Spacing is the maintenance of areas free of other animals, most commonly, conspecifics. Alternately, animals may be free to enter such areas, but there are restrictions on the behavior they may emit while present. The free area may be fixed in space as some form of territory, or it may be portable, so that animals merely keep others from approaching within a certain distance. The restrictions on entering these spacing areas may apply to all conspecifics, or there may be varying degrees of exclusiveness. Thus a male may exclude only other males, admitting females or young, or both; alternatively there may be entry only by certain females, those with whom he is affiliated.

Aggression is the most common behavior used to control spacing areas. It may be overt, or formalized into mild threats and avoidance. The stimuli releasing aggression are never simply those from conspecifics, but always include a distance component, that is, the neighbor must be within the spacing area. This distance component of aggressive stimuli is so general, that one has little difficulty in arguing that intraspecific aggressiveness evolved to keep conspe-

53

cifics spaced for any of the many functions served by spacing.

Animals normally have responses which prevent aggression by
neighbors, or halt it once it has started. We call such behavior
submission. The most general form is avoidance or flight to the
edge of the controlled space. This may be to the border of a territory or to the limits of a personal area around the individual.
Flight is less appropriate among animals living in groups, and these
species have generally evolved alternative forms of submission, often
involving "out of context" behavior, usually sexual or infantile [9].
Submission is only seen within the distance at which conspecifics
constitute aggressive stimuli. Flight removes subordinates from
these areas, while the other submissive behaviors enable neighbors
to remain within these areas without evoking aggressive responses.

SOCIAL SYSTEMS

Spacing is observed within the normal context of animal societies,
and is responsible for the characteristic patterns of these societies.
A minimum definition of an animal society requires that animals are
distributed non-randomly in physical space as a result of their spacing behavior to conspecifics [10]. There are many spacing patterns
in animal societies, but all appear to be variations on four main
themes, and these can now be discussed briefly.

Spacing Patterns

In any season, most animals restrict their activities to some
fixed area (or areas) of land. Some use aggressive behavior to exclude others from the whole area, with the borders marked to communicate to potential trespassers; this is the fixed defended territorial
system. Other animals defend the area around a nest, with the intensity of defense diminishing with distance from the nest, to give an
overlapping territorial system. Here the neighbors show what Allee
called peck dominance when they meet [1]; dominance then depends upon
where the encounter takes place relative to the two neighboring nests
or territorial centers [2,16]. It seems that the essential feature
of any of the territorial systems is that the stimuli which release
aggressive behavior of the territorial animal are not simply those
from its conspecific, but include the position of both animals on
fixed space.

Other species attach to fixed areas of land but do not defend
it. They remain solitary (or as separate groups) by preventing
others using the same area from approaching within a certain distance
in any direction; that is, they maintain a personal sphere. This is
the home range system, where an undefended range is used, but only
the portable personal sphere is defended against intrusion. In behavioral terms, the stimuli releasing aggressive behavior are the approaching animal and its distance.

The third pattern of spacing is found in animals living in groups, the gregarious species. Spacing is still present within the group, with individuals maintaining personal fields and avoiding entering the fields of neighbors. (The personal field was originally called a social force field [9]). These fields do not have an equal radius in each direction as do the personal spheres, but are greater directly in front of the face. This was demonstrated in a flock of domestic hens, where most of the birds' movements were concerned with avoiding the personal fields of dominant neighbors [13].

To simplify terminology, personal area is used to refer to either personal spheres or fields. Personal spheres refer to the area around solitary individuals or isolated affiliated groups on home ranges. The personal distance refers to the distance from an animal to the limit of its field or sphere.

Organization of Societies in Time

Animals do different things at different times. Each of these periods of activity is functional within the species, so that we may say that animals divide social labor in time. To make these changes in activities, animals generally change the organization of their societies, for each form or organization evolved separately as a setting for the particular functional activity. Naturally, any organization at the social level arises from organized behavior at the individual level. One important component of the societal organizations of animals is the spatial architecture, with the individuals varying their spacing behavior in each. We cannot equate spatial with functional organizations, but we can hardly doubt that the spatial structures evolved as a functional setting for the particular activities. There are two main types of social organization in time, the social phase and subphase.

Social phases are major divisions of societies, involving fundamental reorganizations of behavior in animals for long periods of time, certainly longer than a few days and usually seasonal. There is usually a social phase for the breeding season and one for the non-breeding season. There may also be a migratory phase separating these. Animals commonly take up territories in the breeding season, perhaps only for nesting, but sometimes for all of their activities. The same species may then reorganize into groups for the rest of the year. If there is any generalization possible, it is that animals, particularly males, tend to become more aggressive when breeding. This also means that spacing tends to be strongly enforced during the breeding phase.

Within these social phases, animals still order their behavior diurnally. This is seen in both solitary and gregarious species, but, in the latter, there is synchronization of behavior into a series of social subphases. Each activity of the group is associated with a

different structure in space; the common subphases are movement,
sleep, resting, body care, alarm and feeding. Social subphases are
the basic unit of social organization for gregarious animals, and
whenever we talk about spatial structure, we specify a time, and thus
a subphase.

Organization of the Behavior of Animals

Organization of animals at the social level depends upon organization of the behavior of individuals. In particular, the spatial
structure of societies depends upon the organization of spacing behavior among conspecifics. If we examine the behavior of animals, we
see a hierarchical organization at a number of levels, of which three
concern us here, since they profoundly affect spacing between individuals. These levels are caste, role, and interaction.

Caste is the major organic organization of behavior, maintained
by long term endocrine secretions. There are three types of caste,
each representing a functional organization of the behavior of individuals, and a division of social labor within the society. The three
types of caste are age, sex, and seasonal.

Animals pass through a series of reasonably discrete stages, or
castes, as they grow and mature. The behavior of animals is organized
in each to adapt them for their way of life at that particular age.
There are generally also morphological changes accompanying and marking caste changes; for example, young primates change color as they
pass from infants to juveniles, and birds undergo a series of feather
molts.

Sex is a basic organic division of reproductive labor, but it is
usually much more than this. The social behavior and morphology of
most vertebrate species is differently organized in males and females.
When this occurs, the sexes are different social castes. When the social labor of the sexes is divided equally, and the behavior repertoire is the same, then sex is not the basis for caste differentiation. Here sex is only organized as an interaction. The unequal but
complementary division of labor is more common, with each sex organized for a different way of life, as sex castes. This difference in
behavior affects all types of social behavior; very little is in any
way directly concerned with mating. Thus the term "sex hormones" is
inappropriate, for these hormones are social organizers, with sex
only a small part of their effects.

The third type of caste is seasonal and concerns the adult.
The adult males and females change caste to bring about the changed
societal organization of the seasonal phases. Thus the sexes may be
separate castes in the breeding phase, yet may reorganize into a
single caste in the non-breeding phase. The seasonal castes are often
different in morphology as well as in behavior.

It can be seen that the term caste is used here in the sense of
an organic division of labor between individuals, as it is used in
the social insects. It is differently used by sociologists and anthropologists.

We can hardly consider the spacing behavior of animals without
reference to castes. The spacing between individuals of each caste
is usually different, as it is between members of different combinations of castes. Because of this it is usually possible to use spacing as a minimum objective definition of caste.

The spacing behavior of gregarious animals is constant within
each social subphase, changing with subphases. Thus groups may
spread out while feeding, or aggregate in different ways for alarm,
resting, or when moving. The behavior of individuals is organized
differently in each subphase, both in spacing and in the repertoire
of interactions available to members of each caste. The term role
is used to describe this organization of behavior, with subphases
changing as a result of role changes. There is a limitation on the
range of interactions in each role; thus mating and agonistic behavior are not seen in the movement or alarm subphases of many species.

The roles of animals are determined mainly by caste and to some
extent, social rank. The alpha animal of each caste may have a special role in each subphase. A dominance hierarchy is not simply a
set of dominance-subordinate relationships, (though it may be little
more than this in small confined groups). Particularly in the alpha
rank, dominance contributes only a small part of the various roles,
in which it may be compounded with such behavior as leadership, sen-
try duties, initiation of subphase change, group defense and territory maintenance, in an organized system of roles.

The next level of individual organization is the interaction.
Interactions are programmed sequences of responses which are shorter
than the subphases in which they occur. Interactions are initiated
by alerting responses as individuals move into each others' personal
areas [11]. Agonistic interactions are concerned with expelling the
opponent from this area or forcing him to submit; in either case a
dominance-subordinate relationship is established, thereafter expressed spatially. Other types of interactions involve conciliatory
or appeasement behavior, enabling animals to remain without each
other's personal areas, examples are affiliative behavior in prebond
or precopulatory courtship, or bond servicing by allogrooming, allopreening or allofeeding. Interactions between animals serve a wide
range of functions, but they all have a spatial structure, including
orientation.

The important point is that behavior is always organized into
units at various levels, and it is these units which provide the organization of animal societies. The units here are caste, role and

interaction; though smaller units may also be described. Each of
these units specifies sets of behavior at lower levels of organization and imposes restrictions on other types of behavior. Thus
caste specifies sets of roles available to gregarious animals, while
roles specify sets of spacing behavior and repertoires and interactions. It seems important to identify units into which behavior is
organized, for one often sees such terms as sexual, aggressive behavior, or innate and learned behavior. In these cases, what is described are rather heterogeneous categories of well organized interactions, or highly confounded coding systems. I can find no unit of
behavior called aggressive or instinctive, yet one can see many types
of interactions. Some of these may be aggressive, but include sub-
routines "borrowed" from feeding, nest building or sexual interactions. Yet each component is appropriate and a regular part of the
aggressive interaction.

Group Structure

     The concept is spatial. It states that the distance between
flockmates is less than that between members of different groups.
Groups are aggregates of two or more animals. With some exceptions,
groups are not simple congregations of anonymous animals, but are
formed and maintained actively by affiliative behavior. The important
exception is the shoal system of many fishes. The affiliated group
may be closed to varying degrees. The relationship between animals
within a closed group is called a bond. The stimuli which identify
group members may be a group or hive scent, or there may be individual recognition.

     Members of affiliated groups have two sets of relationships with
conspecifics of each caste, one with flockmates and the other with
strangers. Personal fields are maintained within the group, while
there is a large group personal sphere maintained against intrusion
by strangers. Thus the group is a unit of lowered aggressiveness;
other conspecifics are normally attacked should they enter this
sphere. In this way groups remain discrete and maintain exclusiveness of membership.

     Membership of a group is further ensured by the observance of
a social distance, defined by Hediger as the maximum distance an animal will move away from the group [6]. Gregarious animals normally
move in a living space between the personal fields of neighbors and
the social distance. Basically, it is the observance of these two
distances which gives a group its characteristic spatial architecture
in any subphase.

     The individual distance, as defined by Hediger [5], appears to
be one particular form of the personal distance, measured during the
resting subphase when it is a constant. Hediger divided animals into
contact and distance species, depending upon whether or not they ob-

served individual distance. However, the difference appears to depend upon the shape of the personal field. If the field extends to the side as well as to the front of the animal, then an individual distance is seen when the animals are resting. But, when the personal field is only at the front of the face, then neighbors may come into contact when resting. Yet, they still do not rest in contact in the face to face orientation; that is, they still maintain the personal field in front of the face.

It is in groups that we see the most complex organization of spacing behavior. Firstly, there is a separation from other groups. Within the group, each subphase has a characteristic set of personal and social distances for animals of each caste, in their relationships with others of the same caste, and also with neighbors of each other's caste in the group. The result is a separate array of spacing distances in each subphase.

In small groups affiliated on the basis of individual recognition, two additional types of spacing behavior may be found. In a flock of 15 hens, the alpha bird tended to remain in the center of the flock, with decreasing rank associated with increasing distance from the center. Along with this structure, each bird maintained a characteristic average distance from each other bird in the flock. In a large flock of hens, each bird moved over a limited area of the pen, so that it only came into contact with recognized flockmates with which it had well-established dominance relationships [12]. Within such complex spacing structures, each bird moves so as to avoid entering the personal fields of dominant neighbors [13].

This relationship between dominance and spacing appears to be a general one. An individual territory is a hierarchy of one with the owner dominant over all others entering the territory, but subordinate when it moves off this space. Home ranging animals are dominant over a personal sphere, though there may be a fixed hierarchy among animals moving over the same area. No one appears to have observed how home ranging animals behave off their ranges. Within affiliated groups, the priority in the control of personal fields is determined by rank in the hierarchy.

We do not know whether the home range system is open or closed to entry by outsiders. Young cats appear to be attacked as they reach sexual maturity, entering the adult home range system only after repeated fights [7]. This suggests that the home range pattern can be a system of recognized neighbors, closed to entry by strangers.

THEORETICAL CONSIDERATIONS

So far, I have talked as if all the spacing behavior of animals were concerned with repulsive social forces between animals, in the maintenance of personal areas and territories against neighbors.

There are, however, important social forces tending to bring conspecifics together.

Schneirla has presented a simple general theory of animal spacing [15]. He postulated two spacing vectors, A and W, the tendency to approach and withdraw respectively. (He used these terms to avoid the implications of attract and repel, though it is difficult to see the importance of the distinction).

Schneirla presented a vector model, with the A vector increasing with increasing distance between neighbors, while the W vector decreases. Animals tend to space at the distance at which the magnitude of the two vectors is equal. As animals move from this equilibrium point, one vector or the other becomes dominant, thus tending to move the animals back to the equilibrium spacing. Schneirla suggested that this model is most suitable to describe the behavior of extremely simple animals.

There seems to be little ground for quarrel with the concept of two vectors to describe the spacing behavior of animals; but Schneirla's simple model fails to describe the range of spacing behavior described above. Further, we have reasonable descriptions of the operation of the W vector, especially the use of intraspecific aggressiveness in its maintenance, but our knowledge of the A vector is much more sketchy.

The clearest manifestation of the A vector is in the operation of the social distance. The concept of social distance merely states that the A vector increases rapidly beyond this distance. Yet there is a broad neutral area, the living space, between the personal and social distance, rather than an equilibrium point. Within the personal distance, the W vector increases rapidly.

Fraser Darling suggested that the territories of solitary species were also aggregates [4], implying an A vector between neighbors. Leyhausen reached a similar conclusion in his discussion of the subject [7]. It seems necessary to postulate an A vector here, but good evidence is needed.

The A vector seems to be most prominent in aggregates, particularly in affiliated groups where it is clearly organized around group or individual stimuli. The affiliative process has never been studied systematically, but appears to have components actively reducing the W vector and increasing the A vector. Affiliation does not seem to be a passive association as it is in a shoal of fishes, but the group is maintained actively by a series of bond-servicing interactions fostering A responses.

The W vector decreases during group formation by the formalization of aggressive responses into a dominance hierarchy. Appropriate

spacing is learned, and individuals habituate to each others' presence at close distance within the group. There is also coordination of activities in the subphase system, and, in large groups, individuals may actively avoid meeting strangers [12]. Yet, even the
large affiliated group is closed, since every individual forms part
of an interlocking network of affiliations, though it may be treated
as a stranger if it moves to another part of the group.

Of more importance is the active development of the A vector in
a number of interactions. Affiliative interactions may be directly
and obviously reinforcing, as by allofeeding or allogrooming, while
sexual behavior is used in non-reproductive situations in a number
of species, including our own. Play is a common reinforcing interaction among young animals, as are most allelomimetic and contact behaviors, though their reinforcing effects are less obvious. Gregarious information becomes communication when discriminated by neighbors,
who then respond by appropriate movements which bring the spatial
structure of the group into equilibrium. Minimum spacing responses
are evoked when all animals are in living space, but the communicative
responses become alerted as animals approach personal or social distances. The regulatory effects of such behavior are thus maximum at
these two extremes. This is no unitary stimuli model, but a complex
system regulated by automatic behavioral feedback. There is no equilibrium point, but a living space.

This regulatory model is a minimum for gregarious animals. The
pattern becomes more complex when the spacing pattern must include
neighbors of different castes and social rank. Thus there is not
only discrimination of the regulatory stimuli, but also discrimination
of species, caste and individual stimuli of the regulating neighbors.

Behavior involves the discrimination of stimuli from a continuous stream of sensory input, the attachment of responses to these
stimuli, and the shaping of these responses into functional behavior,
appropriate to the social system. This entire process may be genetic
or learned, or the discrimination of conspecific's stimuli may be imprinted. These are not discrete categories, for the evolutionary process is "concerned" only that animals acquire the behavior necessary
to create and maintain their societies. The behavior may be genetically coded by natural selection, or the society may be so organized that
appropriate and inappropriate behavior are positively and negatively
reinforced. More commonly, both coding systems operate together. For
example, piglets move away from their dam and huddle together when she
first stands. The behavior is not completely determined genetically,
so that piglets may walk back to the sow, who vigorously rejects them,
sometimes throwing them back to the litter group [8]. The social system "teaches" behavior already coded genetically.

Imprinting plays a part in the discrimination of species stimuli
in many animals, though there is generally also some genetic coding.

Young chicks appear to learn much of the spacing behavior of each other's caste in the area, and much of this must be relearned when they change caste with sexual maturity. There must be learning of an individual or a group scent in any affiliated group.

FLIGHT AND FIGHT DISTANCES

Though it is the responses to conspecifics which organize animals into societies, it should not be thought that animals organize their spacing only to conspecifics. In fact, animals space themselves relative to most of the other species they normally encounter. There seems to be little gained but complexity by postulating a separate system of spatial organization; it seems adequate to postulate only a modification of normal spacing behavior.

Spacing distances are naturally greater for potential predators than for neutral species. Where species intermingle and compete for some resource, such as food, it is quite normal to find the same sorts of interspecific spacing patterns as one finds intraspecifically. There may be interspecific territories [14], and interspecific dominance hierarchies are extremely common, for example, when birds congregate around a feeding site. The dominance is expressed in spacing behavior as it is within species, and this is very easy to see in such congregations.

It is hard to determine which species regulates the magnitude of the spacing distances, whether by the aggressive behavior of the dominant species or by the timidity of the subordinate; one might expect both species to contribute. Predators are a special case of dominant species; and there are generally well organized spacing responses in prey species, perhaps inherent, but partly learned from the behavior of parents and conspecifics, or from experience. The stimuli of the potential predator are important, so that individuals flee from a hunting animal, but otherwise remain surprisingly close. Predatory animals are, in fact, treated as through they were dominant neighbors with large personal spheres, observed by avoidance or flight.

Man is treated as a potential predator by animals of most species, and spacing behavior to man is well organized.

Submission, if it can be so called, is always flight to the limits of his personal sphere and generally beyond. Hediger first recognized the regularity of this type of behavior, and introduced the term "flight distance" to describe it [5]. He first showed how the flight distance was used in many ways to manipulate the behavior of animals, especially by animal trainers and zoo keepers. Droving or mustering is explicable in terms of flight distances. A man on a horse is able to control a group of sheep or cattle from behind; he accelerates them by moving close to them and slows them by moving back to just within the flight distance. The flight distance has

one property in common with the personal field, it is greater in front
than at the sides. Thus animal groups may be steered by slight
changes in the orientation of the horse. Sheep dog trials provide one
of the finest examples of the control of small flocks of sheep by spacing and orientation movements of a dog.

When animals are cornered, they are unable to observe the flight
distance from an approaching man, and are forced within his normal
sphere. Should the man continue to approach, he eventually passes a
critical distance from the cornered animal. This critical distance is
the interspecific equivalent of the personal distance of the cornered
animal, for the normal rules apply. The animal cannot maintain its
personal area free from intrusions by flight, so it must either submit
or fight. Hediger first recognized the regularity of the observance
of this critical distance and named it the "fight distance" [5]. Again,
he drew attention to its importance in the handling of animals.

There may be a territorial equivalent to the flight distance in
those species which defend a territory around a nest. Because the
nest cannot be moved, the owners behave as though cornered when approached. Many birds and mammals attack a man intruding within a critical distance from the nest, and cease the attack when the intruder
passes once more beyond the critical, or fight distance.

Territories and personal spheres are different manifestations of
normal spacing behavior, differing in their use of fixed space. Aggressive responses are used in both to keep out intruders. Because
of this, it is not surprising to find that each has an interspecific
equivalent, the fight distance.

SPACING IN MAN

The maintenance of spacing is as much a feature of human as animal behavior. Man is extremely flexible and variable in his behavior,
and has incorporated almost every type of spacing into his societies.
Man differs from other species in not having a single form of society,
but has produced a wide range of cultures. One can observe many types
of spacing behavior in each of these cultures. It is of interest that
each human acquires a full knowledge of the spacing rules of his culture, yet most of these appear to be learned without the use of man's
unique gift of speech. We all know how closely we can approach our
neighbors, strangers or acquaintenances, of any caste and from any direction. Yet, in English, we have not yet developed a specific vocabulary to discuss this universal feature of our behavior.

Man's greatest specialization in spacing behavior is seen in his
ability to form groups at will, for any of his specialized functional
activities. Other gregarious species live in the one group and reorganize into different subphases for each activity; the basic set of
affiliations remains constant. Man also uses this technique in many

of his groups, but characteristically forms new groups for each specialized activity. These groups often assemble only for one or two
subphases. People then move physically between groups to change activities. The mass movements between work and family groups twice
a day is a spectacular example of this behavior. Other species tend
to specialize organically by castes, while man is able to specialize
into groups within each caste. Naturally we still use caste as the
basis for much functional specialization, especially the sex castes,
even when the sex differences are irrelevant for the job!

Man usually lives in a colonial nesting system, with homes on
territories. His "harvesting" activities are carried out in groups
meeting daily in special activity sites. Full time association in
single groups is rare. Other family territories include both nesting
and harvesting space, as farms. At a higher level, whole societies
usually occupy and defend marked group territories, as nations.

Man builds shelters for his families (and other groups). In essence the shelters require only four walls and a roof, but this is
normally considered inadequate. Instead, considerable resources are
often expended to create a highly inefficient spacing system which
suits man's nature. Each person uses the one bed, preferably in a
separate room which is used only for sleeping and some toilet activities. This room is treated as highly personal territory with restrictions on entry. Each other room is specialized for certain activities, a kitchen, bathroom, laundry, dining and living room. It
would be a simple technical task to incorporate all of the family activities in a single room, but the demand for such designs is totally
absent. Our home plans are certainly wasteful but this is never
questioned! Aggressive chaos can easily be generated by sitting in
the "wrong" chair at a meal, or by sleeping in the "wrong" bed.

Man's facility in forming groups depends upon a wide range of
affiliative interactions, most depending on the use of speech. Yet
in prebond courtship, the offering of gifts or food and allogrooming
are interactions common throughout the animal kingdom. They foster
the A vector in pair formation and are bond-servicing in the maintenance of the bond. Sexual behavior is one of the most powerful
bond-servicing interactions in the human pair bond. This is possible
because the estrus period has been extended by natural selection to
allow sex to serve this function throughout the year. Mating occasionally leads to reproduction; but this is a trivial proportion of
mating activity. Man also mates promiscuously for pleasure at times.
But the major proportion of copulatory activity occurs within socially organized mating bonds. Here it appears to be affiliative, or
bond-servicing, as it is in many other species which form mating
bonds throughout the year, as in the feral chickens, or during the
breeding season, flying foxes for example.

In other groups, affiliations between roles are often specified

by the structure and function of the group. These affiliations are
then developed by the individuals occupying the roles. Man can be
affiliated in many groups, and develop affiliations of a wide range
of intensities, from closed bonds to slight acquaintanceships. The
maintenance of any close relationship requires regular servicing interactions. The absence of such interactions can have strong alerting stimulus properties. We seldom distinguish between role affiliations and interpersonal affiliations, but the friendship bond appears
to emerge only when people are affiliated in more than a single pair
of roles.

Man may also associate with many strangers daily in various congregations, particularly when travelling between groups. Here behavior is available to respect the spacing requirements of neighbors,
with some standard interactions to deal with occasional intrusions
into personal fields; the most common is the apology, a submission
or conciliatory sequence. Failure to observe these integrative behaviors is rude; it contains elements of aggression and evokes similar responses.

Flight and fight distances describe the behavior of animals as
man approaches. Yet it should be clear that we also observe both
flight and fight distances when approached by a potentially dangerous
animal. We even use the territorial type of fight distance when we
attack an obnoxious animal within a certain distance from our home.

The social distance is best seen within the family, where the
young are kept within a specified distance from the mother (or someone occupying the role) by their retrieval when they stray too far.
The social distance increases with the age of the child. Modern communications has allowed us to remain affiliated with groups, though
separated by great distances. Most long distance communication is
taken up by, such regular "location calls," servicing the affiliations.

DISCUSSION

I have described various patterns of animal spacing, very briefly,
and sometimes with more confidence than is really justified. Spacing
behavior is so general and obvious that it has escaped attention, and
very few attempts have been made to study it. Attention has been focused upon a few distinctive features, such as territoriality, where
controversies have developed. It has seldom been recognized that the
dominance hierarchy is largely organized spacing behavior, though several workers have recognized the essential similarity of dominance
and territoriality [e.g., 3,16].

Before concluding, I would like to say a few words on the functions of spacing. It is probable that animals use the ability to
control space as a means of distributing various resources intraspecifically. This distribution is seldom uniform, but resources are

controlled by those able to exclude others from access to them.

When some or all of the resources by animals are available within a restricted area of land, then one of the various forms of territoriality evolves. When resources are distributed over a large area
with concentrations at several points at different times, then the
home range pattern emerges. Access to the resource is controlled at
any time by the defense of the portable personal sphere. Within a
group, dominance is used to exclude neighbors from a personal field
so that resources within the field are denied to subordinates. Space
control is the way animals exert priority of access to food, water,
nest sites, shelter, toilet facilities and sometimes sex. In groups,
the control of space provides a degree of privacy, or freedom from
interference and disturbances; it gives access to the center of the
group and priority in flight distance from intruders. It is always
dominance which distributes these priorities, but the mechanism is
space control. The priorities divide animals into "haves" and "have
nots."

Though the range of spacing behavior is wide, most can be described in terms of variation in four main themes, social phase,
caste, groups and the spatial patterns of all combinations of the
three. These four patterns of organization must provide the basis
for any descriptive taxonomy of animal societies, and also for the
study of social evolution throughout the animal kingdom [10], including man. The important point is that these are all concepts which
can best be described in spatial terms at this stage of our knowledge.
For the study of animal societies has reached the stage reached by
anatomy in the 19th century, when it was possible to describe structure, though the understanding of function was limited, except at a
very general level.

Simple statements on the spatial structure of animal societies
are seldom possible; for example, it is generally an oversimplification to say that this species is territorial or that species has a
dominance hierarchy. This is well illustrated by a study just completed on a population of feral fowl.

The males of this species show a range of spacing behavior in
the breeding season. Alpha males defend fixed territories against
other alpha males, but not against subordinates. There are two types
of semiterritorial males holding partial territories within the territories of alpha males. Other males formed a hierarchy but were
free to move across territorial boundaries on a home range pattern.
The omega cock kept off the territories during the day.

For the remainder of the year, alpha males with their flocks
used overlapping home ranges with fixed dominance between neighbors,
while subordinate males still moved between flocks. The alpha males
controlled the behavior of subordinate males within a personal sphere

with a radius of about six meters, and inhibited agonistic behavior among their flock females within a sphere of a radius of about three meters. Naturally these distances vary with subphase, as does the social distance of the females.

Broody females left the flock in the breeding season to become solitary animals on home ranges (overlapping the males' territories) while they incubated and reared their brood. Their personal spheres had a radius of six meters while feeding, and the fixed dominance was retained on the overlapping home range. The chicks increased their social distance with age from a few centimeters up to 18 meters at six weeks. At this age the chicks first developed personal fields within the brood. Later the social distance diminished to about four meters as the hen increasingly rejected them. She finally drove them off at about 12 weeks of age and returned to the male. The broods remained as isolated groups with a hierarchy, moving over the established home range. Broods maintained isolation by aggressive behavior within a group personal sphere. At about 18 weeks the broods amalgamated into a single flock, then this flock broke up as, first, the males and then the females reached sexual maturity, and moved into the adult system.

This all adds up to a very complex spatial structure, involving the full range of spacing, territories, home ranges and hierarchies; separate systems for castes and phases, and a range of group structures. All this can be readily described in spatial terms, but is not at all easy to understand. Yet, it seems that careful descriptions of structures will be necessary before we can hope to understand social organization.

This Symposium can do much to focus attention on the significance of spacing behavior.

REFERENCES

1. Allee, W.C.: Dominance and hierarchy in societies of vertebrates. In P.P. Grasse, ed., Structure et Physiologie des Societes Animales, Collegues Internationaux, 34. Centre Nationale de la Recherche Scientifique, Paris, 1952.
2. Castoro, P.L. and Guhl, A.M.: Pairing behavior of pigeons related to aggressiveness and territory. Wilson Bull., 70:57-69, 1958.
3. Davis, D.E.: The role of density in aggressive behavior of house mice. Anim. Behav., 6:207-210, 1958.
4. Darling, F.F.: Social behavior and survival. Auk, 183-191, 1952.
5. Hediger, H.: Wild Animals in Captivity. Butterworth, London, 1950.
6. _____: The evolution of territorial behavior. In Washburn, S.L., ed., The Social Life of Early Man. Methuen, London, 1963.

7. Leyhausen, P.: The communal organization of solitary mammals.
        Symp. Zool. Soc. Lond., 14:249-264, 1965.
8. McBride, G.: The teat order and communication in young pigs.
        Anim. Behav., 11:53-56, 1963.
9. _____: A general theory of social organization and beha-
        vior. Univ. of Qld. Vet. Sci. Pap. 1:75-110, 1964.
10. _____: Society evolution. Proc. Ecol. Soc. Aust., 1:1-13,
        1966.
11. _____: On the evolution of human language. Studies in
        Semantics. (in press).
12. _____ and Foenander, F.: Territorial behavior in the do-
        mestic hen. Nature, 194:102, 1962.
13. _____, James, J.W., and Shoffner, R.N.: Social forces de-
        termining spacing and head orientation in domestic hens.
        Nature, 197:1272-1273, 1963.
14. Orians, G.H., and Wilson, M.F.: Interspecific territories in
        birds. Ecology, 45:736-745, 1964.
15. Schneirla, T.C.: Aspects of stimulation and organization in
        approach/withdrawal processes underlying vertebrate be-
        havior development. Advances in the Study of Behavior,
        1:1-74, 1965.
16. Shoemaker, H.H.: Social hierarchies in flocks of canary. Auk,
        56:381-405, 1939.

Inter-Animal Control of Space

John Le Gay Brereton

ABSTRACT. The inter-animal control of space is here illustrated by comparative studies. Related species of parrots which are found from wet to semi-arid and arid habitats are investigated. As the habitat becomes more arid the species become more gregarious. Social complexity however follows a quite different course. It is low in·the wet habitats but rises rapidly to a maximum in the semi-arid habitats, and from there falls gradually as aridity and gregariousness increase.

Gregariousness is measured by flock size and social index. Data for flock size comes from the number seen flying together and feeding together. Social index is the subjective assessment of morphological and behavioural characteristics. The more similar the sex and age groups are, the higher is the index.

Complexity of the social system is assessed by studying the communication system, and the role of definable individuals and groups in the system. For example, the semi-arid adapted species (platycercus eximius) has at least 27 distinct auditory signals, while the arid adapted species (Barnardius barnardi), has 16 and the wet adapted species (P. elegans) has 20. The semi-arid adapted species is composed of a core population of dominant pairs and a secondary population which forms groups within a flock. The groups are arranged in a hierarchy, and the individuals within a group are also arranged in a hierarchy. Species of the wet forests and the arid areas have fewer recognisable social entities.

*This work was aided by a grant from the Australian Research Grant Committee.

**I wish to acknowledge the help of Mr. Robert Pidgeon and Mr. Ernst Madeley in the formulation of this paper.

69

INTRODUCTION

Rather than attempt to review the topic across a wide spectrum
of animal species, I intend to confine myself to a few taxonomically
related forms. First I wish to outline the inter-animal control of
space in the eastern rosella. This is an interspersing species, by
which I mean that it is neither fully territorial nor fully gregarious. Social groups of the population intersperse with each other in
a complicated manner. I wish then to discuss some communication and
other endogenous and exogenous correlates of the population life
cycle of this species. From here I shall consider more closely how
the communication system is related to the regulation of the population life cycle. I wish to infer that the degree of complexity of
the social system is reflected in the degree of complexity of the
communication system. From here the intention is to compare the
auditory communication system of gregarious species of the more arid
areas with that of the interspersing species of savannah woodland.
In this way, social complexity and inter-animal control of space can
be compared for species adapted to habitats of increasing sparsity
and dispersion of food and other essential resources.

INTER-ANIMAL CONTROL OF SPACE IN AN INTERSPERSING SPECIES

The eastern rosella (<u>Platycercus eximius</u>) is a parrot of the
savannah woodland of the highlands of south-eastern Australia. Its
taxonomic affinities have been studied most fully by Watters, and
reference should be made to this work to understand the relationship
of the eastern rosella to other parrots considered in this paper
[16]. The eastern rosella will be referred to here as an interspersing or core-subsidiary species, to distinguish it from territorial and gregarious (flocking) forms.

The eastern rosella is chiefly a grain eating bird; it is thus
easy to trap at most times of the year. However, there are times
when it concentrates on eucalyptus flowers and on young eucalyptus
fruits, and at these times it is difficult to trap. For a detailed
study seven traps were placed in an area of 800 acres. The traps
are used as permanent free feeding stations and individuals and
groups can be watched at these stations. The greater part of the
population is flagged so that most individuals may be recognised.
Of course, individuals may be observed away from the feeding stations. A summary will now be given of the daily life of these birds
in the breeding and non-breeding season as learned from trap-
recapture, and observation of flagged individuals.

During the middle of the day they rest, hidden in the center of
large evergreen eucalyptus trees. Two to four birds will be scattered in one tree, and other trees in an area up to three acres will

also have birds, making a group total of 10 to 20 birds. As the
afternoon moves along, they change from full rest or near full rest
to maintenance mood during which they preen, defecate and care for
the feet and beak. Then they climb to positions from which they
fly out to trees above favoured feeding places. These flights involve one or two birds, rarely more. Others move to trees near the
feeding places, and from here they land up to 20 yards from the
other feeding birds. The group may now be said to have passed from
resting mood through a maintenance mood to a feeding mood. The individuals have moved in a coordinated but varied and widely spaced
manner; I do not regard this as a flock movement.

It has already been suggested that spacing is wide during feeding. Birds do tend to move as pairs and here the individual distance is less than for other groups. Occasionally aggression is
seen under these circumstances. Mild forms of alarm lead to one or
a few individuals raising the head while the body is kept motionless.
An increase in alarm leads to silent flight to a perch hidden by the
foliage of the tree. From here they may return to the same feeding
area, or they may move to a different area. Sudden danger causes
flight accompanied by a pinging call by one or several birds. There
is a tendency to a short flock flight with the birds landing in a
tighter bunch, or they may make a longer flight spreading out and
landing widely spaced and close to a new feeding area.

As the shadows lengthen rapidly, alarm leads to flights towards
the current roosting area. Feeding flocks tend to increase in number. Pairs and groups of slightly larger numbers tend to go off to
trees in the close proximity of the roosting trees where preening
and beak and foot care take place. Incipient roosting takes place,
with up to four individuals in a tree. Aggression and supplanting
is common; individuals and pairs change trees and position in trees,
and there may be much irregular flying accompanied by the pinging
call. There is also much location calling.

Maintenance mood is dominant after the sun disappears from the
feeding place. There is a tendency to assemble in dead trees or on
the dead branches of living trees, at the top, where the sun still
tips the trees. When the sun has sunk, roosting activity and calling is at its maximum. Gradually the group settles down as individuals climb into the fine twigs among leaves, the individuals of some
pairs tending to be almost touching. The group has moved from feeding mood interspersed with alarm mood to maintenance mood and finally
resting mood.

Eastern rosellas show very little activity in the morning until
the sun touches their trees. They then tend to climb to the top of
the tree and to preen there. As the sun spreads to the ground, they

fly in small dispersed groups to a tree near a feeding area. Hence
they move quite silently from resting mood to maintenance to feeding mood. The pattern from here on is like that of the afternoon,
but day resting is usually at a different site from roosting.

Alarm can of course occur at any time and is basically similar
always, but the threshold appears to be highest in rest and to decrease through maintenance to feeding. Drinking occurs during
feeding and maintenance mood, particularly towards the end of the
feeding period.

We may summarise here that this species moves through the day,
and the area familiar to it, via a well marked succession of moods
(Fig.1). Mood is discussed more fully at the end of this section.

FIGURE 1.   A GENERALISED DIAGRAM FOR SUCCESSION IN MOOD

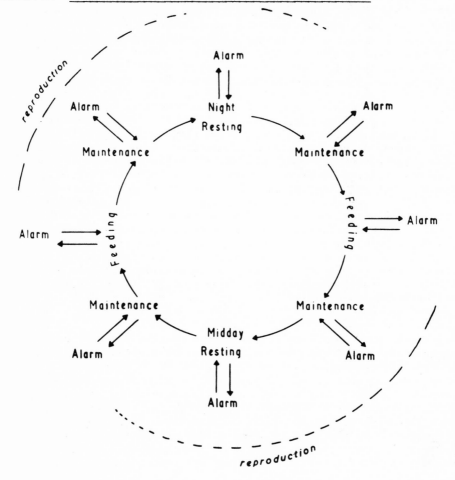

So far no reference has been made to reproductive mood. When spring comes, it fits into the daily pattern in the later part of feeding and the beginning of maintenance. Of course, when incubation and rearing of nestlings develops, the pattern of moods becomes more complex. It can be noted that reproductive mood may occur on certain favourable days in autumn when some reproductive behaviour will be seen. Later in the year it becomes an increasingly common part of the behaviour. As this proceeds, the group and individual relationships change.

There is no space here to present even an outline description of the reproductive behaviour leading to selection of nest holes, cooperative feeding, and copulation. We shall therefore commence with incubation. This is carried out solely by the female. The male either feeds or remains hidden up to 30 yards from the nest. He gives a piping call to tell the female of his presence and to entice her out. When she flies out, he follows, and they usually fly to a feeding ground or a tree near the nest. Here, the male may pass food beak to beak to the female. When the chicks hatch, the female continues to be the only one to enter the nest hole for about three weeks. In the last week of the nesting stage, the male also enters the hole and feeds the chicks.

When the chicks are ready to fly, they may be seen one or two at a time at the entrance to the nest hole. Both the male and the female try to entice them from the hole by calls and short flights. Ultimately one fledgling flies, and immediately the male and female close in on each flank and wheel it in some desired direction. Often the fledgling lands in a sapling, but sometimes it lands on the ground. Then the parents land beside it and guide its walk to a tree, which it then climbs for some distance. It sometimes takes several days to get all the young from the nest hole. This requires very complex coordination by the male and the female, especially when the young are scattered. The male marshalls the fledglings and feeds them, and the female tends the remaining nestlings. Eventually all the young are together and the male and female both can then leave them for short periods. At this time the young give abundant evidence of very close bonds with each other and with their parents.

After about two weeks, the female begins to show signs of resenting the presence of the young. The male may continue to tolerate the juveniles and even to feed them for up to four weeks past this time. During this period of marked aggression by the female to approaches by the juveniles, and to an alternation of care with aggression by the male, the young form some new associations. The nest mates are no longer seen always together, and it is typical to see new groups of four to six or more young, composed of individuals from different nests. As this process proceeds, the juveniles tend to get further from the nest site and the parents,

and they join up with a growing band of juveniles and young adults.
At this time (Figure 2[c]), the eastern rosella may appear to be a
mildly flocking species, and loose groups of up to 75 individuals
have been seen.   During this period, the parents will be in their
original area, moving as coordinated, solitary and rather silent
pairs, while the flocking birds will be noisy and relatively conspicuous, and away from the solitary pairs.

New groups appear to form in these juvenile and young adult
flocks.   A hierarchy in the groups may be detected by watching them
at feeding stations where the spatially concentrated food does not
allow normal individual distance.   Further, a hierarchy of groups
develops so that the mere presence of members of a higher status
group in a tree above a feeding station is enough to cause flight
by a feeding group.   Over and above the highest status group are
the adult pairs.

The formation of groups within the flock gradually corrodes and
destroys the flock.   The groups disperse from the region of the
flock, finding their way back sometimes to the area where they were
hatched (Fig.2[d]).   It is at this time that group status differences
are observed at feeding stations.   The composition of the group
generally includes one or more young adults and a number of juveniles;
it is not entirely stable and changes from time to time.   Within the
groups a detectable arrangement of pairs is seen, though these pair-
ings are not firm and permanent.   Presumably it is at this stage,
months before sexual fighting and nest-hold searching and other
clearcut sexual behaviour begin, that pair bonds slowly form.

It needs to be emphasized here that, while each individual lives
very largely in a circumscribed area and each group and pair has
also ill-defined boundaries, groups are not divided territorially
inside the area.   Individuals, groups, and pairs may be said to
have site attachments and these may change through the year.   Groups
have preferred feeding and other sites which may be high on the preference list of other groups, and only if the two groups happen to
meet together at one of their preferred sites is there any agonistic
behaviour.   This is generally manifested by the quiet departure of
the lower status group, but sometimes it involves threat.   This form
of inter-animal control of space is here called <u>interspersion</u>.

As the winter passes, threat and even fighting develops, and the
incipient pairs of the earlier groups tend to become more distant
from the other members of their group.   Antagonism within the groups
as well as between groups increases, occurring first most notably at
the feeding stations and at roosting, but later being solely over
nesting areas and over nest holes.

A digression on mood is now necessary.   Mood here means that the
physiological state of the animal disposes it to accept certain

classes of stimuli (exogenous or endogenous) rather than others,
and that the response to these stimuli will tend to be or will be
in certain classes rather than others. Endogenous factors, environment and other individuals of the group, affect mood and thus
mood plays an important part in the coordination of individuals.

The mood of individuals affects individual distance. Pidgeon
has shown that the distances between members of a pair and between each parent and a fledged offspring in the galah (Cacatua
roseicapilla) are significantly different and vary with mood [12].
In cage studies of non-breeding galahs the minimum distance apart
is 5.6 inches in resting, 3.0 inches in feeding, and zero in
drinking. The resting and feeding distance is reduced for the
members of a breeding pair and increased between parents and their
fledged offspring in the breeding season (28 and 9 inches respectively). A generally similar pattern of results though several
times greater in magnitude was obtained by Pickett with caged
hooded parrots (Psephotus dissimilis) [11]. These results are consistent with field observations of individual distance and are related also to flock and group size. As the individual distance
goes down for non-breeding activities or moods the numbers in the
flock or group go up.

SOME COMMUNICATION AND OTHER ENDOGENOUS AND EXOGENOUS CORRE-
LATES OF THE POPULATION LIFE CYCLE OF AN INTERSPERSING SPECIES

From observation of flagged birds of known age and from the
capture-recapture data, it can be inferred that the population
has two components: a reproductive and high status core of rather
solitary and sedentary pairs accompanied for about six weeks by
juveniles, and a subsidiary element often spatially separated from
the core. This subsidiary element is at first, more cohesive than
the established adults. It is composed of young adults and immatures. The dynamics of this group are summarized in Figure 2.
During a protracted period in late autumn and early winter, the
flock breaks into loosely bound groups which disperse. Some of
these groups find their way back into the core population. As the
breeding season develops these tend to form pairs and to disperse
out of the core.

In estimating the population size (Figure 3), no attempt has
been made to separate the core from the subsidiary population.
This separation can only be made by observation of known individuals.
It will be seen that the whole population has decreased, which is
attributed to drought conditions resulting in decreased breeding
since 1965. An analysis of survival of immatures and adults shows
no significant variation between drought years and normal, though
there is significant variation for juveniles. This is interpreted
to mean that, when conditions are good for breeding, a prolific
crop of juveniles is produced and most of them disappear from the

FIGURE 2.

THE INFERRED DYNAMICS OF THE EASTERN ROSELLA POPULATION SYSTEM

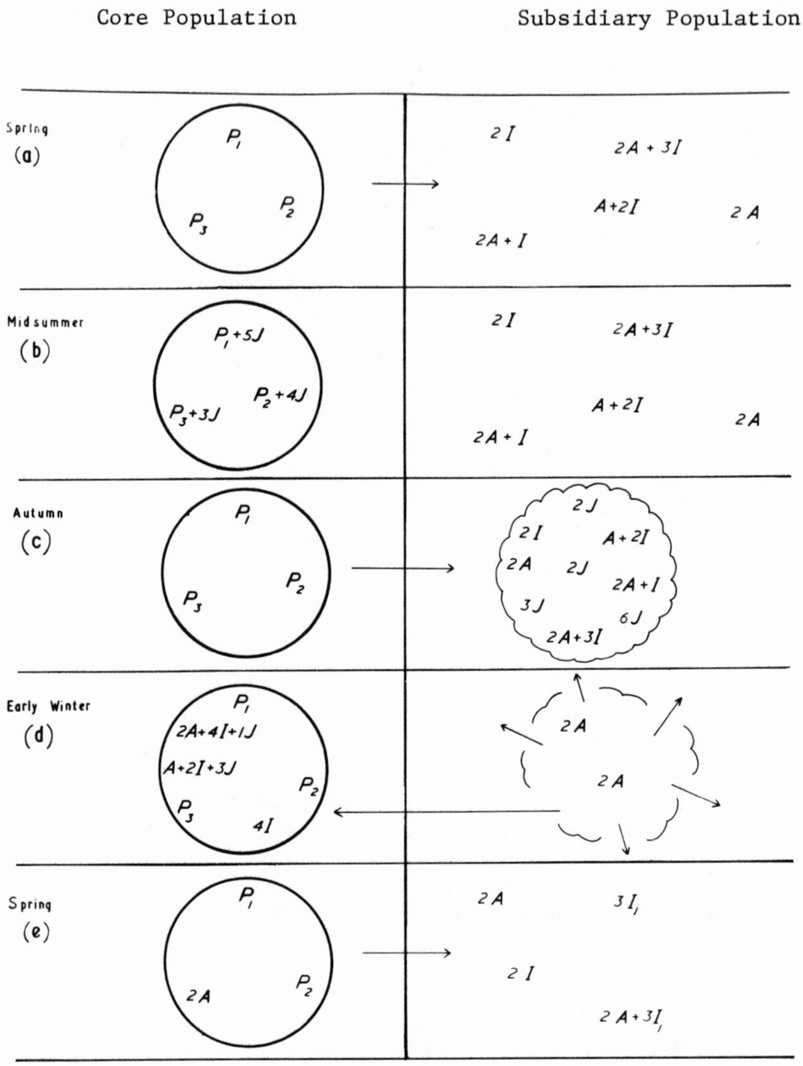

Core Population   Subsidiary Population

Pl, 2,3,- Parental pairs   I- Immatures recently changed
I- Immatures   from Juveniles
J- Juveniles

A- Adults

population, but, if they gain entrance, their survival as immatures
is not demonstrably different from adults.

FIGURE 3.   CORRELATES OF AN EASTERN ROSELLA POPULATION

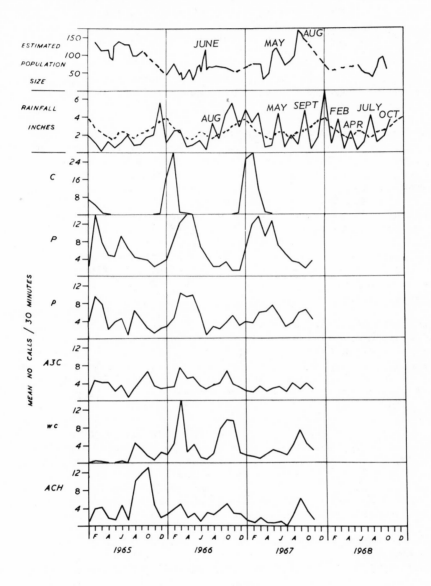

For explanation and abbreviations, see text.

In 1965, there were many juveniles owing to favourable conditions for breeding. The survival of the juveniles over the succeeding four years was significantly less than that of the adults over
the same years (χ^2 = 22.8, n = 3, $P < 0.001$). However, these juveniles did not have a significantly different survival curve from
adults after their first year (χ^2 = 1.01, n= 2, $.7 > P > .5$). In
1964-1965 breeding was poor; there were few juveniles and their survival was not then demonstrably different from adults (χ^2 = 4.34,
n = 3, $.5 > P > .4$).

Some manifestations of the inter-animal control of space, which
occur during the seasonal changes involved in this pattern, may be
briefly considered now.

Flocking in the subsidiary population occurs approximately when
the adults are moulting, and it breaks up about the time the juveniles are moulting. In February and March choying (C), the juvenile
food-begging and cohesion call, is at its maximum occurrence rate
(Fig.3), and at this time immatures are moulting into adult plumage,
and established adults are also moulting. This is shown in Fig.4
by the decrease in immatures and the increase in adults in February.
Gradually choying (C) gives way to pinging (P), and piping (p)
(Fig.3). The P call is a flight alarm - cohesion call, and the p
call is a perch location call; these calls are most common during
the flocking phase of the subsidiary population. The flock breaks
up in May and June, and at this time the juveniles are moulting into
immatures (Fig.4).

Internal changes are also occurring at this time as has been
shown by Hall in his study of seasonal changes in the adrenals and
testes of eastern rosella adult males [8]. The cortical tissue of
the adrenals is active during the reproductive phase and during the
time the juveniles are moving with their parents, but it is at a
low level in the winter when the core is most tolerant of young
adults and immatures.

Having considered how the C, P, and p calls are correlated
with the population life cycle, some attention must now be given
to the other calls shown on Fig.3. Of course, it is impracticable
to consider all 25 calls here because of their low occurrence rate
and close similarity in structure and function to most of the calls
shown. ACH is a strong call given only when perched, and generally
when P is heard in the distance. It seems to function to bring groups
which are flying to perch near the caller. The wc call appears to
be a call given largely by the male to his mate. It is given to
draw the female from the nest log and to investigate possible nesting sites. It had high occurrence rate in 1966 when, after a poor
breeding season in the spring, favourable conditions for breeding
appeared in the autumn. The A3C call is certainly an aggression call
as shown by its context. It is used by the male to rival males and

FIGURE 4.   <u>MOULT PATTERNS IN THE EASTERN ROSELLA</u>

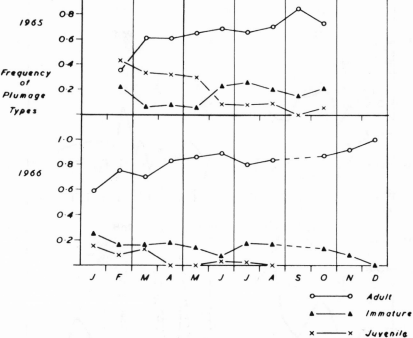

by one group to another. It is initiated normally by the group
leader, but often all members of the group join in to vanquish rivals.
Its pattern is similar to that of wc, but its function is quite different.

While discussing this phase of the population pattern, it is
relevant to mention peer play. This occurs to a slight degree if
it occurs at all. Occasionally juveniles will be seen to touch.
It looks like incipient allopreening or feeding, but sometimes it
appears to be aggression. Peer play may occur in juvenile Australian
magpies (<u>Gymnorhina</u>), in the kookaburra (<u>Dacelo</u> <u>gigas</u>) [10], in the
galah (<u>Cacatua</u> <u>roseicapilla</u>) [12], and also seems to occur in the
Quaker parrot (<u>Myiopsitta</u> <u>monarchus</u>). It is reported of the Quaker
parrot, which is peculiar in building a communal stick nest, that
the young after leaving the nest "all play together, pulling tails
and chasing one another" [14]. On the whole, however, the concept
of peer play does not have the same role in the ethology of birds
that it has in mammals; either because its observation is neglected,
or because it is a rare phenomenon in the class Aves.

FIGURE 5,   ESTIMATED POPULATION SIZE AND THE PROPORTION OF
            UNFLAGGED EASTERN ROSELLAS IN EACH CATCH

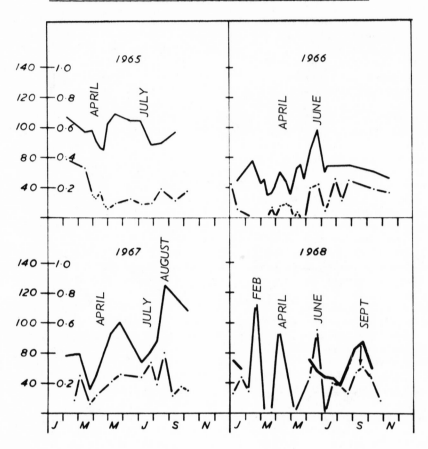

    While trapping is conducted regularly throughout the year, the
catch varies greatly and with a detectable pattern. It is highest
when the flock birds return to the core. Numbers feeding at the
free-feeding trap sites follow the same course. The estimated population does not fluctuate so widely, though formation of the flock
and dispersion before nesting do influence the size of the population (Fig.5). Availability of favoured natural food may be a large
factor in trappability, as the birds are seen to switch from ground
feeding to canopy feeding when some eucalyptus trees are blossoming
and then their fruits are still green. Social factors also can be
seen to influence the capture rate. As aggression increases at the
time of nest selection and nesting, individual distance at the trap
sites increases and the feeding place comes to be dominated by one

pair, or in a non-breeding area, by a dominant immature or young
adult. It seems that the proportion of unflagged birds also increases according to a pattern. In early winter, many juveniles
and new immatures are flagged. This is the result of large numbers
of nestlings which cannot be reached to be flagged in the nest hole,
but also presumably because immatures originating from other cores,
infiltrate the core. At the time of breeding, the proportion of
unflagged birds also rises. It is inferred that these are immatures and paired young adults dispersing from other cores.

The survival of juveniles, immatures, and adults has some relationship to dynamics of the population phase changes. Of 57 flagged
nestlings, none have been followed longer than 60 days. They disappeared at the time of the formation of the flock. In a good breeding year, survival, as shown by disappearance rate, falls markedly
below survival of immatures and of all adults taken irrespective of
their age. It can be concluded that disappearance rate is determined in some measure by the core population. Some juveniles and
immatures do not attempt to return to the hatching area, but move
off in groups and winter in other core populations. Unflagged
individuals occur in groups which return to the core under study;
some of these probably originated in other cores. The core, however, does not accept an unlimited number of newcomers. Groups returning to the core are lead by young adults having higher status.
The demonstration of pressure to enter the core comes from commercial trapping data. Three cases are known of over 300 individuals
being taken from one trap, whereas in the capture-recapture systems
the population is estimated to be about 100 individuals in 800 acres
from five traps. There is little doubt that 300 or more individuals
could be taken from any one of these traps if they were removed from
the area permanently instead of being returned to the area at each
trapping. This tension presumably accounts for the greater disappearance rate of juveniles and immatures when they are numerous in
good years. It also accounts for the stability in composition and
numbers of the winter core, and for the comparative lack of infil-
tration of birds from other areas.

COMMUNICATION SYSTEMS AS A MEASURE OF SOCIAL REGULATION OF SPACE

The communication system of parrots includes auditory, visual,
tactile and perhaps olfactory transmission. The complexity of the
communication system is an expression of the complexity of the population life cycle, or in other words, the social system. It is thus
a very important factor regulating the use of space. It is not
possible to consider all the signal media, so that here the auditory
communication will be stressed.

The aim here is to compare the auditory communication systems of
related parrots which occur along a climate-vegetation gradient. The
gradient here is arranged from the northeastern New South Wales wet

cool tablelands down the western slopes and westwards across the
hotter and more arid western plains. The vegetation goes from forest
to savannah woodland, with changes in species composition and degree of aridity. The species considered are the crimson rosella
(<u>Platycercus elegans</u>), the eastern rosella (<u>Platycercus</u> <u>eximius</u>),
and the buln buln (<u>Barnardius</u> <u>barnardi</u>). These are considered to
be closely related forms, and this opinion is strengthened by the
extensive taxonomic work of Watters on the Psittaciformes in general [16]. The habitats of these forms are: crimson rosella ......
highland grassy forest (rainfall, c.34 inch/year), eastern rosella..
highland woodland savannah (rainfall, c.29 inch/year), buln buln....
lowland woodland savannah (rainfall, c.14 inch/year).

The eastern rosella has been studied in greatest detail, and
thus it is possible to a higher degree to relate the calls to events
in the social system. However, extensive studies have been made of
the calls of the other species, and observations strengthen the view
that the population systems are closely similar. While it is unsatisfactory to attempt a comparison without a complete inventory of
visual, tactile, and auditory signals, an approximation to the total
repertoire may be made from the known visual, tactile, and vocal
behaviour and the coordinated behaviour essential to the population
system. After a detailed study of the auditory signal system, this
method was adopted to estimate the minimum number of messages required for such a system. It is assumed that, given the right mood
and context, a given signal or group of signals will produce a relevant response. Coordinated behaviour by individuals or groups brings
about events. A message is required to initiate an event and to
coordinate behaviour.

With the described population system of the eastern rosella, it
was postulated that the population system would require 18 events
for non-reproductive behaviour and 34 for reproductive behaviour.
Each event required a message or series of messages, and it is estimated that non-reproductive behaviour requires 20 visual and tactile
signals and 18 auditory signals to produce these 18 events. Reproductive behaviour needs 40 visual and tactile signals and 19 auditory ones in order to initiate and control 34 events. Therefore, it
is claimed here that a total of 52 messages made unique by mood and
context is a sufficient minimum to operate this population system,
and that these messages can be formulated and sent by having 67 discrete and unique signals. This is a surprisingly inefficient signal
system when it is remembered that the Morse Code uses only two different signals arranged in groups of not more than four in order to designate the 26 letters of the alphabet. Moreover, it must be remembered
that these 67 signals appear to require that the mood of the recipi-
ent be appropriate and that the context also be known.

The 67 signals may be divided into 42 visual and tactile signals
and 25 auditory signals. Of the 42 visual and tactile signals, 6 are

exclusive to non-reproductive behaviour and 21 are exclusive to reproductive behaviour. Of the 25 auditory signals, six are exclusive to non-reproductive behaviour, and seven are exclusive to reproductive behaviour. This means that 15 visual and tactile signals and 12 auditory signals are common to non-reproductive and reproductive behaviour. This commonness reinforces the point that mood and context are essential concomitants to obtaining a relevant response to a message. The rhesus monkey appears to have a much richer repertoire of signals. Altmann described 123 social behaviours which seemed to be communicative [1]. The fact that many eastern rosella signals are common to messages in non-reproductive and reproductive behaviour suggests that mood is a much greater factor in communication in this animal than it is in the rhesus monkey. Social coordination in the rhesus monkey may be much less dependent on mood, and therefore more plastic and more rapidly adaptive. It would also require more information diversity.

If coordination of mood is of such importance, it is worthwhile to speculate how it is brought about. To what degree is it laid down in the genotype; to what degree is it determined by non-social environmental factors; and to what degree is it the result of social communication?

The predictability of mood succession (resting, maintenance, feeding, maintenance....), regardless of weather and caging, suggests that it is to a large degree a deep-seated internal rhythm. It appears to occur also in all parrots, and indeed prevails in greater or lesser degree in all birds and mammals. On cold or hot, cloudy or bright days, the sequence is the same, and in drought or plenty the pattern remains. Even throughout the breeding season it persists. One sees also when birds are alarmed and fly into trees, that maintenance very frequently occurs before feeding recommences.

However, it is also true that individuals are not tied to an unmodifiable succession of moods. Alarm shows that the sequence can be interrupted and restarted, and that the mood adjusts to environmental events after restarting. Lastly, the sequence appears to be subject to alteration through social factors, as Armstrong has pointed out [2].

The foregoing discussion shows how the communication system is related to the population life cycle. It is estimated that 67 signals are required to bring about 52 events. A surprisingly large proportion of signals are required in the non-reproductive phase, showing that social structure is almost as complex then as it is in the reproductive phase. Of the 67 signals, 37 per cent are auditory ones. It is now necessary to consider the auditory communication system of related parrots in other habitats, with a view to assessing the social complexity of these forms.

The catalogue of discrete recognizable and definable calls of the eastern rosella is 25. The total for the crimson rosella is 21, and for the buln buln 16. Thus the data show that the eastern and crimson rosellas have richer auditory communication systems than the buln buln. It needs to be noted that many of the calls of the eastern rosella are very similar, and there appears to be more differentiation in related calls of the crimson rosella. It is far from clear what subtleties of information transfer are communicated by these variants; much of it may have to do with transferring degrees of mood.

The lesser vocabulary of the buln buln suggests that it has a less complex social system than the eastern and crimson rosella. This inventory was made during four visits of five days each by two observers, given over almost wholly to collecting on tape a full catalogue of the calls and other communication behaviour. Although this work is not complete, there is no reason at present to think that the catalogue is incomplete, nor is there reason to think that the fewer calls are compensated for by visual or tactile signals. Lacking more detailed evidence on the population life cycle of this species, it becomes necessary to examine the social and communication systems of species adapted to still more arid habitats. This is taken up in the next section.

THE USE OF COMMUNICATION SYSTEMS TO COMPARE SOCIAL COMPLEXITY IN INTERSPERSING AND GREGARIOUS SPECIES

In Australian parrots, a trend towards reduction in polymorphism occurs with increasing aridity, and an increase in flock size also occurs. The following three groups of parrots are listed in order of decreasing plumage polymorphism, and this order agrees with one of increasing aridity of habitat and increasing gregariousness:

    (I)   crimson rosella (Platycercus elegans)
           eastern rosella (P. eximius)
           buln buln (Barnardius barnardi)

    (II)   redback parrot (Psephotus haematonotus)
           mulga parrot (P. varius)
           blue bonnet (P. haematogaster)

    (III)   king parrot (Alisterus scapularis)
           crimson wing (Aprosmictus erythropterus)
           superb parrot (Polytelis swainsoni)
           regent parrot (P. anthopeplus)
           rose-throated parrot (P. alexandrae).

While these groups present a good taxonomic sequence, they are not sufficiently common to allow an easy assessment of flock size for various moods. However, the species of Table 1 occur in

semiarid and arid habitats, are common and allow large bodies of
data to be collected. Though they are not of close taxonomic affin-
ity, comparison of flock feeding, flying and perching indicates that
they have much in common, and that all are far more gregarious than
the eastern rosella. Apart from the doubtful case of the quarrion,
they also show a great deal less sexual and age-group variation.

Table 1

Variation in gregarious tendencies in four species of parrot shown
by major differences in group size in perching, feeding and flying

	Perched	Feeding	Flying
Eastern Rosella			
Total seen	391	1145	2010
Number Groups	103	340	706
Av. group size	3.80	5.00	2.84
Largest group known	14	75	22
Galah			
Total seen	887	2830	1569
Number Groups	70	153	304
Mean group size	12.70	18.50	5.16
Largest group known	60	350	500+
Quarrion			
Total seen	171	300	3873
Number Groups	11	2	182
Mean group size	17.10	150.00	21.26
Largest group known	80	150	1000
Budgerigar			
Total seen	2070	1818	5303
Number Groups	7	11	106
Mean group size	295.71	165.27	50.00
Largest group known	1200	1200	1200

The mean group size for the eastern rosella, the galah (Cacatua roseicapilla), the quarrion (Nymphicus hollandicus) and the
budgerigar (Melopsittacus undulatus), are shown in Table 1. The
number of groups observed for perching and feeding in the quarrion
and budgerigar are too few to be reliable, but in all other categories a trend is detectable. Not only do the galah and the quarrion
have low individual distances, as pointed out earlier, but they have

much greater group sizes. Moreover, these groups move as flocks and
not in the dispersed fashion of the eastern rosella. A further demonstration of increase in gregariousness emerges from an alalysis of
frequency of flock flight size. In almost 94% of cases, group flight
size in the eastern rosella is less than five individuals (Table 2).

Table 2

Variation in gregarious tendency in four species of parrot
as shown by frequency of size of flocks in flight

Flight Group Size

	1-5	6-10	11-15	16-20	21
Eastern Rosella	93.7	6.1	8	.2	.2
Galah	33.0	5.9	7.2	5.7	48.2
Quarrion	8.9	10.7	6.4	3.5	70.5
Budgerigar	1.1	4.2	5.2	6.0	83.5

However, with the galah the distribution is noticeably bimodal,
suggesting that there is an optimal size larger than 21 and another
optimum below five. The quarrion and budgerigar both have their
optima over 21 individuals. The data supports the contention that
the arid zone galah, quarrion and budgerigar are gregarious flocking
species in contrast with the very slightly flocking eastern rosella.

Since there is a trend towards gregariousness with increase in
aridity, it might be expected that social complexity would also increase. Social complexity can be assessed through studies of the
communication system as outlined in the previous section. Although
the total communication systems of the eastern rosella, the galah
[12], and the budgerigar [5,6,3], are fairly well known, it is not
possible at this time to assess rigorously the whole communication
system. It is possible, however, to evaluate the auditory system
quite accurately. Results of detailed studies do not suggest that
visual signalling becomes more important in the more arid areas; in
fact, in the preliminary work with the buln buln it appears to be
reduced. For these reasons it is assumed that complexity of vocal
communication is closely related to total communication complexity.

As already stated, the number of auditory signals of the eastern
rosella is 25. Its close relative of the sclerophyll forest, the
crimson rosella, has 21, but the buln buln of the more arid savannah
woodland has only 16 calls. The quarrion has 8 known calls [17],
though more may be discovered as this study was largely conducted

with caged birds. The galah has a total of 11 calls [12], while the
budgerigar has 8 [5,6].

It is a notable feature of the galah as well as the budgerigar
that its vocalizations are not as discrete and definitive as those
of the platycercines. Variation and merging occur, much as is seen
in the vocalizations of the primates. The function of grading in
contrast to stereotypy has been discussed by Marler and Hamilton
[9]. They suggest that the two types may be related to the types of
information conveyed, and that stereotypy may be necessary for error
avoidance when species are sympatric. In the context of this research, grading may be the result of degradation of stereotypy as
the species becomes more gregarious, or it may be the result of imperfect differentiation of the basic parrot vocalization, screeching.
On the other hand, for agonistic communication and for mood transfer,
grading would be advantageous. In the sense that degree of mood can
be transmitted, stereotypy as well as grading is almost equally
effective. The richness of variants of A3C and p calls in the platycercines may be interpreted in this way. Even with grading, the
galah and budgerigar do not appear to have as diverse a repertoire
as the interspersive species. These results then, taken with qualitative observations, suggest that the more gregarious species of the
more arid areas have a less complex social system.

We have compared a non-territorial non-flocking (interspersing)
species with progressively more gregarious forms distributed toward
the more arid areas. It becomes of interest to go toward wetter
areas where we may expect territorial species. No known Australian
parrots fit into this category, though the king parrot (Alisterus
scapularis) of wet sclerophyll forest and rainforest comes closest.
Only four auditory signals are known. The kookaburra (Dacelo gigas),
which is a territorial species in the breeding and non-breeding
season and which has the social complication of having auxiliaries
which aid in incubation and feeding the chicks, has only seven calls
[10]. Grading and variants, however, may raise this number. This
species is said by Parry to "communicate more by vocal signals than
by visual signals."

To summarize, as gregariousness increases from wet to arid habitats, social complexity, as indicated by auditory communication, first
increases and then decreases. It is postulated therefore that a territorial system does not require great social complexity; that an
interspersing system which is intermediate between a territorial one
and a flocking one has greatest complexity, and that as flocking increases, social complexity decreases.

One of the conspicuous observations of the arid zone is the
contrast in numbers of gregarious species in good seasons and bad.
This is no doubt partly a consequence of their capacity to find distant isolated patches rich in resources, but it is also related to

their capacity to increase their numbers rapidly. Hence their populations wax and wane greatly as the conditions change. For this reason, it can be postulated that population size relative to resources
is self-regulated by the territorial and the interspersed system,
and this is progressively lost as gregariousness develops. This
means, that in territorial and interspersing forms population regulation is largely endogenous to the population, while in gregarious
forms it is largely exogenous; i.e., the population fluctuates markedly as a result of marked changes in the non-social environment.
The inter-animal control of space, and it is space which contains
the resources, gradually deteriorates to the point where the environment and not the group is regulating population size.

When territorial species adapt to more widely scattered food,
a number of steps are involved. First, the female starts to look
like the male and to assist in territory defense. In this way a
longer territory boundary can be patrolled. Next, the juveniles
are found to assist in various aspects of reproduction and territory
defense [15,7,13,10]. As the need to expand territory size increases under a regime of increasing aridity and hence more scattered
food, the complexity of the social system increases. Complex forms
of inter-individual and inter-group tolerance develop, and the
system tends more to one of regulation through social hierarchy and
less to geographical exclusiveness. Territory boundaries disappear,
and interspersion with complex social stratification occurs. Social
status is highest for the breeding group. Waxing of hormones of
aggression in the autumn leads to lower status elements being ex-
pelled from the presence of the parents, and they transfer their
parental bond to their peers. This recrudescence of the adult gonad
and various endocrine correlates does not occur in juveniles and
immatures, and for them the genetic and learned social tendencies
increase cohesion to the point of flocking. In this way a core and
a subsidiary population develops.

Within the flock, however, older members under developing aggression move apart, each followed by submissive younger members.
These groups return to the breeding area where wide interspersion
and social stratification permit some coexistence. As the breeding
season advances, increased aggression associated with increased reproductive mood and condensation of groups onto feeding areas close
to nest sites gives rise to many conflicts and to scattered dispersal
from the core. No flocking is possible, because of the heightened
aggression of the now older secondary population.

The social adaptation to even more widely spaced food can lead
to further reduction in aggression and increased tolerance, so that
the parents no longer become aggressive to the juveniles at the end
of the breeding season, but tolerate them or are tolerated by them
in moving to feeding areas. Social categories which became complex
in the interspersed or core-subsidiary phase (mate, offspring, rival

pairs, rival groups, stratification within groups, stratification
between groups) are reduced in selective value. In the core-
subsidiary phase, the immatures needed to look different from adults
as this allowed bonding with other tolerant immatures; the tendency
to social bonding is largely learned from the parents and other
nestlings. Flocks find localized food and water and adults tend to
join them. Acceptance depends on looking like other members of the
flock, and there is a mutual advantage in looking alike. The social
pressure which once regulated the size of the core in the non-
breeding season has now disappeared. The size of the flock can
increase almost without restriction. However, limitations to flock
size do exist. When a flock in flight becomes very large, it breaks
up frequently into smaller groups during manoeuvres. This phenomenon
may lead to the "budding-off" of sub-groups. When resources such as
watering places are extremely localized, limitations to flock size
may occur. There may also be limitations owing to a shortage of
perches for the alarm loop when flocks become very large. These
limitations suggest that accidental budding with geographical
separation may be important in dispersing the population and relieving pressure on essential limited resources. Indeed, this may
be the initial step in the evolution of refined migratory patterns.
If only one dispersal radial is favourable to survival, the breeding
area becomes untenable in winter, and the tendency to return to the
breeding area as seen in the eastern rosella is maintained, it is
easy to see how migration could evolve.

    Permanent budding tends not to occur despite what has been said,
because of the high social tendency of gregarious species. The
sight of another group releases the tendency to join it. This is
commonly observed. Because of dispersed food, however, scattering
of a big flock does occur during the feeding mood; but, as the groups
commence to return to the flock roosting site, amalgamation of small
flocks increases rapidly and flock sizes may become very great. The
transition between feeding and resting mood, called here maintenance
mood, is characterized by seemingly non-adaptive flight not unlike
"Zugunruhe," as well as typical maintenance activities. As a large
flock wheels and turns, budding and rejoining is seen repeatedly.
This manifestation of manoeuvering difficulty and imperfect coordination seems to come about through the size of the flock, and
I do not interpret it as relating the population to its resources.

    Under the regime of climate change, which seems to have oc-
curred in Australia, some species of parrots have adapted to an environment in which food and water is sparse and distantly scattered
with only occasional short periods of abundance. Intermediate forms
living in a more regular climate of dispersed food have become very
complex in their social systems. Increased gregariousness would
endanger these species with overpopulation. Forms living in permanently favourable areas, where food sources are close and abundant,
tend to a territorial system of simple social structure. These more

aggressive forms have the most certain type of population regulation,
or, in other words, the most precise inter-animal control of space.

Lastly, it becomes necessary to discuss briefly colonial nesting. In species with degenerate social systems, coordination of
behaviour is by mood transfer or through environmental and endogenous effects on mood. This dependence on coordinated mood may require
social displays in reproductive mood. Obligate sociality for nesting
occurs in the budgerigar [4,3] and may be necessary during nesting and
courtship in other birds [2]. Suitable nesting sites adjacent to very
rich food sources are required, and tolerance at the feeding site may
carry over to tolerance at the nesting site, so that population regulation is still further reduced.

I have endeavored to show how inter-animal control of space
changes in a series of related organisms ranging from wet forest
through woodland to arid shrub savannah. It is claimed that gregariousness increases along this spectrum of habitats, and that social
complexity gradually falls. As it falls, the capacity of the population to regulate its numbers also falls, so that, ultimately,
population size is controlled by density independent catastrophy.

It seems plausible to suggest that the primates form a similar
array ranging from the gibbons, which are territorial in rainforests,
to the more gregarious chimpanzees in fringing rainforest, to man in
savannah woodland. In this analogy, man is a very gregarious species
with little capacity to regulate his numbers, and having secured
himself very largely from the catastrophes of the environment, he
is now increasing to the point where he over-exploits resources and
pollutes his surroundings.

REFERENCES

1. Altmann, S.A.: Sociobiology of rhesus monkeys. II. Stochas-
        tics of social communication. J. Theor. Biol.,
        8:490-522, 1965.

2. Armstrong, E.A.: Bird Display and Behaviour. Lindsay Drummond
        Ltd., London, 1947.

3. Bergin, T.: Breeding biology of the budgerigar (Melopsittacus
        undulatus Shaw). University of New England, Armidale,
        N.S.W., Australia, Honours Thesis, 1968.

4. Brockway, B.F.: Ethological studies of the budgerigar (Melop-
        sittacus undulatus): non-reproductive behaviour.
        Behaviour 22:193-222, 1964

5. _____: Ethological studies of the budgerigar (Melop-
        sittacus undulatus): reproductive behaviour.
        Behaviour 23:294-324, 1964

6.   Brockway, B.F.:   Social influences on reproductive physiology
     and ethology of budgerigars (Melopsittacus undulatus):
     Anim. Behav., 12:493-501, 1964.

7.   Carrick, R.:   Ecological significance of territory in the
     Australian magpie (Gymnorhina tibicen).   Proceedings
     XIII International Ornithological Congress, 740-
     753, 1963.

8.   Hall, B.K.:   The annual inter-renal tissue cycle within the
     adrenal gland of the eastern rosella (Platycercus
     eximius).   (Aves: Psittaciformes).   In press.

9.   Marler, P. and Hamilton, W.J.:   Mechanisms of Animal Behaviour.
     John Wiley & Sons, New York, 1966.

10. Parry, V.:   Sociality, Territoriality and Breeding Biology of
     the Kookaburra, Dacelo gigas (Boddaert).   Monash
     University, Clayton, Vic., Australia, M. Sc.
     Thesis, 1968.

11. Pickett, P.J.:   Aspects of Social Distance in Some Species of
     Parrots.   University of New England, Armidale, N.S.W.,
     Australia, Honours Thesis, 1967

12. Pidgeon, R.:   Ecology and Behaviour of the Galah (Cacatua
     roseicapilla).   In M.S.

13. Rowly, I.:   The life history of the superb blue wren (Malurus
     cyaneus).   Emu, 64:251-297.

14. Shepherd, P.:   Some notes on breeding the Quaker parrakeet
     (Myiopsitta monarchus).   Avicult. Mag., 74:
     210-211, 1968.

15. Skutch, A.F.:   Helpers among birds.   Condor, 63:198-226, 1961.

16. Watters, P.:   An Integrated Numerical and Orthodox Approach to
     the Taxonomy of the Order Psittaciformes.   University
     of New England, Armidale, N.S.W., Australia,
     Doctoral Thesis, 1968.

17. Zann, R.:   Behavioral Studies of the Quarrion (Numphicus
     hollandicus).   University of New England, Armidale,
     N.S.W., Australia, B.S. Honours Thesis, 1965.

Spacing as Affected by Territorial Behavior, Habitat and Nutrition in Red Grouse (Lagopus l. Scoticus)*

Adam Watson and Robert Moss

INTRODUCTION

This essay reviews studies of how red grouse (<u>Lagopus lagopus</u> <u>scoticus</u>) behave so that they space themselves out, and considers how this social behavior is related to the regulation of populations. Ecologists are becoming increasingly aware that changes in social behavior and population numbers are often associated, and that food shortage, predation, disease and bad weather are often not sufficient to give a full explanation of changes in numbers. Some workers consider that changes in food supply are needed to cause fluctuations in numbers, but others that they are not necessary. One of the difficulties is that food quality in biochemical or nutrient terms, as distinct from mere quantity of material, has been greatly neglected in ecology, despite its well-established importance for the survival, weight, physiology, reproduction and behavior of domestic animals and man. Furthermore, the different views of Andrewartha & Birch (1), Wynne-Edwards (20), Lack (6) and Chitty (3), show that theoretical views on the mechanics of population control are widely different. Anyone surveying the literature will rapidly conclude that remarkably few studies have been done on the inter-relationships between behavior, population, and food or other features in the environment. There are plenty of studies on any one of these aspects, and quite a number on population-food relations, but few on population-behavior relations, very few on food-behavior relations, and hardly any on all three aspects together.

*We thank D. Jenkins and A.N. Lance for helpful comments on the manuscript, and acknowledge the encouragement and support given to our work by Professor V.C. Wynne-Edwards.

92

Our study on red grouse has involved quantifying population density and dispersion, population processes such as mortality survival and breeding, spacing patterns, social status, amount of strife, quantity and quality of food, weather, and physical features in the environment. These descriptive studies led to correlations and predictions, and later to experiments.

GENERAL DESCRIPTION

Red grouse live all year round on open moorland where their diet consists almost entirely of one food plant, the heather (Calluna vulgaris). They are active only in daylight. The total number present can be counted accurately using trained dogs, which also find nests, broods, and about 50% of the carcases of grouse that die. On average, cocks weigh about 650-700 g and hens 550-600 g. Red grouse are a subspecies of the circumpolar willow ptarmigan or willow grouse, the main differences being that they do not turn white in winter and lack white primaries. They inhabit treeless moors in Britain and Ireland, wherever heather, a dwarf shrub seldom reaching a man's knees in height, is common. Grouse in northeast Scotland eat mostly heather shoots in spring, heather shoots and flowers in summer and autumn, and almost entirely heather shoots in winter. They live from sea level up to the arctic-alpine zone, where the closely related rock ptarmigan (Lagopus mutus) replaces them in the stunted vegetation on Scottish mountains. Unlike the arctic willow ptarmigan which move long distances in winter, red grouse are resident in Scotland, and populations move locally only in deep snow. Only 3% of 1275 recoveries of grouse ringed as chicks and later shot were recovered beyond 5 km, the distance that grouse are often driven by beaters during normal shooting. The territorial cocks divide up the suitable habitat between them, and court and pair with hens on the territories. These monogamous pairs feed entirely on the territory in spring, and hens nest in the territories while the cocks keep guard. Territorial behavior virtually disappears after the chicks hatch, and families often move outside the territories. The cocks frequently help to look after the young, which appear fully grown in the field at 12 weeks. Cocks and hens breed in their first year.

POPULATIONS AND NUTRITION

Grouse were counted on study areas which averaged about 100 ha each and which ranged from sea level up to the artic-alpine zone, over rocks and soils of different fertility. The main findings were as follows (7,9):

1) **Breeding success** Year to year variations in breeding (the number of full grown young reared per old bird) depended mainly on changes in chick survival and very little on changes in clutch size. Breeding success, which varied from 0.0 - 3.3 young reared per adult, was correlated with the adults' survival in spring, and with adult survival

in the same summer, but not with variations in summer weather after the chicks hatched. When eggs were taken from the wild and the young were hatched and reared under standard conditions in captivity, chick survival in captivity paralleled that in the wild (9). This showed by experiment that factors before hatching were important for chick survival, and suggested that the quality of the eggs was an important link between the parents' condition and the viability of their chicks.

2) Breeding success was correlated with the condition of the heather at the beginning (r^2 = 22% and end (r^2 = 17%) of the previous winter (10); and was correlated (r^2 = 37%, P<0.1 but with only eight degrees of freedom) with the date when heather showed obvious new growth in spring before egg-laying (8).

3) <u>Annual fluctuations in breeding stocks</u> Changes in the density of the breeding stock from one spring to another – and so changes in the mean size of territories chosen by cocks in autumn (Fig.1,2) were not correlated with changes in heather growth in the intervening summer (10). In other words, the size of territories chosen in autumn was not directly adjusted to the current summer's heather growth.

4) Changes in breeding stocks from one spring to another were correlated with breeding success in the intervening summer on moors over rocks of poor (r^2 = 44%) and intermediate fertility (r^2 = 52%), but not (see 5 below) over base-rich rocks.

5) <u>Differences between areas</u> Average breeding stocks over several years were higher on moors where more of the ground was covered by heather, and particularly by more young heather (10). On moors over fertile, base-rich rocks, breeding stocks were higher than was expected from the amount and age of the heather, but the heather there was richer in phosphorus and certain other nutrients. Breeding success was never poor there (lower than one young reared per old bird), probably because the parent grouse were getting more nutritious food.

These findings have the defect, common to many population studies of being based largely on correlations and changes in percentages. However, two experiments have tested some of the findings mentioned in 1) to 5) above.

1. Nitrogen fertiliser was spread on an area of heather in early summer, and all grouse were shot so that colonisation would not be affected by any traditions from previous residents. Fertilising increased the heather's growth and nutrient content. Grouse colonising in autumn took territories of the same size on experimental and control areas, showing that territory size was not determined by the quantity or quality of food in autumn when territories were chosen. Subsequently, territorial grouse which had been there all winter reared larger broods on the fertilised than on the control areas, showing that breeding success was influenced by nutrition. This was followed next

autumn by smaller territories on the experimental than on the control area. There were two years of better breeding and three of smaller territories.

2. An area of largely uniform old heather was changed by burning many small fires over three years from 1962-65, thus creating a patch-work of heather of different ages. Young heather regenerated in the first summer after burning (i.e., within a few months). Territory size decreased in autumn 1964 and again in autumn 1965, to about half what it had been and what it still was on the control area. This in-crease occurred without the intermediate step of good breeding, and therefore appeared to be different in kind from the mechanism of in-crease in the fertiliser experiment.

Turning now to the research on nutrition, Moss showed that, by agricultural standards, heather is deficient in phosphorus, nitro-gen, sodium and calcium(11). Grouse are well adapted to this poor woody food; they have long caeca and can digest lignin and cellulose. There is a great excess of potential food, and grouse usually eat only 1-5% of the total amount of annual growth (the part of the plant usu-ally eaten) that is available. The total amount of annual growth of heather was not associated with grouse numbers; indeed one area with a low grouse stock had the highest heather production (12). In terms of energy flow, the secondary production of grouse bore no relation to primary production.

There is no shortage of energy in the food, and most of the heather is adequate for maintenance. This explains why territorial grouse do not starve or suffer much mortality during periods of heavy snow lasting for months, when nearly all the heather is buried and un-available. However grouse are selective, especially for heather high in phosphorus and/or nitrogen and are more selective where the heather generally available is less nutritious than usual. Nevertheless, no matter how much an excess of green edible heather is present, it may often be inadequate in nutrients or food "quality," for the birds to lay eggs of high quality likely to produce viable chicks that survive well.

AIMS AND METHODS OF BEHAVIOR RESEARCH

The central aims of the work on social behavior are to understand the mechanisms controlling (a) the size and timing of seasonal de-creases over winter and so the density of breeding stocks, (b) annual fluctuations, and (c) differences in populations between areas.

A Land Rover was used as a mobile hide to cruise around study areas of up to 50 ha, and to survey the open habitat from good vantage points. Grouse paid little attention to the car, and could usually be watched behaving naturally at 50 m or less. On these areas every grouse could be seen and counted, and most were marked with numbered

plastic tabs that were easily read at 50-100 m. Their survival could
therefore be followed accurately, and about half of those that disappeared were later recovered dead. Over 1500 have been tabbed individually on these areas, and about 13500 were ringed as chicks by us
and during a cooperative scheme elsewhere in Scotland.

TERRITORIAL BEHAVIOR

Certain cocks were consistently found on the same small parts of
the moor, often standing on the same stone or mound in places where
they had their territories. From these lookouts, they launched out
on frequent song flights, rising 5-10 m high to give a cackling call
easily heard at 1 km. Neighboring cocks usually responded and often
two neighbors met to parade in threatening postures described as
"walking in line" (18), 0.5-1 m apart along their common boundary.
Occasionally up to five cocks met, "walking in line" into a common
corner. Sometimes they fought, or showed brief agonistic encounters
involving displacement of one bird by another. By plotting these
"walking in line" encounters on a vegetation map, boundaries could be
drawn of each cock's plot of ground or territory (Fig.1), which it
defended against its neighbors. On this plot it was dominant over all
other cocks, which were evicted if noticed. Some hens were consistently paired with territorial cocks, and although they did not defend
any boundaries, they often attacked and drove away any strange hens
that came into the territory. However the most interesting early discovery was that many grouse of both sexes had no territories and did
not pair up or show courtship, thus forming a distinct lower social
class. These often went on to the territories, but were usually
driven out by the territorial birds when noticed.

The amount of hostility or strife was measured by counting the
frequency of agonistic encounters and each individual's aggression
by scoring separately the frequency and the results of its encounters
with other known birds. Measuring the result was easy with encounters
involving displacement of one bird by another, or involving a fight.
"Walking in line" encounters were more evenly balanced, and were
basically "draw situations" where neither bird was at a complete advantage. Both showed postures and calls varying from escape to attack,
and the same bird often changed from escape to attack from one second
to another. The outcome could sometimes be predicted by seeing which
bird gave a higher frequency of attack calls or postures relative to
those of escape. The result was occasionally that the other bird
withdrew slightly on its side of the line, but this was seldom followed
by further incursion by the "winner." Fuller details about these
postures and calls were given earlier (18).

SEASONAL CHANGES IN BEHAVIOR, SOCIAL CLASS AND POPULATION

In summer, cock and hen looked after their young in a closely-
knit family party. In August, the old cocks resumed territorial

FIGURE 1.   TERRITORIES OF RED GROUSE

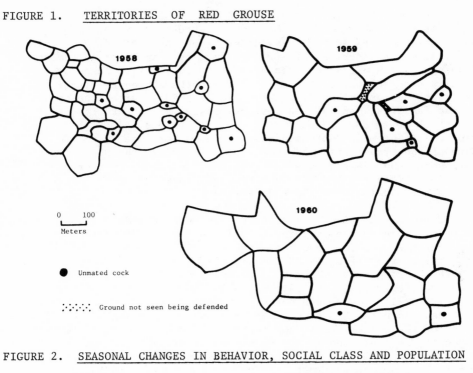

FIGURE 2.   SEASONAL CHANGES IN BEHAVIOR, SOCIAL CLASS AND POPULATION

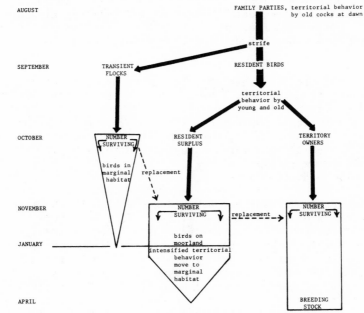

behavior briefly after dawn (Fig.2), rejoining their families later
in the morning. Subsequently, the families broke up, usually in September, but sometimes as early as August or as late as October. This
change followed an increase of strife within the family group, among
both young and old birds, and was not due to territorial behavior.
It usually occurred before the first young cocks showed territorial
behavior, though occasionally the two did coincide. After the break-
up of the families, many of the less aggressive birds gathered in
flocks which moved about locally ("transient" birds). The resident
population on the moor decreased sharply in number, due to the departure of the transients which now lived mostly off the moor, in
fields, scrub and other places which were not defended by territorial
cocks. They often visited the moor to feed, especially in late afternoon when territories were least defended.

In October, the first young cocks – now with gonads as large as
those of old cocks – challenged old cocks on their territories, and
some young hens displaced old hens that were already paired. There
was a complete reshuffle in the number, shape and size of territories,
and in the pairing attachments of cock and hen. Many young birds
failed to get territories or pair up, and some old birds were evicted
from their territories though not necessarily from the moor. This
showed that old birds had no obvious advantage over young birds. For
the rest of the winter these "non-territorial residents" lived mainly
on the moor, but were submissive to the territorial birds and were
often chased by them out of the territories on fine mornings, when
territorial behaviour was most vigorous. From October to January,
there were therefore three social classes:- (1) territorial cocks and
hens, (2) non-territorial residents, and (3) the non-territorial transients whose social class had usually been determined earlier, in
September.

The transient grouse (Class 3) suffered heavy mortality, and
hardly any were left by January. Many were killed by predators and
some by striking wires; others simply died and were found in poor
condition, with or without parasite infestation. Class 2 grouse also
suffered fairly heavy mortality, but very few territorial birds died.
These changes in social behavior and population occurred irrespective
of shooting, which in any case generally took only a small proportion
of the surplus crop available.

There was a social order in each class. The very few class 1
grouse that died or disappeared over winter (about 10%) were usually
replaced (Fig.2) by the most aggressive Class 2 grouse, and some
Class 2 birds that died were replaced by Class 3 birds. From October
to January, Class 2 birds were free to feed on the moor for most of
the day. Usually they were chased out by territory owners only on
fine mornings, and on windy, snowy or heavily-overcast mornings they
were again free to feed on the moor, usually with very little interruption. During fine calm weather, usually in January or February,

there was a sudden change and territorial behavior went on all day. Following this increase in territorial behavior, Class 2 grouse were now forced off the moor to marginal habitats on scrub and fields where they were seldom attacked by territory owners. The resident population on the moor suddenly decreased due to the departure of the Class 2 birds. Not more than 1% of the evicted Class 2 birds survived the summer. By contrast, about 90% of the territorial grouse present in spring were alive next August, and only 20% of territorial birds died over the winter and summer together. Territorial grouse were almost immune to predation, and only 1% of territorial cocks were found killed by predators.

Thus the spring breeding stock was determined by an annual contest for territory six to seven months earlier. Accurate predictions were made in October-November of the size of the spring stock and fairly accurate predictions even of the fate of each individual bird. Any extra birds in November died before the spring, no matter how many were present. Although reductions from October to April were known to be due to mortality and not to migration to other moors, this mortality came only after changes in social behavior formed the social classes and made birds in certain classes much more vulnerable. By contrast, territory owners and their full-grown young suffered almost no mortality in late summer and early autumn, before the change in behavior.

At the next annual contest for ground, some territorial birds kept their territories for a second season but many were evicted. The survival of these evicted birds now became as poor as that of Class 2 or Class 3 birds which had never got a territory in the first place (17). The annual mortality rate of all classes of red grouse combined was about 65% and few birds bred twice. The short life was partly due to frequent evictions of established birds. Furthermore, any grouse that gave up their territories in winter survived very poorly thereafter, and in some cases died within a week. Such birds rapidly lost condition and fed very little, even though - as also occurred in autumn - they were free to feed anywhere in the afternoons, and even though food in the shape of heather, berries, grass seeds and oats was super-abundant. These examples again show the importance of social status for survival.

The above conclusions were tested by 13 experiments in which part or all of the population was removed from certain areas of moor up to 40 ha at a time, involving a total of 128 grouse (19). The hypothesis derived from the descriptive studies was that removed birds would be replaced by non-territorial birds. If this hypothesis were incorrect, the outcome of the experiments would have been that no replacement would occur. In fact new birds readily took territories on these vacant areas, and the population next spring was usually about the same as before shooting. Neighboring territory owners sometimes deserted their territories to occupy vacant ground, but most colonising birds had not previously had territories. The latter subsequently

survived the winter and summer well, and bred successfully. Again,
while young cocks never took territories before late September in
unshot populations, young cocks only 12 weeks old took territories
at the beginning of August if old birds were removed. Almost no
changes in replacement or ownership occurred on unshot control areas.

These results provide experimental evidence, supporting the conclusions from the descriptive studies, that (a) the size of breeding
stocks was limited by the presence of territorial birds, and (b)
that lower-class birds were capable of showing territorial behavior
and of breeding, if the inhibition due to the presence of established
upper-class birds was removed. It was clear that social dominance
affected land tenancy and inhibited others from settling.

DIFFERENCES BETWEEN INDIVIDUALS

In any one year, cocks with the biggest territories had two hens
but most had only one. Cocks with very small territories had no hens
but most of them survived the summer and so had another chance at the
annual contest for territory in the following year when some of them
did obtain a hen and breed. (Fig.2) The most aggressive cocks (as
measured by scoring the frequency of agonistic encounters together
with the result of encounters with their territorial neighbors) had
the largest territories (18); and the least aggressive territory
owners were unmated. The few territory owners that died or disappeared over winter usually had smaller territories (20). Territory size was also correlated with visibility or poor cover, territories being small among moraines or hillocks and big on open ground.
By partial correlations, it was found that territory size was primarily correlated with aggression, but also with secondary local
variation according to cover (18). When a bird's territory size
changed from one year to another, its aggression changed correspond-
ingly.

There was no correlation between the number of young reared and
territory size. Nor did territory owners which had a big territory or
good breeding success one year necessarily do as well in the next year;
many of the more aggressive territory owners lost their territories and
became non-territorial in a second year.

Does a cock have a big territory because it is more aggressive, or
is it more aggressive because it has a bigger boundary to defend? The
conclusions in the last paragraph, about territory size and aggression,
are based only on correlations. But these findings have been tested
experimentally by altering birds' aggression, using implants of sex
hormones (17). Two territorial cocks implanted with androgen became
much more aggressive, almost doubled their territory size, spent more
time in courtship and paired with one or two hens instead of none or
only one. Another territorial cock implanted with oestrogen lost its
hen and eventually its territory. Finally, two non-territorial cocks

FIGURE 3.   <u>RELATION BETWEEN POPULATION AND TERRITORY SIZE</u>
Annual fluctuations within one area in breeding stocks and
in the mean territory size of cocks of different age.

Breeding Stock on
460 ha (birds/km^2)

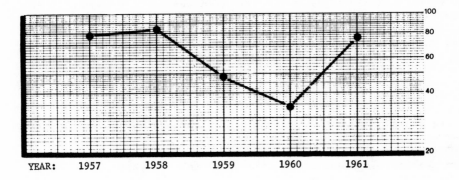

YEAR: 1957   1958   1959   1960   1961

Territory Size
in ha in Spring

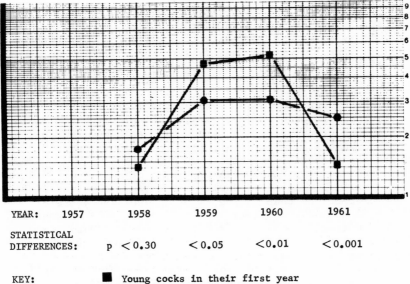

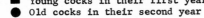

YEAR: 1957   1958   1959   1960   1961

STATISTICAL
DIFFERENCES: $p < 0.30$ < 0.05 < 0.01 < 0.001

KEY: ■ Young cocks in their first year
                ● Old cocks in their second year

in poor body condition, which were implanted with androgen, regained
good condition and drove back existing territory owners to take entirely new territories. Although both remained unpaired that year,
they survived the summer. One cock paired up with a hen in its territory next year and bred, paired again for the following season, and
was an unmated territory owner in its fourth year. Without the im-
plant, it is almost certain that these cocks would have died in their
first winter. These experiments supported the conclusions from the
field observations, that a bird's chances of survival and breeding
depended largely on its social status, and that changes in aggression
caused changes in territory size and status. Social status was
greatly influenced by the bird's physiology, which is probably most
important in autumn when the social classes are first formed.

DIFFERENCES BETWEEN YEARS

The whole of each moor, wherever heather was the dominant plant,
was occupied each year by grouse territories, so changes in spring
breeding stocks were due to changes in mean territory size (Fig.1),
and not to certain areas being unoccupied in some years.

Jenkins et al.(8, Table 6) showed that on average 52% of the
grouse alive in August failed to get territories. As the average
annual mortality rate was 65%, most mortality was socially induced.
A higher proportion became non-territorial in years when population
density was high, and the proportion was higher in years when populations were decreasing (mean 61%) than when they were increasing
(mean 38%). One intensively studied fluctuation was due mainly to
changes imposed by each year's new crop of young cocks (Fig.3); old
cocks were more conservative, and after the summer did not change
their territory size till the annual reshuffle of territories in
October-November.

Jenkins et al. (8) showed that breeding stocks usually increased
after good breeding success in the preceding summer, and usually decreased after poor breeding. At first glance, this might be explained
by a simple effect of numbers: the better the breeding, the more birds
available to compete for territories, and vice versa. However, some
examples with the highest proportion that failed to get territories
were during declines when population density had already dropped considerably, to quite low levels. During one intensively-studied fluctuation, the proportions that failed in two successive years of
decline were 67% and 60%, compared with only 19% in the subsequent
year of increase (Fig.4). No matter how poor the breeding was, a
considerable proportion of the grouse alive in August always failed
to get territories later, even though the breeding stock might be
declining in number from year to year. Thus good breeding was by
itself of no consequence to the population, and the key or bottle-
neck was again aggression in autumn. It did not matter how many
potential recruits were available, because territorial behavior set
a variable ceiling to the level of recruits that could get into the
breeding population each year.

FIGURE 4.   % LOSS BETWEEN AUGUST AND THE FOLLOWING SPRING
            NOTE: This figure shows that winter losses were not
                    simply proportional to density, but varied
                    according to whether the population was in-
                    creasing or decreasing.

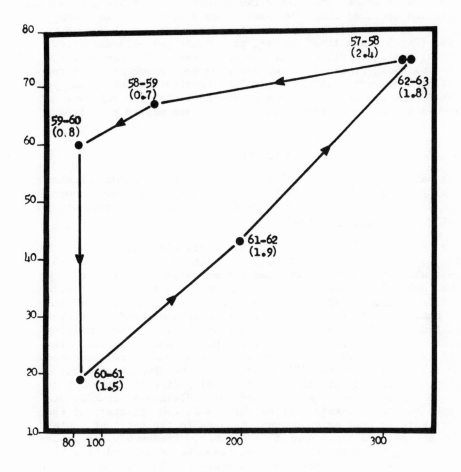

Population density in August   (birds / km^2)

Percentage losses from August to April compared with
August population density, during one fluctuation (number
of young: 1 old in parentheses).

For these reasons, the correlation between breeding success and subsequent changes in mean territory size and in the next spring's breeding stock was not direct cause and effect. Instead, changes in breeding success and then in mean territory size and breeding numbers, may be different consequences of a common antecedent. Territorial young produced in a year of good breeding may be of different type from those produced in a year of poor breeding. Detailed study of one fluctuation showed that after two summers of poor breeding during a population decline, these two year-classes of territorial young were more aggressive (not significant in one year), took bigger territories (Fig.3), and lived longer, than other year-classes (i.e., old birds) taking territories at the same time (17). Conversely, territorial young produced in two years of good breeding, when the population increased again, took smaller territories than other year classes. From one of these years of increase when the relevant measurements were made, they also were less aggressive and lived a shorter time.

DISCUSSION

We have concluded that territory size is the proximate factor regulating the density of breeding stocks in the red grouse, not only in different years within areas but also in differences of population level between areas.

We can say that territory size is relatively small (i.e., spacing is denser) (1) on rich soils, (2) on fertilised areas, (3) on areas where the heather has been burned in many small patches up to 2 ha, and (4) on hillocky areas with good cover or poor visibility. Effects (1) and (2) appear to be similar and result from improved nutrition of breeding birds, and consequent good breeding associated with the production of young which later take small territories. Nutrition appears to affect spacing only indirectly in (1) and (2), by affecting the behavior of the young birds produced. Unlike (1) and (2), effect (3) can occur in the absence of good breeding, and thus apparently affects spacing directly, causing a change in the territorial behavior of the individuals actually present upon an area. Burning causes changes in the structure of the heather sward as well as subsequent changes in the nutrient content, ease of access, and gross amount of heather. Presumably the grouse are responding to an increase in some resource associated with burning. We have not yet identified this resource, but we know it is not the gross amount of edible heather present, nor is it simply the presence of heather of high nutrient content; regenerating heather is highest in nutrients in the first summer after burning but territory size did not change till two and a half years after the first fires. Effect (4) also appears to be the cock's direct response, in this case to the physical structure or topography of the area.

As a generalisation from these conclusions, we can say that, considering differences between areas, spacing in red grouse (i.e., mean territory size) changes in relation to the resources (e.g., quality - but not quantity - of food, cover, etc.), but that the relation to food is apparently not immediate or directly adaptive. A certain minimum area may well be required; but below this density, space per se appears to be less important for population regulation than the resources per unit area.

Although we have shown that numbers sometimes vary with resources, it is not impossible that at other times numbers may vary independently of resources, as a result of changes within the population. This view has been expressed most strongly by Chitty who considers that changes in numbers of animals from year to year within areas may sometimes occur because of genetic changes within a crowded population at high density, in the absence of a preceding deterioration in food, weather, or other features in the environment (3). This view does not conflict in any way with the fact that territorial behavior is the <u>proximate</u> mechanism of regulation in red grouse.

Given that breeding stocks are controlled by territorial behavior, the general question we have to ask is: how are changes in territorial behavior induced by changes in resources? A more specific question is: why do young birds produced in years of good breeding take small territories, whereas young produced in years of poor breeding take big territories? We have already shown that in one fluctuation over several years within one area, there was an inverse association between breeding success and the later spacing behavior of those young which subsequently got territories. This observation also explains the correlation observed on a number of other areas (see Populations and Nutrition) between breeding success in one year and subsequent spring densities. If this is generally true, it may be speculatively explained in several ways; these hypotheses are not necessarily exhaustive or mutually exclusive.

1. Poor nutrition for the parents may depress breeding success and also cause surviving young that get territories to be more aggressive, or at any rate to take larger territories. This direct effect of nutrition on behavior would not necessarily be wholly phenotypic, since parents with different genetic backgrounds might differ in susceptibility to poor spring nutrition, and since the heavy mortality involved in poor chick survival may involve genetic selection.

2. Family size per se may affect aggression, with small broods (i.e. poor chick survival) leading to more aggression, irrespective of the quality of young in these broods. Why broods are small in the first place would still be an open question, with hypotheses 1 or 3.

3. At high densities, there may be a genetic selection for more aggressive types of animals from a polymorphic range (3). These aggressive animals would be favored during the strife resulting from

high density, and may also depress the survival and reproductive rate of later generations. Poorer food, or any other change in the environment, would not be a necessary prerequisite for this selection to occur, even though it might be sufficient to cause a decline in numbers on some but not all occasions.

A requirement now is to get more data, experimental if possible, which will establish or refute the idea that parental nutrition affects the quality and behavior of the young (Hypothesis 1), and subsequently territorial behavior and population regulation. We are currently measuring the nutrient content of the main food throughout the spring on eight study areas - six for red grouse and two for rock ptarmigan. This is to test hypothesis 1, but it may incidentally provide evidence about hypothesis 3, by detecting any cases where the heather's nutritive value decreases or increases without the population showing the response predicted from correlations and experiments so far; or equally, where a population changes - particularly where it declines - without a preceding change in nutrition. So far, we have some evidence that nutrition is important (see Populations and Nutrition), but no proof that it is the only factor operating or that it can explain everything that happens.

Intraspecific Strife

So far, we have used the term "aggression" rather loosely to include those behavioral characteristics which determine whether a cock grouse gets a territory or not, and what size that territory is. What was actually measured in the field was a) the mean result of encounters with other birds, which is a measure of relative dominance, but also separately b) the frequency of agonistic encounters and songs, which are measures of the amount of interaction and strife. Measures a) and b) are correlated in the same individual. But an important point is that we know that b) may vary independently of the inherent aggressive drive of an individual, according to a variety of other factors which are discussed below.

Before giving examples, an important qualification is that the amount of strife is usually a consequence of prior events at the previous annual reshuffle of territories. We assume that later strife (called resultant strife below) is a continuation of earlier events and may reflect them. Causal strife was seen only when observations were made continually enough - in fact almost daily - to detect exactly when numbers changed seasonally (see Seasonal Changes in Behavior).

Differences in Strife Between Areas

Resultant strife was measured at densities from 2-80 cocks per 100 ha. There was much strife on areas consistently at highest density and almost none at lowest density. Birds were so distant on low-density areas that there were rarely enough stimuli from others to cause interaction. On high-density areas, they were so near that they usually saw and heard their neighbors very clearly.

On an area A with a consistently high density, cock X with a big territory of 4 ha is more aggressive than its average neighbors with 2 ha each (see Differences between Individuals). But is cock Y, with a 10 ha territory on area B where density is consistently low and the average territory is 10 ha, any more aggressive than X? Y may simply have a different "aggressive response curve" (13) from X. Thus, X drives out intruders 100 m away, but ignores them at 200 m or 300 m; whereas Y reacts strongly up to 300 m. Densely packed birds with small territories may be more tolerant than birds in sparse populations where territories are bigger, yet densely-packed birds show more frequent strife. The frequency of strife is an erroneous measure of aggression if it is merely a result of the degree of contact between neighbors.

Another variable is that strife and aggressive response curves may vary directly with habitat, for example when a bird moves between areas with different cover or visibility, such as hillocks compared with flat ground; or within an area following a major change in that area, caused by the burning of heather in many small patches.

Differences Between Years in Strife Within Areas

Within one area where numbers fluctuated from year to year, grouse showed more strife when at peak numbers than when increasing from low numbers. But strife did not lessen during the decline, and was indeed greater then, even when numbers had already dropped considerably and when one might expect that pressures due to "crowding" would have been relieved. Watson also found this in a study of fluctuating rock ptarmigan in Scotland (16). Also, the proportion of grouse failing to get territories was as great (and in some cases much greater [Fig.4]) when populations were decreasing as when increasing. The word "crowding" is unsatisfactory; the effects of other animals may be as great, if not greater, when the crowd is thinner, because the animals may have different behavioral characteristics.

In these examples, variations in strife were not directly related to variations in density. Hence either the nature of the aggression shown by the birds altered during these fluctuations, or else the capacity to withstand aggression altered. By ejecting less successful year-classes, young cocks which got territories during a decline probably showed more inherent aggression as well as more tolerance of it. Inherent aggression was presumably enhanced in cocks after hormone implants, because they increased strife in the experimental area and had higher aggressive response curves, and because they gained larger territories by driving back their neighbors.

Comparison with Current Population Theories

The number of breeding grouse was in no case reduced by birds showing non-breeding. Although the density of the breeding stock was inversely correlated with breeding success in the same summer, this effect was negligible for population turnover compared with the numbers that later failed to get territories. Thus non-breeding and "density-dependent" poorer breeding were unimportant, unlike some other animals (20).

Population regulation did not occur through "density-dependent" mortality as a direct result of starvation and food shortage, as suggested for great tits (Parus major) by Lack (16). Most mortality was socially induced and occurred secondarily, only after changes in social behavior affected the status and behavior of certain categories of birds so that they became more vulnerable to all mortality factors. The immediate factor controlling spring breeding stocks was the number of birds taking territories in the previous autumn. Thus the work confirms some ideas of Errington (5) and Wynne-Edwards (20) about mortality, and of Tinbergen (14) about territory. The size of territories taken by red grouse in autumn was not correlated with the total quantity of potential food at the time. Furthermore, the fertiliser experiment showed no immediate adjustment of the territory size taken by incoming birds to the quantity or quality of food in autumn. To sum up, the evidence at present is that mean territory size - and thus spring population density - was not directly adjusted to the food's quantity or nutritive value, as suggested as a general principle by Wynne-Edwards (20) and Lack (6). An exception may be the case of heather burning (see Populations and Nutrition), but we are not sure of the mechanism involved here.

Fluctuations in breeding success, and in breeding stocks via changes in the behavior and viability of the young, occurred against a background of changes in the parents' nutrition in the previous spring and winter. Changes in nutrition in turn were affected by weather. Adjustments therefore occurred to change in the nutritional state of the heather, but they were indirect in time.

Territorial cock grouse from a year-class reared during one decline took bigger territories and were more aggressive than territorial grouse from other year-classes at the same time. This might support Chitty's ideas about genetic selection for aggression in declining populations (3). But the more aggressive year-class of grouse survived better when they were territorial adults and so appeared more viable than other year-classes, whereas Chitty expected selection against some other attribute, such as viability or survival. However, he suggested survival only as a likely possibility and not a necessary part of the hypothesis; perhaps some other attribute was selected against. Alternatively, even assuming that selection did occur in grouse, the changes postulated may not be genetic.

Poorer food or other environmental features might affect the chicks'
inherent behavior through inherited (but not genetic) maternal effects
that may persist over several generations (2,4). Chitty does not
deny that any one of various environmental factors such as worse
weather or food can cause declines in numbers (3). However he considers it is not always a necessary predisposing cause of them.
There is no evidence for this consideration in red grouse, but none
against it. Future work is designed partly to look for evidence for
this idea, as well as to test more rigorously the statements made in
the previous paragraph.

SUMMARY

The way in which animals use space is part of the wider problem
of how populations are regulated in relation to nutrition and other
features of the environment. Space, per se, appears to be less important for population regulation than the resources within a given
space, at any rate in the species mentioned below.

Research on red grouse (Lagopus lagopus scoticus) on heather
(Calluna vulgaris) moorland in Scotland involved studies of spacing
patterns and mechanisms, social status, population processes, and
nutrition and other features of the environment. Field observations
and experiments showed that the density of the breeding stock was
limited by the number of birds occupying territories after an annual
contest in the previous autumn. This contest also established a class
system, with upper-class 1 birds getting territories. Every autumn,
there was always a surplus of middle-class 2 or lower-class 3 grouse
(varying from year to year but on average over 50%), which failed to
occupy territories, and which were evicted from the moor by the territory owners when these were defending their territories vigorously.
These Class 2 and Class 3 birds gathered into flocks, moved more
widely, and spent more time in scrub and other undefended ground where
their main food supply of heather shoots was scarce. Subsequently
they nearly all died from predation, accidents and other causes before the next spring, while Class 1 territorial cocks and hens paired
with them suffered very little mortality in the following year.

Seasonal decreases in the moor's resident population were preceded by sudden increases in strife, irrespective of changes in nutrition, but associated either with changes in weather (winter) or
in the birds' gonad maturation (autumn). The most aggressive Class
1 cocks took bigger territories and paired with two hens, while the
least aggressive Class 1 cocks took small territories and remained
unmated. Experiments with hormone implants showed that increased
aggression enhanced the individual's consequent social status, territory size, survival, body condition and chances of breeding.

All suitable habitat was occupied, and fluctuations in breeding
stocks from year to year within areas occurred due to changes in the

size of territories occupied by young cocks. During one fluctuation,
young cocks that took territories during two years of decline – after
summers of poor breeding – also took bigger territories, survived
better, and were more aggressive than territorial cocks from other
year-classes over the same period. Conversely, young cocks after
summers of good breeding, took smaller territories and survived
worse than other year classes over the same period. Poor breeding
in years of decline was correlated with factors occurring before the
eggs hatched, in particular with poorer nutrition of the parents before egg laying. Experimental improvement of the parents' nutrition
by fertilising the heather caused good breeding and subsequent small
territories. However, mean territory size after the annual reshuffle
of territories in autumn was not correlated with either the heather's
quantity or nutrient content in autumn. An experiment showed that
birds coming on to a vacant area which had been fertilised did not
adjust their territory size to the quantity or quality of food at
this time. Therefore the present evidence is that territorial behavior in autumn was not directly adjusted to either the quantity or
the quality of the food available then. Several hypotheses to explain these findings are being considered, but the main one at present is that the territorial behavior of young birds may be affected
by their parents' nutrition, which is a direct link between the environment and the mechanism for spatial and population regulation.

Considering differences between areas, low mean territory size
was associated with consistently better breeding, and with higher
nutrient content of the heather (but not with greater total quantity)
on moors over base-rich rocks, than on poorer moors of lesser underlying fertility. Low mean territory size was also correlated with
differences in habitat structure (lower visibility or better cover
on areas with hillocks) and with changes in the physical structure,
availability and nutritive value of the heather sward after rota-
tional burning.

REFERENCES

1. Andrewartha, H.G. and Birch, L.C.: The Distribution and Abun-
       dance of Animals. University of Chicago Press, Chicago,
       1954.
2. Barnett, S.A.: Some effects of breeding mice for many genera-
       tions in a cold environment. Proc. Roy. Soc. Ser. B.
       Biol. Sci., 155:115-135, 1961.
3. Chitty, D.: The natural selection of self-regulatory behaviour
       in animal populations. Proc. Ecol. Soc. Aust., 2:51-78,
       1967.
4. Cowley, J.J. and Griesel, R.D.: The effect on growth and behaviour
       of rehabilitating first and second generation low protein
       rats. Anim. Behav., 14:506-517, 1966.
5. Errington, P.L.: Of population cycles and unknowns. Cold Spring
       Harb. Symp. Quant. Biol., 22:287-300, 1957.

6. Lack, D.: _Population Studies of Birds_. Oxford University Press, Oxford, 1966.

7. Jenkins, D., Watson, A. and Miller, G.R.: Population studies on red grouse (Lagopus lagopus scoticus) in north-east Scotland. _J. Anim. Ecol._, 32:317-376, 1963.

8. _____, _____ and _____: Population fluctuations in the red grouse (Lagopus lagopus scoticus). _J. Anim. Ecol._, 36:97-122, 1967.

9. _____, _____ and Picozzi, N.: Chick survival in captive and wild red grouse. _Trans. Sixth Cong. Int. Un. Game Biol._, 63-70, 1965.

10. Miller, G.R., Jenkins, D. and Watson, A.: Heather performance and red grouse populations. I. Visual estimates of heather performance. _J. Appl. Ecol._, 3:313-326, 1966.

11. Moss, R.: Probable limiting nutrients in the main food of red grouse (Lagopus lagopus scoticus). In Petrusewicz, K., ed., _Secondary Productivity of Terrestrial Ecosystems_. Warsaw, 1967.

12. _____: A comparison of red grouse (Lagopus lagopus scoticus) stocks with the production and nutritive value of heather (Calluna vulgaris). _J. Anim. Ecol._, 38:109-122, 1969.

13. Patterson, I.J.: Timing and spacing of broods in the black-headed gull. _Ibis_, 107:433-459, 1965.

14. Tinbergen, N.: The functions of territory. _Bird Study_, 4:14-27, 1957.

15. Watson, A.: Aggression and population regulation in red grouse. _Nature_, 202:506-507, 1964.

16. _____: A population study of ptarmigan (Lagopus mutus) in Scotland. _J. Anim. Ecol._, 34:135-172, 1965.

17. _____: Social status and population regulation in the red grouse (Lagopus lagopus scoticus). _Roy. Soc. Pop. Study Group_, 2:22-30, 1967.

18. _____ and Jenkins, D.: Notes on the behaviour of the red grouse. _Brit. Birds_, 57:137-170, 1964.

19. _____ and _____: Experiments on population control by territorial behaviour in red grouse. _J. Anim. Ecol._, 37:595-614, 1968.

20. Wynne-Edwards, V.C.: _Animal Dispersion in Relation to Social Behaviour_. Oliver and Boyd, Edinburgh, 1962.

Prepared Contributions for Discussion of Session II: Space and Contact Behavior

INTERGROUP RELATIONS IN RHESUS MONKEYS *(MACACA MULATTA)*

H. M. Marsden

I have been concerned with social relations between social groups of rhesus monkeys (<u>Macaca</u> <u>mulatta</u>). My studies have a distinct relationship with the major topics of the first two sessions of the Symposium, even though spatial parameters per se have not been the data of choice; instead, social interactions have been recorded.

The experimental set-up consists of two 1/4 acre enclosures, each holding a small social group of rhesus monkeys. The two enclosures are connected by a tunnel which has a barrier at the midpoint ("doors") which can be raised or lowered to permit or eliminate contact between the two groups.

Major and pertinent results from four recent studies include the following:

1. The normal intergroup relationship in the rhesus monkey with respect to competition for use of space is one of intergroup dominance and not territoriality. In the enclosures as in the field [1,2, 4], contact between a dominant and a subordinate group results in condensation and retreat by the subordinate group, regardless of location. In the enclosures this would include all the space within the home enclosure of the subordinate group.

2. Instability in intergroup dominance can be experimentally induced by the removal or introduction of young, "peripheral" males. Under these conditions of instability, or incomplete dominance, a form of group defense of territory emerged. It now became clear that each group had a clear advantage in its own home enclosure, when previously, under the usual conditions of complete dominance, no such advantage appeared to exist.

3. The frequency of agonistic interaction within each group during intergroup contact was remarkably different and appeared to be a function of the intergroup dominance relationship. Compared to baseline data taken during periods of no contact, aggression increased in the dominant group but decreased in the subordinate. These results were remarkable because, during contact, the dominant group was able, literally, to double its usable space, while the subordinate group, tightly condensed and retreating before the advance of the dominant group's members, was restricted to an area of less than 1/16 that of its own home enclosure.

4. Southwick has found that, under conditions of food deprivation, aggression within a social group of rhesus monkeys decreases [3]. The animals spread out and spend much of their time searching for the sparse food distributed throughout their enclosure. Southwick's results have been confirmed (in my first pilot study) for each of the two groups in my enclosures. Importantly, a similar situation appears to result with food deprivation during intergroup contact; here the intergroup aggression decreases.

REFERENCES

1. Altmann, S.A.: A field study of the sociobiology of rhesus monkeys (Macaca mulatta). Ann. N.Y. Acad. Sci., 102:338-435, 1962.
2. Southwick, C.H.: Patterns of intergroup social behavior in primates, with special reference to rhesus and howling monkeys. Ann. N.Y. Acad. Sci., 102:436-454, 1962.
3. _____: An experimental study of intragroup agonistic behavior in rhesus monkeys (Macaca mulatta). Behaviour, 28:192-209, 1967.
4. Vessey, S.H.: Interactions between free-ranging groups of rhesus monkeys. Folia Primat., 8:228-239, 1969.

THE REGULATION OF TERRITORIAL MARKING

IN THE MONGOLIAN GERBIL*

D. D. Thiessen

Notable progress has been made in the study of territoriality in the field and theoretical advances are forming the basis for greater understanding. Regretfully, however, laboratory studies have lagged far behind, primarily because the concept of territoriality in the laboratory is vague at best, and because the domesticated species usually studied do not lend themselves to naturalistic observations or interpretations.

*Supported by NIMH Grant No. MH 14076-02 and by NIMH Research Development Award MH 11; 174-02

Because of these difficulties, our laboratory group has turned to the Mongolian gerbil (Meriones unguiculatus) for study. The gerbil combines qualities necessary for laboratory work with a discrete territorial response associated with its midventral scent gland. Our global intentions are to 1) define the characteristics of the territorial response, 2) describe the environmental regulation of the behavior, 3) uncover the physiological mechanisms of control, and 4) unravel the social significance of the behavior. Some advances made in these directions during the past two years are summarized here. In general, we are interested in introducing a species and techniques which may serve as prototypes for the laboratory study of territoriality in mammalian species.

Gerbils mark objects in their environment by pressing a midventral sebaceous gland on the objects, leaving a sebum which is oily to the touch and musky in odor. Males mark pegs in an open field about twice as frequently as females, which corresponds to differences in gland size.

Both marking and the gland pad regress in adult male gerbils following castration and can be reinstated by the injection of 80-640 μg of testosterone propionate injected twice a week. Moreover, the testes must be present for the normal development of both the marking and gland morphology. Behavior and gland growth are facilitated in the female with testosterone but ovariectomy does not necessarily lower marking.

Androgens from the male gonads probably control marking by stimulating sites in the central nervous system. 1.25 μg testosterone propionate infused into the lateral ventricles of castrate males elicits marking in four to six days after infusion but does not result in obvious systemic changes. Importantly, when the testosterone is combined with actinomycin D (.001 μg per injection) that is not itself toxic, marking is not stimulated. Actinomycin D, which is generally known to bind DNA and prevent its transcription of RNA negates the effects of the hormone. Our tentative hypothesis is that steroids from the gonads depress segments of DNA in specific sites of the central nervous system allowing templates of critical RNA to stimulate cytoplasmic enzyme formation involved in the final motor response.

We assume that there is a signaling feature to the sebum deposited on objects. The gland could support a host of functions, including the definition of territorial limits, attraction and alarm, recognition of individuals and species and establishment of dominance-submissive relations. It appears that males coming into a marked field are more hesitant in marking, sniffing of objects, and general activity. In both triplet and paired fighting contests the dominant animal is also the one that marks more. These data give the added information that dominance formation is ordinarily predetermined by the physiological and marking status of the individual, and not the reverse. Increasing density in adult male gerbils from isolation groups of five and ten decreases marking, urination and seminal vesicle weight. General activity is increased. These data are consistent with the earlier findings that group stresses or low social status are associated with depressed territorial marking and a lowered level of androgen secretion.

Androgen may be the primary hormone of territorial control in the gerbil. Ordinarily androgen is thought of as fundamentally a male sex hormone. However, the same hormone may also control aggression, and in the case of the male and female gerbil, territorial signaling. Our studies further suggest that androgen acts by triggering gene activity within the central nervous system with its subsequent stimulation of motor activity. External stimuli, social and otherwise, modulate this activity in various ways.

MAPPING HUMAN MOVEMENT WITH THE AID OF A COMPUTER

R. E. Herron

It might be of interest to outline a method which was originally developed [4,5] in connection with research similar to that reported over the years by Esser [1,2,3].

Our method is based on using Cartesian coordinates to describe the location of individuals within an observed area at selected points in time. After we had completed a feasibility study, a remarkably similar technique used by Siniff and Tester [6] to map the movements of wild animals under natural conditions came to our attention. Although there are a few elemental differences, both techniques are based upon the same principle--reduction of spatiotemporal data to coordinate form for convenient computer processing.

In one application, we used an automatically-operated camera (with a fish-eye lens), centrally mounted in the ceiling at a height of approximately nine feet, to completely photograph the floor of an indoor playroom at intervals of ten seconds throughout 15 minute play sessions. The area was marked off in a grid of three feet squares with masking tape so that it was possible to read coordinates for the position of each child in each photograph. These data and coordinates for the areas occupied by equipment or areas surrounding the equipment served as input to the computer.

A relatively simple program was then written to produce the fo_-lowing types of information automatically:

1. Each child's changes in position during each play session displayed graphically, in chronological order, on a plan view of the play area.

2. The distance represented by the total changes in position of each child per play session and the mean distance for each child over all sessions.

3. The aggregate distance between each child and each of the other children for each exposure and for each play session.

4. The mean distance between each child and each of the other children during each play session computed and displayed as a function of time (with succeeding play sessions).

5. The frequency of entry of each child into each of the specified territories for each play session computed and displayed as a function of time.

6. The frequency each child is alone in each territory per play session and the incidence of solitary activity computed and displayed as a function of time.

7. The frequency each child is accompanied by selected permutations of the other children in each territory per play session computed and displayed as a function of time.

8. The aggregate frequency of all children into each of the specified territories for play session computed and displayed as a function of time.

The above list is not exhaustive--other data manipulations can readily be devised as required to answer questions raised in a particular investigation.

The above method is feasible for studying any area in which the individuals' locations at specific points of time can be recorded in Cartesian coordinate form. An asset of photography for this purpose is the fact that it tends to promote high reliability and it also yields a permanent, visible record at relatively low cost--its major drawback is the tedium of manual scanning of the photographs, for want of an inexpensive automatic analyzer.

Among other considerations, there is a need to further explore such matters as sampling rates and the use of random versus regular intervals between observations. Such decisions will be influenced greatly by the exigencies of each experimental situation.

We are now applying this method to a study of hospital design and it seems that the method has potential for use in a wide variety of other situations involving documentation and analysis of human spatial behavior.

REFERENCES

1. Esser, A.H., Chamberlain, A.S., Chapple, E.D. and Kline, N.S.:
        Territoriality of patients on a research ward. In
        Wortis, J., ed., Recent Advances in Biological Psychiatry,
        Vol. VII. Plenum Press, Inc., New York, 1965.
2. _____ and Etter, T.L.: Automated location recording on a
        psychiatric ward: Preliminary notes on continuous moni-
        toring of posture and movement of all individuals in an
        observation area. (Abstract). Amer. Zool., 6:251, 1966.
3. _____: Interactional hierarchy and power structure on a
        psychiatric ward: Ethological studies on dominance be-
        havior in a total institution. In Hutt, S.J. and Hutt, C.,
        eds., Behaviour Studies in Psychiatry. Pergamon Press,
        Oxford- New York, 1970.
4. Herron, R.E.: Computer analysis and display of movement patterns.
        Proceedings of 21st American Congress on Engineering in
        Medicine and Biology, 1968.
5. _____ and Frobish, M.J.: Computer analysis and display
        of movement patterns. J. Exp. Child Psychol. 8:40-44,
        1969.
6. Siniff, D.B. and Tester, J.R.: Computer analysis of animal
        movement data obtained by telemetry. Bioscience, 15(2):
        104-108, 1965.

USE OF TELEMETRY AS A MEANS OF STUDYING

SPACING AND BEHAVIOR OF ANIMALS*

J. R. Tester, D. B. Siniff and C. R. Jessen

Understanding how wild, unrestrained animals utilize space in
their natural environment implies knowledge of their precise location
over a given period of time. In addition, to consider the social interactions of spacing one must have knowledge of the locations of many
animals simultaneously. The recent development of telemetry techniques has made it possible to obtain excellent data for the study of
movement patterns and the concept of home range for many species of
vertebrates. A research team at the University of Minnesota has developed an automatic radio-tracking system located at the Cedar Creek
Natural History Area in east-central Minnesota. This system continually monitors and records movements of animals carrying miniature radio transmitters [14,2]. Animal position and activity data, recorded
minute-by-minute for up to 52 animals, have been utilized for the
study of many mammal and a few bird species [12,6,7,5,3,11]. The
purpose of this paper is to introduce the reader to types of informa-

*This research was supported by the U.S. Atomic Energy Commission
(COO-1332-48) and N.I.H. Training Grant No. 1 TO1GMO1779 from the
National Institute of General Medical Sciences.

tion which can be obtained with this technique and to relevant published literature.

The most detailed analyses of movements and relation to spacing have been with data on larger mammals such as red fox, snowshoe hare and white-tailed deer. Computer programs have been developed to handle the large amount of data generated by the system. Siniff and Tester described initial attempts at computer analysis of radio-tracking data [9]. At present an extensive "software" system has been specifically designed for the analysis of position and activity data on a CDC 6600 computer.

Analysis of these data has required new methods both in terms of data handling and data processing. The home range patterns we have observed, which are not adequately described by past models [1, 12] have led us to consider other models and approaches. Within a home range there are usually several areas of intensive utilization or centers of activity; these may shift in time, depending on individual or environmental variables. For mammals which are established in a particular area, the home range is a stable entity where the animal stays year after year. Juveniles have been observed to have often a dispersing pattern where they appear to be searching for some "unoccupied" area in which to become established. Usage patterns in general are contagiously distributed; however, the exact nature of a satisfactory mathematical model is not clear at this time. Therefore, we have initiated work in the area of computer simulation to measure some of the characteristics of an adequate home range model [10]. These attempts derive their basis from the probability distributions we observed utilizing telemetry as the animal traveled in its normal daily activity. The simulation we have carried out is stochastic in nature and through its use we have established certain guidelines which help interpret animal movement patterns. The movements of animals we have observed were not of a classical random-walk nature and thus the simulation model we have formulated required that certain areas were utilized with higher probability than other areas in the home range. Parameters of the negative binomial probability distribution have been used to compare the simulated movement patterns to those observed by telemetry. In general, the negative binomial distribution is a good approximation for telemetry data and the values of the various estimated parameters suggest a method for intra- and inter-species comparisons.

The simulation model is a method which appears to have numerous applications in the study of spatial and temporal aspects of animal behavior. Simultaneous simulation of several individuals in an area provides guidelines for evaluating social interaction. Interpreting whether avoidance or attraction is taking place requires some "yardstick" for comparison, and it is anticipated that this simulation procedure may provide such a criterion. Certainly it is now possible to more fully understand what is meant by random contact between individuals, given that the pattern of movement is contagious.

Although the automatic radio-tracking system at the Cedar Creek Natural History Area is unique in terms of its scope and automation, many investigators associated with this project are now using portable tracking equipment to study movement and activities of animals at other locations. Because the transmitter makes it easy to locate individuals even after death, some studies have been made attempting to evaluate mortality factors. Hessler and Schladweiler have utilized telemetry techniques to study mortality of artificially propagated pheasants and mallard ducks, respectively [4,8]. Other studies are now in progress utilizing portable equipment to study social spacing and mortality in wild populations of waterfowl and upland game birds. Recently we have had inquiries concerning the possibilities of placing radio-transmitters on humans to study special aspects of their behavior, and future studies may be made in this area.

We have also utilized telemetry methods to study the effects of low level radiation on animal behavior. It is evident that one of the problems of the future is the greater risk of exposure to ionizing radiation. Possible effects of ionizing radiation on the behavior and breeding biology of lower mammals is important to the understanding of possible effects on human populations. With the telemetry system it is possible to capture wild mammals, expose them to a sub-lethal radiation dose, and then monitor their behavior after release. We have carried out work of this nature on raccoons and snowshoe hares to determine changes in movement and activity rhythms [13]. Since we have been faced with detecting changes in behavior, it was necessary to develop suitable methods of analysis prior to attempting to evaluate effect of sub-lethal radiation. With the simulation model we anticipate gaining further insight into changes in behavior and are now proceeding with the analysis of such data.

REFERENCES

1. Calhoun, J.B. and Casby, J.U.: The Calculation of Home Range and Density of Small Mammals. 1-24, U.S. Department of Health, Education and Welfare, Public Health Monograph No. 55, U.S. Government Printing Office, Washington, D.C., 1958.
2. Cochran, W.W., Warner, D.W., Tester, J.R. and Kuechle, V.B.: Automatic radio-tracking system for monitoring animal movements. Bioscience, 15(2):98-100, 1965.
3. Heezen, K.L. and Tester, J.R.: Evaluation of radio-tracking by triangulation with special reference to deer movements. J. Wildlife Manage., 31(1):124-141, 1967.
4. Hessler, E.W.: Survival of Ring-Necked Pheasants Released in Selected Habitats in Minnesota. University of Minnesota, Minneapolis, M.S. Thesis, 1968.

5. Mech, L.D., Tester, J.R. and Warner, D.W.: Fall daytime resting
        habits of raccoons as determined by telemetry. J. Mammal.,
        47(3):450-466, 1966.
6. Nicholls, H.T. and Warner, D.W.: Biotelemetry - a valuable tool
        in bird study. Passenger Pigeon, 28(4):127-131, 1966.
7. Rongstad, O.J. and Tester, J.R.: Movements and habitat use of
        white-tailed deer in Minnesota. J. Wildlife Manage.,
        33(2):366-379, 1969.
8. Schladweiler, J.: Survival and Behavior of Hand-Reared Mallards
        Released in Minnesota. University of Minnesota, Minnea-
        polis, M.S. Thesis, 1969.
9. Siniff, D.B. and Tester, J.R.: Computer analysis of animal move-
        ment data obtained by telemetry. Bioscience, 15(2):104-
        108, 1965.
10. _____ and Jessen, C.R.: A simulation model of animal move-
        ment patterns. In Cragg, J.B., ed., Advances in Ecologi-
        cal Research. In press.
11. Sunquist, M.E., Montgomery, G.G. and Storm, G.L.: Movements of
        a blind raccoon. J. Mammal., 50(1):145-147, 1969.
12. Tester, J.R. and Siniff, D.B.: Aspects of animal movement and
        home range data obtained by telemetry. Trans. N. Amer.
        Wildlife Matur. Resour. Conf., 30:379-392, 1965.
13. _____ and Rongstad, O.J.: Effects of
        radiation on behavior of unconfined raccoons and snowshoe
        hares determined by telemetry. Amer. Zool., 7(4):404,
        1967.
14. _____, Warner, D.W. and Cochran, W.W.: A radio-tracking
        system for studying movements of deer. J. Wildlife Ma-
        nage., 28 (1):42-45, 1964.

Discussion of Session II:
Space and Contact Behavior

PANEL: J. A. Lloyd (Chairman), S. A. Altmann,
E. M. Banks, G. McBride, H. M. Marsden,
E. W. Menzel, W. Sheppe, J. G. Vandenbergh

Lloyd:

In reference to how space should be structured for the use of urban populations, I would like to mention that in some of the large Eastern cities this past summer an attempt was made to control aggression in a very real sense by trying to, as it were, "cool it", as regards tense situations existing in many neighborhoods and many areas in large cities.

In Philadelphia, practically every public square in the city was utilized during July and August. In the city, almost every evening, these public areas featured events, from chamber concerts and esoteric plays in Rittenhouse Square to jazz-concerts and teen dances, thus providing a wide variety of activity throughout the city. Street areas in certain neighborhoods were utilized by traveling players. The plays were, ostensibly, for children. It turned out that they involved entire communities. Residents from the local communities were invited to participate in the plays. In many instances, hostility to other segments of the community was acted out verbally, and the entire situation became somewhat therapeutic.

Now, one can argue whether these activities had anything to do with controlling outbursts of violence in the cities in which these things were done. Many people feel that it helped. We do not know whether it will continue to work or not.

But my point in mentioning this is that we desperately need to start studying, methodically and intelligently, how we can better use public space to improve the quality of life and to control aggression in our society. I think this is an urgent problem.

I think a corollary problem to this is: as a species, what are
the limits to which, in terms of the numbers and kinds of stimuli,
we are capable of adapting? Also, how can we learn to structure our
environment so that we reduce noxious stimuli and increase stimuli
that are not physiologically or behaviorally damaging to us?

Another question in my mind: What is the minimum amount of space
needed by an individual to maintain mental health (for want of a better term)?

Altmann:

Dr. McBride and Dr. Brereton have described in detail the intimate structures of spacing relations among animals. Then Dr. Watson
jumped up a couple of levels and told us about the relationships between territorial size, home range, population density and reproductive success, and the effects of the habitat on these processes. For
several years, in our field work on yellow baboons, Papio cynocephalus,
on the savannahs of East Africa, we have been working at an intermediate level that bridges the gap between the structure of spacing on
the one hand and survival or reproduction on the other. Essentially,
we have been asking, what is the function or adaptive significance of
the particular way in which the animals utilize the space in which
they live?

We are working with animals that live in social groups and that
have no territories, either individually or collectively. They have
a very large home range. We have kept detailed records of where they
went and what they did in the various parts of their range, and have
been piecing together the story of how the movements and other activities of these animals enable them to survive. I will simply state
four of our hypotheses relevant to the theme of this Symposium. For
details, see Altmann and Altmann [1]. We believe that these generalizations apply to the various species of baboons; on the basis of the
literature, they appear to be applicable to several other species of
primates. How much more widely they are applicable remains to be seen.
They are as follows:

1. For any set of tolerable ecological conditions, the movements
and other adaptive activities of baboons tend toward some equilibrium
distribution beyond which reproductive success is lower or mortality
rate is higher, or both. Each portion or sector of a group's home
range has a certain utility to the animals, namely, the difference between what they gain from the sector, in terms of access to those resources that will enhance survival and reproduction, and what they
lose as a result of hazards to life encountered therein. Perpetuation
of a group depends upon its ability to allocate the distribution of
its activities among the areas of its home range so that the net utility of the range to the animals is positive, or at least non-negative.

   This generalization has an important research implication: In
analyzing the utilization of home range, we must consider not only
those portions that animals enter frequently or remain in for long
periods of time, but also those that are seldom and briefly entered.
More precisely, we must consider the distribution of sector utilization and its relationship to the distribution of both hazards and natural resources among sectors.

   2. The amount of home range overlap between groups depends primarily on those essential natural resources that have the most restricted distribution in space. Consequently, home range overlap
will be low in relatively uniform environments, and will be extensive
wherever several essential resources have very restricted distributions.

   3. The amount of time that groups are simultaneously in the
overlapping portions of their home ranges will depend on those essential natural resources whose availability is most restricted in time.
As a result, simultaneous occupation of overlap zones will be long
wherever the most slowly utilized resources have the most restricted
period of availability, and conversely will be brief if those resources that require the longest to utilize are continuously available.

   Thus, an essential natural resource is a restrictive factor in
home range separation, in time or space, to the extent that increasing its dispersion in time or space will reduce home range overlap.

   4. Home range size has an upper and a lower bound. It is limited to that area within cruising range of the essential resource
with the most restricted distribution in space. The animals cannot
wander beyond this limit without jeopardizing their lives. The lower
limit on home range size depends upon those essential natural resources that are most sparsely distributed. The animals must cover
enough ground to obtain a subsistance amount. Where these two limits
are close to each other, they will be the primary factors that determine home range size.

REFERENCE

1. Altmann, S.A. and Altmann, J.: Baboon Ecology: African Field
            Research. No. 12 of Series of Biblioteca Primatologica.
            S. Karger, Basel; also University of Chicago Press,
            Chicago, 1970.

Banks:

   My interest in the study of how animals move in space has taken
the form of an examination of aggressive behavior in one of the (microtine) rodents, the collared lemming, Dicrostonyx groenlandicus.
This particular rodent has a very well-studied population cycle of

three to five year duration; and my particular interest was to see whether I could come to grips with behavioral concomitants of changes in population size.

The manner in which we proceeded was to study the fine structure of aggressive behavior in animals that we have kept in captivity [1]. This includes the motor-patterns and, much more recently, we have considered very closely the roles of vocalization, both audible and ultrasonic, during agonistic encounters among males.

Our plan was, after having established basic information on the motor-patterns of aggressive behavior, to proceed into the field situation and attempt to evaluate the relative levels of aggression of males one could find in nature. Our site was on Hudson Bay at Churchill, Manitoba, and we have spent a number of consecutive summers attempting to proceed with our grand scheme.

One of the problems we faced at the outset was that, although we could readily trap these animals in the tundra in great numbers, we were rarely able to observe them above ground out of their burrows, so that the idea of attempting to evaluate inter-male aggression in animals with this particular habit seemed to be a lost cause.

We turned to a consideration of the home range problem. Could one, perhaps, get at inter-male aggression by looking at home-range characteristics of the species?

The first summer we used standard techniques of trap-mark and trap. We found this technique to be very unsatisfactory. Last summer we turned to a new technique which is good for animals of this size and this particular habitat. We are using a radio-tracking system: a radio transmitter, which is placed on the back of the animal, allows us to monitor movements with a small receiver. We had a dozen transmitters last summer and were able to monitor the movements of both males and females. For the first time, we were able to see these animals above ground where they do spend a considerable amount of time. However, their visual acuity is very good, so if one is as close as 300 yards and makes a slight movement, an animal that is perched surveying the area, immediately goes down into a burrow.

There are a number of fascinating problems that have been opened up by this radio-tracking system. It is quite clear, from our first year's work, that the animals know the terrain in great detail. When they move from one burrow entrance to another, they do so very rapidly. They do not hesitate at all to run from one burrow 150-200 yards away to another burrow and go right down it as if they "know" this is an empty burrow and their sudden appearance will not be an affront to an animal that is already there.

There are some other details that will have to be accounted for in future studies; but it is clear that the males have a much more extensive home-range (three to five acres) than the females (one to two acres). This is not uncommon in microtines. Females and males live in separate burrow systems; females tend to stay very close to the burrows during nursing and suckling periods, whereas males wander extensively, presumably in search of estrous females.

We hope to be able to do some experimental work on the question of territory of the animals by introducing radio-transmitter-tagged animals from distant points to a study site, and to observe interactions between those introduced animals and resident individuals.

REFERENCE

1. Allin, J.T. and Banks, E.M.: Behavioural biology of the collared lemming (Dicrostonyx groenlandicus). I. Agonistic behaviour. *Anim. Behav.*, 16:245-262, 1968.

Menzel:

I agree with those speakers, including Dr. McBride, who have said that concepts such as territory are not terribly useful empirically. But my objection to taking "territory" over-seriously would extend to most of our current "space-like" concepts in the area of behavior. None of the terms in use today--including life space, home range, exploration, fixed action pattern, personal space, approach-withdrawal, social distance, flight distance and dominance--reflect completely independent elements, monads or hard and fast atomic units of psychological life. At best these terms point in a more or less general way to some class of object, activity, or functional relation which we might otherwise overlook in our drier inductive analysis. At their worst some of the terms obscure the fact that all students of behavioral phenomena, whether they be ecologists, geographers, sociologists, psychologists, or ethologists, face a common empirical problem, perhaps a single problem: Simply to account for the variance of animal locations-across-time as such. In short, I would go further than any of the speakers, and perhaps even further than Skinner [13] and say that there is no dire necessity, beyond that imposed by technical convenience and verbal habit, to introduce any special response concept or stimulus concept at all.

At least in principle, it should be possible to study species distribution, group locations, locations of individuals within the group, locations of body parts within the individuals, and changes in all of these locations across time, simultaneously. Some of the principal barriers to achieving an integrated account of various behaviors and various "levels of analysis" arise simply because in order to deal with the continuous flow of spatio-temporal events, we chop it up into arbitrary chunks in the first place. The entire question of how "behavior" relates to "space" is thus in a sense an artificial question: for behavior is itself a locational concept.

I do not know of any objectively defined response pattern or behavioral unit which is anything more, operationally, than a statement about how one rather arbitrary reference point (which can be a group's centroid, an individual, a body part, or a test object such as a lever in a Skinner box) locates itself or changes its location with respect to some other reference point (which can be another individual or group, a test object, the subject's own body axis, or the absolute coordinates of Newtonian physics).

Psychologists in particular have been accused of emulating physics and of being spuriously operational; but perhaps the truth is that we have not tackled the theoretical aspects of space-time seriously enough, even in this Symposium devoted to space. Perhaps we actually can, as Einstein stated the case for physics, make do with a single "space-like concept" alone. What I am therefore attempting to do in my own research on chimpanzees and monkeys [8,9] is to develop a "bona fide field-theoretic" approach to behavior--to borrow Hull's [3] phrase--for an objective analysis extended to handle multidimensional space and multiple reference points or "levels of analysis" simultaneously. This sort of approach differs from the phenomenological field theories of the 1930's [6,4,5] and from approach-avoidance [12,10,3: ch.8, possibly 15] or "distance" accounts [1:pp. 365-385, 2], but is not basically incompatible with any of them. The analytical "units" are not such things as stimuli, responses, or individual animals per se, but rather the simultaneous configuration of all selected reference points at a given instant in time (e.g., a map or a scored photograph of objects and animals is the unit). The problems of analysis are, then: a) To account for where all movable reference points are now, exactly as they are positioned in the "real" ecological field; and to control or predict in detail how the configuration will change next. Here, of course, the total variance of all locations across time must eventually be partitioned into components, and we must account for the movements of each pair of reference points with respect to each other, just as we might in a more conventional approach-avoidance analysis. However, "location" can be seen to be a fluid, multilevelled and relativistic concept, and its partitioning into components is systematic rather than haphazard. b) To transform the coordinates of measurement from our initial, arbitrary and "absolute" Newtonian ones to more meaningful, psychophysical ones. c) To thus determine the proportion of the total variance in the data that is explicable, and how many independent factors are necessary to account for the data. This, it seems to me, would tell us eventually what are the parameters and boundaries of the ecological niche or, as psychologists might say, the psychological environment, Umwelt, cognitive map, or behavioral life space.

In the vocabulary of information theory, the total uncertainty in a given behavioral event, as it occurs in nature, is equal to the number of choices we would have to make to completely describe and predict the condition of all our chosen reference points, on all spatio-temporal levels of analysis [7,14]. The goal of theory and research is to be able to reduce this total uncertainty to the maximum extent possible, with a minimum number of choices or theoretical summary statements. A basic objection one could raise about all past or present behavior theories, including my own, is that in their attempts to arrive at a minimum number of summary statements they usually choose the procrustean technique of throwing out all levels of information which do not fit into their one formula: that is, they deal with an artifically bounded space, and a parochial concept of location or movement. In this respect perhaps we should be tolerant of others' concepts (even sloppy, intuitive, or common sense ones such as territory and dominance) if they continue to alert us to aspects of events which our own conceptualizations have missed.

I would like now to ask two leading questions of Dr. McBride. The main explanatory concepts that students of behavior seem to have put forth to account for why animals are where they are within a group are bipolar psychological directional concepts: aggregation-dispersion, approach-withdrawal (i.e., movement toward or away from a reference point), attraction-repulsion, etc. As you commented, by far the greatest emphasis in field interpretations of animal social behavior is on the withdrawal side of the equation. But please comment further on the following:

1. Is it really true, as you said, that we have little data on the approach side of the equation? It seems to me that the entire laboratory work on imprinting and maternal-infant interactions, as well as field information on group cohesion or schooling during travel, flocking behavior, and defense, is both voluminous and relevant. Species differences in ecological niche and stimulus preference would also be relevant; for common goals in the way of safe places, food, shelter, places to rest, and so on would certainly be a highly important factor producing apparent mutual approach and cohesion. In other words, group members go together not only because they like each other, but also because they tend to go toward or away from the same things in the "non-social" environment [16]. Such ecological bases of grouping certainly deserve more respect than social theory per se has given them.

2. The second question is somewhat more theoretical. What evidence do we have that approach and withdrawal are in fact bipolar and independent of each other, especially in social situations? For one thing there is considerable experimental difficulty in establishing what objects are controlling a response in any given situation (and statements about approach and withdrawal imply a unitary reference point, and a known reference point). Matters are difficult enough even in tightly controlled laboratory discrimination or conditioning studies, but in studies of group behavior the analytical task is even more formidable. For another thing, as Nissen said, it is logically possible to translate any descriptive statement about approach into

a statement about withdrawal, and vice versa [11]. All this amounts to is changing your reference point, or transforming your coordinates of measurement. Thus, for example, when one observer talks about how a subordinate animal withdraws from a dominant animal, another observer could in most cases just as convincingly argue that the subordinate is actually approaching a less crowded place, or going to that nearby tree, or is suddenly attracted to his mother. I wonder if the terms "approach" and "withdrawal" actually tell us much more here than that certain components and a certain proportion of the variance in the subordinate's location are predictable, once we know the location of the dominant animal or the tree or the mother.

REFERENCES

1. Carpenter, C.R.: Naturalistic Behavior of Nonhuman Primates. Pennsylvania State University Press, University Park, 1964.
2. Hediger, H.: Studies of the Psychology and Behavior of Captive Animals in Zoos and Circuses. Criterion, New York, 1955.
3. Hull, C.L.: A Behavior System. Yale University Press, New Haven, 1952.
4. Kohler, W.: The Mentality of Apes. Harcourt Brace, New York, 1925.
5. Koffka, K.: Principles of Gestalt Psychology. Harcourt Brace, New York, 1935.
6. Lewin, K.: Defining the "field at a given time". Psychol. Rev., 50:292-310, 1943.
7. Margalef, D.R.: Information theory in ecology. Gen. Systems, 3:36-71, 1958.
8. Menzel, E.W.: Primate naturalistic research and problems of early experience. Develop. Psychobiol., 1968.
9. _____: Naturalistic and experimental approaches to primate behavior. In Willems, E. and Raush, H., eds., Naturalistic Viewpoints in Psychology. Holt, Rinehart and Winston, New York, 1969.
10. Miller, N.E.: Liberalization of basic S-R concepts: Extensions to conflict behavior, motivation, and social learning. In Koch, S., Psychology: A Study of a Science. Vol. 2. McGraw Hill, New York, 1959.
11. Nissen, H.W.: Description of the learned response in discrimination behavior. Psychol. Rev., 57:121-131, 1950.
12. Schneirla, T.C.: An evolutionary and developmental theory of biphasic processes underlying approach and withdrawal. In Jones, M.R., ed., Nebraska Symposium on Motivation. University Nebraska Press, Lincoln, 1959.
13. Skinner, B.F.: Cumulative Record. Appleton-Century-Crofts, New York, 1961.
14. Slobodkin, L.B.: Growth and Regulation of Animal Populations. Holt, Rinehart and Winston, New York, 1961.

15. Tolman, E.C.: <u>Purposive Behavior in Animals and Men.</u> Appleton-
        Century, New York, 1932.
16. Wynne-Edwards, V.C.: <u>Animal Dispersion in Relation to Social
        Behaviour</u>. Hafner, New York, 1962.

McBride:

I think my comment that we "know" about withdrawal systems is
based on the fact that I think we know more about W systems. In approach systems we certainly know that imprinting is involved. We do
not understand, we know that it is.

The thing that I think that we know least about is: What are
the processes of developing affiliations, that make groups, that make
bonds between individuals - closed bonds or open bonds, whatever sorts
of affiliation that we find. We know that there are processes associated with bringing animals together: They have to close distances,
they have courtship behaviors, pre-bond courtships, they have behavior associated with appeasement when coming close together. We know
also, once they are together, that there are whole hosts of interactions in which they can now engage; many are bond-serving, such as
allofeeding or allogrooming. But we do not really understand how
this system works. We have never put this into a systematic social
context, so we never really set out systematically to study affiliations. Yet we have put enormous amounts of effort into a quaint thing
called aggression, without recognizing that this is also organized.
So much for that.

For the A-W system I think I said the model is a useful one, but
it does not imply any simple control, for it ignores the fact that
there are A-W systems between groups, between the individuals within
the group, between males and females, between males and young females,
and young, and so on. This is how the behavior seems to be organized;
I do not think that we expect to find the same balance existing in
each of these systems.

The point that you make about whether the same factors are involved in A and W, I do not think we can specify. For example, Darwin suggested that the sorts of character that males use to repel
each other were also sexual. (He was talking on the descent of man
and selection in relation to sex.) That is, the same sorts of characters that were attractive to females were used in competition between
males; in other words, he postulated some economy ideas. So in this
sense the same character may have a double function. Whether it has
exactly the same double function in A-W in the same caste, for example, I do not know. I suspect that a lot of the territorial crowding which is threatening to neighbors is also locating, telling others
that they are there, keeping them close. This brings up the whole
theory which Fraser Darling first introduced: Is there an A as well
as a W force between territories when they adjoin, and are both the

result of the same stimuli, or is there a different set of stimuli for each?

Sheppe:

I think that there are other possibilities for studying the use of space. There has been a great emphasis on social behavior in recent years, and, of course, an overemphasis on territoriality; and one thing that has been largely overlooked is the actual relation of the individual animal to his physical environment, established by means of exploratory behavior. We need to know what types of stimuli produce exploration, and what sort of change there is at the edge of the home range to cause the animal not to explore farther. There has been work with exploration by animals in the laboratory, but not nearly enough with animals in real life.

Another approach to the use of space that is totally different from anything we are accustomed to working with has been developed by the locational geographers*, after being stimulated by work done by animal ecologists, especially Lee Dice. They have attempted to study the location of human structures and activities by means of mathematical models. I have, in the past few years, made some non-professional observations on the locational behavior of the Bantu tribes in Central Africa. It is highly variable, depending on environmental conditions and population density. In the Tonga tribe it is quite elaborate, with an elaborate pattern of breakdown and utilization of space.

Vandenbergh:

Both McBride and Watson described animals to us in which the male of the species plays an extremely important role in the distribution of the animals in the environment, as well as in their social structure. I think I ought to rise to the defense of females by discussing a species in which females play an important role in the distribution of animals in space.

We were able to study the formation of social groups in rhesus monkeys when about 200 animals were brought from India and released on an island off the coast of Puerto Rico, at La Parguera in 1962. The females that were released formed small groups of two to five animals very promptly, whereas males remained quite scattered throughout the island. These small groups of females, if dominated by a male (and here is where we have to agree that the male role is important), remained as cohesive social groups and grew in size by the addition of new members. Those bands that were not dominated by an adult male dispersed and the individuals joined other bands.

*e.g. P. Haggett, Locational Analysis in Human Geography, St. Martin's Press, New York, 1965 (Editor)

Another feature of the female influence on dispersal was shown by observations at La Parguera which indicated that males moved from band to band frequently and that even the dominant adult could move from one band to another without any artificial intervention. As a consequence of such movements there were no changes in the social rank of that band relative to other bands on the island. It appears that it is the basic group of adult females in the central portion of the band that essentially holds the rank of the band. The dominant member, even though he shifts from a higher-ranking to a lower-ranking band, does not carry the rank of the band with him.

Marsden:

Vandenbergh has nicely introduced the comment I would like to make. McBride introduced a concept which, I believe, was reinforced by Watson's comments, which may have led in many of your minds to a misconception.

The concept which was introduced was that the change from breeding season to non-breeding season results in major changes in social structure. This is certainly true for many birds, and it is true for many mammals; the cottontail rabbit shows a fantastic change in social behavior between the breeding and the non-breeding season.

However, in the specific example of the rhesus macaque groups which Vandenbergh discussed, family units comprise groups (a family contains a female and her offspring). The family is the basic social unit of the rhesus macaque group. And this does not change in any fundamental way between the breeding and non-breeding seasons.

In Puerto Rico, where Vandenbergh worked, and where I am at present, we have distinct breeding seasons, and yet the groups maintain their intragroup integrity throughout the year, and such organization is not limited to the breeding season.

McBride:

My only comment is that it is very obvious that all animals do not have social phases. Many animals do not have sex castes. I am trying to introduce a number of general comments on the sorts of ways that societies are organized, not specifying, of course, that all societies have all these properties. I was trying to be totally theoretical and deal with a system of imposing order into the organization of societies. I never meant that anyone would assume that all societies had social phases. Obviously, many males and females are not different at all. Sex can be a whole caste for a season, it can be a single role, or just a single interaction, as it is in the many shoaling fishes, for example. It is in these three levels of organization (the interaction, the role and the caste), where I see the behaviors organized; but not in the same way in all species.

Marsden:

My remark was intended for the audience, not as a direct comment on McBride's work. Zuckerman introduced years ago the concept
that sex is what holds the primate social group together, and this
is something that recent work has shown to be an erroneous generali-
ty.

Lloyd:

During this session attention has been drawn to the wide range
of factors that operate among various species to influence the utilization of space by animals. Examples of situations in which territory, aggression, flocking, family structure and rank operate to influence the distribution of animals in space have been reviewed.
These factors have been shown to have an effect on population density
through their influence on the size and effectiveness of breeding populations. The components of social organization are also involved in
the process of spacing of animals. The characteristics of a given habitat may also play a major role in setting limits on the ability of
animals to exploit their environment.

The discussion has brought an awareness that since there is considerable variation among species with respect to the factors influencing spacing, generalizations regarding these factors are extremely
risky; factors having a major influence in one species may not be involved at all in another instance. It has also been shown that our
fundamental knowledge of the components of social structure and organization is still extremely limited for most species, including
man. Thus, this session has been very valuable in providing investigators with an awareness of the need for more descriptions of the
spacing patterns across a wide range of species, and of the need for
intensive study of the social structures and organizational patterns
of a large number of species.

Physiological Effects of Continued Crowding

David E. Davis

INTRODUCTION

During the past decade many studies have considered the effects
of crowding on behavioral and physiological phenomena in mammals
and birds. However, most of these studies have considered short-
term effects and hence the problems associated with prolonged crowding have rarely been considered. This review will consider the information available that might help us to understand the physiological effects of continued crowding. Also, an attempt will be
made to put these effects into perspective for the whole life of
the individual. Since most of the information available concerns
mammals, this review will, with a few exceptions, limit the examples
to mammals. The extension of work on mammals to other species, even
birds, is questionable since it appears that at least some of the
physiological phenomena are entirely different in birds [22].

The term crowding is perhaps unfortunate since crowding per se
does not affect animals; something associated with crowding produces
changes. Indeed, the term crowding resembles such a word as altitude
which is known to be correlated with various phenomena in animals
and plants, but, of course, the altitude per se is not the causative
factor; something associated with altitude produces the effect.
Animals whether crowded together or not produce stimuli that affect
other animals. If these stimuli reach a rather high level of intensity then the effects on other animals may be obvious and perhaps severe. In many cases the stimuli are chemical and in an aqua-
tic environment these chemicals can accumulate. For example, water
that contained a large number of tadpoles can be transferred to
another aquarium containing a single tadpole which will show some

133

of the effects of crowding such as inhibition of growth [35]. Sounds,
of course, cannot be accumulated in such a manner and, therefore,
cannot be stored. In a terrestrial environment both chemical and
acoustic signals are used but can only reach a high density at the
time of high crowding. Thus, the animals react to the immediate
situation rather than to some past occurrence. The significance of
this situation for continued crowding is that for an effect to continue the signals must continue at a high level. The reduction in
the effects of crowding can occur if either the numbers of signals
are decreased or instead the animals themselves are able to adapt
to a high number of signals. It will be seen during this presentation that both a reduction of the number of stimuli and an adaptation to the stimuli occurs in continued crowding.

The only significant means for the production of signals is
behavior of one sort or another. When two or more individuals wish
the same item, their behavior becomes aggressive and one individual
gets the item. The types of behavior involved in settling disputes
have been described and reviewed numerous times; perhaps the most
useful recent review is given by Scott [48]. It is important at the
start to exclude the types of fighting that are involved in predation
or defense against a predator. Presumably the predator itself when
attacking a prey does not endure the same type of stimuli as in true
aggression. Also, the prey itself receives a different set of stimuli
although some physiological and psychological responses may be similar.

Another important point that has not yet been solved is whether
the response to aggression is innate or learned through experience.
It does appear that the actual procedures of fighting (for example,
the method of biting or standing) is innate. However, the object
attacked may be learned during early life. In any case, the details
of the aggressive behavior differ even within one species. For example, Levine et al., compared two strains of mice and found that
one was superior in fighting but slower to get started than the other
[32]. Thus, not only measurements of the results but of the latency
were needed to describe the differences.

The role of isolation in contrast to crowding needs to be considered. However, this topic will receive little attention here because isolation is not the normal situation and does not present the
problems that crowding does. Isolation can be obtained by simply
separating adults for a matter of weeks. When these animals are put
together again, they will usually fight rather severely but in a short
period of time settle down to an apparently peaceful rank organization.
Isolation at weaning or perhaps earlier is even more effective and
may result in the appearance of very severe fighting especially if
the animals are not put together in groups until they have attained
sexual maturity. In rats, the isolation of adults must last for
three to six months before being effective but in mice a mere three

weeks will produce results [49]. Isolation produces various changes
such as the amount of activity [80]. It must not be overlooked that
long-term isolation may produce physiological stress reactions in
animals at almost the level of those produced by crowding [24]. Thus,
thirteen weeks of isolation of rats resulted in dermatitis, enlarged
adrenals and small thymi. Also, there were some changes in the toxicity of certain drugs. As emphasized by Sigg et al., extreme isolation or density produces many homeostatic adjustments [49]. From
studies of isolation and of crowding it is clear that there must be
some population size at which the physiological processes can be considered at a normal or minimum level.

    The problems of measuring the effects of crowding are very great.
In the first place crowding acts on individuals through stimuli such
as sound and smell whose effects may be confused or confounded. In
the second place a number of physiological measures are available,
some of which last a short period of time and some of which develop
only after a long period of time. In addition there may be great
differences between the genotypes. Thiessen compared the weights
of adrenals for six strains of mice, subjected to identical conditions of crowding of either 10 or 20 individuals in a cage [51].
The cages differed in size so that the area per mouse was identical.
In some of these domesticated strains the size of the adrenal increased with crowding and in others it did not. Other studies show
that there may be a differential response according to strain of mouse
in the level of corticosterone in the plasma [31]. The significance
of these problems of measurement is that experiments that fail to
confirm some report or that seem to differ may be merely the result
of the strain of individual or the criteria that were selected for
measurement. Great caution must be exercised in claiming the existence of differences.

    This review will exclude work on the effect of crowding on pop-
ulations. Thus, the studies of self-regulation of mammalian populations have been reviewed at various times [14,18]. It is clear that
there are very great effects on rates of reproduction, growth, and
mortality. These effects occur not only under conditions of captivity but in such natural phenomena as the lemming cycle in which the
levels of corticosterone are low at low densities of mice and then
increase at high densities [1]. Another topic that will be passed
over is a discussion of social rank as such. It is assumed that
everyone now realizes that many kinds of animals including invertebrates arrange themselves in some sort of ranking which is established
by some sort of aggressive behavior. Since under the conditions of
social organization there may be survival value for aggressiveness,
it seems likely that over a period of time selection will alter the
genotype of the species. So far genotypic change has not been demonstrated [40] although probably many more studies should be made before
the hypothesis is rejected. Perhaps the selection occurs over centuries rather than a year or two as has been suggested.

THE DEVELOPMENT OF STRESS

The crowding of animals, through the stimuli produced by the individuals, produces physiological reactions that have been lumped together under the term stress. This term has been widely used in a most sloppy manner so that it has come to mean simply that something is going wrong with the individual. However, in its original meaning it was meant to imply that some divergence from the normal occurs which presumably, through homeostatic mechanisms, will eventually be brought back to the original level. It is very important to note that the effects of several stressors are roughly additive. For example, Boulouard reported that the corticosterone in normal rats was 26.7 mg/100 ml of plasma [7]. In animals that were starved it was 34.6 mg/100 ml. Rats kept in the cold produced 37.0 mg/100 ml. Rats both starved and put in the cold produced 46.8 mg/100 ml. The phenomenon has been reported numerous times and was one of the items in the original formulation of the theory of stress. While there must be a point beyond which the adrenal cannot increase the output of hormones, nevertheless for our interest it is important to recognize that we may assume that chemical and auditory stimuli are probably additive in their effect on other animals in a crowded situation.

A variety of conditions can produce stress. For example, Arguelles found that in men auditory stimuli produced an increase in the cortisol in the plasma [2]. It was noted that patients suffering from anxiety had a great increase but depressive patients had only a small increase. Of particular relevance to our discussion here is the fact that surgical procedures, through the stimuli of anticipation and the actual pain or wounding, may produce an increase in the activity of the adrenals. This activity is superimposed upon the circadian rhythm causing an increase whether the daily activity is at a low period or a high period [21]. Another common cause of stress is a strange situation produced, for example, by captivity in animals or a change of location in humans. This stress may deplete the adrenal reserve over a period of time and thereby result in a condition where the added stress of surgery will result in adrenal insufficiency and perhaps physiological derangement leading to death [41]. While perhaps the chemical and acoustic stimuli have been most frequently studied, there is evidence that visual stimuli may be effective [39]. The viewing of an unpleasant film resulted in an increase in the heart rates, skin resistance and respiration in a number of normal subjects.

Fortunately mammals have developed feedback processes to regulate the effects of derangements. Within limits the corticoids, produced by stimulation of ACTH from the pituitary, depress the release of ACTH thereby acting as a negative feedback. This effect may prevent excessive physiological derangements that might cause overt illness. However, the existence of occult responses may be important in the long-term physiological responses.

In recent years the astounding effects of early experiences in altering the reaction of an animal when adult to stress have been extensively studied. For example, McIver found that trivial handling of the infant for a three-minute period at ages two to five days had great effects in the reaction of glucose level to stress when the animal was an adult [38]. The rats that had been handled showed in response to stress a prompt increase in the glucose level and then a rapid lowering. In contrast, the animals that had not been handled as infants showed little change over a period of an hour. It seems that the first reaction is physiologically more useful to the individual. In another study Barrett and Stockham compared the effects of housing conditions and some other experimental procedures on the response of the rat after a sharp noise [5]. Grouped individuals showed a much greater response than did isolated. Also, such simple procedures as weighing, injection of saline and several drugs produced rather striking increases in the corticosterone in the plasma. The effects of earlier experience can be extended to the prenatal condition. Certain stresses before mating of the parents resulted in changes in the behavior of the progeny when they were exposed as adults to various stresses. To add complications to the situation is the fact that different genotypes react differently to these conditions. A further complication is the fact that there is recent evidence to indicate that when high levels of corticoid are maintained either by the injection of ACTH or hydrocortisone then the individuals have a high level of learning [33]. The separation of the physiological and psychological effects will take a long time.

An additional factor mentioned above that adds complications is the fact that the output of corticoids from the adrenal follows a circadian rhythm. The rhythm seems to have functional value since the output of corticoids increases around dawn thereby tuning up the animal for the activity of waking up and getting started for the day's activities. In nocturnal species the circadian rhythm differs by approximately 12 hours. These changes in corticoid levels are accompanied by many changes in other physiological phenomena such as the levels of sodium and potassium. Important for our interest is that experiments must be done either at the same time of day or with consideration to the circadian rhythms, to allow interpretation or comparison.

PHYSIOLOGICAL REPERCUSSIONS

Crowding through a variety of stimuli excites the central brain mechanisms to stimulate the hypothalamus which releases the hormones from the anterior pituitary. The study of these endocrine effects has produced extensive results recently reviewed [14]. Bronson has reviewed the topic with special interest in reproduction, and the short term production of adrenal hormones [9]. It should be noted that ACTH although having its major effect on the adrenals can produce some effects directly [13].

The distinction between acute and chronic stimuli is important because the results differ markedly. An acute stimulus (loud noise, wounds, fright) produces an immediate chain of reactions resulting in prompt release of hormones from the adrenal and other glands and then a return to normal without a change in the average level. In contrast a chronic stimulus (regular noise, daily conflict, persistent infection) results in a gradual (one to two weeks) increase of release of hormones until a new, higher, level is attained.

As has been mentioned before most studies last only a few days or weeks at the most. However, an important point is that minor changes in the conditions may bring about these adrenal changes. For example, Barrett and Stockham found that small changes of cage conditions resulted in very high levels of corticosterone in the plasma and in the adrenal [5]. However, conditioning by handling or simply weighing the animals reduced the responses to further treatments. The essence of this type of study is that continued change or variation in living circumstances can permit a mammal to become accustomed to change. These changes really are part of the homeostatic mechanism that comes into action as various stimuli persist. Even such things as the arterial pressure in mice can be affected. Henry and Stephens measured systolic pressure of mice under several different conditions [26]. The pressure in mice six to a cage was 126 mm of mercury. When eight were in a small cage the pressure rose somewhat but when 50 were put into a 4-foot square box, the pressure rose after five months from 136 to 164 and was maintained at approximately that level. Thus, the homeostatic mechanisms were readjusted to a different position. Innumerable studies of this type have been performed showing that the changes occur but that adjustment results. It would be out of place here to describe these in detail.

However, another type of change is important for our considerations. Among the many effects of corticoids is an inhibition of the production of antibodies to foreign protein. This reduction in antibodies may result in an increase in overt disease among mammals suffering this change. Again, the literature is extensive [6], but a few recent examples may be mentioned. Hill et al., immunized a kind of monkey with albumin [27]. Then the monkeys were exposed to noise and light and to sudden movements. These individuals had a delayed formation of antibody in contrast to monkeys that were not exposed to these environmental stresses. Also, the stressed individuals had higher levels of cortisol. In another study the levels of interferon decreased in mice that were stressed by being exposed to a shuttle box [29]. However, mice whose adrenals had been removed also had a decrease under these conditions suggesting that a change in levels in adrenal corticoids is not the whole story. A difficult problem to surmount in studies of this type is that the actually measured antibodies or substances such as interferon are not necessarily involved in immunity to disease. However, ample evidence is available to show that disease is exacerbated when animals are exposed to stresses of the type that occur in crowding [12]. A final set of effects that needs to be mentioned is the altered sensitivity to a variety of drugs. Welch and Welch [53] have recently summarized some of these effects from the immense literature. One of the drugs most frequently studied is amphetamine which differs greatly in its effect on mice that are grouped in contrast to mice that are kept singly. Apparently, most of these effects act through the catecholamines. In some cases the effects alter the metabolism of precursors [52]. A sedative such as reserpine may prevent adaptation to certain types of stress [45]. The important point to recognize in all of these studies is that the environmental situation produces a level of response that may differ according to the particular stimuli. Thus, we can expect that when an animal changes to a different situation, then it will have to change its basic level of environmental stimulation.

A major effect of high levels of corticoids is inhibition of various reproductive functions. The details have been described [9, 12], and need not concern us here, except to point out that chronic stress may result in prolonged diestrus, regression of testes and other changes. These disturbances may add to the difficulties of an animal and, in the case of humans, the problems of diagnosis and care.

Age after maturity seems to have little relation to the physiological repercussions. However, the overt changes (e.g., reproduction) mimic the changes occurring with advanced age. Thus, premature senility would be the apparent result of chronic stress resulting from crowding.

The above discussion has concerned principally studies of short term effects or at least studies that were carried out during a short period of time. One report indicates that restraint of rats for five weeks causes no adrenal response, even though a response occurred at five days [42]. As indicated above, very few long-term studies of adaptation are available. However, some recent work suggests that the long-term effects begin immediately after birth [33]. Rats that were handled for 10-20 days shortly after birth showed a reduction in the adrenal hormones in the plasma at the time of weaning. Of further interest is the fact that if the female was handled while she was pregnant, there was also a reduction even though the progeny themselves were not handled [34]. To translate these results into a crowded situation, one can suppose that if many animals are in a small area then the young are exposed to a variety of stimuli and thus become less responsive to stimuli when they are adults.

This same phenomenon perhaps is responsible for an aspect that has been important in the study of the effects of density on popu-

lations. For many years it has been known that rodents born at
high density have a low survival as adults even when they were
maintained at a low density. Furthermore, the young born to such
parents also had a low survival. The importance for populations
has been that after a striking reduction in numbers the increase
was delayed for surprisingly long periods of time. DeLong showed
that house mice had a remarkably different survival as adults depending on whether they were born at a time of high density or at
a time of low density [19]. Thus, again the long-term effect is
quite striking. At least some chronic disease conditions perhaps
result from these high levels of adrenal activity. Christian showed that a renal disease occurs in mice after treatment with ACTH
for a matter of many weeks [13]. Other chronic conditions such as
response to angiotensin may also be induced by behavioral stimulation [47]. This increased response may be a factor in the production of kidney disease.

Another long-term effect concerns the growth of the individuals.
For many species it has been clearly demonstrated that corticoids
inhibit growth, and animals in crowded situations grow at a lesser
rate. A possible explanation, of course, is that such individuals
do not get an adequate supply of food. However, recently Imms carefully measured and regulated the food and water intake of rats [28].
Various artificial stresses such as injections, forced choice, and
surgery slowed the growth independently of intake of food and water.
Presumably, the oxidative metabolism must have been increased under
these circumstances.

BEHAVIORAL ADAPTATIONS

The profound physiological effects of changes in the environment have encouraged the development of behavioral adaptations to
mitigate any unfortunate results. Animals have developed a system
of social organization that is exemplified by territorial or social
ranks behavior. While in practice these two types often seem very
different, nevertheless, they are simply modifications of the same
basic organization. A territorial individual defends a particular
area from which it excludes other individuals. He could be considered as the sole member of a group or as a member of a group of
several individuals, none of which actually come into physical contact with each other except in the early phases of establishment of
territory. In contrast, social rank is the arrangement of individuals into a sequence with the dominant individual at the top. Presumably, the same physiological effects occur in territorial species
as in social ranks species, but so far studies have not been performed on the former. Some interesting variations occur, such as
the woodchuck which has a social organization but only exerts social pressure when individuals are above ground. Thus, an individual, although usually subordinate, may be dominant if the top ranking individuals are asleep in the burrow. This example is only one

of the multitude of variations within the general topic.

The conditions of crowding produce many behavioral changes. Naturally, there are more contacts among the individuals and a frequent result is that many animals will huddle together in groups or even piles. Indeed, as a population of individuals in a cage increases, there may suddenly be a change from relatively individual behavior to huddling [12]. Presumably, all of the individuals in a group can identify each other so that individual recognition is possible. Naturally, there are very many stimuli from the other individuals. The variety of sounds, smells and motions increases as the number of individuals increases. If we remember the old law of family interaction, we will note that the number of interactions increases approximately as the square of the number of individuals, at least after relatively high numbers are attained. Thus, the change from 100 to 200 mice in a large cage results in an increase by four in the number of stimuli. The adjustment to crowding consists of organization into behavioral groupings. It is important to remember that animals can identify only a certain number of individuals and thus at very high densities the organization may collapse simply because the individuals cannot learn the characteristics of all others. Equally important in this crowded situation is the possibility that the chance of encountering the same individual enough times to learn his characteristics becomes very low. Under these circumstances again the individual does not know the other individuals in the group. Thus no possibility exists for a stable organization of any sort. There are suggestions from recent studies on mice that this extreme condition actually occurred, and since there is no organization there are no physiological inhibitions of breeding and the mouse population increases to astronomical numbers.

A long time ago it was shown that the top ranking mice had normal adrenal glands [17], and, more recently, Louch, et al. have confirmed that the corticosterone in the plasma of dominant individuals is at a lower level than that of the subordinate [37]. In this experiment, the weight of the adrenals also was lower in the dominant individuals though the difference was small. It now appears likely that the weight of the adrenals greatly underestimates the differences in the production of corticoids in animals of different rank. An important feature of this relationship is illustrated by Bailey [31]. He kept mice in groups of 2, 4, 8, 16, and 32 in cages of varying sizes so that the space per mouse was identical for all groups. The adrenals of single mice were smaller than those of mice in groups, but the adrenals of mice in groups of 32 were not different from groups of 2. Thus the real change is between an isolated individual and individuals that are together in groups.

The significant aspect about social rank is that an organization is produced that results in stability. However, if the dominant individual is replaced by a new individual then the stability is destroyed and a new rank has to be developed [44]. Generally the introduced animal has little chance of succeeding, but Christian reports that if four or more individuals are introduced then the disruption of the social organization may be sufficient so that some of the aliens can establish themselves in the ranking [15]. Although in mice the location of food and water seem to have little effect on the development of rank, in some species (domestic swine), the social organization among gilts only develops when the feeding space is inadequate [43]. Perhaps, however, in this case the organization was present but not sufficiently conspicuous to be noticed under circumstances of adequate feeder space. Among wild species the aggression may change during the year [10, 25]. Generally the adult males are most aggressive in the springtime. In the woodchuck the aggression declines rather rapidly after breeding in May, but in the deermouse the aggressiveness is maintained throughout the mating season until Fall. The organization of social rank and the seasonal changes in aggression are devices to reduce the social strife. A result is that groups become compatible and can live together in peace because each knows his place. Thus behavioral adaptation reduces the physiological repercussions.

The above information shows that mammals can adapt to crowding through the development of social organization that mitigates the ill effects. Another obvious behavioral adaptation is to emigrate. Many species use this device [16]. Indeed Lidicker [36] emphasized that some species might have a selection value for emigration. Thus individuals that move out of an area that was too crowded would have a chance for survival by starting over somewhere else. Among humans this factor was probably important in movements in past centuries, but since the world is now essentially full of human beings, this factor can no longer be regularly used. Indeed, the humans have now reached the stage where they must recognize that they are living in a closed environment that is essentially full to capacity.

The above types of behavioral adaptations consist of patterns that involve the history of each individual in respect to other individuals. However, the individual himself may produce adaptation through learning or habituation. Komaromi and Donhoffer tested the effect of a reward on the response to intravenous injection of saline into individual rats [30]. The measure of effect was the depletion of adrenal ascorbic acid (AAA). The reference individuals had a level of 467mg/100g of AAA. Animals that had no pretreatment or warning of the injection showed a depletion to 367 mg. Animals that were injected every day for a period of time became somewhat habituated and showed only a slight depletion to 410 mg. However, individuals that were rewarded after each injection by a morsel of food showed no depletion whatsoever. Thus there may be situations

in which reward should be presented at the time of a noxious stimulus. This reward would overcome the effects in terms of physiological repercussions.

CONSEQUENCES

The main result of crowding in wild species is the elimination
of low ranking individuals [15]. Through disease due to the lowered resistance and through emigration the individuals that have
not been able to attain a high rank will disappear from the population. It must be noted that in most cases the organization of
the species into a rank does not require severe fighting so that
direct injuries are relatively rare. However, in some cases the
injuries are sufficiently severe perhaps to cause death, at least
to increase the risk of infection [50, 46]. Individuals that are
not sufficiently low in the organization to die or to move away
may adapt to the situation. In some cases the adaptation is physiological resulting in an increased but steady level of reactions.
Presumably such animals are able to exist although not as securely
as the dominant ones. Another type of adaptation is a withdrawal
of the individual so that he does not receive any stimuli. It is
not uncommon in mouse populations to find some very low-ranking
individuals with small adrenal glands and other evidences of lack
of stress. When watched closely these individuals remain in corners and rarely exert themselves to join the group. They may be
considered as having withdrawn completely from the situation.

APPLICATION TO MAN

The translation of studies of other mammals to man is fraught
with danger. However, there is no doubt that at least the methods
of study can be used for important discoveries about man. Furthermore, the results of studies of other animals may suggest hypotheses
to be tested. The first conclusion that may be applied to man is
that new and unusual stimuli may produce physiological effects [23].
Indeed, this conclusion has been amply documented by psychosomatic
studies. For example, Brady reports severe and prolonged gastric
disturbances resulting from various stressors [8]. The most common
study is the reaction of medical students to examinations where again
and again it has been shown that adrenal function is increased. The
significance for humans is simply that for many apparently normal
individuals the reaction to stressful situations may be excessive
and that their health may be impaired by this situation. Crowding
with its increase in the level of stimulation produces a variety of
conditions that alter the physiological function.

Several possible ways exist to mitigate the ill effects of
crowding. The information about the social organization of animals
indicates the importance of stability; individuals must be fully
aware of their position in an organization. Disruption of organiz-

ations will produce very severe effects on persons. Another very important consideration is the relationship between the size of the group and the complexity of the social organization [11]. Studies of various types of human populations show that as the number of individuals increases the number of social units increases. This division apparently arises from the necessity of maintaining social interactions, without increasing the difficulties of communication and thereby the stress.

For mental hospitals reduction of stress should be fostered by dividing the group of patients into small units. The recent procedure of division into treatment teams ("unitization") certainly would improve the care of the patient by developing stability within the social organization. Another suggestion is to use rewards in reducing the ill effects of a stressful situation. Thus, a new psychiatrist in a hospital should reward each patient by some device to reduce the physiological effects of his being a stranger. As another example, the change of an individual from one building to the next or from one room to the next should be accompanied by some favorable stimulus. Also when a patient is introduced to a new social group some reward or benefit should be available. The effects of such applications from animal studies have not been adequately tested.

REFERENCES

1. Andrews, R.V.: Daily and seasonal variation in adrenal metabolism of the brown lemming. Physiol. Zool., 41:86–94, 1968.
2. Arguelles, A.E.: Endocrine response to auditory stress of normal and psychiatric subjects. In Bajusz, E., ed., An Introduction to Clinical Neuroendocrinology. Williams and Wilkins Company, Baltimore, Maryland, 1967.
3. Bailey, E.D.: Social interaction as a population-regulating mechanism in mice. Canad. J. Zool., 44:1007–1012, 1966.
4. Barrett, A.M. and Stockham, M.A.: The effect of housing conditions and simple experimental procedures upon the corticosterone level in the plasma of rats. J. Endocrinol., 26:97–105, 1963.
5. _____ and _____: The response of the pituitary-adrenal system to a stressful stimulus: the effect of conditioning and pentobarbitone treatment. J. Endocrinol., 33:145–152, 1965.
6. Beisel, W.R. and Rapoport, M.I.: Inter-relations between adrenocortical functions and infectious illness. New Eng. J. Med., 280:541–546, 1969.
7. Boulouard, R.: Effects of cold and starvation on adrenocortical activity of rats. Fed. Proc., 22:750–753, 1963.
8. Brady, J.V.: Behavioral stress and physiological change. Trans. N.Y. Acad. Sci., 26:483–496, 1964.

9. Bronson, F.H.: Effects of social stimulation on adrenal and
        reproductive physiology of rodents. In Conally, M.L.,
        ed., Husbandry of Laboratory Animals. Academic Press,
        New York, 1964.

10. _____ : Agonistic behavior in woodchucks. Anim. Behav.,
        12:470-478, 1964.

11. Carneiro, R.L.: On the relationship between size of population
        and complexity of social organization. Southwest J.
        Anthropol., 23:234-243, 1967.

12. Christian, J.J.: The pathology of overpopulation. Milit. Med.,
        128:511-603, 1963.

13. _____ : Glomerular renal disease in mice after chronic
        ACTH treatment. J. Endocrinol., 28:6-7, 1964.

14. _____ , Lloyd, J.A. and Davis, D.E.: The role of endo-
        crines in the self-regulation of mammalian populations.
        In Pincus, G., ed., Recent Progress in Hormone Research,
        Vol. 21. Academic Press, New York, 1965.

15. _____ : The potential role of the adrenal cortex as af-
        fected by social rank and population density on experi-
        mental epidemics. Amer. J. Epidemiol., 87:255-266, 1968.

16. Clough, G.C.: Social behavior and ecology of Norwegian lemmings
        during a population peak and crash. Norwegian State Game
        Res. Instit., 2:1-50, 1968.

17. Davis, D.E. and Christian, J.J.: Relation of adrenal weight to
        social rank of mice. Proc. Soc. Exp. Biol. Med.,
        94:728-731, 1957.

18. _____ : Integral Animal Behavior. Macmillan, New York, 1966.

19. Delong, K.T.: Population ecology of feral house mice. Ecology,
        48:611-634, 1967.

20. Essman, W.B.: The development of activity differences in isolated
        and aggregated mice. Anim. Behav., 14:405-409, 1966.

21. Estep, H.L.: Neuroendocrine aspects of surgical stress. In Ba-
        jusz, E., ed., An Introduction to Clinical Neuroendocrin-
        ology. Williams and Wilkins Company, Baltimore, 1967.

22. Frankel, A.I., Graber, J.W., Cook, B. and Nalbandov, A.V.: The
        duration and control of adrenal function in adenohypo-
        physectomized cockerels. Steroids, 10:699-707, 1967.

23. Friedman, S.B. and Ader, R.: Adrenocortical response to novelty
        and noxious stimulation. Neuroendocrinology, 2:209-212,
        1968.

24. Hatch, A., Balazs, T., Wiberg, G.S. and Grice, H.C.: Long-term
        isolation stress in rats. Science, 142:507, 1963.

25. Healey, M.C.: Aggression and self-regulation of population size
        in deermice. Ecology, 48:377-392, 1967.

26. Henry, J. and Stephens, P.: Effects of the social environment
        on the arterial pressure of CBA mice. Fed. Proc., 23:515,
        1964.

27. Hill, C.W., Greer, W.E. and Felsenfield, O.: Psychological stress,
        early response to foreign protein and blood cortisol in
        vervets (monkey). Psychosom. Med., 24:279-283, 1967.

28. Imms, F.J.: The effects of stress on the growth rate and food
                 and water intake of rats. J. Endocrinol., 37:1-8, 1967.
29. Jensen, M.M.: Transitory impairment of interferon production in
                 stressed mice. J. Infect. Dis., 118:230-234, 1968.
30. Komaromi, I. and Donhoffer, S.: The effect of habituation and
                 reward on adrenal ascorbic acid depletion in response
                 to the intravenous injection of physiological saline
                 in the rat. Acta Physiol., 23:293-295, 1963.
31. Levine, S. and Treiman, D.M.: Differential plasma corticosterone
                 response to stress in four inbred strains of mice.
                 Endocrinol., 75:142-144, 1964.
32. Levine, L., Daikow, C.A. and Barsel, G.E.: Interstrain fighting
                 in male mice. Anim. Behav., 13:52-58, 1965.
33. Levine, S. and Brush, R.F.: Adrenocortical activity and avoid-
                 ance learning as a function of time after avoidance
                 training. Physiol. Behav., 2:385-388, 1967.
34. _____: Maternal and environmental influence on the adreno-
                 cortical response to stress in weanling rats. Science,
                 156:258-260, 1967.
35. Licht, L.E.: Growth inhibition in crowded tadpoles: intraspeci-
                 fic and interspecific effects. Ecology, 48:736-745, 1967.
36. Lidicker, Jr., W.Z.: Emigration as a possible mechanism permit-
                 ting the regulation of population density below carrying
                 capacity. Amer. Natur., 96:29-33, 1962.
37. Louch, C.D. and Higginbotham, M.: The relation between social
                 rank and plasma corticosterone in mice. Gen. Comp.
                 Endoc., 8:441-445, 1967.
38. McIver, A.H.: Reactivity to stress in rats as a function of in-
                 fantile experience. Proc. Soc. Exp. Biol. Med.,
                 119:757-759, 1965.
39. Mordkoff, A.M.: The relationship between psychological and physio-
                 logical response to stress. Psychosom. Med., 26:135-150,
                 1964.
40. Myers, K.: The effects of density on sociality and health in
                 mammals. Proc. Ecol. Soc. Aust., 1:40-64, 1966.
41. Nagle, J.P., Cammock, E.E., Nyhus, L.M. and Harkins, H.N.: Evi-
                 dence for adrenal insufficiency in acutely stressed
                 captive monkeys. J. Appl. Physiol., 20:131-133, 1965.
42. Pfeiffer, C.J.: The physiologic effects of restricted activity
                 in the rat: Stress effects of chronic restraint. Exp.
                 Med. Surg., 25:201-217, 1967.
43. Rasmussen, O.G., Banks, E.M., Berry, T.H. and Becker, D.E.: So-
                 cial dominance in gilts. J. Anim. Sci., 21:520-522,
                 1962.
44. Reimer, J.D. and Petras, M.L.: Breeding structure of the house
                 mouse (Mus musculus) in a population cage. J. Mammal.,
                 48:88-99, 1967.
45. Rosecrans, J.A. and De Feo, J.J.: The interrelationships between
                 chronic restraint stress and reserpine sedation. Arch.
                 Int. Pharmacodyn., 157:487-498, 1965.

46. Rothballer, A.B.: Aggression, defense and neurohumors. UCLA Forum Med. Sci., 7:135-170, 1967.
47. Sapira, J.D., Lipman, R.L. and Shapiro, A.P.: Hyperresponsivity to angiotensin induced in rats by behavioral stimulation. Proc. Soc. Exp. Biol. Med., 123:52-55, 1966.
48. Scott, J.P.: Agonistic behavior of mice and rats: A review. Amer. Zool., 6:683-701, 1966.
49. Sigg, E.B., Day, C. and Colombo, C.: Endocrine factors in isolation-induced aggressiveness in rodents. Endocrinology, 78:679-684, 1966.
50. Smith, M.S.R.: Injuries as an indication of social behavior in the weddell seal (Leptonychotes weddelli). J. Mammal., 30:241-246, 1966.
51. Thiessen, D.D.: Population density, mouse genotype, and endocrine function in behavior. J. Comp. Physiol. Psychol., 57:412-416, 1964.
52. Welch, B.L. and Welch, A.: An effect of aggregation upon the metabolism of Dopamine-1-^{3}H. In Himwich, H.E. and Himwich, W.A., eds., Progress in Brain Research, Vol. 8. American Elsevier, New York, 1964.
53. _____ and _____: Sustained effects of brief daily stress (fighting) upon brain and adrenal catecholamines and adrenal, spleen, and heart weights of mice. Proc. Nat. Acad. Sci., 64:100-107, 1969.

The Effects of Varying Density and Space on Sociality and Health in Animals

K. Myers, C. S. Hale, R. Mykytowycz
and R. L. Hughes

ABSTRACT. This paper represents data on two experiments (using
31 replicates) in which populations of wild rabbits were exposed to
different conditions of density and living space within the confined
areas of a natural habitat. The analysis offered at this stage relates only to treatment effects.

1. Living space varying - population density held constant.

Under this regime, the most detrimental effects were measured in
rabbits in the smallest living space, despite the fact that this was
accompanied by a decrease in numbers of animals in the group. There
were changes in index organs (liver, spleen, kidney), adrenal morphology and zonation, and behaviour and reproduction. In the
smallest space, rates of sexual and aggressive behaviour increased
significantly, especially among females, and wounding was higher.
There was a fall-off in reproductive capacity in females - lower
ovulation rates and smaller numbers of corpora lutea.

2. Living space varying - numbers of animals in population constant.

There was great improvement of the quality of individual animals
in each group as living space increased. Index organs and endocrines
all showed the development of harmful effects in individual rabbits
when living space was restricted. Sexual and aggressive behaviour
decreased and reproductive capacity increased with increasing space.

The effects of changes in living space were also measurable at
embryonic, nestling and young animal levels. In the smallest living
areas, the younger classes in the population were severely stunted.

Adult rabbits of both sexes which had been born 12 months previously into high density populations were significantly different, qualitatively, to those born in low density situations.

Such animals were sexually and aggressively very active, but possessed large adrenals and other attributes indicative of ill-health.

Survival in adults followed the trends set by physiological indices. In the young, mortality due to social factors was greatest where group size was largest, irrespective of space.

The data are discussed in relation to other findings. We conclude that the "density syndrome" in mammals is a reality. It is a reaction to a rise in numbers; but in the individual mammal, it is not a response to group size per se but to some form of spatial restriction, either in the form of space itself or some configuration of animals behaving in space.

The response of the individual mammal to this stimulus depends upon its genotype, physiological equipment, and previous social experience. Of the three, we believe that upsets in the physiological homeostases during development could rank, over the short term, as the most important by altering the biological qualities of successive generations.

INTRODUCTION

There is a growing emphasis in the study of mammal populations on those processes which operate in relation to changes in density. This work had its roots in early considerations of the causes of cycles in arctic mammals [43] and was established as an important field for study and conjecture by the works of Christian [22], Calhoun [14] and Chitty [18,19]. With the inclusion of the later but equally significant contribution of Wynne-Edwards [127], this group of workers provides one of the most challenging theses of our age. In the words of Christian [25], "each population has an upper asymptote of growth based on its sociobehavioral structure, which will operate even in the presence of a great superfluity of all environmental needs." Each of the above-mentioned workers places different emphases on the processes involved, but Christian's statement epitomizes the main theme which links their work.

The definition of "crowding" or "density" in relation to mammalian populations is accompanied by conceptual difficulties. Several variables are involved - numbers of animals (group size), numbers of animals per unit space (density), reaction of individuals to other individuals in the living area ("social space"), and space itself. Many ecologists ignore the last two in the belief that, in nature, space never or rarely limits. On the other hand, it is just as common for laboratory workers in many fields to ignore living area when they vary cage size to keep floor space per animal constant [104,123,116,5]. Differences in treatment means are then ascribed to increase in group size since density remains unaltered.

The inherent difficulty in studying space per se as a variable in mammalian populations is reflected in the paucity of published data on the subject. The only ones of substance we have been able to find are those of Eleftheriou et al. [42], Petrusewicz [99], Petrusewicz et al. [100,101], and Southwick]109].

Eleftheriou et al. used variable cage size as a physical, environmental stimulus when testing the effects of strange male Peromyscus maniculatus bairdii on implantation rates. In the largest cages, the stud male performed better and strange males had less effect on blocking pregnancies. Since group size was held constant, the space-density effect, although not commented on, was obvious[42].

Petrusewicz and his colleagues compared beetles (Tribolium spp.) and white mice in cages of different sizes. Both the insects and mammals, when censused as adults, showed a lower mean density in the larger containers in which they lived. Petrusewicz was led to suggest that, in the media of smaller size, the structural organization of the populations was simpler, the probability of contacts of the type inhibiting population growth was less, and productivity was therefore greater [99]. Absolute number of individuals was thus more important than density.

Southwick, studying a balanced, social group of 17 rhesus monkeys in a large pen in N. India, measured the increase in agonism which occurred when new juveniles, adult females and adult males were introduced into the population, and when the group was crowded into half the space by partitioning the cage [109]. Crowding of the animals caused a twofold increase in intragroup aggression (11.6 to 22.8 acts/hour), but social changes caused increases in aggression of up to tenfold. Social changes thus had a greater impact on aggression than decrease in space. This agrees in general with the ideas expressed by Petrusewicz [99], Bailey [5], and others mentioned above, but shows, in addition, that rates of aggression are also a function of space itself.

THE RABBIT

The rabbit is a positively gregarious mammal. It is also a highly social one [73,84,85,88,89,90,91]. The social unit of rabbit populations is the breeding group, a small assemblage of one to three males and one to five females which, together, protects an area of land in which feeding, resting and breeding takes place, and which fulfills all the requirements of territory. Within the group, one male is always dominant over the other one or two present and one female usually dominates her colleagues.

Group formation is a function of mutual attraction between females [85]. The breeding group of females is a compact, social unit. The males are attached to the group by attraction to the females. The number of rabbits in a group appears to be determined by the ability of the animals to recognize, or at least associate with, a limited number of other rabbits.

Territorial behavior is accompanied by aggression. In rabbits within the group, there occur acts of aggression between dominant and subordinate males, and to a less extent, between females, and a varying amount of aggression between members of the group and strangers either from neighbouring groups or attached to no group at all.

Successful reproduction is a fundamental function of group activity. Within the balanced social atmosphere of the group, the female rabbit breeds with little hindrance and, while physical conditions remain favourable, her young appear and grow vigorously in a regular succession of litters.

If living space is held constant and population numbers are permitted to increase, a sequence of events occurs which significantly alters this situation [81]:

i. There is an increase in the number of breeding groups and a significant decrease in the size of group territory. At very high population densities, group size increases.

ii. Rates of aggression increase. In males, this is due mainly to an increase in extra-group encounters. In females, there is an increase in fighting between members of the same group.

iii. Reproduction is depressed, mainly due to interruptions in breeding in females (resorptions of embryos, inhibition of oestrous behaviour, upsets in maternal behaviour). Depression in reproductive performance commences as soon as density starts to increase. The main effect occurs when there are between 10 and 50 breeding adults per acre. A further increase in density has less effect.

iv. A wide variety of physiological changes occurs in both adults and young, typified by significant changes in the morphology, zonation, and lipid content of the adrenal glands and in the weights of various organs.

In this paper, we examine the population response to a variable living space, both when density is held constant and when size of population remains unchanged.

METHODS

The design of the experiment was as follows:

i. Living Space Varying - Numbers of Animals Constant.

Treatment	Number of Replicates	Population Size		Size of Enclosure (sq. yds.)	Density (Rabbits/Acre)
		♂	♀		
A1	5	2	3	450	50
A2	5	2	3	225	100
A3	12	2	3	112.5	200

ii. Living Space Varying - Population Density Constant.

Treatment	Number of Replicates	Population Size		Size of Enclosure (sq. yds.)	Density (Rabbits/Acre)
		♂	♀		
B1	3	8	12	450	200
B2	6	4	6	225	200
B3	12	2	3	112.5	200

Treatment 3 is common to both analyses.

KEY TO TABLES

Category	Abbreviation used	Explanation
KIDNEY	Glom.	Presence of glomerulonephritis (index 1-8, see text)
	Kidney scar.	Scar tissue on kidneys (index 1-8, see text)
	Kidney fat	Kidney fat (index 0-3, see text)
REPRODUCTION	Ovulations	Number of recent ovulations
	Corpora Lutea	# of functional corpora lutea present
	D. Corpora Lutea (mm)	Diameter in millimeters of corpora lutea
	Litter #	Numbers of litters born per unit female
	Litter size	Mean litter size at birth
	Corp. Alb.	Corpora Albicantia (index 1-2, see text)
	D. Corp. Alb. (mm)	Diameter in millimeters of Corpora Albicantia
	Palp. pregn.	Number of pregnancies ascertained by palpation during experiment
	Successful pregn.	Percentage of palpated pregnancies terminated successfully
	Young ♂	Number of young produced per unit female
	Burrow length	Mean length of feet of burrow excavated per animal
	Young mort.	Young mortality total in all litters (index 1-9, see text)
	Young survival	% of total number of days each rabbit lived
	Sperm.	Stage of spermatogenesis (index 1-8, see text)
BEHAVIOR	Aggression	Total aggressive behavior (acts/min.)
	Avoidance	Total avoidance behavior (acts/min.)
	Activity	Total activities behavior (acts/min.)
	Sex	Total sexual behavior (acts/min.)
	Scratches	Number of skin scratches (per rabbit)
	Wounds	Number of wounds in body (per rabbit)
	Status	Status (index 1-3, 1=dominant, see text)
	Survival	Per cent of total # of animals that survived
	Rel. Mort.	Relative mortality rate per rabbit
WEIGHT	B.W. (g)	Body weight in grams (g)
	% B.W. change	Per cent body weight change
	A.W. (g)	Adrenal weight in grams (g)
	Rel. A.W.	Adrenal weight (g)/Body weight (kg)
	S.W. (g)	Spleen weight in grams (g)
	Rel. S.W.	Spleen weight (g)/Body weight (kg)
	L.W. (g)	Liver weight in grams (g)
	Rel. L.W.	Liver weight (g)/Body weight (kg)
	Skin W.	Skin weight in grams (g)
	Rel. Skin W.	Skin weight (g)/Body weight (kg)
	T.W. (mg)	Testis weight in milligrams (mg)
	P.W. (mg)	Pituitary weight in milligrams (mg)
	M.G.W. (g)	Dry weight of mammary gland in grams (g)
	O.W. (g)	Ovary weight in grams (g)
	Thyr. W. (g)	Thyroid weight in grams (g)
ADRENAL	# adrenal nod.	Number of nodules on adrenal per rabbit
	Lipofuscin F-R	Lipofuscin in Z. Fasciculata-reticularis (index 1-12, see text)
	Alveol. F-R	Alveolation of Z. Fasciculata-reticularis (index 1-12, see text)
	Lipid F-R	Lipid in Z. Fasciculata-reticularis (index 1-10, see text)
	Lipid G.	Lipid in Z. Glomerulosa (index 1-15, see text)
	Alveol. G.	Alveolation in Z. Glomerulosa (index 1-5, see text)
	W.B.C.	White blood cells in cortex and medulla (index 1-9, see text)
	Adrenal area	Total area of median cross-section of adrenal (mm^2)
	Area F-R	Area of Z. Fasciculata-reticularis in per cent of adrenal area
	Area G	Area of Z. Glomerulosa in per cent of adrenal area
	Area M	Area of adrenal medulla in per cent of adrenal area

TABLE 1

RELATIONSHIPS BETWEEN ASSIGNED SOCIAL STATUS

AND BEHAVIOR IN MALE RABBITS

Behavior (Acts/minute)	Social Status			Significance of Differences between Means Deg. Fr. 2/130
	1 n = 49	2 n = 17	3 n = 67	
Threats	0.071	0.022	0.001	p<.001
Chases	0.040	0.023	0.005	p<.001
Avoidance of Threats	0.021	0.063	0.037	p<.01
Avoidance of Chases	0.009	0.021	0.033	p<.001
Territorial Chinning	0.360	0.044	0.012	p<.001
Sexual Following of Female	0.029	0.011	0.002	p<.001
Sexual Inspections of Female	0.129	0.056	0.009	p<.001
Precopulatory	0.012	0.000	0.000	p<.01
Total Sex Activities	0.170	0.067	0.011	p<.001

The 31 replicates were comprised of adult rabbits caught in natural populations in surrounding fields and a small number of animals (28 males, 27 females) bred in enclosures in 1963 [81]. Rabbits were weighed and assigned randomly to their replicates, except for those bred in enclosures which were distributed evenly among Treatments B1, B2 and B3.

Animals which died during the experiment were immediately replaced by a similar adult drawn from reserve populations held in neighbouring enclosures.

Excess food was present throughout the experiment in the form of a spring flush of pasture grasses (principally ryes and clovers), and abundant supplements of oaten grain and green and dry alfalfa scattered twice a week throughout each enclosure to give all animals equal access. Water was presented ad lib.

Each population was caught once per month for physical examination and births, deaths, and behaviour were measured as previously described [85,86]. Behaviour was measured on a time-numbers basis, each replicate receiving periods of observation proportional to the numbers of rabbits present. Replicates A1, A2, and A3 (B3) received 60 minutes of observation; replicate B2, 120 minutes and B1, 240 minutes. Each replicate was observed on at least six separate evenings. The categories of behaviour measured were: in males, acts of aggression, threats, chases, avoidances, territorial marking, inspections of females, sexual following and pre-copulatory activities; in females, acts of aggression and avoidances. On the basis of these measurements and taken in conjunction with the known dominant-subordinate relationships [84], each rabbit was then classified as dominant (social status 1), subordinate-high sexual activity (status 2), subordinate-low sexual activity (status 3).

The differences between the social categories in males are shown in Table 1. The data on females show similar trends.

The experiments were terminated on November 17-19, after 140-142 days, at the peak of the breeding season. All adults alive on that date were sacrificed and a series of observations made. Most of those relating to weights and counts raise no ambiguity in the following tables and need no further description. Some of the variables, however, need mention.

The crystalline eye lens was fixed in formalin, dried in an oven at 80°C for 72 hours and weighed to give an estimate of age [41,83].

Since the rabbits in each replicate were subjected to a variable amount of handling and chasing when being captured, no attempt was made to measure circulating corticoids. Stress was inferred by

measuring morphological changes in the adrenal gland known to be
associated with pituitary-adrenal stimulation. Where it seemed
profitable, we have not hesitated to make subjective estimates of
some variables.

A median, transverse section of the regularly shaped, right
adrenal gland was cut at 15μ stained in hematoxylin and a 50:50
mixture of Sudan III and IV, and examined for the following information:

i. Areas of the zona glomerulosa, zona fasciculata-reticularis
and medulla were measured by planimeter on enlarged photographs.
The Z.fasciculata-reticularis hypertrophies under the stimulus of
increased ACTH secretion [26].

ii. The lipid content in each adrenal zone was estimated
[Index 1-5 for the Z. glomerulosa: 1=cytoplasm of cells containing
sparse lipid granules; 3=cytoplasms of cells half full; 5=cytoplasms
of cells crammed full with lipid. In the same manner, index 1-10
or 1-12 was used for the Z.fasciculata-reticularis]. Lipid stores
in the adrenals are steroid precursors and disappear rapidly with an
increase in ACTH secretion [36].

iii. Lipofuscin content of the Z.fasciculata-reticularis was
estimated. [Index 1-12: 1=no lipofuscin present, 12=lipofuscin very
abundant.] Lipofuscin is an insoluble ceroid material which increases in the adrenal cortex with increasing age [36] and reproduction [73] and under stimulus of circulating estrogens [8].

iv. Alveolation of each adrenal cortical zone was estimated
[73] [Index 1-5 used in Z. glomerulosa: 1=cells of strands arranged
in thin fascicles 2 cells wide; 5=cells of strands arranged in large
multicellular alveoli. Index 1-12 was used for the Z. fasciculata-
reticularis] Under ACTH administration, the adrenal cortical cells
become compact and arranged in alveoli [110]. In severely stressed
glands, the whole cortex is reorganized. When this occurs, the cortex stains strongly for alkaline and acid phosphateses, dehydrogena-
ses and other enzymes; mitochondria become abundant and steroido-
genesis occurs.

v. Abundance of small, undifferentiated, white blood cells in
the different adrenal zones was estimated [Index 1-9: 1=white cells
absent, 9=cells very abundant.] White blood cells first appear in
the medulla and inner cortical zones and later spread to the outer
cortex. The adrenals may become the site of blood cell formation
in any situation when hematopoiesis is markedly stimulated in the
adult mammal [36].

In the healthy adrenal, the balance between glycocorticoid and
mineralocorticoid secretion appears to be satisfied by the process

of nodulation whenever the Z. fasciculata-reticularis is stimulated
by ACTH. The accessory adrenals thus formed are composed predominantly of glomerulosal tissue and probably secrete aldosterone predominantly.

Kidney damage occurred, apparently as a glomerulonephritis [27],
indicated by profuse inflammation and pitting of the kidney surface.
Scar tissue, in the form of raised, white, fibrous material on the
surface of the kidneys, was also common. In both cases, for each
kidney, an index measure of 0-4 (total 0-8) was used to attempt to
quantify the condition (1=no disease, 4=surface completely covered).

Kidney fat, which in the rabbit extends from the front of the
kidney to the pelvic region, was used as an index of condition
(0-3) (0=no fat present, 3=kidney completely covered with fat, fat
extending to pelvic region).

In males, the testes were sectioned at 10μ, stained with Giemsa,
and the most terminal stage of spermatogenesis noted according to the
following index:

          Spermatogonia present - 1. Resting
                                   2. Moderate mitotic division
                                   3. Active mitotic division

          Spermatocytes present - 4.
             Spermatids present - 5.
                 Sperm present - 6. Few only
                                   7. Moderate numbers
                                   8. Very large numbers

In females, in addition to other reproductive data, the absence (1) or presence (g) of corpora albicantia was noted, and their
diameters in mm. measured.

Young rabbits were removed from each replicate when 30 days of
age, in order to maintain the structure of the populations unchanged.

Animals which lived for less than 21 days are not included in
the analysis, since regressions of data on physiological changes on
time indicated that the period of adjustment to the respective
treatments was of this order.

Mortality is expressed as mean deaths per rabbit in each treatment. Survival is the period lived by each rabbit expressed as per
cent time available to live. Mortality in the young is analysed
simply by assigning a numerical value to each dead animal, such
that low numerals represent ecologically determined and high numerals
socially determined causes of death (1 = Drowned; 2 = Flooded out;
3 = Exposure to Damp and Cold; 4 = Bird Predation, 5 = Starved-

Mother Ill or Dead; 6 = Interference by Strange Female; 7 = Failure
of Early Parental Care; 8 = Deserted by Parent, 9 = Aborted).

The analyses presented here are confined almost completely to
treatment effects on the principal variables measured. Since comprehensive analyses showed that, with minor exceptions, there were
no significant differences between replicates, we have pooled the
data and present them as simple one-way and two-way analyses of
variance in relation to sex and treatment. Insignificant data have
generally been omitted except where they appear important for explanation.

Data derived from this experiment pertaining to the role of the
scent glands in population behaviour have been published [92]. Other
analyses, to be presented elsewhere, will deal with data on parasites
(J.D. Dunsmore), blood counts (E. Hesterman), and adrenal dynamics,
behaviour and health (K. Myers). The analyses were carried out on a
CDC 3600 computer.*

RESULTS

Mortality

Rabbits which died during the experiment exhibited a syndrome
which varied little between the sexes (Tables 2 and 3), irrespective
of whether death followed severe "social persecution" (by direct
aggression) or, in the absence of strong aggression, whether death
followed the development of diarrhoeia, unkempt pelage and chronic
inflammation and infection of scratches and wounds ("pathological").
Post-mortem examinations revealed miliary-type necrotic lesions on
the livers of many rabbits in the latter category, and a Pasteu-
rella sp. was isolated from some.

There was a tremendous loss in body weight, and significant
losses in skin, liver weights and fat reserves on the kidney. Kidney weight increased slightly due to the development of renal disease
and scarring of the kidney surface. Spleens increased in weight in
males, but decreased in females, a difference noted earlier [81].

In both sexes, adrenal weight increased significantly, and the
quantity of lipid in the adrenal cortical zones was markedly lower.
The areas occupied by each of the adrenal cortical zones in median
cross-section also showed significant differences, the adrenals of
living animals possessing lower proportions of zona fasciculata-

* We are indebted to Mr. Neil Gilbert, Division of Mathematical
  Statistics, C.S.I.R.O., Canberra, for assistance during
  this work.

TABLE 2

RELATIONSHIPS BETWEEN INDICES OF CONDITION, BEHAVIOR, AND

MORTALITY IN MALE RABBITS

| Variable | Type of Death | | | | Significance of Differences Between Means Deg. Fr. 3/127 |
	Sacrificed at End of Experiment	Social Persecution	Pathological Symptoms	Unknown	
n	87	17	23	3	
Survival	100	50.5	63.4	64.2	$p < .001$
Weight at Death (g.)	1469	1156	1150	1066	$p < .001$
% B.W. Change	-6.1	-24.9	-26.1	-29.8	$p < .001$
P.W. (mg.)	4.42	-	2.25	-	$p < .001$
A.W. (g.)	0.45	0.62	0.56	0.64	$p < .001$
Lipid G	1.91	1.41	1.35	1.00	$p < .001$
Lipid F-R	9.07	5.18	5.44	4.25	$p < .001$
Adrenal Area	31.56	40.48	36.62	40.63	$p < .001$
Area G	10.2	7.0	7.0	7.5	$p < .001$
Area F-R	83.9	87.5	87.7	89.1	$p < .001$
# Adrenal nod.	1.25	0.41	0.44	0.00	$p < .01$
Alveol. F-R	7.44	10.12	10.35	8.50	$p < .01$
W.B.C.	1.03	4.65	5.13	4.25	$p < .001$
Glom.(Index 1-8)	2.82	4.06	5.33	5.67	$p < .05$
Status	2.05	2.74	2.04	2.35	$p < .05$
Aggression	0.055	0.035	0.070	0.017	$p < .01$
Sex	0.079	0.020	0.073	0.016	$p < .05$

TABLE 3

RELATIONSHIPS BETWEEN INDICES OF CONDITION, BEHAVIOR, AND

MORTALITY IN FEMALE RABBITS

| Variable | Type of Death | | | | Significance of Differences Between Means Deg. Fr. 3/172 |
	Sacrificed at End of Experiment	Social Persecution	Pathological Symptoms	Unknown	
n	115	12	45	4	
Survival	100	49.6	69.0	67.3	$p < .001$
Weight at Death (g.)	1608	1103	1127	945	$p < .001$
% B.W. Change	8.4	-27.03	-24.09	-35.88	$p < .001$
K.W. (g.)	11.84	12.45	12.98	8.12	$p < .05$
S.W. (g.)	7.92	5.32	6.23	2.92	$p < .001$
A.W. (g.)	0.40	0.52	0.48	0.53	$p < .001$
Lipid F-R	7.91	6.17	6.02	6.00	$p < .001$
Adrenal Area	25.01	32.89	33.05	34.07	$p < .001$
Area G	13.3	8.5	8.2	8.5	$p < .001$
Area F-R	79.5	84.2	84.5	85.7	$p < .001$
Area M	6.9	8.6	8.6	8.8	$p < .01$
Alveol. F-R	6.92	8.58	8.62	8.75	$p < .01$
W.B.C.	1.13	4.67	3.98	3.75	$p < .001$
Glom.(Index 1-8)	2.95	3.33	4.41	5.50	$p < .01$
Scar Tissue on Kidneys (Index 1-8)	0.09	0.17	0.48	0.00	$p < .05$
Palp. Pregn.	2.87	0.67	1.35	1.21	$p < .001$
Successful Pregn.	92.8	50.0	65.2	90.0	$p < .001$
Scratches	3.7	13.5	5.5	9.6	$p < .1$
Status	2.15	2.58	2.5	2.58	$p < .05$
Aggression	0.032	0.025	0.014	0.009	N.S.
Avoidance	0.027	0.030	0.021	0.006	N.S.

reticularis and medulla and a much larger proportion of zona-
glomerulosa. In a solid model, such differences as measured here
would involve extremely large differences in the weight of secret-
ing tissues; and differences of this order in the rabbit have already been shown to be correlated with varying rates of corticoid
secretion [9]. Nodulation (formation of adrenal cortical adenomas
[82]) was suppressed in the sick animals, the cells of the cortex
were clumped into distinct alveoli, probably signifying a switch
in secretion from corticosterone to cortisol [68], and the cortex
was invaded by small white blood cells with large, dense nuclei
and sparse cytoplasm (probably lymphocytic).

It is to be noted that, in males, little difference existed
between the fate of the more subordinate animals, which died under
strong aggressive attack, and the more dominant rabbits which merely
exhibited cachexia (columns 2 and 3, Table 2). In females this
trend is not as marked.

The data pose several interesting problems, requiring multiple
regression analysis for their solution.

The best individual variables for predicting survival in males
(Deg. Fr. = 1/133) are white blood cells in Z. fasciculata-reticularis (F = 154), lipid in Z. fasciculata-reticularis (F = 124),
weight change (per cent) (F = 87), relative adrenal weight (F = 46),
and renal disease (F = 33); and, in females Deg. Fr. = 1/188),
white blood cells in Z. fasciculata-reticularis (F = 82), weight
change (per cent) (F = 65), relative adrenal weight (F = 53), and
lipid in Z. fasciculata-reticularis (F = 44).

Many other variables also show significant and important regressions on survival.

Rabbits in Confined Populations : Living Space Varying - Numbers
         of Animals in Population Constant

In this experiment, we studied the biological reactions of
adult and young rabbits in breeding populations, in which the numbers of animals were kept constant when maintained in three different sizes of enclosure. The main physical variable was living space.
Treatment A 1 comprised a balanced, social group in four units of
space; Treatment A 2, a social group in two units of space and
Treatment A 3, one group in one unit of space (112.5 sq. yds).

The living conditions for all the rabbits were harsher in terms
of density and spatial restriction than those which might be expected
in nature, even in Treatment A 1.

TABLE 4

DIFFERENCES IN BEHAVIOR IN ADULT WILD RABBITS IN CONFINED POPULATIONS:

VARIABLE LIVING SPACE - NUMBERS OF ANIMALS IN POPULATION CONSTANT

Behavior (Acts/minute)	Males				Females				Analysis of Variance Deg. Fr. 2/150		
	Living Space			Significance of Differences between Means	Living Space			Significance of Differences between Means	Sex	Treatment	Interaction
	4 Units	2 Units	1 Unit		4 Units	2 Units	1 Unit				
n	13	17	36	Deg. Fr. 2/63	18	22	50	Deg. Fr. 2/87			
Territorial Marking	0.094	0.108	0.100	N.S.	0.025	0.034	0.030	N.S.	N.S.	N.S.	N.S.
Total Sexual Behavior	0.089	0.112	0.131	p<.1	-	-	-	-	-	-	-
Total Aggressive Behavior	0.017	0.032	0.059	p<.05	0.018	0.029	0.049	p<.05	N.S.	p<.01	N.S.
Total Avoiding Behavior	0.020	0.033	0.053	N.S.	0.040	0.050	0.046	N.S.	p<.1	N.S.	N.S.

TABLE 5

DIFFERENCES IN INDICES OF CONDITION AND SURVIVAL IN ADULT WILD RABBITS IN CONFINED POPULATIONS:

VARIABLE LIVING SPACE - NUMBERS OF ANIMALS IN POPULATION CONSTANT

Variable	Males				Females				Analysis of Variance Deg. Fr. 2/150		
	Living Space			Significance of Differences between Means	Living Space			Significance of Differences between Means	Sex	Treatment	Interaction
	4 Units	2 Units	1 Unit		4 Units	2 Units	1 Unit				
n	13	17	36	Deg. Fr. 2/63	18	22	50	Deg. Fr. 2/87			
*Body Weight	1401	1434	1414	N.S.	1623	1482	1448	p<.05	p<.05	N.S.	p<.05
*%B.W. Change	-6.5	-13.0	-11.6	N.S.	8.3	-3.7	-6.3	p<.05	p<.01	N.S.	N.S.
Glom. (Index 1-8)	2.82	3.26	3.43	p<.01	2.75	3.25	3.22	p<.1	N.S.	p<.01	N.S.
Kidney Scar. (Index 1-8)	0.00	0.00	0.30	N.S.	0.06	0.44	0.43	N.S.	N.S.	N.S.	N.S.
Kidney Fat (Index 0-3)	0.90	1.00	0.77	p<.1	1.15	1.15	0.85	p<.1	p<.05	N.S.	N.S.
L.W. (g.)	44.30	43.56	43.34	N.S.	63.92	59.46	55.17	p<.001	p<.001	p<.05	N.S.
S.W. (g.)	0.466	0.521	0.490	N.S.	0.856	0.886	0.684	p<.05	p<.001	p<.1	N.S.
*P.W.(mg.)	4.11	4.18	3.59	p<.001	6.29	6.06	5.61	p<.001	p<.001	N.S.	N.S.
*Thyr. W.(g.)	0.118	0.084	0.097	p<.01	0.131	0.108	0.111	N.S.	-	-	-
Scratches	3.00	4.00	5.18	N.S.	2.62	1.69	3.83	p<.05	N.S.	N.S.	N.S.
Wounds	0.00	1.11	5.00	p<.05	0.77	3.46	1.21	p<.1	N.S.	N.S.	N.S.
Rel. Mort.	0.30	0.87	0.87	p<.05	0.30	0.66	0.90	p<.01	N.S.	p<.01	N.S.
Survival	91.7	80.1	83.9	N.S.	88.3	87.1	80.1	N.S.	N.S.	N.S.	N.S.

* Corrected for regression on age.

i. Behavior (Table 4).

   When the numbers of animals in the group were constant and
space varied, the behavioral response was straightforward. Decrease in living space for the group led to a threefold increase
in rates of aggression in both sexes. In males, there was a barely
significant increase in sexual behavior.

ii. Indices of Condition (Table 5).

   Most of the indices measured indicated a progressive improvement in health as living space increased, especially among female
rabbits. Weight loss was less in Treatment A 1: females in that
treatment actually gained during the experiment and the kidneys
showed less surface inflammation and scarring. The perirenal fat
reserves increased, along with liver and spleen weights, and there
were significant increases in the weights of the pituitary and
thyroid glands in both sexes, suggesting decreased stimulation and
rates of secretion. The lower rates of aggression mentioned earlier
(Table 4) were reflected in lower numbers of scratches on the skin,
and fewer body wounds.

   Relative mortality rate was significantly lower in Treatment
A 1, and this was reflected in a higher survival rate for those
animals living longer than 21 days.

iii. Changes in Morphology of the Adrenal Glands (Table 6).

   Differences in the morphology of the adrenal glands of rabbits
under different treatments add to the data of the preceding section
by showing that decrease in living space adversely affected the
health of the animals in Treatments A 2 and A 3, especially in females. Total adrenal weights and the area of median cross sections
of the right adrenal gland were significantly larger in females.
The lipid content of the cortex was lower, lipofuscin content
higher, and there were significant changes in adrenal morphology
indicative of ill health (increase in the per cent area of Z.
fasciculata-reticularis and decrease in that of the Z. glomerulosa,
increase in clumping of the cortical cell strands, suppression of
nodule formation, and a slightly higher score for white blood cell
density).

   Few of these indices show significance in the males, although
almost all of them follow the same trends.

iv. Reproduction (Table 7).

   The increase in reproductive behavior exhibited by males in
Treatment A 3 was correlated with a significant increase in degree
of sperm development, despite the fact that testis size tended to
be smaller.

TABLE 6

CHANGES IN MORPHOLOGY OF ADRENAL GLANDS IN ADULT WILD RABBITS IN CONFINED POPULATIONS:

VARIABLE LIVING SPACE - NUMBERS OF ANIMALS IN POPULATION CONSTANT

	Males				Females				Analysis of Variance Deg. Fr. 2/150		
	Living Space			Significance of Differences between Means	Living Space			Significance of Differences between Means			
Variable	4 Units	2 Units	1 Unit		4 Units	2 Units	1 Unit		Sex	Treatment	Interaction
n	13	17	36	Deg. Fr. 2/63	18	22	50	Deg. Fr. 2/87			
*A.W. (g.)	0.45	0.51	0.48	N.S.	0.31	0.41	0.38	$p < .05$	$p < .001$	$p < .05$	N.S.
Rel. A.W.	0.32	0.39	0.36	N.S.	0.21	0.32	0.29	$p < .001$	$p < .001$	$p < .05$	N.S.
Lipid G.	1.29	1.16	1.68	$p < .01$	1.24	1.28	1.60	$p < .001$	$p < .05$	$p < .001$	N.S.
*Lipid F-R	7.95	7.74	8.24	N.S.	7.59	6.94	6.81	$p < .01$	$p < .01$	$p < .1$	N.S.
*Lipofuscin F-R	1.91	2.56	2.06	N.S.	3.16	7.21	5.47	N.S.	$p < .001$	N.S.	N.S.
Adrenal Area	33.41	35.74	34.56	N.S.	23.67	30.54	28.67	$p < .05$	$p < .001$	$p < .1$	N.S.
Area G	9.9	9.8	9.6	N.S.	15.0	11.2	10.6	$p < .001$	$p < .001$	$p < .01$	$p < .05$
Area F-R	83.9	84.8	85.1	N.S.	77.6	82.4	82.8	$p < .001$	$p < .001$	$p < .001$	$p < .1$
Area M	6.2	5.4	5.2	N.S.	7.4	6.4	6.6	N.S.	$p < .001$	$p < .1$	N.S.
W.B.C.	2.21	1.80	2.03	N.S.	2.41	2.06	2.77	$p < .01$	N.S.	N.S.	N.S.
# Adrenal Nod.	1.08	0.67	0.82	N.S.	0.94	0.89	0.70	$p < .1$	$p < .02$	N.S.	N.S.
Alveol. F-R	6.42	8.73	9.29	$p < .05$	5.71	7.28	7.81	$p < .05$	$p < .001$	$p < .001$	N.S.

* Corrected for regression on age.

TABLE 7

REPRODUCTION IN THE WILD RABBIT IN CONFINED POPULATIONS:

VARIABLE LIVING SPACE - NUMBERS OF ANIMALS IN POPULATION CONSTANT

	Males				Females			
	Living Space			Significance of Differences Between Means	Living Space			Significance of Differences between Means
Variable	4 Units 13	2 Units 17	1 Unit 36	Deg. Fr. 2/63	4 Units 18	2 Units 22	1 Unit 50	Deg. Fr. 2/87
*T.W. (mg.)	1849	1752	1643	N.S.	-	-	-	-
*Width Seminal Vesicles (mm.)	62.2	56.6	63.6	N.S.	-	-	-	-
*Sperm.	7.2	7.4	7.8	$p < .001$	-	-	-	-
*W.G.M. (g.)	-	-	-	-	11.78	10.16	11.91	N.S.
*O.W. (mg.)	-	-	-	-	530	523	509	$p < .1$
*O.D. (mm.)	-	-	-	-	10.7	-	6.8	$p < .001$
*Ovulations	-	-	-	-	1.15	0.77	0.75	$p < .01$
*Corp. Lutea	-	-	-	-	6.38	5.92	4.03	$p < .001$
*D. Corp Lutea (mm.)	-	-	-	-	7.18	6.55	4.15	$p < .001$
*Corp. Alb.	-	-	-	-	1.28	1.09	1.30	N.S.
*D. Corp Alb.(mm.)	-	-	-	-	0.68	0.60	0.71	N.S.
Palp. Pregn.	-	-	-	-	3.01	2.36	2.30	N.S.
Successful Pregn.	-	-	-	-	85.0	87.1	79.9	N.S.
Litter #	-	-	-	-	2.37	2.00	2.12	$p < .05$
Litter Size	-	-	-	-	4.55	4.50	4.95	N.S.
Young #	-	-	-	-	10.8	9.00	10.5	N.S.
Burrow Length	-	-	-	-	12.9	9.1	6.4	$p < .001$
Young Mort.	-	-	-	-	4.0	9.0	9.8	$p < .001$

* Data taken from rabbits sacrificed at end of experiment.

Total productivity varied little between treatments during the experiment. The largest mean number of litters born per female breeding unit (allowing for mortalities within the group) occurred in Treatment A 1. Mean litter size at birth, however, tended to be largest in Treatment A 3. Females in Treatment A 1 also had a higher mean number of pregnancies, ascertained by palpation during the four - weekly censuses (gestation in the rabbit lasts 28-30 days), and a greater percentage of the palpated pregnancies terminated successfully. Due to the small differences in mean litter size between treatments, the mean number of young produced per female was unaltered from treatment to treatment.

Examination by dissection of the females alive at the end of the experiment showed that the mammary glands of females in all the treatments were large, but the ovaries of the females in Treatment A 1 were significantly heavier and larger than those in Treatment A 3. Furthermore, the numbers of recent ovulations and functional corpora lutea and the sizes of the corpora lutea were much larger in Treatment A 1 than in Treatment A 3. These data are to be analyzed more critically elsewhere, but are included here to emphasize the differences in endocrine status of the females in each treatment. In Treatment 1, the main barrier to higher reproduction appeared to be loss of eggs. Follicle stimulation and egg release were uninhibited. In Treatment 3, on the other hand, the numbers of eggs shed were depressed, and rates of embryonic resorption increased. Differences in the oestrogen-progesterone balance were probably involved.

Mortality in the young rabbits differed quite dramatically between treatments. Almost all the deaths of kittens which occurred in Treatment 1 were of an ecological nature (drowning, bird predation). In Treatment 3, there was a higher proportion of deaths caused by social factors (disturbance by strange female, failure of maternal care, etc.). This was correlated with a significantly lower amount of burrow shelter in the latter treatment.

v.   Indices of Condition in Embryos, Nestlings
     and Weaned Young (Table 8).

The better health enjoyed by their mothers was reflected in the condition of all of the younger stages in the populations. Thus all embryos taken from pregnant females in Treatment A 1, corrected for regression on age, showed significantly heavier weights of body reserves, organs and larger body proportions.

The differences were also strikingly apparent in nestlings still dependent upon the females for sustenance, and in weaned young shortly after emerging from the nest to feed on the surface; although in the latter group, the differences were far less significant.

TABLE 8

INDICES OF CONDITION IN EMBRYOS, NESTLINGS AND WEANED YOUNG RABBITS BORN IN CONFINED POPULATIONS:

VARIABLE LIVING SPACE – NUMBERS OF ANIMALS IN POPULATION CONSTANT

| | Embryos | | | | Nestlings | | | | Weaned Young | | | |
| | Living Space | | | Significance of Differences between Means Deg. Fr. 2/40 | Living Space | | | Significance of Differences between Means Deg. Fr. 2/86 | Living Space | | | Significance of Differences between Means Deg. Fr. 2/28 |
Variable n	4 Units 17	2 Units 11	1 Unit 15		4 Units 13	2 Units 23	1 Unit 53		4 Units 11	2 Units 8	1 Unit 12	
*Body Weight(g.)	25.21	19.70	16.61	$p < .01$	122.54	100.73	85.86	$p < .001$	290.83	318.57	286.25	N.S.
*Neck Fat(mg.)	639.78	551.03	272.17	$p < .001$	1.91	1.57	1.40	$p < .001$	1.98	1.81	1.50	N.S.
*Thymus(mg.)	28.60	17.20	15.20	$p < .001$	217.7	200.4	163.0	$p < .05$	739	691	567	$p < .05$
*Liver(g.)	1.80	1.65	0.96	$p < .001$	–	–	–	–	1.65	1.47	1.36	$p < .05$
*Adrenal(mg.)	–	–	–	–	8.65	7.39	7.53	$p < .01$	397	316	328	$p < .01$
*Kidney (mg.)	149.01	128.30	83.60	$p < .01$	1.19	0.95	0.94	$p < .001$	4.23	3.71	3.19	$p < .01$
*Tarsus Length(mm.)	14.96	14.15	12.02	$p < .05$	–	–	–	–	–	–	–	–
Spleen(mg.)	–	–	–	–	–	–	–	–	200	175	145	$p < .05$
Area F-R	–	–	–	–	–	–	–	–	66.84	66.58	65.29	N.S.
Area M	–	–	–	–	–	–	–	–	15.57	18.37	19.00	$p < .05$
Alveol. G.	–	–	–	–	–	–	–	–	2.13	3.61	4.05	$p < .05$
Alveol. F-R	–	–	–	–	–	–	–	–	4.5	4.6	6.00	N.S.

* Corrected for regression on age.

TABLE 9

DIFFERENCES IN BEHAVIOR IN ADULT WILD RABBITS IN CONFINED POPULATIONS:

VARIABLE LIVING SPACE – DENSITY CONSTANT

| | Males | | | | Females | | | | Analysis of Variance Deg. Fr. 2/257 | | |
| | Living Space | | | Significance of Differences between Means | Living Space | | | Significance of Differences between Means | Sex | Treatment | Interaction |
Behavior (Acts/ minute) n	4 Units 33	2 Units 40	1 Unit 36	Deg. Fr. 2/106	4 Units 55	2 Units 49	1 Unit 50	Deg. Fr. 2/151			
Territorial Marking	0.023	0.059	0.100	$p < .01$	0.005	0.016	0.030	$p < .01$	$p < .01$	$p < .01$	N.S.
Total Sexual Behavior	0.031	0.090	0.131	$p < .001$	–	–	–	–	–	–	–
Total Aggressive Behavior	0.032	0.069	0.059	$p < .01$	0.006	0.021	0.049	$p < .001$	$p < .001$	$p < .01$	N.S.
Total Avoiding Behavior	0.036	0.057	0.053	$p < .1$	0.004	0.022	0.046	$p < .001$	$p < .001$	$p < .01$	N.S.

It is to be noted that the weight of the adrenal gland in the weaned young still varied in sympathy with the weight of all the organs in general. Despite this, the adrenal exhibited significant differences on a morphological level in the proportion of the gland occupied by the medulla and in the alveolation of the cortical strands, showing that the young animals in Treatment A 3 differed from their confreres in the larger living areas also in respect to basic physiologic functioning.

Rabbits in Confined Populations:
Living Space Varying - Population Density Constant

In this experiment, we studied the reactions of adults and young rabbits in breeding populations maintained at a constant, high density, in enclosures of three different sizes. The two main physical variables were group size and living space. Thus Treatment B 1 was comprised of what would have constituted four balanced social groups (at lower densities) in four units of space, whereas treatment B 3 represented one balanced group in one unit of space.

The living conditions for all the rabbits were undeniably harsh, in an ecological sense.

i. Behaviour (Table 9)

The rabbits in each replicate of Treatment B2 and B3 behaved as single social groups. The groups existing in Treatment B2 ($4\,\delta\delta$ - $6\,\female\female$) were slightly larger than normal [86].

In Treatment B1, the rabbits in each replicate split into social groups, which marked out and defended territories in the usual manner [84].

In one replicate, there were two groups ($3\,\delta\delta$ - $5\,\female\female$; $3\,\delta\delta$ - $6\,\female\female$); in the second replicate, two groups ($6\,\delta\delta$ - $6\,\female\female$; $2\,\delta\delta$ - $4\,\female\female$); and, in the third replicate, three groups ($2\,\delta\delta$ - $5\,\female\female$; $4\,\delta\delta$ - $4\,\female\female$; $2\,\delta\delta$ - $3\,\female$). In terms of functional, social groupings, group size thus decreased more or less with the treatments.

The frequency of occurrence of the more important acts of sexual and aggressive behaviour varied significantly with treatment. In males, there was a large, three to fourfold, increase in sexual behaviour and territorial marking in the limited living space in Treatment B3. Aggression on the other hand, barely doubled. In females, all forms of measured activity were depressed in the large population - living space complex of Treatment B 1, and dramatically heightened, six to eightfold, in Treatment B 3.

The highest mean rates of aggressive and sexual activities thus occurred when normal social groups were restricted spatially. Lower rates occurred where group size was larger than normal although

TABLE 10

DIFFERENCES IN INDICES OF CONDITIONS AND SURVIVAL IN ADULT WILD RABBITS IN CONFINED POPULATIONS:

VARIABLE LIVING SPACE – DENSITY CONSTANT

Variable	Males				Females				Analysis of Variance Deg. Fr. 2/257		
	Living Space			Significance of Differences between Means	Living Space			Significance of Differences between Means	Sex	Treatment	Interaction
	4 Units	2 Units	1 Unit		4 Units	2 Unit	1 Unit				
n	33	40	36	Deg. Fr. 2/106	55	49	50	Deg. Fr. 2/151			
*Body Weight (g.)	1375	1390	1414	N.S.	1448	1445	1431	N.S.	N.S.	N.S.	N.S.
%B.W. Change	-14.1	-10.9	- 9.0	N.S.	- 2.1	- 0.75	- 4.4	N.S.	$p<.001$	N.S.	N.S.
Glom. (Index 1-8)	2.85	2.74	3.37	$p<.01$	2.92	2.95	3.28	$p<.01$	N.S.	$p<.01$	N.S.
Kidney Scar (Index 1-8)	0.10	0.31	0.30	N.S.	0.04	0.09	0.43	$p<.05$	N.S.	$p<.05$	N.S.
Kidney Fat (Index 0-3)	0.86	0.88	0.77	N.S.	1.36	1.57	0.85	$p<.001$	$p<.001$	$p<.001$	$p<.1$
L.W. (g.)	47.70	43.32	42.97	$p<.001$	60.67	56.57	55.17	$p<.001$	$p<.001$	$p<.01$	N.S.
*S.W. (g.)	0.418	0.504	0.490	$p<.01$	0.607	0.566	0.552	$p<.001$	$p<.001$	N.S.	$p<.1$
Scratches	7.91	7.46	5.18	$p<.1$	3.43	4.73	3.83	$p<.1$	$p<.001$	$p<.01$	N.S.
Wounds	1.59	3.33	5.00	$p<.1$	0.00	1.21	1.50	$p<.01$	$p<.001$	N.S.	N.S.
Rel. Mort.	0.50	0.75	0.87	$p<.01$	0.77	0.75	0.90	$p<.01$	$p<.01$	N.S.	N.S.
Survival	86.0	85.2	84.0	N.S.	90.0	86.5	80.1	$p<.05$	N.S.	N.S.	N.S.

* Corrected for regression on age

TABLE 11

CHANGES IN MORPHOLOGY OF ADRENAL GLANDS IN ADULT WILD RABBITS IN CONFINED POPULATIONS:

VARIABLE LIVING SPACE – DENSITY CONSTANT

Variable n	Males				Females				Analysis of Variance Deg. Fr. 2/257		
	Living Space			Significance of Differences between Means	Living Space			Significance of Differences between Means	Sex	Treatment	Interaction
	4 Units 33	2 Units 40	1 Unit 36	Deg. Fr. 2/106	4 Units 55	2 Units 49	1 Unit 50	Deg. Fr. 2/151			
A.W.(g.)	0.48	0.50	0.48	N.S.	0.34	0.39	0.39	$p<.01$	$p<.001$	N.S.	N.S.
*Rel. A.W.	0.37	0.37	0.32	N.S.	0.26	0.29	0.28	N.S.	$p<.001$	N.S.	N.S.
*Lipid G	2.10	1.86	1.68	$p<.01$	1.85	1.71	1.47	$p<.001$	$p<.05$	$p<.001$	N.S.
*Lipid F.R.	8.37	8.12	8.24	N.S.	7.57	7.47	6.81	$p<.01$	$p<.01$	$p<.1$	N.S.
Lipofuscin F-R	1.94	2.56	2.06	N.S.	3.12	5.46	5.09	N.S.	$p<.001$	N.S.	N.S.
Adrenal Area	32.83	33.40	34.56	N.S.	26.60	28.67	28.81	N.S.	$p<.001$	N.S.	N.S.
Area G	8.2	9.2	9.6	N.S.	11.8	12.1	10.6	$p<.1$	$p<.001$	$p<.05$	$p<.05$
Area F.R.	86.1	85.0	85.2	N.S.	80.9	81.1	82.8	$p<.05$	$p<.001$	N.S.	N.S.
*W.B.C.	1.37	2.23	2.03	$p<.01$	1.53	1.64	2.70	$p<.001$	N.S.	$p<.01$	N.S.
*#Adrenal nod.	1.62	0.89	0.99	$p<.01$	0.69	0.76	0.70	N.S.	$p<.02$	N.S.	$p<.1$
Alveol. F-R	7.10	8.95	9.29	$p<.01$	7.22	7.81	8.27	$p<.1$	$p<.05$	$p<.001$	N.S.

* Corrected for regression on age.

still living within restricted areas.

ii. Indices of Condition (Table 10).

Several indices showed that reduction in living space, despite
the accompanying reduction in group size, was detrimental to some
aspects of health. In both sexes, there were minor but significant
decreases in kidney fat and liver weight. Spleen weight increased
in males and decreased in females, in typical fashion. Females
were clearly more affected than males. Indeed, in some data there
are suggestions, although mostly insignificant, that increase in
group size in the larger space affected males adversely. In Table
10, for example, the data show an increase in scratches on the skin
and greater loss of body weight in males in Treatment B 1. Despite
this, there was a great increase in the amount of wounding in both
sexes in Treatment B3, and relative mortality rates climbed accordingly. Survival rate also decreased in the smaller space.

iii. Changes in Morphology of the Adrenal Glands (Table 11).

Examination of the adrenal glands disclosed much the same situation as evidenced by the other index organs. Almost all the indices measured suggested that female rabbits were more adversely
affected by the imposed limitations of living space than males.
Thus they possessed larger adrenals, with a higher proportion of
zona fasciculata-reticularis, an increased level of alveolation of
the fasciculate strand cells, and a significantly higher index of
white blood cell density. These were accompanied by decreases in
the lipid content of the cortex and by the proportion of the adrenal
occupied by the zona glomerulosa.

In males, some of the indices suggested detrimental effects of
decreased space. There were slight decreases in the cortical lipids
and in the numbers of nodules on the adrenals. Clumping of the
fasciculate strands and the density of white blood cells in the
adrenal also increased in Treatment B 3. On the other hand, in
Treatment B 1, the data show a tendency towards an increase in zona
fasciculata-reticularis and relative adrenal weight and a decrease
in zona glomerulosa.

Of interest is the significant increase in lipofuscin in the
zona fasciculata-reticularis in female rabbits. It has been shown
that the production of this ceroid material is stimulated in the
mouse adrenal gland by high titres of oestrogen in the blood [8].

iv. Reproduction (Table 12).

Data collected during the four months of the experiment showed
few significant differences between the treatments in terms of productivity. The numbers of pregnancies, ascertained by palpation

TABLE 12

REPRODUCTION IN THE WILD RABBIT IN CONFINED POPULATIONS:

VARIABLE LIVING SPACE - DENSITY CONSTANT

	Males				Females			
	Living Space			Significance of Differences Between Means Deg. Fr.2/106	Living Space			Significance of Differences Between Means Deg. Fr.2/151
Variable n	4 Units 33	2 Units 40	1 Unit 36		4 Units 55	2 Units 49	1 Unit 50	
*T.W. (mg.)	1749	1611	1641	N.S.	-	-	-	-
*Width Seminal Vesicles (mm.)	60.3	62.5	63.6	N.W.	-	-	-	-
*Sperm.	7.4	7.5	7.8	p<.01	-	-	-	-
*W.G.M. (g.)	-	-	-	-	8.97	7.70	11.91	p<.001
*O.W. (mg.)	-	-	-	-	474	484	509	p<.1
*Ovulations	-	-	-	-	1.07	0.90	0.75	N.S.
*Corp. Lutea	-	-	-	-	5.52	5.35	3.89	p<.01
*D. Corp. Lutea (mm.)	-	-	-	-	5.35	5.94	4.00	p<.01
*Corp. Alb.	-	-	-	-	1.07	1.20	1.30	p<.01
*D. Corp. Alb. (mm.)	-	-	-	-	0.39	0.68	0.71	p<.1
Palp Pregn.	-	-	-	-	2.05	2.14	2.30	N.S.
Successful Pregn.	-	-	-	-	88.3	83.0	79.9	p<.05
Litter #	-	-	-	-	2.14	1.99	2.12	N.S.
Litter Size	-	-	-	-	4.74	4.81	4.95	N.S.
Burrow Length	-	-	-	-	1.6	3.7	6.4	p<.001
Young Mort.	-	-	-	-	14.00	11.50	9.80	p<.01
Young Survival	-	-	-	-	22.18	32.26	28.8	p<.01
Young #	-	-	-	-	10.1	9.6	10.5	N.S.

* Data taken from rabbits sacrificed at end of experiment.

TABLE 13

INDICES OF CONDITION IN EMBRYOS, NESTLING AND WEANED YOUNG BORN IN CONFINED POPULATIONS:

VARIABLE LIVING SPACE - DENSITY CONSTANT

	Embryos				Nestlings				Weaned Young			
	Living Space			Significance of Differences between Means Deg. Fr. 2/55	Living Space			Significance of Differences between Means Deg. Fr. 2/132	Living Space			Significance of Differences between Means Deg. Fr. 2/27
Variable n	4 Units 29	2 Units 14	1 Unit 15		4 Units 28	2 Units 54	1 Unit 53		4 Units 5	2 Unit 13	1 Unit 12	
*Body Weight(g.)	22.11	22.38	16.61	p<.01	92.90	97.51	85.86	p<.001	342	291	259	N.S.
*Neck Fat(mg.)	650.52	708.13	272.17	p<.001	1.67	1.74	1.40	p<.001	1.73	1.58	1.50	N.S.
*Thymus(mg.)	21.52	20.04	15.20	p<.001	182.8	181.7	163.50	p<.05	668	529	567	p<.05
*Liver(g.)	1.56	1.62	0.96	p<.001	3.67	3.79	3.43	p<.01	1.53	1.37	1.36	p<.05
*Adrenal(mg.)	-	-	-	-	9.21	7.94	7.53	p<.01	355	357	328	p<.01
*Kidney (mg.)	126.03	124.69	83.60	p<.01	1.09	0.99	0.94	p<.001	3.49	3.01	3.19	p<.01
*Tarsus Length(mm.)	14.1	13.9	12.0	p<.05	-	-	-	-	-	-	-	-
Spleen(mg.)	-	-	-	-	74.2	52.4	50.8	p<.01	201	168	145	p<.05
Area F-R	-	-	-	-	-	-	-	-	70.38	65.29	63.42	p<.01
Area M	-	-	-	-	-	-	-	-	11.98	17.01	19.00	p<.01
Alveol. G	-	-	-	-	-	-	-	-	2.64	4.07	4.05	p<.05
Alveol. F-R	-	-	-	-	-	-	-	-	4.2	5.2	6.00	N.S.

* Corrected for regression on age.

during the four-weekly censuses, showed a slightly higher pregnancy
rate in Treatment B3. The females in that treatment, however, lost
more of their embryos by uterine resorption. Mean litter size
tended to be largest in Treatment B 3 and smallest in Treatment B 1,
but the mean number of young produced per female breeding unit (making allowances for deaths) was similar for each treatment.

Examinations by dissection of the females alive at the end of
the experiment disclosed significant differences of an important
nature. In the males in Treatment B3, although the testes tended
to be smaller, the seminal vesicles were slightly larger and spermatogenesis more advanced. In females in that treatment, the mammary
glands and ovaries were larger, there was a higher rating for the
presence of corpora albicantia and those bodies were also significantly larger. On the other hand, the numbers of recent ovulations
and functional corpora lutea present were smaller, so were the sizes
of the corpora lutea.

The data point to significant differences in endocrine status
between the treatments. Females in Treatment B1 were exposed to a
low rate of sexual advances by males, probably resulting in low
titres of pituitary and gonadal hormones in the blood. In Treatment B3, the opposite was undoubtedly true. Reduction of liver size
in the latter treatment (Table 10) suggests that inactivation of
circulating oestrogens by that organ may have been affected and,
together with the heavy secretion of ACTH and adrenal corticoids,
severe upsets in hormone balance must have occurred feeding back
both on the pituitary to inhibit follicle rupture and directly on
the corpora lutea to affect the well-being of the embryos.

Survival of the young rabbits to 30 days was significantly
lower in Treatment B 1. In that treatment, females excavated only
1.6 ft. of burrow per animal and shelter was thus limited. Under
such conditions, mortality of the young was mainly due to social
disturbances, e.g., scratching out of nest, or being savaged by
strange females. In Treatment B 3, with its small group size, mortality occurred under more natural conditions, e.g., wet burrows.
In that treatment, there was more burrow shelter for the young
(mean 6.4 ft. per female).

v. Indices of Condition in Embryos, Nestlings and
    Weaned Young (Table 13).

The measurable differences at the adult level were much more
significant in embyros, nestlings and weaned young. In Treatment
B 3, measurements of all of the organs, including the adrenal
glands, the fat deposits and body proportions clearly pointed to a
significant retardation in development. This retardation was still
in evidence when the young rabbit was weaned and started life on
the surface.

TABLE 14

RELATIONSHIPS BETWEEN ORIGIN OF MALE RABBITS AND THEIR BIOLOGY AS ADULTS

Variable n	Born in Confined Population			Born in Natural Population 102	Significance of Differences between Means Deg. Fr. 3/126
	High Density 6	Medium Density 10	Low Density 12		
Survival	75.8	68.3	84.4	86.8	p<.1
B.W. (g.)	1200	1225	1389	1375	p<.1
%B.W. Change	-21.0	-22.0	-9.1	-12.0	p<.05
Rel. K.W.	10.41	8.91	8.69	8.20	p<.1
Rel. A.W.	0.421	0.483	0.315	0.363	p<.1
F-R	5.67	5.80	8.33	8.07	p<.001
Adrenal Area	32.85	37.96	31.12	33.76	N.S.
Area G	8.7	8.2	9.2	10.3	N.S. (but climbing)
Area M	6.7	4.1	4.8	5.8	p<.05
W.B.C.	3.67	4.40	2.42	2.04	p<.01
#Adrenal nod.	0.17	0.40	0.83	1.08	N.S.
Alveol. F-R	10.17	9.20	9.42	8.01	N.S. (but climbing)
Status	1.83	2.10	1.67	2.25	N.S.
Aggression	0.122	0.082	0.072	0.039	p<.1
Avoidance	0.053	0.059	0.019	0.051	N.S.
Sex	0.136	0.069	0.136	0.083	N.S.
Activity	0.311	0.210	0.227	0.173	p<.01
T.W. (mg.)	2045	1846	1944	1615	N.S.
Sperm	8.0	7.63	8.0	7.51	N.S.

TABLE 15

RELATIONSHIPS BETWEEN ORIGIN OF FEMALE RABBITS AND THEIR BIOLOGY AS ADULTS

Variable n	Born in Confined Population			Born in Natural Population 167	Significance of Differences between Means Deg. Fr. 3/191
	High Density 9	Medium Density 9	Low Density 9		
Survival	69.5	85.7	89.7	87.2	p<.05
B.W. (g.)	1404	1442	1345	1439	N.S.
%B.W. Change	-5.2	-11.1	-7.3	-3.3	N.S.
Rel. A.W.	0.383	0.397	0.269	0.273	p<.05
L.W. (g.)	73.67	60.40	51.75	58.17	p<.05
Lipofuscin F.R.	1.44	0.55	0.79	0.38	p<.05
Adrenal Area	35.12	34.96	31.32	27.00	p<.01
Area G	9.9	10.3	11.4	12.0	p<.05
Area F-R	84.4	84.3	82.5	80.1	p<.01
W.M.G. (g.)	12.41	15.69	5.24	9.51	p<.01
O.W. (g.)	694	604	449	475	p<.05
Ovulations	2.67	0.60	0.00	0.89	p<.01
Corp. Lutea	8.00	5.20	4.25	4.88	N.S. (but climbing)
Litter #	2.4	2.1	2.0	1.8	p<.1
Litter Size	5.4	4.7	4.1	4.8	p<.1
Aggression	0.023	0.036	0.019	0.024	N.S.
Avoidance	0.028	0.005	0.017	0.026	N.S.

It is also to be noticed that some morphological characteristics of the adrenal, which correlated with adult ill-health, were
present in the adrenals of the young. The adrenal cortex of the
young rabbits born in Treatment B 3 was highly alveolated or
clumped and there was a tremendous increase in the proportion of
the glands occupied by the medulla. Unlike adult rabbits, however,
the area occupied by the zona fasciculata-reticularis was greatest
in Treatment B 1. The state of the adrenal of the young rabbit
born into a stressful situation thus suggests that catecholamines,
as well as cortical hormones, are important. The retardation of
growth of the adrenal in the young rabbit up to 30 days further
suggests that the pituitary had not yet started to function in an
important manner in response to stress.

Relationships between Origin of Rabbits and Their Biology
As Adults (Tables 14 and 15).

A sample of 28 males and 27 females born during the spring of
1963 in confined populations of different densities [81] were included in the experiments described in this paper, distributed
evenly among Treatments B1, B2 and B3. During the 12 months preceding the experiment, they were kept in enclosures in separate,
large, male and female colonies, and all received exactly the same
management with regard to food, etc.

The males born into high density populations were very active
animals as adults, displaying high rates of aggressive and sexual
activities. They had large adrenal glands (relative to body weight)
and were of relatively high status. Testis weight and stage of
spermatogenesis both testified to physiological reproductive capability. However, the low body weights and large loss in body weight,
the lack of lipid in the adrenal, the reduced proportion of the
Z. glomerulosa, the lack of adrenal nodules, and the lower survival
rate all point to a loss of fitness in the group as a whole. Male
rabbits born into what is here called a medium density population
(an unbalanced social group with excess males) showed similar trends.
The animals born in the low density treatments (of one balanced
social group) and those that were collected from low to medium
density natural populations exhibited superior qualities relating
to health and survival.

The differences between the female groups tended to be less
significant in some respects. Like the males, the females born in
high density populations were very active as adults, although not
particularly aggressive or dominant. Unlike the males, they maintained good body weights, possessed heavy livers, mammary glands
and ovary weights, and showed a superior breeding capability in
terms of rates of ovulation, numbers of functional corpora lutea
on the ovaries, numbers of litters born and mean size of litters.

TABLE 16

RELATIONSHIPS BETWEEN ASSIGNED SOCIAL STATUS AND

BIOLOGICAL ATTRIBUTES OF MALE RABBITS

Variable n	Social Status			Significance of Differences Between Means Deg. Fr. 2/136
	1 49	2 17	3 67	
Survival (per cent)	90.1	93.7	79.4	p<.05
Body Weight (g.)	1148	1204	1068	p<.01
Weight Change (per cent)	-11.1	-6.0	-15.9	p<.05
Liver Weight (g.)	46.89	48.08	42.25	p<.01
Skin Weight (g.)	63.95	60.87	54.04	p<.001
Relative Adrenal Weight (g./Kg.)	0.342	0.313	0.403	p<.05
Numbers of Nodules on Adrenal Glands	1.14	1.47	0.72	p<.05
White Blood Cells in Adrenal Medulla	0.99	0.60	1.12	p<.05
Skin Scratches	0.36	6.67	11.10	p<.001
Weight of Testes (g)	1.89	1.76	1.41	p<.001
Stage of Spermatogenesis	7.69	7.58	7.44	N.S. but climbing

TABLE 17

RELATIONSHIPS BETWEEN ASSIGNED SOCIAL STATUS AND

BIOLOGICAL ATTRIBUTES OF FEMALE RABBITS

Variable n	Social Status			Significance of Differences Between Means Deg. Fr. 2/166
	1 43	2 36	3 90	
Survival (per cent)	92.7	94.6	82.6	p<.001
Body Weight (g)	1531	1512	1354	p<.001
Weight Change (per cent)	11.6	14.4	-8.13	p<.01
Skin Weight (g.)	43.59	39.56	38.19	N.S.
Relative Adrenal Weight (g./Kg.)	0.241	0.256	0.312	p<.05
Pituitary Weight (mg.)	6.00	5.53	5.37	N.S.
Number of Litters per Female	2.2	2.1	1.6	p<.01
Number of Kittens Born per Female	10.5	10.2	7.7	p<.05
Skin Scratches	0.48	4.32	5.82	p<.01
Wounds	0.00	0.53	1.56	p<.1

Like their male counterparts, however, they possessed heavy and large adrenal glands, relative to body weight and alterations in adrenal zonation (increase in Z. fasciculata-reticularis and decrease in Z. glomerulosa) indicative of ACTH stimulation. They also possessed a greater amount of lipofuscin in the adrenal, suggesting higher oestrogen levels in the blood. Like the males, they also exhibited a tendency towards a lower survival rate.

Relationships between Assigned Social Status, Health and Survival (Tables 16 and 17)

The healthiest males in the enclosures were those subordinates assigned social status 2. They had a slightly higher survival rate, heavier body and organ weights, and adrenal indices suggestive of better health - including smaller relative adrenal weights. Their dominant companions bettered them only in terms of a slightly superior reproductive capability.

The differences for social status 2 were less marked in the case of females, where a more linear arrangement held (Table 17).

DISCUSSION

Stress in Adult Mammals

Although several studies of natural populations of mammals [108,21,94,32] have tended to negate some aspects of the general hypothesis, a large amount of evidence has now been presented to affirm that crowding in laboratory and field populations of many mammals causes significant changes in behaviour and physiology [for reviews: 30,114,81,1,10,20; for recent papers: 72,105,113,124,38,59,2]. The rabbit is no exception.

In earlier experiments [85,86,81] and in the work described in this paper, adult rabbits of both sexes have been shown to respond to crowding in ways similar to those measured in other species of mammals. There is a large loss in body weight and changes in the weights of index organs vitally concerned with metabolic function (e.g., spleen and liver). The kidneys become inflamed, pitted and scarred with lesions caused by a systemic disease, clearly similar to that measured in mice, deer, and other mammals where it has been shown to be ACTH induced [27,30]. There is an impairment of reproductive condition, in ways which agree, in general, with the findings of Varon and Christian [120] and Christian [26], that ACTH at high physiological levels suppresses gonadotrophic secretions, follicle growth, ovulation and luteinization, and that adrenal androgens suppress the formation of large graafian follicles and corpora lutea, thus leading to failure of implantation, resorption of embryos, depression of libido, foetal dysgenesis, upsets in lactation and abnormal maternal behaviour. In males, the testes tend to atrophy.

The adrenal glands hypertrophy and lose their lipid steroid precursors. The zonation of the adrenals alters to favour increased secretion of glycocorticoids and suppression of mineralocorticoids, possibly causing natriuresis, and upset Na:K ratios in the body. It seems likely that the findings of Aumann [3] and Aumann and Emlen [4], where the densities of rodent populations in North America are correlated with soil sodium levels, may be related to this phenomenon. In stressed rabbits, adrenal nodulation is suppressed thus exacerbating problems relating to the Na and K metabolism already posed by pituitary secretion of ACTH. The adrenal cortex is invaded by small, undifferentiated, white blood cells and the cortical tissue reorganized into alveoli separated by prominent sinuses pointing to increased rates of secretion. Similar structural change is described in other stressed mammals - Microtus [29], Cervus [25] and man [111].

Other than noting that the pituitary and the thyroid glands lost weight in stressed animals, we made no attempt to look at one other very important aspect of physiology relating to stress in mammals. This might be called brain activity. Evidence incriminating brain-hormonal relations at a population level is hard to come by. Despite this, several lines of work are converging on the problem. Central nervous system stimulants like amphetamine are found to be more toxic in dense populations of mice and rats [34,53] but this toxicity is reduced when tranquilizers are fed [24]. In natural populations of wild mice, tranquilizers are found to stimulate fresh population growth [122]. Brain chemistry is affected by the numbers of mammals living together. Grouped rats and mice respond with decreases in cortical cholinesterase and increases in subcortical cholinesterase [67,117]. Group size also causes fluctuations in brain catecholamines, serotonin and dopamine [125,126]. This kind of information adds importantly to our understanding of population processes.

Heightened activity of the pituitary - adrenocortical system during emotional stress has also been demonstrated in a number of studies of man. During competitive sports, anticipation of surgery, exposure to shame and emotional disturbances of various kinds, especially where fear of physical injury is involved, the adrenal cortical hormone level in the plasma rises, and increased amounts of 17 - hydroxycortico-steroids are excreted in the urine. When distress passes, the circulating corticoids decrease substantially [69]. There is little doubt that emotional distress in man is associated with adrenal activity.

Factors Affecting Young Mammals

The effects of stressful factors in the population are not confined to adults. In this study, it has been shown that at embryonic, nestling, and young animal levels, the well-being of the baby rabbit in all stages of development is utterly dependent on and varies with the health of the mother. And the health of the mother is not dependent on food alone. It has further been shown, that the young rabbit, born under crowded conditions, carries into adulthood the imprint of its early environment in terms of behavioural and physiological aberrations.

The mammalian foetus is not in nirvana. The maternal pregnancy hormones, oestrogens and androgens, cross the placenta and can interfere with foetal development, attacking foetus, uterus and placenta, causing foetal death or impairment of growth [63]. The stage at which hormones act is most important. In later stages of embryonic life the effects may be only transient.

Adrenal hormones also cross the placental barrier and appear in the foetal blood [106,62], causing cleft-palate [101] and affecting the foetal adrenal and pituitary [33,63]. ACTH, vasopressin, or adrenalin injected into rat and rabbit foetuses less than 19 days old cause haemorrhages, necrosis, congenital amputations and other prenatal abnormalities. The foetal adrenals are extremely sensitive to extraneous stress hormones [76].

Behavioural and physiological stress to pregnant female mice and rats produces permanent changes in the physiology and behavior of their offspring [28,119,64]. The offspring's emotionality is positively associated with the mother's level of emotionality, both pre- and post-natal [97]. Hormones appear to be implicated in the transfer of behavioral stress to offspring, since similar changes in the young occur when pregnant females are injected with epinephrine and hydrocortisone [119,129]. It has been shown that even the stress of sound, affecting female rats during the second semester of pregnancy, conditions the behavior of the offspring by increasing their emotionality rating on day 25 postpartum [79].

Maternal diets also disturb embryonic development [122,48]. This phenomenon is well known to breeders of livestock [45], as is the fact that the earlier in life the shortage occurs, the greater and more persistent is the effect.

Stimulation of the neonatal mammal has large effects on its behavior and physiology as an adult. A voluminous literature now testifies to the fact that environmental and social factors during the post-natal period are more profound in their effects than during any other period of the animal's history. Thus, handling rats as nestlings significantly reduces their emotionality in adulthood and changes the activity of the pituitary-adrenal response to stress [55,71,93,39]. In this connection, it is of interest to note that there is some correlation between adrenocortical activity and stimulation and inhibition of the central nervous system [73]. Aggressiveness in lactating female rats, extinguished by treatment with estrone, can be re-established by administration of corticosteroids [44]. The close parallel between the corticosteroid content of peripheral blood and catatonia in schizophrenia is well known [54].

Imbalances in the titre of sex hormones in the neonate modifies adult physiology and behavior, including rates of aggression [17,46, 51,11], and there is good evidence that development is also altered by abnormal quantities of pituitary and adrenal hormones in the new-born young [107,98,60]. Such phenomena may be related to the long-lasting effects measured in young mice and rats reared by stressed or foster parents [40,97,110] either as a result of impaired lacta-tion or abnormalities in maternal behavior. In any case, it is clear that adult patterns of neuroendocrine activity regulating ACTH secre-tion and some aspects of behavior are formed very early in life, and occur during sensitive periods in the development of the organism. The proposition [56,129], that hormones directly affect the central nervous system during development to produce permanent changes in physiology and behavior in later life, still stands as the most likely explanation for these phenomena. Recent papers which show that the hypothalamus takes up circulating corticosterone differentially [130], and that morphological changes occur in the hypothalamus when stress hormones are administered neonatally [98], give promise of exciting advances to be made in this field during the next decade.

Alterations in the early social environment also play an import-ant part in quality control of the adult mammal. Thus, deermice [112], dogs [75], rabbits and rats [130], reared in social isolation, exhibit all sorts of abnormalities as adults, including lower sociability and defective care of young. Interferences with the mother-neonate bond in sheep, goats and monkeys also greatly affects later social and other behavior [59,52].

There must be, of course, a genetic component in these processes. Levine and Wetzel [70] have shown that different strains of rats handled during early life react differently in avoidance learning as adults; and Thompson and Olian [118], Thompson et. al. [119], De Fries [37], and Joffe [61] have shown that offspring from stressed pregnant female rats display differential behavioral responses as adults, the response being a function of genotype. It is also common knowledge that behavioral and physiological response to density differs between species and between strains of the same species [15,12,115].

The embryonic, neonatal and weaned life of the young mammal is thus open to a whole array of stimuli which bear importantly on its health and behavior as an adult. Many of these stimuli, especially those relating to foetal dysgenesis, imbalance of maternal endocrines, abnormal maternal behavior, and physical disturbances in the neonatal environment are most likely to occur in crowded conditions. We have shown in this paper that stimuli present in crowded populations cer-tainly affect the young rabbit and predetermine in important ways cer-tain qualities of its adult life.

There is as yet little general awareness that such processes
are important in man, but evidence is mounting to show that human
existence still is predominantly determined by its biological basis.
Emotional state in the human female, physical agents, nutrition,
drugs, maternal diseases and age have all been shown to affect the
developing human foetus [77,78], causing congenital malformations [49],
neonatal death rates and birth weights [50] and seasonality in the
births of the mentally deficient [66]. Developmental abnormalities of
an important kind do occur in man.

Mechanisms

Changes in physiology and behavior elicited by rise in numbers
have been shown to occur in many mammalian species. The mechanisms
involved, however, have still to be substantiated. Several variables
need to be considered - especially group size, space, and quality of
animals concerned (genetics, physiology, behavior).

Group size in the rabbit is fixed by evolution to one to three
males and one to five females. It is only at very high densities,
indeed, that those limits are exceeded; the only significant response
to this that we have been able to measure has been suppression of
sexual and aggressive behavior and atrophy of the ovaries in the female members of the group. This agrees with Whitten's [127] and
Bruce's [13] observations that, in large groups of mice, many females
become anoestrous. In males, there is an increase in numbers of
"omega" animals [6]. Group size is thus not an important stimulus in
the rabbit other than to suppress gonadotrophin secretion in the female.

It is difficult to obtain biological meaning from much of the experimental work pertaining to group size in other mammals. Most workers thrust together varying numbers of individuals of either sex without thought of basic group structure. Apparently the social unit of
the wild mouse is one to four males and two to five females [103].
Except by chance, this is not usually duplicated in experiments, since
most workers erroneously accept group size and total numbers as being
synonymous.

Deliberations on the way in which space is important in mammalian
populations usually involve ideas of home-range and territoriality,
and especially the ways in which the latter operates as a spacing mechanism per se. There is a tacit assumption in all this that the sizes
of home-range and territory remain relatively fixed. This is not true
for birds where size of territory is readily compressible in many species [31,95,65,7] and, although there is a little information on the
subject it does not appear to be generally true for mammals. Frank
describes plagues of the vole, Microtus arvalis, in Germany [47]. He
states that population increase in that species depends decisively on
a group of behavior mechanisms which he calls "condensation potential"

- including a reduction in size of home-range and a large increase in the numbers of adult females in the breeding group. "Space becomes scarce" and competition among females restricts reproduction, causes embryonal resorptions, infertility, and young mortality.

Barbehenn's (unpublished) data on the house shrew, Suncus murinus, on Guam presents strikingly complementary information. He indicates that size of home range in that species expands and compresses with remarkable ease. In large home ranges, pregnancy and lactation rates are high, young females are rapidly recruited into breeders, and immature males are abundant. In small home ranges, the opposite picture prevails.

Territories in rabbit populations are also readily compressible [85] and a decrease in size of territory in that species, like the vole and shrew above, is followed by changes in behavior and physiology [81,84,85,90,91], although in large living areas such changes may not reach pathological proportions [80,87].

The key to reaction to density in rabbits appears to lie not in increase in numbers per se, but in some qualitative decrease in living space. This may be intrusion by other members of the group into what Davis [25] calls "individual tolerance limits", or what is called "ego space" or "personal space" by other workers. Critical discussions in this area by Calhoun [16] and McBride (this Symposium) certainly accord with the ideas suggested by our findings.

The data presented in this paper indicate that there is a significant overall effect of living space on biology. They also show that stimuli arising from the stress of a restricted living area affect individuals differently. There is little doubt that some of this variability must be genetic in origin, and further work exploring this possibility should be done. Highest survival rates and health were invested in the group of animals which were behaviorally dominant. Behavior thus looms large in the analysis of causal factors. Initial correlation and regression analyses, however, have shown that there is not a highly significant positive relationship between aggression, health and survival. Some of the most aggressive animals were also very sick. The same analyses, on the other hand, show strikingly significant correlations between physiological attributes, behavior and survival. Such analyses, which are to be presented elsewhere, point to a principle which has as yet not gained sufficient credence and understanding at a population level. Besides the genetic and psychological (experiential) processes which shape the nature of the individual adult mammal, there is an important organic component, rooted in developmental homeostases.

Organic changes in the young mammal born under crowded conditions can alter the biological quality of the generation to which it belongs, dictating patterns of behavior, health and survival as adults. Qualitative changes of this magnitude may explain cyclic oscillations in mammalian populations in nature. In man, they merely add to the frightening variability which permits "culture" to flourish at the expense of evolutionary reality.

SUMMARY

Adult rabbits of both sexes respond to crowding in ways similar to those measured in other mammalian species. There are large losses in body weight and in the weights of organs concerned with metabolic function, an impairment in reproductive condition, and significant changes in adrenal morphology which point to increased rates of secretion of corticoids.

The effects of stressful factors are also measurable at embryonic, nestling and young animal levels. Young rabbits born to stressed mothers show severe stunting in all body proportions and organs. Furthermore, the young rabbit born under crowded conditions tends to be behaviorally and physiologically different, when adult, from those rabbits born under more favorable circumstances.

The effects of crowding are most severe when living space is decreased. Although stress is elicited as a reaction to a rise in population numbers, in the individual it is not a response to group size per se, but to some form of spatial restriction either in the form of space itself or in the quality of animal behavior in space.

The data are discussed in relation to other findings, and it is concluded that upset homeostases in the physiology of development probably play an important part in preconditioning the adult mammal and in changing the qualities of successive generations of mammals in natural populations.

REFERENCES

1. Adler, J.H.: Aspects of stress in animals. In Conalty, M.L., ed., Husbandry of Laboratory Animals. Academic Press, New York, 1967.
2. Andrews, R.V.: Daily and seasonal variation in adrenal metabolism of the brown lemming. Physiol. Zool., 41:86-94, 1968.
3. Aumann, G.D.: Microtine abundance and soil sodium levels. J. Mammal., 46:594-604, 1965.
4. _____ and Emlen, J.T.: Relation of population density to sodium availability and sodium selection by microtine rodents. Nature, 208:198-199, 1965.
5. Bailey, E.D.: Social interaction as a population-regulating mechanism in mice. Canad. J. Zool., 44:1007-1012, 1966.
6. Barnett, S.A.: An analysis of social behaviour in wild rats. Proc. Zool. Soc. Lond., 130:107-152, 1958.
7. Bendell, J.F. and Elliot, P.W.: Behaviour and the regulation of blue grouse. Can. Wildlife Service Rep. Ser., 4:1-76, 1967.

8. Bern, H.A., Nandl, S., Campbell, R.A. and Pissoti, L.E.: The
        effects of hormones and other agents on weight changes
        and on ceroid deposition induced by oestrogen administra-
        tion and by hypophysectomy in the adrenal glands of
        BALB/c Crgl. mice. Acta Endocrinol., 31:349-383, 1959.
9. Blair-West, J.R., Coghlan, J.P., Denton, D.A., Nelson, J.F.,
        Orchard, E., Scoggins, B.A., Wright, R.D., Myers, K. and
        Junquiera, C.L.: Physiological, morphological and be-
        havioural adaptation to a sodium deficient environment
        by wild native Australian and introduced species of ani-
        mals. Nature, 217:922-928, 1968.
10. Bronson, F.H.: Effects of social stimulation on adrenal and re-
        productive physiology of rodents. In Conalty, M.L., ed.,
        Husbandry of Laboratory Animals. Academic Press, New
        York, 1967.
11. _____ and Desjardins, C.: Aggression in adult mice: Modi-
        fication by neonatal injections of gonadal hormones.
        Science, 161:705-706, 1968.
12. _____ and Eleftheriou, B.E.: Adrenal responses to crowd-
        ing in Peromyscus and C57BL/10J mice. Physiol. Zool.,
        36:161-166, 1963.
13. Bruce, H.M.: Continued suppression of pituitary luteotrophic
        activity and fertility in the female mouse. J. Reprod.
        Fert., 4:313-318, 1962.
14. Calhoun, J.B.: The social aspects of population dynamics.
        J. Mammal., 33:139-158, 1952.
15. _____: A comparative study of the social behaviour of
        two inbred strains of house mice. Ecol. Monogr.,
        26:81-103, 1956.
16. _____: The social use of space. In Mayer, W. and van
        Gelder, R., eds., Physiological Mammalogy. Vol. 1.
        Academic Press, New York, 1963.
17. Campbell, H.J.: Effects of neonatal injections of hormones on
        sexual behaviour and reproduction in the rabbit.
        J. Physiol., 181:568-575, 1965.
18. Chitty, D.: Adverse effects of population density upon the via-
        bility of later generations. In Cragg, J.B. and Pirie,
        N.W., eds., The Numbers of Man and Animals. Oliver and
        Boyd Ltd., Edinburgh, 1955.
19. _____: Self-regulation of numbers through changes in via-
        bility. Cold Spring Harbour Symp. Quant. Biol., 22:277-
        280, 1958.
20. _____: The natural selection of self-regulatory behaviour
        in animal populations. Proc. Ecol. Soc. Aust., 2:51-78,
        1967.
21. Chitty, H.: Variations in the weight of the adrenal glands of
        the field vole (Microtus agrestis). J. Endocrinol.,
        22:387-393, 1961.
22. Christian, J.J.: The adreno-pituitary system and population
        cycles in mammals. J. Mammal., 31:247-259, 1950.

23. _____: Adrenal and reproductive responses to population size in mice from freely growing populations.
Ecology, 37:258-273, 1956.

24. _____: Reserpine suppression of the density-dependent
adrenal hypertrophy and reproductive hypoendocrinism in
populations of male mice. Amer. J. Physiol., 187:353-356,
1956.

25. _____: The pathology of overpopulation. Milit. Med.,
128:571-603, 1963.

26. _____: Effect of chronic ACTH treatment on maturation
of intact female mice. Endocrinology, 74:669-679, 1964.

27. _____: ACTH-induced renal glomerular disease in intact,
adrenalectomized and castrate male mice. Proc. Soc. Exp.
Biol. Med., 126:152-157, 1967.

28. _____ and LeMunyan, C.D.: Adverse effects of crowding
on lactation and reproduction of mice and two generations
of their progeny. Endocrinology, 63:517-529, 1958.

29. _____ and Davis, D.E.: Endocrines, behaviour and population. Science, 146:1550-1560, 1964.

30. _____, Lloyd, J.A. and Davis, D.E.: The role of endo-
crines in the self-regulation of mammalian populations.
In Pincus, G., ed., Recent Progress in Hormone Research.
Vol. 21. Academic Press, New York, 1965.

31. Clarke, C.H.D.: Fluctuations in numbers of ruffed grouse (Bonosa
umbellus [Linne]), with special reference to Ontario.
Univ. Toronto Biol. Ser., 41:5-118, 1936.

32. Clough, G.C.: Viability of wild meadow voles under various conditions of population density, season, and reproductive
activity. Ecology, 46:119-134, 1965.

33. Courrier, R., Colonge, R.M. and Baclesse, M.: Action de la cortisone administree a la mere sur la surrenale du foetus
de rat. C.R. Acad. Sci., 233:333-336, 1951.

34. D'Arcy, P.F. and Spurling, N.W.: The effect of cortisone and
corticotrophin on amphetamine toxicity in mice under
crowded and non-crowded conditions. J. Endocrinol.,
22:35-36, 1961.

35. Davis, D.E.: The role of density in aggressive behaviour in
house mice. Anim. Behav., 6:207-211, 1958.

36. Deane, H.W.: The Adrenocortical Hormones. Vol. 1 of Handbuch
der Experimentellen Pharmakologie. Springer-Verlag,
Berlin, 1962.

37. De Fries, J.C.: Prenatal maternal stress in mice. J. Hered.,
55:289-295, 1965.

38. De Long, K.T.: Population ecology of feral house mice. Ecology,
48:611-635, 1967.

39. Denenberg, V.H.: The effects of early experience. In Hafez, E.S.,
ed., The Behaviour of Domestic Animals. Williams and
Wilkins, Baltimore, 1969.

40. _____ and Whimbey, A.E.: Behaviour of adult rats is
modified by the experiences their mothers had as infants.
Science, 142:1192-1193, 1963.

41. Dudzinski, M.L. and Mykytowycz, R.: The eye lens as as indicator
        of age in the wild rabbit in Australia. CSIRO Wildlife
        Res., 6:156-159, 1969.
42. Eleftheriou, B.E., Bronson, F.H. and Zarrow, M.X.: Interaction
        of olfactory and other environmental stimuli on implanta-
        tion in the deer mouse. Science, 137:764, 1962.
43. Elton, C.: Voles, Mice and Lemmings. Oxford University Press,
        Oxford, 1942.
44. Endroczi, E., Lissak, K. and Telegdy, G.Y.: Quoted in Lissak, K.
        and Endroczi, E., eds., The Neuroendocrine Control of
        Adaptation. Pergamon Press, Oxford, 1966.
45. Everitt, G.C.: Prenatal development of uniparous animals, with
        particular reference to the influence of maternal nutri-
        tion in sheep. In Lodge, G.A. and Lamming, G.E., eds.,
        Growth and Development of Mammals. Butterworths, London,
        1968.
46. Feder, H.H. and Whalen, R.E.: Feminine behaviour in neonatally
        castrated and estrogen-treated male rats. Science,
        147:306-307, 1965.
47. Frank, F.: The causality of microtine cycles in Germany.
        J. Wildlife Manage., 21:113-121, 1957.
48. Fratta, I., Zak, S.B., Greengard, P. and Sigg, E.B.: Fetal death
        from nicotinamide-deficient diet and its prevention by
        chlorpromazine and imipramine. Science, 145:1429-1430,
        1964.
49. Gentry, J.T., Parkhurst, E. and Bulin, G.V.: An epidemiological
        study of congenital malformations in New York State. In
        Bresler, J.B., ed., Human Ecology. Addison-Wesley, Read-
        ing, Mass., 1966.
50. Grahn, D. and Kratchman, K.: Variation in neonatal death rate
        and birth weight in the United States and possible rela-
        tions to environmental radiation, geology and altitude.
        In Bresler, J.B., ed., Human Ecology. Addison-Wesley,
        Reading, Mass., 1966.
51. Gray, G.A., Levine, S. and Broadhurst, P.L.: Gonadal hormone in-
        jections in infancy and adult emotional behaviour. Anim.
        Behav., 13:33-45, 1965.
52. Green, P.C. and Gordon, M.: Maternal deprivation: its influence
        on visual exploration in infant monkeys. Science,
        145:292-294, 1964.
53. Greenblatt, E.W. and Osterberg, A.C.: Correlations of activating
        and lethal effects of excitatory drugs in grouped and
        isolated mice. J. Pharmacol. Exp. Therap., 131:115-119,
        1961.
54. Gunne, H. and Gemzell, C.A.: Quoted in Lissak, K. and Endroczi,
        E., eds., The Neuroendocrine Control of Adaptation.
        Pergamon Press, Oxford, 1966.
55. Haltmeyer, G.C., Denenberg, V.H. and Zarrow, M.X.: Modification
        of the plasma corticosterone response as a function of
        infantile stimulation and electric shock parameters.
        Physiol. Behav., 2:61-63, 1967.

56. Harris, G.W.: Sex hormones, brain development and brain function. Endocrinology, 75:627–648, 1964.
57. Hatch, A., Wiberg, G.S., Balazs, T. and Grice, H.C.: Long-term isolation stress in rats. Science, 142:507, 1963.
58. Healey, M.C.: Aggression and self-regulation of population size in deermice. Ecology, 48:377–392, 1967.
59. Hersher, L., Richmond, J.B. and Moore, A.U.: In Rheingold, H.L., ed., Maternal Behaviour in Mammals. Wiley, New York, 1963.
60. Howard, E.: Effects of corticosterone on the developing brain. (Abstract). Fed. Proc., 22:270, 1963.
61. Joffe, J.M.: Genotype and prenatal and premating stress interact to affect adult behaviour in rats. Science, 150:1844–1845, 1965.
62. Jones, C., Jarrett, I.C., Vinson, G.P. and Potter, K.: Adrenocorticosteroid production of foetal sheep near full term. J. Endocrinol., 29:211–212, 1964.
63. Jost, A.: Hormonal factors in the development of the foetus. Cold Spring Harbour Symp. Quant. Biol., 19:167–187, 1954.
64. Keeley, K.: Prenatal influence on behaviour of offspring of crowded mice. Science, 135:44–45, 1962.
65. Kluyver, H.N. and Tinbergen, L.: Territory and the regulation of density in titmice. Arch. Neer. Zool., 10:265–289, 1953.
66. Knobloch, H. and Pasamanick, B.: Seasonal variation in the births of the mentally deficient. In Bresler, J.B., ed., Human Ecology. Addison-Wesley, Reading, Mass., 1966.
67. Krech, D., Rosenzweig, M.R. and Bennet, E.L.: Effects of environmental complexity and training on brain chemistry. J. Comp. Physiol. Psychol., 53:509–519, 1960.
68. Krum, A.A. and Glenn, R.E.: Adrenal steroid secretion in rabbits following prolonged ACTH administration. Proc. Soc. Exp. Biol. Med., 118:255–258, 1965.
69. Levi, L.: Endocrine reactions during emotional stress. In Levi, L., ed., Emotional Stress. Elsevier, New York, 1967.
70. Levine, S., Haltmeyer, G.C., Karas, G.G. and Denenberg, V.H.: Physiological and behavioural effects of infantile stimulation. Physiol. Behav., 2:55–59, 1967.
71. _____ and Wetzel, A.: Infantile experiences, strain differences and avoidance learning. J. Comp. Physiol. Psychol., 56:879–881, 1963.
72. Lidicker, Jr., W.R.: Comparative study of density regulation in confined populations of four species of rodents. Res. on Pop. Ecol., 7:57–72, 1965.
73. Lissak, K. and Endroczi, E.: The Neuroendocrine Control of Adaptation. Pergamon Press, Oxford, 1966.
74. Lockley, R.M.: Social structure and stress in the rabbit warren. J. Anim. Ecol., 30:385–423, 1961.
75. Melzack, R. and Burns, S.K.: Neuro-psychological results of early sensory restriction. Bol. Inst. Estud. Med. Biol. Mex., 21:407–425, 1963.

76. Milkovic, K. and Milkovic, S.: Pituitary-adrenocortical system in the foetal rat. Endocrinology, 71:799–802, 1962.

77. Monie, I.W.: Influence of the environment on the unborn. In Bresler, J.B., ed., Human Ecology. Addison-Wesley, Reading, Mass., 1966.

78. Montagu, M.F.A.: Constitutional and prenatal factors in infant and child health. In Haimowitz, M.L., ed., Human Development. Thomas Y. Crowell, New York, 1966.

79. Morra, M.: Prenatal sound stimulation on postnatal rat offspring open field behaviours. Psychol. Rec., 15:571–575, 1965.

80. Myers, K.: Influence of density on fecundity, growth rates and mortality in the wild rabbit. CSIRO Wildlife Res., 9:134–137, 1964.

81. _____: The effects of density on sociality and health in mammals. Proc. Ecol. Soc. Aust., 1:40–64, 1966.

82. _____: Morphological changes in the adrenal glands of wild rabbits. Nature, 213:147–150, 1967.

83. _____ and Gilbert, N.: Determination of age of wild rabbits in Australia. J. Wildlife Manage., 32:841–849, 1968.

84. _____ and Poole, W.E.: A study of the biology of the wild rabbit (Oryctolagus cuniculus) in confined populations. I. The effects of density on home range and the formation of breeding groups. CSIRO Wildlife Res., 4:14–26, 1959.

85. _____ and _____: A study of the biology of the wild rabbit (Oryctolagus cuniculus) in confined populations. II. The effects of season and population increase on behaviour. CSIRO Wildlife Res., 6:1–41, 1961.

86. _____ and _____: A study of the biology of the wild rabbit (Oryctolagus cuniculus) in confined populations. III. Reproduction. Aust. J. Zool., 10:225–267, 1962.

87. _____ and _____: A study of the biology of the wild rabbit (Oryctolagus cuniculus) in confined populations. V. Population dynamics. CSIRO Wildlife Res., 8:166–203, 1963.

88. Mykytowycz, R.: Social behaviour of an experimental colony of wild rabbits (Oryctolagus cuniculus). I. Establishment of the colony. CSIRO Wildlife Res., 3:7–25, 1958.

89. _____: Social behaviour of an experimental colony of wild rabbits (Oryctolagus cuniculus). II. First breeding season. CSIRO Wildlife Res., 4:1–13, 1959.

90. _____: Social behaviour of an experimental colony of wild rabbits (Oryctolagus cuniculus). III. Second breeding season. CSIRO Wildlife Res., 5:1–20, 1960.

91. _____: Social behaviour of an experimental colony of wild rabbits (Oryctolagus cuniculus). IV. Conclusion: Outbreak of myxomatosis, third breeding season, and starvation. CSIRO Wildlife Res., 6:142–155, 1961.

92. _____ and Dudzinski, M.L.: A study of the weight of odoriferous and other glands in relation to social status and degree of sexual activity in the wild rabbit (Oryctolagus cuniculus). CSIRO Wildlife Res., 11:31-48, 1966.

93. Mullins, R.R. and Levine, S.: Hormonal determinants during infancy of adult sexual behaviour in the male rat. Physiol. Behav., 3:339-343, 1968.

94. Nagus, N.C., Gould, E. and Chipman, R.K.: Ecology of the rice rat (Oryzomys palustris [Harlan]), on Breton Island, Gulf of Mexico, with a critique of the social stress theory. Tulane Stud. Zool., 8:95-123, 1961.

95. Nice, M.M.: The role of territory in bird life. Amer. Midland Natur., 26:441-487, 1941.

96. Noddle, B.A.: Transfer of oxytocin from the maternal to the foetal circulation in the ewe. Nature, 203:414, 1964.

97. Ottinger, D.R., Denenberg, V.H. and Stephens, M.W.: Maternal emotionality, multiple mothering, and emotionality in maturity. J. Comp. Physiol. Psychol., 56:313-317, 1963.

98. Palkovits, M. and Mitro, A.: Morphological changes in the hypothalamo-pituitary-adrenal system during early postnatal period in rats. Gen. Comp. Endocrinol., 10:253-262, 1968.

99. Petrusewicz, K.: General remarks on the productivity of confined populations. Ekol. Pol. Ser. A., 11:617-624, 1963.

100. _____, Tadeusz, P. and Rudzka, H.: Density and size of medium in populations of Tribolium. Ekol. Pol. Ser. A., 11:603-608, 1963.

101. _____ and Przemyslaw, T.: The influence of the size of the cage on the numbers and density of a self-ranging population of white mice. Ekol. Pol. Ser. A., 11:611-614, 1963.

102. Pinsky, L. and DiGeorge, A.M.: Cleft palate in the mouse: a teratogenic index of glucocorticoid potency. Science, 147:402-403, 1965.

103. Reimer, J.D. and Petras, M.L.: Breeding structure of the house mouse (Mus musculus) in a population cage. J. Mammal., 48:88-99, 1967.

104. Rodgers, D.A. and Thiessen, D.D.: Effects of population density on adrenal size, behavioural arousal, and alcohol preference of inbred mice. Quart. J. Stud. Alcohol, 25:240-247, 1964.

105. Sadlier, R.M.F.A.: The relationship between agonistic behaviour and population changes in the deermouse (Peromyscus maniculatus [Wagner]). J. Anim. Ecol., 34:331-352, 1965.

106. Sandler, M., Ruthven, C.R.J. and Wood, C.: Metabolism of (C^{14}) epinephrine and their transmission across the human placenta. Int. J. Neuropharmacol., 3:123-128, 1964.

107. Schapiro, S.: Some physiological, biochemical and behavioural consequences of neonatal hormone administration: cortisol and thyroxine. Gen. Comp. Endocrinol., 10:214-218, 1968.

108. Southwick, C.H.: Population characteristics of house mice liv-
          ing in England corn ricks: density relationships. Proc.
          Zool. Soc. Lond., 131:163-175, 1958.
109. _____: An experimental study of intragroup agonistic
          behaviour in rhesus monkeys (Macaca mulatta). Behaviour,
          28:182-209, 1966.
110. _____: Effect of maternal environment on aggressive
          behaviour of inbred mice. Commun. Behav. Biol., Part A.
          1:129-132, 1968.
111. Symington, T.: Morphology and secretory cytology of the human
          adrenal cortex. Brit. Med. Bull., 18:117-121, 1962.
112. Terman, C.R.: The influence of differential early social ex-
          perience upon spatial distribution within populations
          of prairie deer mice. Anim. Behav., 11:246-262, 1963.
113. _____: A study of population growth and control exhibited
          in the laboratory by prairie deermice. Ecology, 46:890-
          895, 1965.
114. Thiessen, D.D.: Population density and behaviour: A review of
          theoretical and physiological contributions. Tex. Rep.
          Biol. Med., 22:266-314, 1964.
115. _____: Population density, mouse genotype, and endo-
          crine function in behaviour. J. Comp. Physiol. Psychol.,
          3:412-416, 1964.
116. _____: Role of physical injury in the physiological
          effects of population density in mice. J. Comp. Physiol.
          Psychol., 62:322-324, 1966.
117. _____, Zolamn, J.F. and Rogers, D.A.: Relation between
          adrenal weight, brain cholinesterase activity, and hole-
          in-wall behaviour of mice under different living condi-
          tions. J. Comp. Physiol. Psychol., 55:186-190, 1962.
118. Thompson, W.R. and Olian, S.: Some effects on offspring behaviour
          of maternal adrenalin injected during pregnancy in three
          inbred mouse strains. Psychol. Rep., 8:87-90, 1961.
119. _____, Watson, J. and Charlesworth, W.R.: The effects
          of pre-natal maternal stress on offspring behaviour in
          rats. Psychol. Monogr., 76:38, 1962.
120. Ugeno, E.T. and White, M.: Social isolation and dominance be-
          haviour. J. Comp. Physiol. Psychol., 63:157-159, 1967.
121. Varon, H.H. and Christian, J.J.: Effects of adrenal androgens
          on immature female mice. Endocrinology, 72:210-222, 1963.
122. Vessey, S.: Effects of chlorpromazine on aggression in labora-
          tory populations of wild house mice. Ecology, 48:367-376,
          1967.
123. Warkany, J.: Disturbances of embryonic development by maternal
          vitamin deficiencies. J. Cell. Comp. Physiol., 43:207-
          236, 1954.
124. Warnock, J.E.: The effects of crowding on the survival of mea-
          dow voles (Microtus pennsylvanicus) deprived of cover and
          water. Ecology, 46:649-664, 1965.

125. Welch, B.L. and Welch, A.S.: Greater lowering of brain and
         adrenal catecholamines in group-housed than in indivi-
         dually-housed mice administered DL-X-methyltyrosine.
         J. Pharm. Pharmacol., 20:244-246, 1968.
126. Welch, A.S. and Welch, B.L.: Effect of stress and para-chlor-
         phenylalanine upon brain serotonin, 5-hydroxyindole acetic
         acid and catecholamines in grouped and isolated mice.
         Biochem. Pharmacol., 17:699-708, 1968.
127. Whitten, W.K.: Occurrence of anoestrus in mice caged in groups.
         J. Endocrinol., 18:102-107, 1959.
128. Wynne-Edwards, V.C.: Animal Dispersion in Relation to Social
         Behaviour. Hafner, New York, 1962.
129. Young, W.C.: The hormones and mating behaviour. In Young, W.C.,
         ed., Sex and Internal Secretions. Williams and Wilkins,
         Baltimore, 1961.
130. Zarrow, M.X., Philpott, J.E., Denenberg, V.H. and O'Connor, W.B.:
         Localization of ^{14}C-4-corticosterone in the 2-day-old rat
         and a consideration of the mechanism involved in early
         handling. Nature, 218:1264-1265, 1968.

Behavior Under Involuntary Confinement

Henri F. Ellenberger

The psychologist who is studying behavior of humans under involuntary confinement has to deal with manifestations of extraordinary variety and polymorphism. Depending upon the aim of the institution, the administrative system, the kind of inmates, the length of time they spend there, their personal idiosyncrasies and many other factors, we observe an almost unlimited diversity of psychological and psychopathological reactions.

It would be erroneous to take one type of institution with a certain type of administrative system and then to generalize. One could not, for example, describe a mental institution of the "snake pit" type and extend the findings to all other mental institutions, and still less to all other kinds of closed settings. Not only are there basic differences between a monastery, a mental hospital, a jail, a prisoner of war camp, but for each one of these institutions there are wide differences depending on whether the administrative system is tyrannical, paternalistic, or liberal. Let us take the example of the mental hospital. Sullivan used to say that it was "diabolically organized to make the disease incurable"[39]. On the other hand, Esquirol proclaimed that "an asylum for the insane is an instrument of healing in the hands of a skillful physician, it is the most powerful instrument we possess for the treatment of mental patients" [13, p.398]. Both Sullivan and Esquirol were referring to mental hospitals, but apparently they were not thinking of the same ones!

In spite of these intricacies, we will try to bring out the common denominator in the behavioral reactions that can be observed in closed settings, then sketch a comparison between the main types of institutions, and point out the basic approaches toward a scientific treatment of the problem.

GENERAL FEATURES

Our first concern will be to define the general features which are the common denominator of the totality of closed institutions. In that regard we note the existence of three essential features:

1. The first and most conspicuous fact is the existence of a barrier which separates a closed milieu from the outside world.

2. Secondly, this barrier is closed in both directions, though not equally: it may be difficult to enter from outside to inside, but it is still more difficult to pass through from within to without.

3. As a third characteristic, people who are inside are compelled to remain there, whether for a limited or unlimited time.

It is easy to deduce from these general features that three categories of behavioral reactions are to be expected, and, in fact, can be met.

1. Firstly, the crossing over from the outside world to the inside, closed milieu, is bound to bring forth a variety of reactions determined by the separation of the individual from his former life setting. These reactions may at times be very traumatic, but this is by no means always so. One schizophrenic patient will suffer a devastating psychic trauma on account of the commitment, whereas another one will experience the commitment as being a beneficial experience; much depends on the type of illness and above all on how the patient was brought to the mental hospital and whether he understood what was happening to him.

2. Secondly, the sojourn of the individual in the closed setting entails problems of adjustment to his new life, namely adjustment to the confinement situation itself, to the way of life, the administrative system, the personnel, and the forced company of the other inmates. A good adjustment may or may not be reached, but this does not mean that a good adjustment is always necessarily beneficial in the long run. Thus in mental hospitals it all too often happens that a patient who recovers from his illness becomes "rooted" in the institution and increasingly unable to readjust to the outside world. A similar phenomenon can be observed in prisons. There is a type of "model prisoner" who is likely to relapse shortly after his liberation. On the other hand, in many closed institutions a number of inmates will develop a variety of psycho-pathological reactions that can be ranged into neurotic, psychotic, psychopathic, and deterioration reactions. One central problem is to what extent such disturbances can be correlated to the type of institution, the administrative system, the personality of inmates, their idiosyncrasies, or whether a part of these reactions could be interpreted as general reactions to confinement, in other words as reactions that are due to occur in any type of closed setting.

3.   Thirdly, whenever the inmate leaves the closed setting and goes back into the outside world, new behavioral reactions may be elicited.   These reactions may be connected with the lasting effect of the experiences the individual underwent within the closed milieu, or with the difficulty of readjusting to the outside world, or with both.   Here too, it is often a matter of psychopathological reactions, but in other cases the sojourn in the closed milieu is felt as having been beneficial.

We now have to examine whether the great variety of behavioral reactions can be correlated with a few basic variables: the aim of the institution, the kind of inmates, the administrative system, the length of time spent in the institution.

The aim or principle of the institution is expressed in the following classification of the main types of institutions:

INSTITUTION	AIM OR PRINCIPLE
Monastery	Collective sublimation
Hospital	Treatment of patients
Homes	Care of children, aged people, etc.
P.O.W. Camps	Segregate potential enemies
Prisons	Punishment of criminals and delinquents
Extermination camps	Inflict suffering and death to enemies

The classification according to the type of inmates largely covers the preceding one.   Given the purpose of the institution, one will expect to find a religious and moral elite in monasteries, mentally sick patients in mental hospitals, criminals in prisons, etc..   This selection of the inmates will be held as largely responsible for the difference in the behavioral reactions according to the type of institution.   However, things may at times be more complex.   When innocents are thrown into jails and criminals hide themselves in monasteries, one can expect that the atmosphere of the place will not be exactly the same as that of the typical jail and the typical monastery. Nehru tells how he and a group of political prisoners organized a kind of university within the prison and taught each other.   More extraordinary is the story of Heinzgeorg von Heintschel who, with two other companions founded a religious Order which gained several adherents in the prison where they had been thrown by the Gestapo [33].   Conversely, newspapers related some time ago the strange story of a monastery in Southern Italy which had fallen under the control of the Mafia.   No doubt, the behavior of the inmates in Nehru's and von Heintschel's prisons, and the behavior in the Mafia-controlled monastery largely deviated from the ordinary, average prisons and monasteries.

Our third variable is the administrative system.   In a mental hospital it makes all the difference in the world whether it is governed in a despotic and tyrannical way, or in a paternalistic and benevolent one.   In the first case we are likely to find an institution .

of the "snake pit" type, and much aggravation of the psychotic symptoms; in the second case, the patients will be happier and their illness will be less aggravated, but many of them become "rooted" in the
institution. Even wider differences in the behavioral reactions of
the patients will be found in prisons, depending on the administrative
system. It is a well-known fact that the system of cellular isolation
(the socalled "Pennsylvania system") furthers the development of prison psychoses; on the other hand, when prisoners live together in
large rooms and dormitories there will be fewer psychoses but more
psychopathic reactions. It also appears that a very rigid prison discipline will produce more psychoses, and a liberal system more psychopathic behavior.

    As a fourth variable, let us consider the length of time. It
makes a considerable difference whether the inmates are confined for
a definite or indefinite period of time (in that regard prisoners of
war often envy convicts who, at least, know exactly how long they have
to be in prison). Whatever the nature of the institution, behavioral
reactions vary according to the length of time spent there. In that
regard we must distinguish several periods. The immediate reaction to
the entry into the closed setting can vary extremely from one individual to the other, depending on circumstances. It may be experienced as very traumatic or very beneficial, with all possible forms of
transition. The same is true for the initial period of confinement,
that is the first days or weeks. It is not exceptional that some people experience a favorable effect from a short sojourn in a jail or a
prisoner of war camp (we will have to come back to this point), but if
the individual is not soon discharged, a reversal will take place and
psychopathological reactions may appear. When the sojourn is prolonged, the main problems will be those of adjustment or non-adjustment,
and whether adjustment is desirable or not. Some people will not adjust when they should, others will adjust when they should not. Non-
adjustment is likely to further the development of chronic reactions,
which, as already mentioned, may be classified in four groups: neurotic, psychotic, psychopathic, and deterioration reactions. A further
variety of reaction may occur when the inmate is facing his discharge
from the institution, or immediately afterwards; here too, reactions
differ widely from one case to another. And finally, there may occur
more or less lasting sequels, which depend upon the type of the institution, the length of the sojourn, and other factors.

    So far we have considered four major variables, but it must be
added that other factors should be considered, among these the relationships which the inmates keep with the outside world, the stereotyped opinion held in the outside world about the institution, the
personal background and vocation of the personnel, the degree of
crowding within the institution, and so forth.

    At this point, we may draw a first conclusion. Confinement en-
tails a number of variables that will be the starting-point of numerous

possible reactions. The nature and intensity of these reactions will vary according to the aim of the institution, the personality of the inmates, the administrative system, the length of time spent there, and other factors. We must determine to what extent each one of these variables is likely to further the production of specific behavioral reactions, and we must describe the behavioral reactions which are characteristic for each of the major types of closed institutions.

CHARACTERISTIC BEHAVIORAL REACTIONS IN THE MAJOR TYPES OF CLOSED INSTITUTIONS

Monasteries. We begin with monasteries and convents, a type of institution whose aim could be defined as the search for collective sublimation, often associated with some kind of philanthropic activity (hospitals, schools, etc.). In the 5th century A.D. monasteries of the West were afflicted with a widespread epidemic of a peculiar neurosis called acedia [31]. Acedia was a consuming boredom associated with doubts about one's religious vocation and horror loci (repulsion for one's cell). This epidemic was brought to an end largely through a reform by St. Benedict who introduced systematic work into the monasteries. Quite different were the manifestations of collective hysteria in certain convents in the Middle Ages and later, for instance the epidemic of devil possession among the Ursuline nuns in Loudun in 1634 [22]. Today, cases of acedia, or more common forms of depression, are seen occasionally. It would seem that the main problem in convents and monasteries is that of adjustment: mental balance depends on a good adjustment, but a successful adjustment depends on the existence of a true monastic vocation.

General Hospitals. Ancient hospitals were much dreaded places of suffering and hotbeds of contagion. As late as 1911, the writer Remy de Gourmont depicted the contemporary Paris hospital as "a prison for the sick, a laboratory for the physician, and a place of dying for the poor" [8, p.299-302]. We assume that present-day hospitals stand on a higher scientific and humane level. However, certain persons who have spent a long time in general hospitals describe them as places where a human being becomes a "number", a "bed", a "diagnosis", an "interesting case", where the patients' rights are turned into privileges, his family into visitors, and where the outside world becomes increasingly remote [44]. All this means that patients are exposed to a gradual depersonalization. Common depressive and neurotic reactions in hospitals are often associated with a morbid concentration on one's symptoms (whether genuine or hypochondriacal ones). Another phenomenon is that of the patient who recovers but makes the hospital his home and utilizes every possible means to prolong his stay there. This has been called in English the "nestling process" [18].

Tuberculosis Sanatoriums. A peculiar neurosis called the "Magic Mountain Disease" was observed in certain sanatoriums with a cosmopoli-

tan clientele of wealthy tuberculosis patients [21]. (This condition
was described for the first time by Thomas Mann in his novel, The
Magic Mountain, hence the name). These patients shared their time between amorous intrigues and endless talks about every conceivable subject; they were fascinated, as it were, by the thought of death and
the revelation of a new world and became increasingly estranged to
life in the outside world.

Leprosy Institutions. It is well known that in Medieval Europe
leprosy was an exceedingly frequent and much dreaded disease; lepers
were subjected to a rigorous, life-long segregation in special closed
institutions. The halo of mystic horror around such institutions was
well described by Robert Louis Stevenson in the letters he wrote after
visiting the leprosy settlement on the island of Molokai, near Hawaii
[1, p.82-85]. According to reliable authors, the dominant feeling in
these places is the patients' conviction of being rejected by his family as well as by human society at large. This feeling is made worse
by the sight of the mutilations brought about by leprosy in the patient
himself and his fellow-lepers, hence manifestations of despair, or
sometimes mystic effusions [5].

Mental Hospitals. The notion that a patient's stay in a mental
hospital could create a psychopathology of its own is not new. Pinel
himself, speaking of the "insane" bound by iron chains, exclaimed:
"... how can one distinguish the resulting agitation from the symptoms
of the illness proper?", and he demonstrated the rightness of this
view when the patients who were liberated from their chains quieted
down [29, p.63]. For a long time, however, physicians were reluctant
to accept the idea that noxious effects could be exerted by the mental
hospital upon the patients, and it is not easy to distinguish these
noxious effects from the symptoms of the mental illness proper. In
the last few decades, a great number of studies have been devoted to
what is called in English, institutionalization, in French, alienisa-
tion, (i.e., the total effect of the negative factors of the mental
hospital upon the patients). We will content ourselves with enumerat-
ing briefly the main types of these reactions.

1. The trauma of commitment. In certain psychotic patients this
can be extraordinarily severe, especially if it has been accomplished
in a brutal or unethical way. I remember, for instance, the case of
a schizophrenic who was taken to see a physician under the pretext of
having a blood test which in reality was an intravenous injection of
a powerful sedative, and found himself, upon awakening, in a "mad-
house", far from his home. For several years this patient remained
under the shock of his "kidnapping" (as he called it); he developed
a system of delusions of persecution which dominated the morbid condition much more than the mental disturbances which had preceded his
commitment.

2. The "nestling process", has been carefully studied in France

by Daumezon, who called it the *enracinement* (taking roots) in the
asylum of a patient who has recovered [7]. Whatever the initial diagnosis, it is the story of a passive individual, lacking in drive and
ambition, unenergetic, without a sound social integration. He may be
a bachelor or a widower without definite occupation, with a precarious
economic status. As soon as the eventuality of a discharge is mentioned, a relapse occurs. Such patients can succeed in spending their
whole life in a mental hospital.

3. Under the name of <u>morbid mental persistence</u> *(persistance men-*
tale morbide) French authors described the condition of patients who
were admitted to the mental hospital, with, say, a depression or a hy-
pomanic condition, and who, although the condition receded, maintained
a number of attitudes they showed during the acute phase of the illness
proper [23]. In modern terminology, these patients adopt the "role"
of their initial illness. Sometimes the "role" is enforced upon them
by the attitude of the staff or the clinical demonstrations before students or visitors.

4. Kielholz, in Switzerland, pointed out that the "barbed wire
neurosis" (that had been described among prisoners of war) was frequent in certain remote and backward mental hospitals among chronic
patients and even among certain members of the staff [24].

5. <u>Psychotic reactions</u> occur in mental hospitals mostly as aggravation of already existing psychotic conditions. Baruk in France
made a special study of these phenomena, which he relates to two different mechanisms. The first is what he calls *"reactions de presence"*,
(that is a specific reaction occurring only in the presence of a certain individual). A catatonic patient, for instance, will have a fit
of anxiety or agitation when a certain attendant, a certain fellow-
patient, even a certain physician comes into his presence. Sometimes,
as Baruk shows, the reaction can be "invisible", revealed only through
registration of cardiac and respiratory curves [2, p.159-160]. According to Baruk, the mental condition of certain psychotic patients can
be improved when taking these reactions into account. Even more important are the effects of frustrations and social injustice upon psychotic patients. Baruk contends that part of the delusions and hallucinations of chronic ward patients are the result of the oppression
of the weaker patients by the stronger and of the favoritism shown by
the staff [3]. Baruk claims that he observed a noticeable reduction
of delusions and hallucinations after such conditions had been removed.

6. <u>Anti-social reactions</u> can develop in certain mental hospital
wards containing a number of psychopaths, in a form not very different
from that occurring in a prison. When the percentage of psychopaths
reaches a certain level, serious disturbances or riots may take place.
As emphasized by Baruk, the disturbances brought forth by these psychopaths is likely to produce a worsening of the mental condition of
chronic psychotics [3].

7. The most typical form of "institutionalization" is a gradual process of emotional deterioration, culminating in a terminal state of pseudo-dementia (what German authors call *Anstaltsverblödung*). To this condition belong certain symptoms previously considered obligatory manifestations of chronic advanced schizophrenia, prolonged stupor or mutism, stereotyped movements, mannerisms, etc. Such symptoms disappear wherever intensive therapy, including occupational therapy, is applied.

8. Another type of specific reaction may occur when the patient is on the point of being discharged after his recovery. "Rooted" or "nestling" patients are of course more exposed to these reactions, either just before discharge or soon afterwards. French authors described the *"vertige de la sortie"* ("dizziness of discharge") and several other varieties of such reactions [28].

9. Finally, we should mention that persons who have spent a long period of illness in a mental hospital may manifest certain characteristic attitudes, for instance, they will keep secret the fact that they have ever been committed and they may develop a kind of phobia against people learning about it.

In all these reactions one should consider the part of individual predispositions, of the personality of the patient, of the role of the family, and, above all, the attitude of the medical and nursing staff.

Hospitals and homes for infants. A condition was described in the 1890's by a school of German and Austrian pediatricians, Pfaundler, Freund, Czerny, and others, who called it "hospitalism". Freund's definition of hospitalism was: "The sum total of noxious influences of all kinds produced by the crowding of healthy and sick infants in hospitals" [17, p.333-368]. Those infants lost weight, faded away and died in spite of the best dietetic and hygienic conditions, and these pediatricians ascribed it to the monotony, lack of emotional stimulation and lack of exercise. Individual predisposition might also play a role. These investigations did not receive the attention they deserved, but today hospitalism has been rediscovered and reformulated in psychoanalytic terminology with great success [35, p.53-74].

Numerous studies have also been made of homes for children and orphanages. Such are the studies by Goldfarb [20], Stern [37], and many others. A variety of conditions has been described: inferiority, frustration and guilt complexes, depressions, emotional regression, intellectual retardation, disharmony between the psychic functions, maladjustment to life after leaving the institution, and so on. The salient fact is that life within a closed institution is likely to produce perturbations in the emotional, intellectual, and sometimes physical development of a child.

Homes for aged persons. Vittiger, Jaffe and Vogt—a team con-

sisting of a psychiatrist, a psychologist and a sociologist--studied
a home of excellent reputation in Basel, Switzerland. These authors
emphasized the high percentage of maladaptation among the inmates, the
difficulty of taking root in the new setting and tolerating the presence of the others. The role of the individuals's personality and
life history appeared to be the decisive point [45].

Camps for prisoners of war. A Swiss physician, Adolf Vischer,
who visited camps of French, English and German prisoners of war during World War I, gave a classic description of what he called the
"barbed wire disease" [46]. The main symptoms of this neurosis are
the impoverishment and flattening of emotional life, the loss of energy and initiative, a difficulty in concentrating, and irritability.
Vischer ascribed this neurosis to three factors that must coincide:
internment, unknown duration and enforced group living.

Among the best studies which have been devoted, after Vischer,
to the psychopathology of camps and prisoners of war is one by Oswald
Urchs, who spent seven years (from 1939 to 1946) in a camp for 300 to
400 German internees in India [43]. Urchs distinguishes between "collective reactions", "group reactions" and "individual reactions".
Among collective reactions, some concern the long-lasting adoption of
moods, fashions, slang; others are violent but of short duration (in
one instance it was a collective hunger strike). Group reactions consist of the formation of small cliques united by a common purpose.
One of these groups was that of the voluntary civil servants. Under
the tolerant eyes of the British command, a group of volunteers organized an autonomous administration with a heavy hierarchic system;
these volunteers worked for 10 to 12 hours a day, seven days a week
in exchange for insignificant advantages, just for the enjoyment of
their functions. This leads us to wonder whether the "self-government"
of inmates in hospitals or prisons, wherever it exists, is not basically a "group" phenomenon, in other words the manifestation of an ambitious clique. The individual reactions are as multiform as the personalities and idiosyncrasies of the inmates. Neurotic reactions appear very frequently. Homosexuality and sexual perversions seem to
be rather infrequent, in sharp contrast to conditions in penal institutions. Like most authors of similar studies, Urchs emphasizes the
difficulties of readjusting to normal life after liberation from a
military prisoners' camp.

Prisons and penitentiaries. A variety of reactions have been
described by Kraepelin [25, p.1510-1530], Nitsche [27] and many others
after them. Much in this psychopathology depends upon the purpose of
the imprisonment. Obviously, the situation is not the same for the
jailed man awaiting his trial, the man sentenced to death and awaiting
his execution, or the convict who has to "do his time". In the last
case, the reaction will differ, not only as time passes, but also from
the very beginning, whether the individual has to be in prison for a
short term, for two years, five years, ten years or for life. Further-

more, one has to take into account the type of penitentiary system,
the harshness of discipline, the individual predispositions and an
infinity of other factors.

Among the immediate reactions to imprisonment, some could be
called normal: anxiety, despair, anger, depression or even a certain
amount of mental confusion. Some individuals will throw themselves
upon the walls, knock the doors, smash up the contents of their cell.
In contrast, a few neurotic delinquents will show a paradoxical reaction of alleviation in the form of relief from their previous tensions and guilt feelings.

Psychotic reactions may develop during the first days or weeks.
One is the Raecke syndrome, a kind of dull stupor, with mental confusion and a few hallucinations. Another, better known, is the Gan-
ser syndrome: clouded consciousness, disorientation, amnesia; the individual wonders where he is and why. (Asked any question, he will
give absurd answers: two and two are five; how many fingers on his
two hands: eleven; how many legs has a horse: three, and so on). Gan-
ser was the first to show that this condition had nothing to do with
stimulation, but was a specific form of hysterical confusion. It re-
cedes spontaneously within a few days or weeks.

What Kraepelin called "prisoners' insanity" *(Gefangenenwahnsinn)*
is a more severe psychotic condition which usually begins very soon
after imprisonment: the patient behaves histrionically, claims to
hear voices which insult him, sees masked individuals who intrude into
his cell during the night. Then he tells incoherent stories of plots
against him, of being afflicted with an extraordinary illness, of being elected by God for some great mission. These delusional ideas
change from one day to the other. Punishments aggravate this condition, a humane contact brings relief. It usually disappears spontaneously within a few months.

Among psychoses that start after a few years of incarceration,
the most frequent is a systematized delusion of persecution, whose
beginning often follows a punishment or some other unpleasant event.
The individual becomes gloomy, suspicious, irascible, rebellious; his
physical condition becomes worse. He complains of being insulted or
threatened by voices, that there is poison in his food, that he is
visited in his cell during the night by attendants or other people.
The delusions of persecution are directed against the warden, the attendants, the other employees and the inmates. Disciplinary measures
make this condition worse; transfer to a mental hospital brings a
marked improvement or its disappearance. This condition should not
be confused with that of those prisoners whose whole activity is absorbed by a systematic pursuit of legal procedures.

Other types of prison psychoses have been described: systematic
delusions of being innocent or of being pardoned. The latter seems

to be frequent among prisoners condemned to a life sentence: after
many years in jail, they suddenly proclaim that they have been pardoned; they describe how the warden or the judge came and announced
the good news to them; they complain of being kept illegally in prison.

Neurotic reactions are frequent, either in the guise of the
"barbed wire disease" of prisoners of war, or under another form such
as the flight into daydreams. A slow and continuous process of emotional and intellectual deterioration also takes place in the prisoner. Certain political prisoners, who were sentenced to long term imprisonment, give evidence of this. They started their prison life
with a productive philosophical or literary activity, but as years
passed on, they gradually found themselves unable to sustain that activity. This slow impoverishment of emotional life, the breaking of
one's activity and living energy have been described in pathetic terms
in the letters of prisoners like the German writer Ernst Toller [41].

Most characteristic of the prison and penitentiary setting are
the antisocial behavioral disturbances. So much has been written
about the so-called "prison code", the government of prisoners by the
most perverted, the mutual corruption of the inmates, the reign of homosexuality, that we do not need to enlarge upon the matter.

At this point we should note a difference between the psychopathology of the prisoners of war camps and that of the ordinary prisons.
According to practically all accounts, psychoses rarely occur among
military prisoners; homosexuality and other deviations are not frequent
either. This stands in sharp contrast to the frequency of psychotic
reactions and the prevalence of homosexuality and antisocial behavior
in prisons, not to speak of the collective reactions, of which prison
riots are the best known. The personality of the inmates of both institutions seems to be the main factor explaining these striking differences.

On the other hand, prisons and military prisoners' camps have
one feature in common, namely, the importance of the psychopathological reactions at the moment of liberation. In regard to prisons, Cormier goes so far as to assert that discharge from prisons is, for the
prisoner, as great a psychic trauma as had been his admission [6].

We have not as yet mentioned a few atypical psychic reactions to
confinement in prison. One is habituation, the rooting and nestling
of certain prisoners who come to make the prison their home. De Greeff
emphasized the danger of the "good prisoner" who gives no trouble,
whose behavior is faultless, who is well considered by the personnel,
and who is likely to relapse soon after his liberation [9, p.296].

Finally, it should be mentioned that a sojourn in prison is not
always and necessarily harmful. A short term imprisonment may prove

beneficial to certain young delinquents, particularly if it is supplemented with psychotherapeutic intervention. The professional
thief interviewed by Sutherland stated that the average thief was not
likely to learn from a one or two years sentence, whereas a long term
sentence would lead him to reconsider his philosophy of life [38].
We should also recall the story of the German socialist leader, Bebel,
who considered the two and a half years spent in prison as the hap-
piest period of his life: he was relieved from a life of strenuous
work that was killing him, recovered there from pulmonary tuberculosis, and found leisure to write several books, including his master-
piece, the History of the German Peasants' War [4, p.254-267]. Even
though such cases are rare exceptions, they cannot be neglected in
an all-inclusive theory of prisons and other closed setting.

    Extermination camps. Their psychopathology has been made known
by a number of survivors. Among many excellent studies are those by
Kral [26], Rousset [31] and Frankl [16]. The internees' condition
is dominated by the horror of their present situation and the fight
for survival. Psychotic reactions seem to be very rare. According
to all testimony, there is an initial period of psychic shock, followed by a difficult state of relative adjustment. A pervasive anxiety is the main feature of the initial period. It leads some of the
prisoners to an apathetic resignation or to run into the barbed wires,
two forms of disguised suicide. In the phase of relative adjustment,
the individual's activity is absorbed by the fight for survival,
though there is a constant temptation to give up all efforts to survive. Among the main features of the period of adaptation are a growing indifference and apathy, inadequate emotional reactions and the
flight into vivid daydreams. Follow-up studies of former inmates emphasize the frequence and intensity of psychic sequels. Trautman, who
examined a number of survivors of these death camps 15 years after
liberation, found that practically all of them showed a definite syndrome characterized by headaches, dizziness and other vegetative disturbances, chronic anxiety, a permanent feeling of mourning, guilt
feelings ("I am living, they are dead"), stereotyped dreams showing
the last vision they had of beloved dead ones, a kind of emotional
paralysis and the absence of any hate or vengeance feelings [42].
In certain persons, the extraordinary sufferings to which they were
submitted stimulated their way of thinking. Rousset came to elaborate
a new vision of the world [31]; Frankl to devise a new system of existentialist psychotherapy [16]. In such cases, the psychoanalytic concepts of "reaction-formation", "over-compensation", "sublimation" cannot do justice to the higher integration of personality and renewed
creativeness experienced by these men. Perhaps one can more satisfac-
torily account for them by the existentialist notions of "self-tran-
scendence" and "will to meaning".

        TOWARD A SCIENTIFIC TREATMENT OF THE PROBLEM

    The preceding survey shows the extraordinary complexity of the

problem of behavior under involuntary confinement, owing to the differences in the aim of the institutions, the personality of the inmates, the type of administrative system, the length of time spent
in confinement by the inmates, the relationships of the inmates with
the outside world, the stereotyped opinion held in the outside world
about the institution and its inmates, the personal background of the
personnel, the degree of crowding within the institution and no doubt
several other variables. Much time and study will be necessary before
we are able to work out the role of all these factors and to devise an
all-inclusive psycho-sociological theory of closed institutions. What
methods can be used toward the achievement of a comprehensive theory
of that kind?

Probably the oldest method on record was that of subjective description. We possess a great number of letters, diaries, autobio-
graphies written by people who spent a more or less prolonged time
in general or mental hospitals, internment camps, prisons and other
closed institutions. Much in this literature is of great interest.
These documents, however, must be utilized with caution: they may reflect the viewpoint of their authors, but not necessarily that of
their average fellow-inmates. A critical study must always start with
an examination of the extent to which the authors of these documents
do constitute a representative sample of the inmates of their institution and whether the institution is representative of similar ones.
Similar considerations apply to the many publications written by directors, staff members, physicians, chaplains, employees of the same
institutions.

A more objective method is the systematic study of the sociology
or collective social psychology of certain institutions. As an example for the mental hospital we should mention Stanton and Schwartz's
book, The Mental Hospital [36], and for the prison, Sykes' Society of
Captives [40]. These psychological or micro-sociological analyses
bring a valuable contribution to the subject, and provide material
that will be utilized for a wider synthesis.

Another approach is represented in the studies made by people
who brought about reforms of mental or other institutions. Through
trial and error they sought to determine which reforms were efficient
and which were not. When removing the chains of the insane, Pinel
noticed that these unfortunates quieted down [29, p.63]. This gave
him evidence that at least a part of their agitation was due to their
being chained. Pinel's successor, Esquirol, systematically applied
the method of "classifying" mental patients [13, p.398], (i.e., isolating them or grouping them together according to the influence they
exerted upon one another). Later, Simon in Germany demonstrated that
a series of symptoms of "advanced schizophrenia" disappeared when he
introduced his method of work and occupational therapy, hence the conclusion that these alleged schizophrenic symptoms were artifacts resulting from noxious environmental conditions [33]. Baruk in France

demonstrated in a similar way that a part of the agitation, delusions and hallucinations of chronic psychotics originated in the daily frustrations and injustices to which they were submitted. [3]. The therapeutic utilization of space in mental institutions has been demonstrated in France by Sivadon [34].

A further approach is represented by comparative studies. Some of these compare psychopathological reactions in a variety of closed institutions—such is the viewpoint used by Goffman in his book Asylums [19]. Other studies enlarge their basis, e.g., the author takes as starting-point the comparison on psychopathological reactions in closed institutions (notably mental hospitals and prisons) with reactions of animals in zoological gardens [10,11,12]. A further step in these studies is the organization of experiments in closed settings, utilizing concepts from comparative behavior, notably those of territoriality and social hierarchy. This approach has been pioneered by Esser in experimental studies he organized and conducted in the research wards of Rockland State Hospital, Orangeburg, New York [14,15]. The author is presently conducting experimental studies on a similar basis at the Pinel Institute in Montreal. We believe that the systematic application of this method will bring significant progress in the study of the very complex problem of behavior under involuntary confinement. The papers and the discussions of this Symposium will be fruitful to all those who are engaged in these studies.

REFERENCES

1. Balfour, G.: The Life of Robert Louis Stevenson, Vol. 2. Scribner's Sons, New York, 1901.
2. Baruk, H.: Psychiatrie Medicale, Physiologique et Experimentale. Masson, Paris, 1938.
3. _____: Psychiatrie Morale. Presses Universitaires de France, Paris, 1945.
4. Bebel, A.: My Life. English translation. Unwin, London, 1912.
5. Burnet, E.: Le Monde des Lepreux. Flammarion, Paris, 1932.
6. Cormier, B.: Cell breakage and gate fever. Brit. J. Criminol., 317-324, 1967.
7. Daumezon, G.: L'enracinement des malades gueris a l'asile. Hyg. Ment., 36:59-71, 1946-1947.
8. De Gourmont, R.: Le Chemin de Velours. Mercure de France, Paris, 1911.
9. De Greeff, E.: Introduction a la Criminologie. Vandenplas, Bruxelles, 1945.
10. Ellenberger, H.F.: Zoological garden and mental hospital. Canad. Psychiat. Ass. J., 5:136-149, 1960.
11. _____: Jardin zoologique et hopital psychiatrique. In Brion, A. and Ey, H., eds., Psychiatrie Animale. Desclee de Brouwer, Paris, 1964.
12. _____: Introduction biologique a l'etude de la prison. Fourth Res. Conf. Delinq. Criminol., 421-438, 1964.

13. Esquirol, J.E.D.: Des Maladies Mentales, Vol. 2. Paris, 1838.
14. Esser, A.H. et al.: Territoriality of patients on a research
            ward. In Wortis, J., ed., Recent Advances in Biological
            Psychiatry, Vol. 7. Plenum Press, New York, 1965.
15. _____: Interactional hierarchy and power structure
            on a psychiatric ward. In Hutt, S.J. and Hutt, C., eds.
            Behaviour Studies in Psychiatry. Pergamon Press, Oxford
            New York, 1970
16. Frankl, V.: From Death Camp to Existentialism. English transla-
            tion by Ilse Lasch. Beacon Press, Boston, 1959.
17. Freund, W.: Uber den Hospitalismus der Sauglinge. Ergebnisse
            der inneren Medizin und Kinderheilkunde, Vol. 6. 1910
18. Gatto, L.E. and Dean, H.L.: The "nestling" military patient.
            Milit. Med., 117:1-26, 1955.
19. Goffman, E.: Asylums. Doubleday and Co., Garden City, 1961.
20. Goldfarb, W.: Psychological privation in infancy and subsequent
            adjustment. Amer. J. Orthopsychiat., 15:247-255, 1945.
21. Hellpach, W.: Die Zauberberg-Krankheit. Med. Welt., 1-2:1341,
            1425, 1465, 1927.
22. Huxley, A.: The Devils of Loudun. Harpers, New York, 1952.
23. Hyvert, M.: Persistance mentale morbide. Ann. Medicopsychol.,
            100:310-314, 1942.
24. Kielholz, A.: Probleme des Fuhrung in der Anstalt. Die Irren-
            pflege, 23:201-207, 221-232, 1944.
25. Kraepelin, E.: Psychiatrie, 8th ed., Leipzig, 1915.
26. Kral, V.A.: Psychiatric observations under severe chronic stress.
            Amer. J. Psychiat., 108:185-192, 1951.
27. Nitsche, P. and Wilmanns, K.: The History of Prison Psychosis.
            Translated by Francis Barner and Bernard Glueck. Ner-
            vous and Mental Disease Monographs Series, No. 13, New
            York, 1912.
28. Pelletier, A.: Les Rechutes des Malades Mentaux a la Sortie du
            Service Ouvert. Bosc, Lyon, 1949.
29. Pinel, P.: Quoted by Morel, B.A. in Traite des Maladies Mentales.
            Paris, 1860.
30. Revers, W.J.: Die Psychologie der Langeweile. Hein, Meisenberg
            am Glan, 1949.
31. Rousset, D.: L'Univers Concentrationnaire. Editions du Pavois,
            Paris, 1946.
32. Schmidt, W.: Gegenwart und Zukunft des Abendlandes. Stocker,
            Luzern, 1949.
33. Simon, H.: Aktivere Krankenbehandlung in der Irrenanstalt. De
            Gruyter, Berlin, 1929.
34. Sivadon, P.: L'espace vecu. Incidences therapeutiques. Evolut.
            Psychiat., 30:477-499, 1965.
35. Spitz, R.: Hospitalism. Psychoanal. Stud. Child., 1:53-74, 1945.
36. Stanton, A.H. and Schwartz, M.: The Mental Hospital. Basic Books,
            New York, 1954.
37. Stern, E.: L'enfant de la maison d'enfants. Z. Kinderpsychiat.,
            16:17-24, 33-43, 1949.

38. Sutherland, E.H.: The Professional Thief, by a Professional
              Thief. University of Chicago Press, Chicago, 1937.
39. Sullivan, H.S.: Reference unknown.
40. Sykes, G.M.: The Society of Captives: A Study of a Maximum Se-
              curity Prison. University Press, Princeton, 1958.
41. Toller, E.: Letters from Prison. Translated by R. Ellis Robert.
              John Lane, London, 1936.
42. Trautman, E.C.: Psychiatrische Untersuchungen an Uberlebenden
              der Nationalsozialistischen Vernichtungslager 15 Jahre
              Nach der Befreiung. Nervenarzt., 32:544-555, 1961.
43. Urchs, O.: Beobachtungen eines Lagerarztes Uber Psychoneurotische
              Reaktionen. Psyche, 2:181-210, 1949.
44. Vaizey, J.: Scenes from Institutional Life. Faber and Faber,
              London, 1959.
45. Vittiger, G., Jaffe, A., and Vogt, A.: Alte Menschen im Alters-
              heim. Benno Schwabe, Basel, 1951.
46. Vischer, A.: Die Stacheldraht-Krankenheit. Rascher, Zurich, 1918.

Prepared Contributions for Discussion of Session III: Population Density and Crowding

SOCIAL STIMULUS AND METABOLISM OF THE BRAIN*

B. L. Welch

It is reasonable to assume that the endocrine effects of intensified social interaction that were discussed by the preceding speakers are mediated by the brain. For several years, A.S. Welch and I have been studying the effects of different levels of social stimulation upon brain norepinephrine, dopamine and serotonin, amines that are believed to have a primary role in the process of neurotransmission.

Measurable differences exist between the brains of male mice that live in groups and those that live in isolation; further, the effects of different social stimulus conditions are usually graded such that mice living in small groups are intermediate in response between those that are crowded and those that live in isolation. We have used mice because of the great expense that would be involved in experimentation with a higher animal and because of the relative ease and rapidity with which the brain may be removed from mice and chilled in order to slow metabolic processes.

Briefly, the differences that have been found in our laboratory and in other laboratories doing similar work are as follows:

1. Norepinephrine and dopamine are produced and utilized at greater rates in the brains of grouped than in those of isolated mice. This has been inferred from observations that brain levels of these amines decline more rapidly when rate-limiting enzymes for their biosynthesis are inhibited with drugs, and from observations that the amines usually accumulate more rapidly when enzymes for their catabolism are inhibited [16,17,19,20]. Our results are supported by obser-

* The work summarized here was supported by grants from the Air Force Office of Scientific Research, the U.S. Army Medical Research and Development Command, and the National Institute of Mental Health.

vations made in another laboratory that the electro-corticogram is
more readily synchronized by inhibitors of catecholamine biosynthesis
in group-living rats than in rats that live in isolation [10].

2. Serotonin, an indoleamine, is apparently metabolized at higher
rates in grouped than in isolated mice. It has been inferred from the
observation of Garattini et al. [4,5] that the major catabolite of serotonin, 5-hydroxy-indoleacetic acid (5-HIAA), declines more rapidly from
the brains of grouped mice after administration of a monoamine oxidase
inhibitor and from our confirming observation that 5-HIAA is normally
present in higher amounts in the brains of group-living than isolated
mice [13].

3. The livel of N-acetyl-L-aspartic acid is higher in the brains
of grouped mice than isolated mice [8]. In grouped rats, less inter-
peritoneally-administered 3,4-dimethoxyphenylethylamine is taken up
by the brain [12]. The levels of cholinesterase and acetylcholinester-
ase are different [7].

4. Compared with isolated animals, grouped animals are less reactive to most CNS excitatory and stimulant drugs and more affected by
most sedatives and tranquilizers [3,18,21].

5. Grouped animals are behaviorally less excitable, less aggressive and less reactive to electric shock than isolated animals [3].

6. Grouped animals maintain high levels of adrenocortical activity relative to isolates, but the adrenocortical response evoked in
them by stress is relatively small [1]. This probably reflects different levels of tonic activation of cortical inhibitory systems that
restrain subcortical activating systems of the brainstem. Failure to
take these differences in excitability into account in the conduct of
experiments can lead to apparent results that are the opposite of those
that actually exist between undisturbed grouped and isolated animals;
for instance, although isolated male mice normally have smaller adrenals than grouped mice, this difference is reversed if the isolated
mice are caged in pairs and allowed to fight for only five minutes
daily for a few days [3].

7. A lowering of norepinephrine in the pons and medulla oblongata
of the brain, similar to that produced by actually fighting, can occur
in mice that merely witness fighting [14]. Bronson and Eleftheriou [2]
and Mason [9] have shown in mice and in monkeys that psychosocial stimulation causes pituitary-adrenocortical activation. In view of the fact
that norepinephrine apparently has a role in the activating systems of
the brain [6,11,22], it is possible that these peripheral endocrine
effects may be either a direct or an indirect consequence of changes
in the activity of noradrenergic neurons. We have recently observed
that intense daily encounters of short duration between mice that otherwise live in isolation have profound sustained effects upon brain nor-

epinephrine and dopamine and upon heart, adrenal and spleen weight [15]. It is my opinion that, in the future, intensive study of the behavioral and physiological effects of occasional encounters between animals that otherwise live apart may yield more information that is relevant to real life situations than will the study of animals confined under different prescribed conditions for long periods of time.

Our knowledge of the manner in which the use of space by animals and men affects their behavior and the functioning of their brain is yet both primitive and fragmentary. It remains a most challenging area for future research.

REFERENCES

1. Barrett, A.M. and Stockham, M.A.: The response of the pituitary-adrenal system to a stressful stimulus: the effect of conditioning and pentobarbitone treatment. J. Endocrinol., 33:145-152, 1965.
2. Bronson, F.H. and Eleftheriou, B.E.: Adrenal response to fighting in mice: Separation of physical and psychological causes. Science, 147:627-628, 1965.
3. Conslo, S. Garattini, S. and Valzelli, L.: Amphetamine toxicity in aggressive mice. J. Pharm. Pharmacol., 17:53-54, 1965.
4. Garattini, S., Giacalone, E. and Valzelli, L.: Isolation, aggressiveness and brain 5-hydroxytryptamine turnover. J. Pharm. Pharmacol., 19:338-339, 1967.
5. Giacalone, E., Tansella, M., Valzelli, L. and Garattini, S.: Brain serotonin metabolism in isolated aggressive mice. Biochem. Pharmacol., 17:1315-1327, 1968.
6. Hillarp, N.A., Fuxe, K. and Dahlstrom, A.: Demonstration and mapping of central neurons containing dopamine, noradrenaline and 5-hydroxytryptamine and their relations to psychopharmaca. Pharmacol. Rev., 18:727-741, 1966.
7. Krech, D., Rosenzweig, M.R. and Bennett, E.L.: Environmental impoverishment, social isolation and changes in brain chemistry and anatomy. Physiol. Behav., 1:99-104, 1966.
8. Marcucci, F., Mussini, E., Valzelli, L. and Garattini, S.: Decrease in N-acetyl-L-aspartic acid in brain of aggressive mice. J. Neurochem., 15:53-54, 1968.
9. Mason, J.W.: Psychological influences on the pituitary-adrenal cortical system. In Pincus, G., ed., Recent Progress in Hormone Research, Vol. 15. Academic Press, New York, 1959.
10. Pirch, J.H. and Rech, R.H.: Effect of alpha-methyltyrosine on the electrocorticogram of unrestrained rats. Int. J. Neuropharmacol., 4:315-324, 1968.
11. Torda, C.: Effect of changes of brain norepinephrine content on sleep cycle in rat. Brain Res., 10:200-207, 1968.
12. Vogel, W.H.: Physiological disposition and metabolism of 3, 4-dimethyoxyphenylethylamine in the rat. Int. J. Neuropharmacol., 7:373-381, 1968.

13. Welch, A.S. and Welch, B.L.: Effect of stress and para-chloro-
         phenylalanine upon brain serotonin, 5-hydroxyindole-
         acetic acid and catecholamines in grouped and isolated
         mice. Biochem. Pharmacol., 17:699-708, 1968.
14. _____ and _____: Reduction of norepinephrine in the
         lower brainstem by psychological stimulus. Proc. Nat.
         Acad. Sci., 60:478-481, 1968.
15. _____ and _____: Isolation, reactivity and aggres-
         sion: evidence for an involvement of brain catechol
         and indoleamines. In Eleftheriou, B.E. and Scott, J.P.,
         eds., Physiology of Fighting and Defeat. University
         of Chicago Press, Chicago, in press.
16. Welch, B.L.: Discussion of "Aggression, Defense and Neurohumors"
         by Alan B. Rothballer. In Clemente, C.D. and Lindsley,
         D.B., eds., Aggression and Defense, Neural Mechanisms
         and Social Patterns. University of California Press,
         Los Angeles, 1967.
17. _____ and Welch, A.S.: Differential effect of chronic
         grouping and isolation on the metabolism of brain bio-
         genic amines. Fed. Proc., 25:623, 1966.
18. _____ and _____: Graded effect of social stimulation
         upon d-amphetamine toxicity, aggressiveness and heart
         and adrenal weight. J. Pharmacol. Exp. Therap., 151:
         331-338, 1966.
19. _____ and _____: Differential activation by restraint
         stress of a mechanism to conserve brain catecholamines
         and serotonin in mice differing in excitability. Nature,
         218:575-577, 1968.
20. _____ and _____: Greater lowering of brain and
         adrenal catecholamines in group-housed than in individual-
         ly-housed mice administered DL-alpha-methyltyrosine.
         J. Pharm. Pharmacol., 20:244-246, 1968.
21. _____ and _____: Aggression and the biogenic amine
         neurohumors. In Garattini, S. and Sigg, E.B., eds.,
         Biology of Aggressive Behavior. Excerpta Medica Founda-
         tion, Amsterdam, in press.
22. Wise, C.D. and Stein, L.: Facilitation of brain self-stimulation
         by central administration of norepinephrine. Science,
         163:299-301, 1969.

Discussion of Session III:
Population Density and Crowding

PANEL: C. H. Southwick (Chairman), J. L. Brereton,
J. B. Calhoun, D. E. Davis, H. F. Ellenberger,
F. Gehlbach, G. Morgan, U. Olin

Southwick (Chairman):

Our speakers have discussed many aspects of the sociobiology of
confinement and crowding: Myers and Davis presenting experimental
data from animal studies, and Ellenberger, clinical observations from
human experience. I think some of the similarities and disparities
between animal and human studies can now be seen in clearer perspective. We face the difficult scientific task of relating these types
of data. I would like to call upon our discussants for questions or
comments.

Calhoun:

There is a very interesting wholeness to these papers, a wholeness that nevertheless encompasses something missing. The last paper
by Ellenberger focused on the impact on individuals resulting from
their confinement in simplified restricted institutional settings.
In essence he was saying that reduction of the spatial and configura-
tional aspects of an enclosed habitat below some unknown threshold
has rather uniform, predictable deleterious consequences on the inmates. On the other hand, in the paper by Myers, the focus fell
nearly solely on the amount of space available to his rabbit subjects. Decreasing space, particularly if accompanied by increasing
numbers for the available space, produced increased degrees of physiological and behavioral disturbance. He intentionally simplified
the structural configuration of the habitats of his pens so that
this variable would not complicate his results. These and related
studies amply demonstrate a conclusion, which is the wholeness to
which I refer, that continuing reduction of available space precipi-
tates undesirable behavioral and physiological changes.

What I shall now say is not meant as a criticism of

208

these papers; rather they highlight an omission which must receive
high priority in our future research. This has to do with choice
and control. To what degree does a particular environmental setting
provide for an alternate route or means for completing a behavioral
sequence whose initial avenue selected for its expression becomes
blocked? How wide is the opportunity for expressing different kinds
of behavior? To what extent does the individual have opportunity to
manipulate and control its environment? Until more insights about
these types of questions are available, those who are concerned with
designing environments will be unable to judge the degree to which a
particular unit of physical space is confining or liberating.

Southwick:

Regarding structure, I wonder if there have been prison studies
of group behavior in relation to structural features of cellblocks,
room size, dormitory patterns, the distribution of physical amenities,
etc. Have these things, in their effect on individual and group social behavior, been investigated?

Ellenberger:

There have been many lay observations about these problems, but
no systematic experimental studies as far as I know.

Southwick:

I would like to call on each of the discussants to give their
comments.

Olin:

Davis has told us about some of the long-term effects of crowding on animals. He has also pointed out that it is a relatively new
and unexplored field of research. This comment certainly applies to
Homo sapiens. Nevertheless, if only by virtue of being mammals, we
have reason to believe that human reaction to crowding is in principle
similar to that of other mammals. Existing research, although spotty
and incomplete, tends to confirm that this is the case. As it is well-
known that crowding, or rather the behavior associated with crowding,
leads to a decrease in reproductive capacity, it may be appropriate
to comment briefly on the possible implications of crowding for future
population growth, a problem that is of world-wide concern at the moment.

The relevance of this question stems from the universal trend
towards urban, i.e., crowded habitation. In analogy with the findings
of animal research, there would seem to be reason to believe that the
generally observed lower rates of population growth in urban as compared with rural areas are a reflection of a higher degree of nervous

tension. This in turn may be assumed to derive from the greater intensity of social competition that is typical of cities and to a
lesser, but still noticeable extent, also of most smaller towns.

In terms of future population growth, this may well mean that
the economically highly developed and less developed countries face
even more divergent trends than is generally assumed.

In the developed or industrial countries more or less complete
urbanization is within sight. This means that tomorrow's parents
will all come from an urban environment, a new experience in human
history. As there is some question about the ability of any truly
urban population to reproduce itself over any length of time, it
would seem to introduce a new and so far neglected element into the
present concern about future population growth.

To avoid misunderstanding, it may be added that the term urban
comprises a variety of environments, ranging from high-rise apartment
houses near the city center to spacious suburban developments, consisting of one family dwellings with gardens. The latter are obviously far more conducive to child-rearing than the former. It may, however, be noted that suburban expansion appears to contain its own limitations, both in terms of space and water, which in many places are
in short supply, and in terms of the stress and nervous tension imposed
by long-range commuting and related problems. To this may be added the
pollution problems of large-scale, dense habitation as well as many
other problems of child-rearing in modern society, which will have to
be left out of this brief comment.

Altogether, it would seem that the problem of future population
growth in the so-called Western countries is a many-sided problem
that will, among other things, include the creation of an environment
conducive to population control, without going so far as to prevent
reproduction.

By contrast, in most developing countries urbanization has not
progressed very far. In view of its likely indirect effect on population growth, it may perhaps be viewed as the potentially most effective means of population control. This statement in no way intends
to belittle the role of family planning. Quite the contrary. It is,
however, a well-known fact that voluntary family planning will be
adopted readily and on a large scale only in an environment that is
highly conducive to a small family pattern. For practical purposes
this means urban areas and, to a lesser extent, those rural areas
significantly affected by industrial development. Rapid urbanization
in combination with an efficient family planning program would therefore appear to have the greatest potential for rapid population control.

If this hypothesis is correct, a case could perhaps be made for the re-assessment of the high costs of urbanization, particularly if it is borne in mind that urbanization is also a necessary ingredient in industrial development. Needless to say, the question raised is part of a highly complex equation that would have to be studied in detail to determine whether it might be feasible to deliberately speed up urbanization. It might be added that such a policy would require active urban planning with a view to avoiding some of the well-known problems of un-directed urban growth, which often mainly affects one or a few over-sized cities. Another part of the planning would seem to require greater attention to the problem of employment creation. Serious and difficult as all these problems are, they need perhaps not preoccupy us to the point of overshadowing all the positive aspects of an urban environment.

Southwick:

I am very interested in the concept that human populations may be self-limiting. I think to many ecologists this is a very provocative and controversial statement, and I wonder if any of our speakers, panelists, or those who are in the audience would like to comment?

Gehlbach:

As a population ecologist who deals with lower vertebrates, I am concerned that much of what has been said about population limitation has a kind of negative sound to it. Perhaps a positive influence on population regulation may result from crowding--at least temporary crowding. Consider social display in birds or schooling behavior in fishes as positive regulatory factors. "Huddling" in certain mammals and birds, in which the heat content of the group is increased during cold weather, is another example. However, crowds often seem to be temporary in nature and related to particular conditions, especially the environmental carrying capacity.

My studies of ambystomatid salamanders indicate that larval crowding causes cannibalism, which is a positive population regulatory mechanism. Cannibalistic larvae grow at increased rates by consuming smaller larvae that would be lost otherwise, since the pond environment presumably cannot support high larval densities. This produces large metamorphosing salamanders, better adapted to their land environment; because large size effects a favorable surface area/mass relation, hence reduces the terrestrial desiccation problem. Thus, not only does larval crowding cause the adaptive response of cannibalism, but it results in limiting the total larval population within the sphere of environmental resources.

Turning briefly to the human predicament, crowding in industrial centers may exert a positive influence on man in somewhat the same fashion. Cannibalism is not relevant of course, but crowding allows the specialized human close proximity to his resource requirements

(i.e., food, clothing, shelter). Simultaneously, can crowding lower
human reproduction through greater educational opportunity or does
it increase mortality through greater social stress? Either a population declines, disperses, increases its resources, or does some
combination of these three things in adjusting. Let us hope that the
adjustment process is not as violent as cannibalism in ambystomatid
salamander larvae.

Another interesting parallel may be drawn between crowded versus
dispersed humans and some results of my research in collaboration
with J.F. Watkins on blind snakes and ants. Blind snakes are small,
"live-in predators" on ant colonies. A chemical communications system of snake and ant secretions regulates density and presumably optimum feeding conditions. Ant secretions attract blind snakes, while
blind snake secretions deter ant attacks and repel possible competi-
tory and predatory snakes but attract other blind snakes. Similarly,
different socio-economic human groups develop enclaves, like suburbia
versus the inner city, in proximity to various resources. Intolerance
to pollution, i.e., chemical communication, helps create and sustain
suburbia which "feeds upon" the inner city yet resists its rehabilitation.

I am not suggesting that density phenomena in lower vertebrates
are always pertinent to humans, yet these phenomena help to shape our
conceptual thinking. Territoriality, for example, is thought to be
rather universal. However, we cannot find territoriality in our ambystomatid salamanders, the concept is usually inapplicable to snakes,
and territories may not exist in marsupial mammals according to John
Kaufmann. If territoriality has replaced more drastic regulatory
mechanisms like cannibalism and is as important in limiting crowds
among higher mammals as Ardrey and others believe, why is it rare or
absent in many animals?

I would like to see a synthesis in which both positive and negative feedbacks are factors in the equation of crowding, population
control and environmental carrying capacity. If certain mechanisms
that reduce crowding in one animal group are apparently replaced by
others in a more complex group, what does this tell us about their
efficiency? How do these mechanisms relate to relative. complexity of
social systems or the temporal nature of crowds? Perhaps populations
can tolerate drastic crowd-limiting mechanisms, if the crowds are very
temporary and of comparatively little social advantage. But if crowds
are socially more advantageous, thus likely to be longer lived, perhaps populations must evolve the "softer" crowd-dispersal mechanisms.

Morgan:

I would like to raise some basic issues which have not been
brought into consideration. About 20 years ago I posited that human
vitality as a genetic constant is not something we should take for

granted. It may be something subject to erosion from environmental circumstances over a considerable period of years and generations. I was severely criticized by some people, with the objection that genetics is the only hereditary influence, and, consequently, each generation starts afresh. Julian Huxley responded to my interest in this area by saying that there is no such thing as non-genetic biological inheritance.

I think that Myers has effectively proven that this is simply not the case. We must take into consideration deep-seated transmissions of environmental influences upon the newborn and upon youth. There are cumulative effects of environmental influences which may be profoundly influential in human affairs.

Following the publication of my pamphlet "Vitality and Civilization"*, it was suggested to me that India was a strong evidence against my theory. A study of the situation in India was then undertaken in regard to the cumulative effect in particular of urban influences. In trying to find any population which was able to survive more than a few generations of urban living, the Parsees of Bombay were one of the most promising potential exceptions to the rule that large cities have a progressive degenerative effect on subsequent generations. The head of the medical division of a major Indian firm, a Parsee, explained the situation among the Parsees as follows:

A hundred years ago the Parsees were villagers, in villages 50-100 miles north of Bombay. They settled there when they fled from the Muslims during the latter's conquest of Persia, taking their Zoroastrian religion with them. Of course, in Persia they had been associated with one of the oldest urban civilizations in the world. About 100 years ago, when Bombay was a relatively small town, Parsees lived there, and others joined them. The migration continued, but in decreasing numbers, as the village populations became exhausted feeding the city. One hundred years ago, there were 100,000 Parsees in all of India; today there are 90,000, two-thirds of them in Bombay.

The medical specialist put it this way: A man comes from a Parsee village full of energy, and makes good financially and socially. His son also has energy, and betters the position his father has achieved. The grandson shows much less energy, and the great-grandson, if any, is on subsidy. (There is great wealth among the Parsees, and I am told that a considerable part of the Parsee population lives wholly on the subsidy of this wealth).

This is representative of what we have been able to find of urban populations all over the world. The cities are places of exploitation of human resources, accumulated in generations of healthy rural living. It has been our finding, from one study after another, that the migration to the cities is highly selective. Typically, a study covering

* Community Service, Inc., Yellow Springs, Ohio

several years found that out of 20 village high school graduates with
the greatest potential of competence and leadership, 19 went to the
city. In a rural town in Kentucky, the high school superintendent
said that any high school graduate who stayed in the town was considered a failure.

The result is a progressive degeneration - maybe the degeneration is less important - of the culture, the wealth and the whole
hope of these rural communities, to the point that they become sociologically relatively hopeless. People of culture and purpose cannot
abide to live in them. This migration to the cities is taking place
all over the world in response to the deterioration of rural cultures.
The newer migrations, consequently, bring more and more hopeless human material.

One other item of interest: A student at Antioch just made a
study of what happens to the birthrate of Negroes who move into the
large cities from the deep South. Interestingly enough - and this
has wide applicability - the birthrate _increases_ dramatically among
most of the Negroes, characteristic of groups with high unemployment.
But with those who go in for education and occupational advancement,
the birthrate becomes greatly _reduced_.

The effects of urban living stretch over several generations.
We cannot adequately observe this in only one or two generations.
Consequently, demographers, for the most part, do not know what is
taking place. What is required, for one thing, is the study of actual, historical experiences. We have practically no records of
any urban population that has been able to survive. We have a record of one urban population, a small minority group, that did survive; it proved the rule. The Surashtras, a Brahman sect, in Madura,
India survived in that city for long by maintaining a rigorous isolation from the surrounding urban environment. With the decline of
that isolation it is falling prey to the same trend as the rest of
the city.

Southwick:

To return briefly to the point of self-limitation or intrinsic
limitation of human population, I wonder if one of the issues at
hand is whether or not such limitation might occur by tragic or non-
tragic means. I think we agree that, ultimately, limitation will be
occurring in the cities; but the point at hand is how much deterioration of health and behavior might prevail before this limitation
occurs.

Olin:

It is very difficult to say anything in general about the point
Southwick raises. It depends on what resources the urban societies

can muster in order to deal with this problem. An efficient family
planning program in an urban area, properly supported by social workers and designed with the assistance of anthropological study data,
could, quite possibly, keep the population rate down. If other facilities could also be made available, one need not think in terms of
disasters, at least in theory. The big question is to what extent
will any of these things be done. If they are not done varying problems are likely. What is happening in connection with emigrations,
is that they take place because the systems of production, social
competition and organization are being changed. Big population
groups tend to become only partially, marginally integrated into the
social machinery. Stress builds up and accumulates and once it exists on a large chronic scale in a society, then we may have a great
probability of violence, among other things.

Davis:

In relation to Gehlbach's comment: He mentioned the fact that
there is self-limitation in a large number of species. This is, of
course, correct. It is very important here to recognize that many
species have a device for self-limitation. We must also recognize
that the mechanisms differ. It is manifestly absurd to assume that
all species have the same regulating mechanism. Species are clever
in grabbing on to some mechanism that happens to be available. Obviously, insects do not have adrenal glands, and thus I look forward
to the day when we will have adequate information on the insect mechanism producing a self-limiting effect. Let us have more studies on
more species which will clarify the different kinds of mechanisms.

We have also had frequent comments that these adrenal studies
deal only with mammals; actually we have to be very cautious in extending them to birds because their adrenal response differs. Also,
we need to be very careful with mammals. As you are aware, most of
these studies are done with rodents. We do not have adequate studies
on primates. We do know that the stress mechanism occurs in primates,
there is no question about that. The question is whether stress mechanism is tied to behavioral mechanisms stemming from crowding.

Brereton:

The thing which emerged for me from this morning's papers is that
the work on the Selye syndrome for population regulation is tremendous.
It is probably true that there are organisms adapted to environments
that are so widely fluctuating, that their regulation is through the
means of never achieving high population, because they get bounced
back to very low densities periodically. But this is not always the
case. There is a silly, sterile controversy in population theories
between Andrewartha and Birch, on the one hand, and Nicholson, on the
other. There are Andrewartha and Birch-like populations, i.e., they
fluctuate with the goodness and badness of the seasons and it is my
suspicion that, in a range of related organisms (from secure areas to
ones that fluctuate markedly), you will find some that lack self-regu-

lating systems, as Nicholson proposes. I suspect that man is on that
end of the primate range. It is extremely significant, in respect to
man's relation to resources on this earth, that he may lack a self-regulating mechanism. I suppose one way to get at this would be: What
kind of threshold to ACTH release and cortical response does man have
relative to the other primates? The threshold may be very high so
that man will tolerate very high densities before his birth rate falls
and his death rate rises. Hence, when he is shielded from environmental catastrophy, he over-exploits resources and pollutes his environment.

Morgan:

You are speaking of a biologically self-regulating mechanism as
compared to a sociologically self-regulating mechanism.

Brereton:

Well, I would bet that there is no difference.

Morgan:

That is a good question! One of the most ambitious and important
laboratories in human biology, the Peckham Experiment of London, fur-
nished data on biological aspects of human population limitation. It
found of its sample 2000 city dwellers, that "the limitation of families (in urban society) is part of a complex picture of which the physical inadequacy of the individual and the disintegration of his social
environment are the outstanding features." The biological response to
human crowding and devitalization in the large city has led to having
to resort to available forms of family limitation in order to conserve
personal health and sanity. A wide variety of systems of sociological
controls that once prevailed in many human societies in the past have
been documented by the sociologist Carr-Saunders. On last Friday's
AAAS section on "The Control of Fertility", Margaret Mead mentioned
that such systems had prevailed in Japan until the advent of Euro-Ameri-
can influence. She also mentioned, exemplifying the variety of such
controls among other peoples, that in one society a family was not allowed to have a second child until the first was married. These I
would call sociological as contrasted with biological controls.

Southwick:

In closing, we come to the key issues of population ecology--
the interplay of behavior and physiology in altering natality and
mortality. It is apparent that animal studies have much to contribute
in terms of knowledge, insight and perspective, but we still have a
long way to go in understanding the human condition. I would like to
thank our speakers for their excellent papers, and our discussants for
their stimulating comments.

The Role of Orienting Behavior in Human Interaction*

Mario von Cranach

In this paper, we deal with a class of movements and positions observed in human interaction which we have called orienting behavior: the orientation of the eyes, head and the whole body towards the partner. This behavior is based on physical structures in the human body, which, as with all other organisms that move in space, has its organs for input and output located in a distinct frontal orientation.

In man, the eye and the ear are the most important entrances for social stimuli. The ear has so far been neglected in terms of orienting behavior in social interaction; most investigators deal with looking behavior. A reason for this concentration on the eyes may be that, unlike the ear, the eyes, because of their marked directional characteristics, show distinct orientation positions and movements which can be observed directly.** These movements enable the interaction-partner (hereafter called partner), and the observer as well, to draw inferences about the looking-interactant's cognitive or emotional states; they may also serve as communication signals. It is this signal-function of the eyes which will be the focus of our discussion; furthermore, we shall try to relate it to the orienting movements of the body in general.

---

* A German version of this paper appears under the title: "Uber die Signalfunktion des Blickes in der Interaktion", in Sozialtheorie und Soziale Praxis. Festschrift fur Eduard Baumgarten, Hain – Meisenheim/ Glan, 1969.

I am indebted to Agnes v. Cranach and to Dr. William Charlesworth for assistance in preparing the English manuscript.

** It would be interesting to know whether evolution, in those instances where sense organs acquire signal-functions, makes use of directional characteristics, e.g., this might be the case in the development of the white human sclera.

THE GAZE IN INTERACTION

Social Functions of Looking Behavior

In social psychology, the gaze is considered as important social behavior. Argyle and Kendon summarize: "We may distinguish three ways in which visual orientation functions in interactions: 1) to look at another is a social act in itself; 2) to meet the gaze of another is a significant event and may often be an important part of the goal sought in interaction; 3) in seeing another, much important information about him may be gathered, in addition to his direction of gaze" [7].

The present paper deals with the first two of these statements, which maintain that the gaze of one partner is significant for the behavior systems of both partners, thus inferring a communicative function. As stated explicitly: "On the basis of the relationships we shall describe, we shall offer some suggestions as to the function of gaze-direction, both as an act of perception by which one inter-actant can monitor the behavior of the other and as an expressive sign and regulatory signal by which he may influence the behavior of the other" [7].

The assumption that looking behavior functions as a signal can be found in many studies on this subject as an explicit or implicit supposition, determining the design of investigation and the interpre-tation of results. The available empirical studies on the function of looking behavior, especially those dealing with the glance at the face of the partner, will be discussed in regard to the following questions:

> Does the glance function as a signal? Which components of looking behavior are effective under different condi-tions? What is signalled? In which way is looking be-havior integrated into the behavior of the partners of the interaction, especially into the system of the other signals?

No historical survey is intended since it has only been in the last few years that speculation and uncontrolled observation in this field have been replaced by experimental methods. This new trend has been largely influenced by a study-group around Argyle, who has recently reported the present state of research on interactive behavior [4,7]. Today, in this field, social psychology joins with that branch of psy-chiatry which is interested in the interview and in therapeutic situa-tions and with human ethology.

Concepts and Methods in the Investigation of Social Signals

A signal may be defined as the physical substrate of a message [36]. To be received, the signal has to be perceptible, that is,

it has to fall within the range of sensitivity of the receiver's
sense organs. Any detailed description of the signal has to start
with considerations of its connections with properties and behaviors
of the receiver, since in their mutual relationship, signal and receiver constitute the essential units of investigation. Signals can
also be studied for their significance in a shared communication system of two organisms. In this case, their place in the behavior system of the sender is also of importance. Signals of this kind may be
called social agents. (The adjective "social" does not designate any
special kind of signal, but the context in which it is used, viz.,
the existence of a communication system involving sender and receiver).
The analysis of a social signal thus requires the separate study of
receiver, signal and sender. For this purpose, we have to examine
two different aspects of looking behavior as a social signal. First,
the quality: Whether an event is a social signal depends on whether
it is received by the receiver as it originates from the sender. Second, the meaning: What is its function in the behavior (and in man
in his conscious experience) of the sender and the receiver.*

        Research has developed along other lines. Before the signal
qualities of looking behavior were known in detail, numerous authors
studied the function of the gaze in the behavior system of the sender.
It may have been the subjective certainty of the glance being easily
recognized, which made examinations of its signal qualities seem unimportant. Our report does not follow the history of research but
the logic of the problem.

                            Variables of Looking Behavior

        Signals may differ in their degree of complexity. "Any single
event or any common structure-quality of several events may function
as a signal;...we distinguish between sequences of signals (electric
impulses, morse-code, spoken language) and signal configurations
(pictures, letters). Many signal structures are distributed in space
and time" [36].

        In looking behavior, as in most expression movements, we have
to take into consideration the complex structures in the sense just
described. The phenomenon has to be well described; the definition
of variables has to consider the phenomenology of the signal. Most
studies (especially the experimental ones) on the function of the
glance in the behavioral system of the sender omit the latter. Instead, components of looking behavior are taken out of their context
to satisfy certain logical or statistical criteria and used as vari-

---

* For innate social signals, the sequence we propose for research corresponds to the temporal order of phylogenetic development where selection generally lies with the receiver; i.e., in developing the
signal (releaser), the sender adapts to the special capabilities of
the receiver's sense organs [22, p.110; 37, pp.157 ff.].

ables. The following survey lists the concepts used in dealing with
looking behavior:

Onesided look: The sender looks at the face of the receiver, mainly
at the region around the eyes.

Mutual look: Both partners look at each other's faces mainly at the
region around the eyes, thus acting simultaneously as sender and receiver.

Eye-contact: Both partners look into the other's eyes, most probably
into one eye only, and both partners are aware of the mutual look.
(Many authors, however, use the term "eye-contact" as identical to
the "onesided look").

Gaze-avoidance: A person avoids looking at the partner of the interaction and especially so if the latter looks at him, so that eye-
contact does not occur. In this definition, it is only by the intention of avoidance that his behavior is distinguished from the following:

Omission of gaze: One partner does not look at the other one without evidently avoiding to do so.

    The following constitute aspects of looking behavior:

Gaze direction (line of regard): The direction of the gaze of its
receiver is deduced from the position of the eyes in the face of
the sender.

Eye movement (gaze movement): The change of eye position in changing
gaze direction.

Duration of glance, eye-contact, or mutual look: The periods of
time that a certain gaze direction is maintained, especially the period during which the sender looks at the receiver.

               THE ASSESSMENT OF GAZE COMPONENTS BY THE RECEIVER

    We have shown why the analysis of a signal first requires estab-
lishing whether the signal can be assessed by the receiver. Many of
the studies to be reported below have only assumed that the signal
could be assessed by the receiver. Some of the authors justify this
assumption of the basis of a study by Gibson and Pick [28].

        Earlier Studies on the Accuracy of Gaze Recognition

    Gibson and Pick experimentally investigated how well a subject
can recognize being looked at in the face [28]. In their experiment
they used a sender and six receivers at two meters distance. Beside

gaze direction, the head position of the sender was also varied.
Head positions were "straight", or turned 30° to the right or the
left, respectively. The authors reached the conclusion that the
judgement of the receiver is based on two components, the position
of the head and that of the eyes. Variations of both components are
judged in terms of Gestalt-like configurations. Head position alone
produces only a small constant error. They concluded: "The results
suggest that we have good discrimination for the line of gaze of another person, at least with respect to whether or not we are being
looked at. The ability to read the eyes seems to be as good as the
ability to read fine print on an acuity-chart, according to our first
determination" [28].

Cline repeated the experiment using more refined methods, which
included gaze direction to points outside the face as well [14]. His
receivers saw the mirror image of the sender, who fixated target
points distributed around their heads. One of these target points
lay between the receiver's eyes. In one of the experiments, the sender's head was fixed at an angle of 30°. Cline essentially confirmed
the results reached by Gibson and Pick, especially that the receivers
react to a total stimulus from eye and head. He added, however, that
head position and gaze direction interact, the perceived direction
falling between both head and eye positions. There is no constant
error when eye and head are turned in the same direction, whether the
direction be left, right, or straight ahead. If the head is directed
straightforward and the eye position varied, the constant error is determined by the direction of the gaze. As to eye contact, Cline remarks: "As a matter of fact, for most head-positions, the line of
regard directed into S's eyes is discriminated with greater accuracy
than all other lines of regard. The mutual glance is a unique experience, and there are unique judgements coordinated with it" [14].

Our Own Studies on the Signal Character of Gaze Components

The studies just cited led to interesting results, especially
as far as the influence of head position is concerned. However, they
do not allow safe conclusions about the signal character of looking
behavior, mainly because they are restricted to a single variable,
viz., gaze direction. For this reason, we undertook a series of experiments on gaze recognition, using not only a sender and a receiver,
but an impartial observer as well. The behavior of the observer allows inferences as to the gaze recognition by other persons not directly involved in the interaction process; it also permits an examination of experimental methods, which use observers to assess gaze
variables. The receiver's or the observer's statement that the sender looks at the receiver is, forthwith, called "face-reaction".

Kruger and Huckstedt experimentally studied the question whether
eye contact, that is, the mutual glance from eye to eye, can be recognized [35]. The sender looked in a random order at seven target

points distributed at equal distances on the face of the receiver,
two of them being the eyes. The receiver announced his opinion as
to where the sender was looking. The results (35% correct judgements
for the eyepoints at 80 cm. distance and 10% correct judgements at
two m. distance) show that "eye contact" in the sense of the definition given above, cannot be assessed reliably by the receiver, and
thus does not qualify as a measurable variable in studies of social
signals. A repetition of the experiment by Ellgring yielded essentially the same results [23].

In two further experiments, Kruger and Huckstedt investigated
the conditions that lead to the receiver's judgement of the sender's
gaze direction as directed into the face of the receiver [35]. Some
of the target points looked at in a random succession by the sender
were located in the face of the receiver, others were horizontally
and vertically distributed around it. Head position of the sender
was varied (straight, 20-25° turned to the right or the left). The
results show that the receiver, under the given conditions (adjudged
good for many reasons), recognizes most of the gazes directed into
his face, but also frequently reacts to glances at target points outside his face. The frequency of the face reactions increases with
distance and somewhat with gaze-duration. Head position could not
be shown to be an independent factor while there is a clear influence
of head position on judging the gaze direction. On the whole, the
observer differentiates considerably less accurately than the receiver. His position (in relation to the sender-receiver-axis) and
especially the head position of the sender are of importance. Personality differences between observers can, in unfavorable conditions,
lead to different reactions (extraversion score, 9). The effect of
this factor also shows in the reactions of the receivers, although,
statistically, the effect is insignificant. In our context, it is
essential to know that the judgement of gaze direction is no simple
matter, but depends on situational factors and personality properties.

Since the recognition of the gaze direction of the unmoving eyes
does not correspond to the receiver's task in a normal interaction
situation, we tried to assess the effect of the natural stimulus by
analyzing its single components in a series of separate studies. We
included gaze movement in an additional study of gaze recognition.
In this experiment, the sender's head was fixed, while he moved his
glance between a number of target points in and around the face of
the receiver. Two alternative hypotheses were tested: a) Adding
an eye movement would improve the quality of gaze recognitions as a
whole; that is, the glances directed at the face with eye movement
would give more "face-reactions" than when eye movements were not
present, and the glances directed to the side of the face would give
less reactions. In this case, every single glance constitutes a
stimulus configuration of Gestalt-character in which the eye movement and following gaze direction in each instance produce a total
common effect. b) Gaze movement in the direction of the face should

lead to a general reaction tendency, namely an increase of correct
judgements for target points within the face and errors for target
points outside the face. In this case, we can assume additive effect of the two components.

Results support the second hypothesis. Subjects do not reach
a significantly higher number of correct judgements of gazes into
the face compared to judgements of pure gaze direction; this probably occurred because the discrimination had already reached the level
of the asymptote in the latter case. However, target points outside
the face yielded considerably more "face-reactions" if they occurred
immediately after a gaze movement towards the face. For extraverted
subjects, this tendency is stronger for larger angles of gaze than
for smaller ones. Thus, the results are in favor of an additive model.*

In a succeeding experiment, head movements were included as a
further approximation of the natural stimulus [16]. In this experiment, we tested the hypothesis that the "face reaction" of the receiver depends mainly on gaze direction, head movement and the successive head position of the sender. It was assumed that these components cooperate more or less in an additive way, and that their
relative weight is a function of the sender-receiver distance. In
this experiment, gaze direction (seven target points), head position
(five positions) and head movements between these positions were varied for two different distances (one and one half and three meters).
The results confirm our hypotheses on gaze direction and head position for both sender and receiver.

With increasing distance, the discrimination of gaze direction
became worse and its relative influence on the "face-reaction" diminished. The influence of the head position remained unchanged.
In consequence, the latter gained in importance relative to gaze direction. The size of head movement did not affect the receiver's reactions; the observer's reactions were affected only at the three
m. distance condition. On the whole, the reaction tendency of the
receivers diminished under the condition of head movement; however,
the reaction tendency is stronger for the greater distances [35].
Extraverts among our subjects recognized gaze direction more accurately than introverts; they were less influenced by head position. Observers generally discriminated less accurately than receivers and
reacted mainly to head position.

If we summarize the results of these experiments, we come to the
conclusion that, in this special particular experimental condition,
the receiver's judgement of the gaze behavior of the sender is influenced by various stimuli, the combined effects of which are depend-

_____

* Future studies should test whether the ethological concept of stimulus summation can be applied to the components of gaze recognition.

ent on the special conditions of the social situation. In special
cases, judgements may reach a high degree of accuracy, while, in
other cases, gazes directed at the face are not recognized or non-
existing gazes are erroneously perceived. Eye contact, in the sense
of our definition, is not a measurable variable that can be regarded
as a social signal. It should be replaced by the variable "mutual
look" that is equivalent to the "face reaction" in our experiments.
Gaze direction and eye movement are signals only in combination with
other orienting behaviors.

Personality properties of the receiver and observer influence
reaction tendencies. The results obtained for our observers permit
some insight into signal recognition by other persons not involved
in the interaction process. Methodologically, these studies are of
importance because they permit conclusions about the appropriateness
of observation methods for the assessment of variables of looking behavior.

THE FUNCTION OF THE GAZE IN THE BEHAVIOR SYSTEMS OF THE RECEIVER

Gaze Versus the Eyes as Innate Releasing Signals in Early Infancy

The study of innate signals and their recognition is one of the
central problems of ethology. Lorenz' "innate releasing schema" [38]
has been replaced by the term "innate releasing mechanism" (IRM),
which includes the efferent component of the mechanism as well [44].
"The IRM may be understood as a neuro-sensory-mechanism which releases
a special innate behavior pattern in reaction to appropriate environmental stimuli. Like a stimulus filter, the sensory mechanism determines the animal's selective sensibility for these key stimuli" [41,
p.303, ibid. more about the IRM]. The IRM can be modified, especially
restricted, by learning *(Instinkt - Dressur - Verschrankung)* [38].
Nowadays, releasing mechanisms (RM) are classified by their innate or
acquired genesis [45,41]. It is safe to assume that in higher mammals
all IRMs are modified by learning, especially those IRMs found in the
adult humans. At best, we can hope to find a pure IRM in the newborn.
Here, however, we have to keep in mind that only a few hereditary coordinations will be fully developed.

The smile of the newborn baby, as the first communicative act in
ontogenesis, attracted a relatively high degree of attention. Ambrose
discussed in detail numerous studies on this behavior pattern [2].
The smiling response appears already in the first week of life, sometimes only a few hours after birth; at this stage probably no differentiated visual perception exists, much less a visual oriented mother-
child-relation. The newborn baby often smiles with closed eyes; babies
born blind or blind and deaf smile as well, making this behavior pattern especially suited for studies of psychic development. For our
purposes, the eyes in quiescence and in movement are of interest as

releasing stimuli in ontogenesis.

Buhler and others found, that three- and-four month olds smile
mainly in reaction to a glance, while mimic expressions only gain
importance at the age of five months [10,11]. Kaila studied the smiling response of children from two to seven months by means of dummies
[33]. He found that the children, at a distance of 20 - 30 cm. did
not fixate the dummies, which were dark glass spheres, but a point between them (corresponding to the bridge of the nose). If the distance
between the spheres was shortened to half eye distance, the child's
gaze wandered to and fro between them. From this and other findings
he concluded that the smile is not released by characteristics of the
eyes, especially not by the glance, but by the Gestalt of the whole
eye region. While the child grows older, other parts of the face
(mouth-region) gain in importance.

Spitz and Wolf also used the eye and the ocular region in their
extensive study of the smile [47]. They concluded that the Gestalt
character of the face with eyes, forehead and nose is the essential
releasing character. The social quality of the stimulus, a friendly
face or the glance, are of no importance. As the authors, however,
did not experimentally vary these components of the Gestalt "face",
the function of the several elements remains to be proven.

Ahrens was the first to investigate the effect of different releasing stimuli by systematic variation in dummy experiments [1].
One of the purposes of his experiments was to explain the contradictory
results of Buhler et al. on the one side and Kaila as well as Spitz and
Wolf on the other, namely, whether the eye alone or the Gestalt of the
ocular region releases the smile. Ahrens found different optimal optical releasers for different age groups. Up to the age of two months,
several (up to six) eye-sized dots are the best releasers. In the second month, the ocular region with two horizontal eye points has the
strongest effect. From the third month on, the lower part of the face,
not as yet the mouth, gains in importance. Elaborately lifelike dummies are more effective than purely schematic ones. From the fourth
month on, the dummy has to be more and more elaborate, movements of
the mouth begin to be effective, until in the fifth or sixth month
dummies can no longer be used as releasers and the natural face of
the adult is the optimal releaser. These findings are best explained
by the assumption that an IRM is slowly transformed by learning. At
first, eye-sized points are innate releasers (the more the better)
then, step by step, the ocular region is included. Only much later
are the face as a whole and its expressions of importance. "Experience
- the completely modelled human face - is slowly blended over the basic
structure, until finally differentiation has proceeded far enough to
make personal recognition and a progressively differentiated responding smile possible" [41]. On the whole, we find that the cited studies
do not give information on the effect of the gaze as a releaser of the
infant's smile; they do show, however, that the eyes and ocular region

hold an important place in ontogenesis; they are the first optically
effective social stimuli.

Looking Behavior, Distance and Choice of Distance

The perception of the partner's location and distance probably
depends on his looking behavior. Nachson and Wapner studied the conditions that influence the perception of a person's schematic drawing
as being "straight ahead"; they found, that this depends on the perceived gaze direction of the drawing that may, in turn, be influenced
by the elaboration of the drawing or by instruction [39]. Hunt showed
that the distance of a drawing is perceived to be smaller, if the person pictured looks in the direction of the observer [29].

Similar results are to be found in an investigation by Argyle
and Dean [5]. They advanced a theory that forces of attraction and
avoidance result in a state of equilibrium, which acts as a theoretical
value *(Sollwert)* of the desired intimacy. Which state of intimacy is
actually reached depends on, among other things, the distance of the
partners and the frequency of eye-contact. In a series of experiments,
they found that the subjects observe people with closed eyes at closer
range than people with open eyes; in conversations, frequency and mean
duration of eye contact are in proportion to the distance. Thus their
hypotheses were sustained.

Cranach, Frenz and Frey had their subjects choose "the most comfortable distance" to look at social stimuli [15]. In repeated experiments they found that their subjects would rather approach persons who
looked at them closely than those who looked away from them. Castell
found that normal as well as disturbed children advanced close to adults who were looking at them [12]. These results, although contra-
dicting those of Argyle and Dean, do not disprove their theory; we
have to assume, however, that their equilibrium model can be applied
under special conditions only. We cannot specify these conditions in
detail, because the experiments are different in several respects.
Besides, the analysis of these differences is not of interest in this
context; we are concerned with the signal function of the gaze.

The results cited do show that distance not only influences the
assessment of looking behavior, but is also of importance for the
function of the glance in the behavior system of the receiver. The
"most comfortable distance" chosen by normal subjects keeps within
the near range, inside of which a distinction of gaze directions is
still possible.

The Interpretation of the Glance by the Receiver

The receiver's experience of looking behavior or his reaction
to it is probably highly dependent on the special social situation.
Argyle and Williams investigated the conditions under which subjects

feel observed; they came to the conclusion that this feeling depends
on a "cognitive set" rather than on the actual looking behavior of
the sender [8]. Argyle and Kendon report some unpublished studies
which, on the whole, justified the conclusion that the receiver judges
his power or popularity from the gazes received [7]. This reminds us
of the "attention structure" which Chance regards as basic to primate
hierarchy [13].

THE FUNCTION OF THE GAZE IN THE BEHAVIOR-SYSTEM OF THE SENDER

Some of the studies reported here investigate qualities of the
signal as well. Most of them are based on the assumption that looking behavior is used as a signal to regulate communication in one
way or another.

Announcement of Readiness to Communicate

"Gaze fixation, that is, looking directly at another individual,
signifies a readiness for interaction" [30]. Although plausible, this
assumption is as yet only sustained by unsystematic observations and
not by experimental data. Our own observations were systematic, but
not completely standardized; they cannot be regarded as a regular
sample; subjects were patients of a mental hospital; there are no
data on the reliability. We found that the beginning of verbal communication generally is preceded by an orientation of the body, the
head and the gaze. We assume that these behaviors are hierarchically
ordered and express the intensity of readiness to communicate at high
intensities; gaze, head and body are turned towards the partner. One
of the functions of this behavior might be the accurate designation
of the receiver of the communication in presence of several people.

We also found that people who give the general impression of a
readiness to interact respond to changes in the social situation (for
instance, the experience of a new partner) by changes in their body
orientation. In inhibited depressive patients, the increase in orienting reactions seems to announce improvement even before verbal interaction is resumed. These observations are numerous but difficult to
control, because of the complexity of the behavior and the social situations; for these reasons they cannot be regarded as definitive
proof.

The hypothesis that the gaze signals the readiness to communicate
implies that strength or change of social motives or effects is announced by a variation of looking behavior. This hypothesis has been
subjected to experimental investigation. Exline studied the connection between looking behavior and the affiliation motive in competitive and non-competitive situations [26]. He found that the mean duration of eye contact correlates negatively to the competitiveness of
the situation for persons with a high affiliation motive and positively
for persons with a low affiliation motive. In another experiment,

Exline manipulated the subjects' orientation of gaze towards interviewers [26]. The mean duration of gaze co-varied with the critical
attitude of the interviewers towards the senders and thus with the
positive or negative effects that the interviewer induced in them.
In a further study with two interviewers, subjects showed a higher
mean gaze duration with those interviewers held high in their estima-
tion [25]. An investigation by Webb et al. shows that the relation
between effect and gaze duration is not restricted to social stimuli:
the investigators offered the subjects four pictures for simultaneous
observation [49]. Gaze duration for the single pictures co-varied
with their affective content, positive pictures being regarded longer
than negative ones. The results here reported make it more probable
that the function of looking behavior is the signaling of readiness
to communicate.

Announcement of Communication-Avoidance

About the connection between communication avoidance and gaze
variables, two assumptions may be formulated:

1. The absence of visual orientation co-varies with the absence
of readiness to communicate.

2. The absence of visual orientation signals avoidance to communicate in the sender. In this case, the problem much resembles the
above-mentioned case of communication readiness; we come up against a
further difficulty however: a lower intensity of inclination to communicate might be expressed by a mere omission of the gaze. A communication avoidance, a defensive attitude, should be announced by an additional signal. This might be achieved by a special version of looking behavior, for example, by temporal variation or by body movements.

Body movements in connection with gaze avoidance of autistic
children are described by Hutt and Ounstedt [30]. They report turning away of the head, covering of the eyes with the hand, etc. Similar behaviors are described in the ethological studies of different
authors: Tinbergen described the "looking away" of the kittiwake as
an appeasement gesture [48], Chance the "cut-off-acts" of birds and
mammals [13], Riemer in agreement with our assumption, reports two
forms of gaze-abnormality in psychiatric patients: "Excessive eye-
blink, that is eye blink at an unnatural frequency (up to 100/min)
is considered to announce the screening against the environment; the
'averted gaze' has the meaning of communication avoidance." Riemer
continues: "In persons manifesting it, there is also a concomitant
turning away of the body and an aversion of the whole emotional being"
[42]. It should not be overlooked that up to now these variables have
not been defined in an unequivocal operational way. As before, in the
discussion of the facts of body-and-head-orientation, we find that
gaze-variation acquires its meaning as a signal only in connection
with other communication variables.

Hutt and Vaizey investigated the influence of population density in a small room on the behavior of a mixed group of normal, brain damaged and autistic children [31]. In all children but the autistic ones, aggressive behavior increased significantly with density. It was remarkable that autists, though relatively helpless, were not sub-jected to increased attacks. Hutt and Ounstedt explain this by the autistic gaze avoidance which acts as an appeasement gesture [30]. Some of their data, however, suggest other explanations: the fact, for example, that autistic children display less contact, that they retire to the corners or to adults when density increases and that they do not attempt to defend positions or toys. In our own ward, we took movies of a schizophrenic patient who showed a definite ten-dency to hide her eyes. She turned her body and head conspicuously away from her partner or covered her eyes with her hands. If she was sitting at her table with other patients, she hid her glance from the highest in rank. When doing so, she tried to watch her environment through spread fingers. After having received sun-glasses which shielded her eyes from the gaze of other persons, she behaved much more normally.

Exline, Thibaut, Brannon and Gumpert induced their subjects to cheat in a group experiment [27]. In interviews conducted before and after the experiments the frequency of eye contact was measured; this was decreased in the experimental and not in the control sub-jects.

Summing up, it can be stated that there are as yet too few re-liable findings on the meaning of gaze avoidance or gaze omission; these behaviors probably indicate communication avoidance. Gaze avoidance seems to be accompanied by conspicuous body movements or postures in most cases.

Coordination of Partner-Behavior

There are a number of studies showing that looking behavior and talking are coordinated. Nielsen reports that during conversations his subjects looked at their partner mostly when he was talking and less when they were talking themselves [40]. They would glance away when they began to speak, or a few seconds later or, in some rare cases, even a few seconds before they began, to return their glance to the partner only when finishing their utterance. Nielsen offers several explanations: "It was maintained that each particular visual act may have a number of functions. It may be a matter of observing, orientation, inspection, a rhetorical device, an example of expres-sive behavior, a concealment response, an avoidance of distraction or a search for pacification" [40, p.158]. Argyle and Kendon reported an investigation by Weisbrod on looking behavior in a discussion group in connection with coalition formation of the participants: "Weisbrod concluded that to look at someone while he is speaking is to signal a request to be included by him in discussion, and that to

receive looks back from the speaker is seen as a signal from the
speaker that he is including the other" [7, p.74].

The most extensive as well as intensive investigation was conducted by Kendon [34]. He analyzed sound-movie pictures of 14 subjects in conversation. In doing so, he found temporal coordinations
of looking behavior and speaking corresponding to those reported by
Nielsen. The tendency to look away at the beginning of the utterance
is explained as a screen against information during the planning phase
of the communication. Furthermore, he found that subjects looked at
their partners at the end of their utterances, simultaneously assuming a characteristic head position; this he interpreted as a signal
to take over in conversation. If this signal is absent, the answer
is delayed. Argyle, Lalljee and Cook found, that the synchronization
of partners deteriorated as visual conditions got worse: interruptions and pauses increased [6]. Day reports observations from interview situations in which the interviewees, while keeping the heads
quiet, frequently averted their glances from their partners [19];
Duke showed that this behavior accompanied only the answers to difficult questions, but not to those which were easy [20]. This may be
regarded as screening behavior in the sense of Kendon [34].

Thus, looking behaviors which are accompanied by head movements
and speaking are coordinated in their sequence. There is some support for the assumption that this facilitates the cooperation of the
speakers.

The Glance as Component of a Greeting Gesture

Eibl-Eibesfeldt made observations and took movies of a special
behavior pattern, the so-called *Augengruss*, which is shown by men and
women of different cultures, some of whom had no previous contact with
foreign influences, when flirting or exchanging greetings [21,22].
Slow motion pictures of the very quick movement (total duration about
one third of a second) show the following sequence: orientation of
gaze, smiling, lifting of the eyebrows and short headnods of a typical frequency. As he describes in the following chapter, he released
it by looking at his subjects, by a friendly nod, or by waving. The
behavior pattern is very similar in all of the people observed. In
view of this intercultural similarity in the character of this Zeit-
Gestalt of a fraction of a second's duration, Eibl-Eibesfeldt's assumption that the greeting movement is an innate one seems plausible;
the special circumstances of the movement's release have to be experimentally investigated.

As another form of greeting, Eibl-Eibesfeldt describes the *Lid-
Gruss*, a slow lowering of the eye-lids which interrupts the eye-contact for about half a second [21]. He assumes that this interruption
of eye-contact has an appeasing function. It is possible that the
lowering of the eye-lids might be a low intensity form of the head

nod (agreement).

Gaze and Distance in the Behavior of the Sender

The distance between the partners also influences the behavior
of the sender. Argyle and Dean found that their subjects, in interview situations, looked more frequently at their partner as the distance was enlarged [5]. The authors interpreted this finding in
terms of their equilibrium model. Since the sender's glances were
assessed by observers, a repetition of the experiment should perhaps
consider the fact that increasing distances might increase the frequency of the observer's "reaction face" even if the sender's behavior
remained unchanged [16,35].

CONCLUSIONS: THE INTERACTION OF THE COMPONENTS OF ORIENTATION IN SENDER AND RECEIVER

We have reported the results of studies on gaze movement and
on gaze behavior. We shall now attempt to describe the interaction
of the main factors of the complex process in the sender and the receiver as far as our present knowledge justifies.

Gaze Assessment by the Receiver

The studies have shown that an explanation of gaze assessment
is only possible·if many factors are considered, the most important
of which we want to discuss now: Gaze direction (eye position)
is a determining factor only for short distances (up to two m.).
The white sclera of the human eye permits a rather exact judgement
on eye position at short distances.* The judgement of gaze direction
is influenced in a complex manner by other factors. Head position
has hitherto been investigated mainly in terms of horizontal variations. It also is an important factor, already influencing the perception of gaze direction at near distances, and it gains in importance with distance. For distances of three to four m. and more it
is the main factor. It is not known whether body position also plays
a role; an influence of body position on gaze recognition at great
distances is conceivable. Eye and head movement were less effective
in our experiments; the results might have been different, however,
if the exposure times of the steady position following the movement
is shortened. On the other hand, these movements could possibly
function as preparatory signals. In this case, we might distinguish
static stimuli with signal function and dynamic stimuli announcing a

---

* To my knowledge, besides men only gorillas and, in some instances,
chimpanzees have a white sclera. It would be interesting to find
out whether eye communication plays a larger role in their behavior
than in those of other animals. It would also be interesting to
know whether the signal function of the gaze is more marked in dark-
skinned and dark-eyed human races.

change in orientation in the behavior of the sender. Scheflen makes
a similar distinction between "points" or "markers" and "positions"
in his descriptions of the interactive function of body postures [43].
However, there are no empirical results to sustain this interpretation. The influence of facial expressions or gestures in gaze assessment is equally unknown. It can be assumed that looking behavior is
accompanied and its recognition influenced by numerous expressive
movements. For this, the greeting movements described by Eibl-Eibesfeldt are examples [21]. The influence of movements of this kind
might possibly increase with the distance between sender and receiver.
Similar considerations might apply to characteristics of speech.

Personality characteristics of the receiver are undoubtedly of
importance for glance assessment. Their meaning has been proved as
to the dimension of extraversion - intraversion; other dimensions
have not been investigated. Future experiments should control what
degree of attention the receiver dedicates, respectively, to the
stimulus and its several components.

The reported studies on signal assessment by the receiver give
rise to doubts about the results of those experiments which assessed
sender behavior by means of observations made by the receiver or an
impartial observer. We cannot be entirely sure on which of the
sender's behavior patterns the obtained data are actually based.
Most studies use "eye-contact" or "look into the face" as variables.
In those cases in which the distance was small and the spatial position favorable, we can assume that the "look into the face" was actually assessed. In the other cases, it was probably the general
orientation of the sender that was assessed. For this reason, we
should understand the results of these investigations in terms of
the more or less undefined orienting behavior of the sender rather
than in terms of looking behavior. Special problems arise concerning the concept of eye-contact, which has become questionable as a
consequence of the results of the experiments on gaze assessment.
There is no reason to assume that the mutual "meeting of glances" is
reliably recognized. On the other hand, it may be doubted whether
our experimental designs permit conclusions on the significance of
eye-contact in natural situations. This consideration requires further examinations of the sender behavior.

Sender-Behavior: Distribution of Target-Points

In the experiments on gaze assessment, according to the design,
the sender looks in rapid succession at many target points in and
around the face of the receiver, who does not reliably differentiate
between these gaze directions. We can expect considerably better
discrimination, however, if we assume that in real life interactions
the sender looks either into the eyes of the receiver or in an entirely
different direction. Indeed, in real interaction we probably do not
look just past the ear of the partner. What is missing are exact

studies on the distribution of the sender's gaze in real life situations. On the other hand, larger sweeps of the gaze will, in most
cases, be accompanied by head movements, which may serve as signals.
Furthermore, one of our experiments showed that gaze movements are
regularly accompanied by eye-blinks: the bigger the gaze-movements,
the more frequently they are accompanied by an eye-blink [17]. This
probably physiologically caused behavior might too serve as an announcing signal. Only further exact studies on sender behavior can
fully clarify these processes.

Coordination of Orienting Movements

Among the available investigations, the experimental ones do not
offer sufficient behavior descriptions, while the descriptive ones
are not analytical in design. Most of the reported studies do mention
head-and-body postures and movements, but only in a casual way. From
our own observations, however, we conclude that looking behavior is
part of a total system of orienting reactions. This is no new finding.
It is a commonly available experience well known in physiology; to
quote Jung, under the heading "gaze movement and total motoric": "As
has been pointed out in the discussion of vestibular reactions, the
isolation of the optomotoric is an artifact. In men, voluntary gaze
movements are almost never restricted to the muscles of the eye. Neck
and body muscles are involved in auxiliary innervation. Eye movements
and nystagmus are but sections of general orienting movements of the
total motoric" [32].

As far as we know, details of the coordination of head, gaze and
body in active motor behavior have not been described. Specifically,
nothing is known about possible existing special coordinations of
orienting movements in social interaction. We think it safe to assume, however, that gaze movements are almost always connected in social interactions. Since we generally tend either to look markedly
at our partner or markedly not to look at him, horizontal gaze movements are practically always accompanied by movements of at least the
head when interrupting longer periods of looking at the partner or
looking away from him. Vertical downward movements of the gaze are
probably always accompanied by a lowering of the eye-lids and, in
most cases, of the head as well. Upward movements are accompanied
by a lifting of the head.

The Correspondence of Sender and Receiver Behavior

What relationship exists between sender and receiver behavior?
As we have seen, the sender acts as a whole, differing according to
special situational conditions. In his orienting behavior, widely
different components of movement and posture are integrated into one
pattern. The receiver (and the observer as well) reacts according to
special conditions, distance being one which we have studied. His reactions are made to a single or several components of the sender's vi-

sual orientation. On the one hand, the integration of the sender's orienting movements and, on the other hand, the receiver's tendency to evaluate perceived orienting movements of all kinds in terms of visual orientation enable both partners to make do with one communication system for different distance conditions.

For an explanation of the genesis of the receiver's reaction we have to consider the following assumptions: in early childhood, eyes and the ocular region have the function of releasers. This results in a very marked attention to this component of orientation in the further development. The disproportionately high subjective certainty in the judgement of gaze direction might also originate from the innate basis for this reaction. Since visual orientation serves important functions in interaction, attention to it is positively reinforced in the sense of a conditioning process. The same reinforcement might have made it possible that the receiver learns the connection of all orienting reactions which are normally connected in sender behavior. The fact, known from behavior therapy, that orienting behavior can be conditioned, is in favor of this assumption.

The Significance of Orienting Movements

What is the signal function of orienting movements, including the gaze, in interaction? The few investigations on the behavior of the receiver and those on the behavior of the sender mostly suggest regulative functions. Studies show that the interactions of the partners during communication are controlled by orienting movements, the adequate assessment of which may thus facilitate communication and the achievement of communicative goals. From these effects, reinforcement may be induced. Furthermore, we assume that orienting movements reflect affective attitudes toward the partner and thus already indicate the readiness to interact before as well as during interaction. The assessment of these movements might facilitate an estimate of the success of intended communicative acts. However, this assumption is not supported by data and neither the coordination of the orienting movements in question nor the modus of their assessment is known.

The present state of research into orienting behavior is symptomatic for the whole area of interactive behaviors. There are just enough studies to recognize an outline, but nearly all single questions remain as yet unsolved. Theories are unconnected and vague. As the interest in problems of human behavior steadily increases, faster progress may be expected for the future. Future research also will have to include the pathology of interactive behaviors which may possibly yield especially important results.

REFERENCES

1. Ahrens, R.: Beitrag zur Entwicklung des Physiognomie-und Mimiker-
        kennens. Z. Exp. Angew. Psychol., 2:412–454, 1954.
2. Ambrose, J.A.: The development of the smiling response in early
        infancy. In Foss, B.M., ed., Determinants of Infant Be-
        havior. Methuen, London, 1961.
3. _____: The Smiling and Related Responses in Early Human
        Infancy: An Experimental and Theoretical Study of Their
        Cause and Significance. London, Ph.D. Thesis, 1960.
4. Argyle, M.: The Psychology of Interpersonal Behavior. Pelican,
        London, 1967.
5. _____ and Dean, J.: Eye contact, distance and affiliation.
        Sociometry, 28:289–304, 1965.
6. _____, Lalljee, M. and Cook, M.: The effects of visibility
        on interaction in a dyad. Hum. Rel., 21:3–17, 1968.
7. _____ and Kendon, A.: The experimental analysis of social
        performance. In Berkowitz, L., ed., Advances in Experi-
        mental Social Psychology, Vol. 3. Academic Press, New
        York, 1967.
8. _____ and Williams, M.: Observer or Observed? A Reversible
        Perspective in Person Perception. (Mimeographed). In-
        stitute of Experimental Psychology, Oxford, 1968.
9. Brengelmann, J.C.: Deutsche Validierung von Fragebogen der Extra-
        version, neurotischen Tendenz und Rigiditat. Z. Exp.
        Angew. Psychol., 7:291–331, 1960.
10. Buhler, Ch. H. and Hetzer, H.: Das erste Verstandnis fur Ausdruck
        im ersten Lebensjahr. Z. Psychol., 107:50–61, 1928.
11. _____, _____ and Tuder-Hart, B.: Soziologische
        und psychologische Studien uber das erste Lebensjahr.
        Quellen und Studien zur Jugendkunde, Heft 5. 1927.
12. Castell, R.: Physical distance and visual attention as measures
        of social interaction between child and adult. In Hutt,
        S.J. and Hutt, C., eds., Behaviour Studies in Psychiatry.
        Pergamon Press, Oxford, 1970.
13. Chance, M.R.A.: An interpretation of some agonistic postures;
        the role of "cut-off" acts and postures. Symp. Zool.
        Soc. London, 8:71–89, 1962.
14. Cline, M.G.: The perception of where a person is looking. Amer.
        J. Psychol., 80:41–50, 1967.
15. Cranach, M.v., Frenz, H.G. and Frey, S.: Die "angenehmste Ent-
        fernung" zur Betrachtung sozialer Objekte. Psychol.
        Forsch., 32:89–103, 1968.
16. _____, Huckstedt, B., Schmid, R. and Vogel, M.W.: Some
        stimulus components and their interaction in the per-
        ception of gaze direction. (Mimeographed). MPI fur
        Psychiatrie, Munchen, 1969.
17. _____, Schmid, R. and Vogel, M.W.: Uber einige Beding-
        ungen des Zusammenhanges von Lidschlag und Blickwendung,
        Psychol. Forsch., 33:68–78, 1969.

18. _____ and Hucksted, B.: Der Einfluss der Blickbewegung
        auf das Erkennen von Blickrichtungen. To be published.
19. Day, M.E.: An eye movement phenomenon relating to attention,
        thought and anxiety. Percept. Motor Skills, 19:443-446,
        1964.
20. Duke, J.D.: Lateral eye movement behavior. J. Gen. Psychol.,
        78:189-195, 1968.
21. Eibl-Eibesfeldt, I.: Zur Ethologie des menschlichen Grussver-
        haltens. 1. Beobachtungen an Balinesen, Papuas und
        Samoanern. Z. Tierpsychol., 25:727-744, 1968.
22. _____: Grundriss der vergleichenden Verhaltens-
        forschung. Piper-Verlag, Munchen, 1967.
23. Ellgring, J.H.: Die Beurteilung des Blickes auf Punkte innerhalb
        des Gesichts. Munchen, 1969. To be published.
24. Exline, R.V.: Explorations in the process of person perception:
        visual interaction in relation to competition, sex and
        need for affiliation. J. Personality, 31:1-20, 1963.
25. _____ and Winters, L.C.: Interpersonal preference and
        the mutual glance. Technical Report to the Office of
        Naval Research, 13:1964.
26. _____ : Affective phenomena and the mutual glance: Effects
        of evaluative feedback and social reinforcement upon
        visual interaction with an interviewer. Technical Re-
        port to the Office of Naval Research, 11:1964.
27. _____, Thibaut, J., Brannon, C. and Gumpert, P.: Visual
        interaction in relation to machiavellism and an unethi-
        cal act. Amer. Psychol., 16:1961. (Abstract).
28. Gibson, J.J. and Pick, A.D.: Perception of another person's
        looking behavior. Amer. J. Psychol., 76:386-394, 1963.
29. Hunt, S.: Thesis, Clark University. Unpublished.
30. Hutt, C. and Ounstedt, C.: The biological significance of the
        gaze with particular reference to the syndrome of in-
        fantile autism. Behav. Sci., 2:346-356, 1966.
31. _____ and Vaizey, M.J.: Differential effects of group density
        on social behavior. Nature, 209:1371-1372, 1966.
32. Jung, R.: Neurophysiologische Untersuchungsmethoden: Nystagmo-
        graphie. In Von Bergmann, et al., eds., Handbuch der
        Inneren Medezin, Bd. V/I. Springer, Berlin, 1963.
33. Kaila, E.: Die Reaktionen des Sauglings auf das menschliche Ge-
        sicht. Ann. Univ. Aboensis, Ser. B., 17:1932.
34. Kendon, A.: Some functions of gaze-direction in social interac-
        tion. Acta Psychol., 26:22-63, 1967.
35. Kruger, K. and Huckstedt, B.: Die Beurteilung von Blickrichtungen.
        (Mimeographed). MPI fur Psychiatrie, Munchen, 1968.
36. Langer, D.: Informationstheorie und Psychologie. Hogrefe,
        Gottingen, 1962.
37. Leyhausen, P.: Biologie von Ausdruck und Eindruck. Psychol.
        Forsch., 31:113-227, 1967.

38. Lorenz, K.: Betrachtungen uber das Erkennen der arteigenen
          Triebhandlungen bei Vogeln (1932). Der Kumpan in der
          Umwelt des Vogels (1935). Translated in: Lorenz, K.:
          Studies in Animal and Human Behavior. Harvard Univer-
          sity Press, Cambridge, 1970.
39. Nachshon, I. and Wapner, S.: Effect of eye contact and physiog-
          nomy on perceived location of other person. J. Per-
          sonality Soc. Psychol., 7:82-89, 1967.
40. Nielsen, G.: Studies in Self-Confrontation. Munksgaard, Copen-
          hagen, 1962.
41. Ploog, D.: Verhaltensforschung und Psychiatrie. In Gruhle, H.W.
          et al., eds., Psychiatrie der Gegenwart. Springer-
          Verlag, Berlin, 1964.
42. Riemer, N.: Abnormalities of the gaze -- a classification.
          Psychiat. Quart., 29:659-672, 1955.
43. Scheflen, A.E.: The significance of posture in communication
          systems. Psychiatry, 27:316-321, 1964.
44. Schleidt, W.M.: Die historische Entwicklung der Begriffe "Ange-
          borenes auslosendes Schema" und "Angeborener Auslose-
          mechanismus" in der Ethologie. Z. Tierpsychol.,
          19:697-722, 1962.
45. _____: Wirkungen ausserer Faktoren auf das Verhalten.
          Fortschr. Zool., 16:1964.
46. Simmel, G.: Soziologie: Untersuchungen uber die Formen der Ver-
          gesellschaftung. Duncker, Berlin, 1923.
47. Spitz, R. and Wolf, K.M.: The smiling response: a contribution
          to the ontogenesis of social relations. Genet. Psychol.
          Monogr., 34:57-125, 1946.
48. Tinbergen, N.: Comparative study of the behavior of gulls
          (Laridae): A progress report. Behaviour, 15:1-70, 1959.
49. Webb, W.W. et al.: Eye movements as a paradigm of approach and
          avoidance behavior. Percept. Motor Skills, 16:341-347,
          1963.

Transcultural Patterns of Ritualized Contact Behavior

Irenaeus Eibl-Eibesfeldt

Man communicates with his fellow man, not only with speech but also with a number of expression-movements. Whether these signals belong to an innate repertoire of motor patterns which are not learned is a point of controversy. Gehlen is of the opinion that, except perhaps for a few reflexes of the newborn, there are no innate behavior patterns in man [14]. A similar view was expressed by Montagu [21], while Birdwhistell specifically emphasized that there are no inherited facial expressions and gestures in man, and that therefore differences are found transculturally [4,5]. Birdwhistell is very firm about this point, although in his publications concerning cross-cultural evidence he only makes statements.

On the other hand, Darwin already pointed out in 1872 that there are inborn expression-movements in man which occur transculturally, and his opinion has since been widely accepted [3,13]. If we examine the question whether genetically pre-programmed motor patterns can be found in human social behavior from an ethological point of view, we must be aware of the theoretical and practical importance of the answer [8].

In order not to be misunderstood, may I briefly define what ethologists mean by the term "innate" or inherited". (For detailed discussions see 8,20). If we observe a newly hatched duckling, we find that the animal performs a number of well-coordinated acts. It can walk, sift mud with its beak, preen itself and swim. It will demonstrate these innate skills even if brooded by a chicken foster-mother. And, vice versa, a chick will never show an inclination to dabble in the mud, even if its foster-mother is a duck. We must therefore assume that the animals inherited these adaptive behavior patterns; or more precisely, they developed the neuronal structures

238

underlying and coordinating the movements, according to a developmental recipe coded in the genome of the species, just as their organs developed. Thus we say in shorthand description that the behavior patterns are underlined. Many of the inborn behavior patterns mature in the growing animal after birth, as can be demonstrated by isolation (deprivation) experiments. Some birds (juncos, white-headed grosbeaks) develop their species-specific songs and call notes in complete isolation from conspecifics [18,19], and chicks did so even after they were deafened immediately after hatching [17]. The argument that the deprivation experiment is not conclusive, since one can never deprive an animal of all environmental stimuli and thus of all learning possibilities, does not hold. It is simply not necessary to deprive totally. We only need to deprive the animal of relevant information, and relevant here concerns the environmental situation which fits the behavior pattern in question [20]. This becomes clear in the earlier example of the bird song. May I add another: Squirrels hide nuts by burying them in the ground with a stereotyped sequence of movements. They scratch a hole, deposit the nut, tamp it into the ground with rapid blows of the snout and finally pack loose earth over the hole with sweeping and pressing-down movements of the paws. One can easily deprive the animal of the necessary information. It is raised in a wire mesh cage with no conspecifics and without soil or shavings to practice digging and on a liquid diet only. It can therefore neither learn by imitation nor by trial and error. Nevertheless, when such a squirrel is tested as an adult, it will perform all these movements, even when given a nut in a room which provides no opportunity to dig. It will scratch in one corner of the room, deposit the nut, tamp it down with the snout and finally perform the movements of covering the hole with soil, although it has never dug up any earth [7]. The motor patterns therefore must have been adapted for its function during phylogeny: they are inborn.*

Of course, one cannot perform deprivation experiments with humans. There are, however, deprivation experiments performed by nature which can be evaluated. Some children are born blind or deaf or both and, therefore, lack certain developmental experiences. I started my investigation with the study of children born deaf and blind. Film analysis of their behavior shows that a number of expression-movements develop along the same lines as they do in healthy children. The deaf-blind develop smiling, laughing (including the normal utterance of sound), crying and the expression of anger (frowning, stamping of feet, clenching of fists). Frames taken from my film may serve to illustrate some of these motor patterns (Figure 6). From this evidence it is

---

* Besides innate motor patterns, there are other phylogenetic adaptations determining the behavior of animals. Animals are capable of reacting to specific stimuli in a biologically adequate (adaptive) way, which demands special mechanisms which are adapted to this function (Innate Releasing Mechanisms). Animals are, furthermore, fitted with specific motivating mechanisms, and their capacity to learn is presented through phylogenetic adaptations. This paper, however, deals only with motor patterns.

clear that some basic motor patterns, serving human contact, are undoubtedly innate. One could advance the hypothesis that they have
been learned accidentally by touching the mother's face and by getting
social rewards. However, such a hypothesis can be disregarded in the
case of brain damaged children who cannot be taught, in spite of all
efforts, to hold as much as a spoon, but who do laugh and smile and
cry.

However, the information which we can get from the deaf and blind
is limited. Many behavior patterns of man are released by auditory or
visual cues under normal circumstances, and these channels are blocked
in the deaf and blind. Thus, if we want to learn whether our more
complicated behavior patterns contain innate components, we must turn
to trans-cultural comparisons. Since man tends to vary strongly and
to alter his behavior, forming small exclusive groups which are separated by customs, the occurrence of identical or highly similar behavior patterns in different cultures would point to a common heritage.

One might think that it should be fairly easy to answer the question of transcultural similarity in motor patterns, since man is the
most filmed being. It appears that one need only go to the nearest
large scientific film-library and ask for unstaged documentation of,
e.g., angry or flirting Papuans, Samoans, Bantus, Europeans, etc.,
under natural conditions, and thus be able to scrutinize these films
in regard to (culture-independent) invariables. Upon examining ar-
chives, however, one soon realizes that unstaged documentation of natural behavior is rare and is not listed systematically. Many documentary films are like travelogues, providing a glimpse of human interaction here and there. Cultural activities (potting, mat weaving,
hut building, etc.) are more adequately documented.

A couple of years ago, Hans Hass and I began the systematic documentation of human expression-movements. With the use of mirror lenses
we were able to record the behavior of our subjects without their being
aware of it [10]. This is a prerequisite to our endeavor, for it is
well known that humans change their behavior immediately when they realize that they are being filmed. Even people who do not know what a
camera is tend to become uneasy as soon as the lens points at them.
The activities which one wants to document can be taken in the natural
context or brought about experimentally. It is of the utmost importance, however, that a detailed protocol go with each shot, stating
what the person did before and after he or she was filmed and in what
context the filmed behavior occurred. Only this allows an objective
motivational analysis. We usually film facial expressions and gestures
in slow motion. We found also that the speeding-up technique is valuable for documenting events of longer duration, such as social interactions in small groups, etc. [10]. Our films from various parts
of the world* demonstrate clearly variables independent of culture

---

* Uganda, Kenya, Tanzania, various European countries, India, Thailand,
Bali, New Guinea, Japan, Hongkong, Brazil, Peru.

Fig. 1: French lady. The sequence a-d covers 41 frames; b shows the 20th and c the 23rd frame. The eyebrows were maximally raised from frame 19 to 26.

Fig. 2: Samoan girl (Papa, Sawaii). The sequence covers 124 frames. She smiles at frame 41 (b). c shows frame 107. The eyebrows remained maximally raised for 6 frames.

KEY:

Figures 1-5 are greetings with eyebrow flash; Figure 6 shows different facial expressions of a girl born deaf and blind. The photographs are copies from 16 mm. motion pictures taken at 48 frames
per second. Figures 1 and 2 are by H. Hass; Figures 3-6 are by
I. Eibl-Eibesfeldt.

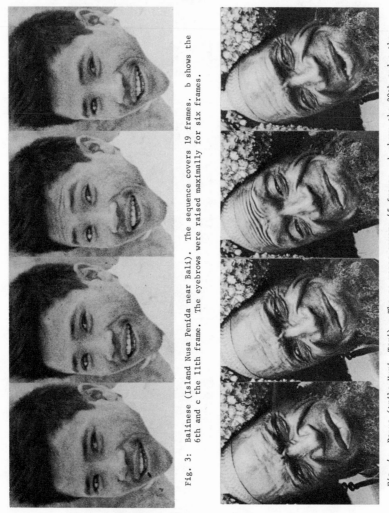

Fig. 3: Balinese (Island Nusa Penida near Bali). The sequence covers 19 frames. b shows the 6th and c the 11th frame. The eyebrows were raised maximally for six frames.

Fig. 4: Papua (tribe Huri, Tari). The sequence covers 45 frames. b shows the 30th and c the 36th frame. The eyebrows were raised maximally for 7 frames.

Fig. 5: Waika Indian. Eyebrow-flash

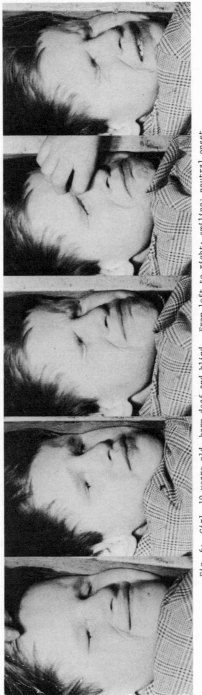

Fig. 6: Girl, 10 years old, born deaf and blind. From left to right: smiling; neutral onset of crying; crying; crying with eyerubbing; full crying (Schreiweinen).

in human greeting and expression behavior. Greeting, as is well known, has an appeasing function. It serves to overcome the aggressive barriers between individuals and helps to form a bond by buffering aggression within social groups. Many culture-dependent rites are involved, most of which, in principle, also show analogies to other cultures and to the greeting rituals in animals [9]. Besides these functional analogies, the examination of the greeting patterns in men of different cultures also reveals a number of homologous patterns. This is true, specifically, in distance greeting. Unless there is hostility, a greeting will take place when two people have approached each other closely enough to recognize each other's facial expressions, or, being already close, establish visual contact for the first time. The greeting pattern consists of a smile, followed by a rapid raising of the eyebrows, which stay raised for approximately one sixth of a second. Finally, there is a nodding of the head, with the smile continuing (Figures 1-5). We have filmed this complete pattern in Europe, Bali, Samoa, New Guinea and Brazil, and we have observed it, without the chance to film it, in Africa, Japan, Hongkong and Peru [9]. We were often able to release this pattern while filming by accidentally looking at the person we filmed and smiling faintly at him.

The smiling response is certainly innate [1,2,11,12,16]. The origin of this pattern is unknown. Some authors connect the smile with a behavior which originally represented threat because the teeth are shown. This is, however, not a convincing argument. The way teeth are exposed in a smile differs from the way teeth are exposed in fury. In the latter case, the corners of the mouth are drawn open. Furthermore, a number of primates expose their teeth with a friendly gesture, derived from grooming (e.g., macaques and some lemurs expose the teeth with a gesture that is reminiscent of grinning, when performing grooming movements in the air). The possibility of our smiling response having a similar origin must be considered. An aggressive component is certainly present in laughing. The sound utterances remind one of the mobbing reactions of a number of primates.

The eyebrow-flash is a very fast, but nonetheless conspicuous, greeting signal. It follows the smiling and is always a signal of the most friendly intentions. In our culture we greet our close friends this way, and we observe it in flirting girls and men. Interestingly enough, we are neither aware that we signal this way nor that we quite regularly respond to it by eyeflashing; the exchange follows as a reflex, and this may be the case why this signal has, so far, escaped the attention of the scientist. Once we became aware of it, we saw it again and again in our culture, also as a gesture of friendly approval. In Samoa it is equivalent to a "yes", whereas in Japan it is considered as indecent and therefore suppressed. Nothing is known about the origin of this pattern. We often raise the eyebrows as a gesture of surprise, be it positive or negative. In the latter case, the eyebrows remain raised for a longer period and a threat stare is added, constituting the expression of indignation.

A similar movement can be observed in some macaques. A friendly
surprise is expressed by the combination of eyebrow raising and smile,
and the eyebrow-flash as a friendly signal ("happy to see you") may
well have derived from this.

The nodding which follows the smiling or the eyebrow-flash, and
which sometimes occurs by itself, is a widespread gesture of approval.
One can consider it as a ritualized gesture of submission [15].

As part of my presentation I will show you a film demonstrating
distance-greeting of people of different cultures. The conformity
of the patterns is evident. We discovered similar cross-cultural
agreements in flirting behavior, gestures of approval and refusal as
well as in the maternal behavior. These, together with the studies
of the deaf and blind, make it evident that phylogenetic adaptation
controls our social behavior in definable ways. Of course, we need
more information about human behavior, and we continue our research
along these lines. We are specially interested in the documentation
of the behavior of the so-called primitives. Cultures, which are
still so remote as to be untouched by the influence of the civilization, are most important for our studies; they are, alas, disappearing at a shocking rate. Although this is well known, concentrated
efforts to documents their natural behavior are so far lacking. We
hope to stimulate an interest in this endeavor in our colleagues in
the different disciplines. We intend, specifically, to build up an
ethological Film Encyclopedia of Man, where films on human behavior
can be archived and published.

REFERENCES

1. Ambrose, J.A.: The Smiling and Related Responses in Early Human
                Infancy. An Experimental and Theoretical Study of their
                Course and Significance. University of London, Ph.D.
                Dissertation, 1960.
2. _____: The development of the smiling response in early
                infancy. In Foss, B.M., ed., Determinants of Infant
                Behavior. Methuen, London, 1961.
3. Asch, S.: Social Psychology. Prentice-Hall, New York, 1952.
4. Birdwhistell, R.L.: The kinesic level in the investigation of
                emotions. In Knapp, P.H., ed., Expression of the Emotions
                in Man. International University Press, New York, 1963.
5. _____: Communication without words. In Alexandre,
                P., ed., L'Aventure Humaine. Paris, 1966.
6. Darwin, C.: The Expression of Emotions in Man and Animals.
                J. Murray, London, 1872.
7. Eibl-Eibesfeldt, I.: Angeborenes und Erworbenes im Verhalten
                einiger Sauger. Z. Tierpsychol., 20:705-754, 1963.
8. _____: Grundriss: der vergleichenden Verhaltens-
                forschung. Piper, Munchen, 1967.

9. _____: Zur Ethologie menschlichen Grussverhaltens.
1. Beobachtungen an Balinesen, Papuas und Samoanern
nebst vergleichenden Bemerkungen. Z. Tierpsychol.,
25:727–744, 1968.

10. _____ and Hass, H.: Neue Wege der Humanethologie.
Homo, 18:13–23, 1967.

11. Freedman, D.G.: Smiling in blind infants and the issue of innate
vs. acquired. J. Child. Psychol. Psychiat., 5:171–184,
1964.

12. _____: Heredity control of early social behavior. In
Foss, B.M., ed., Determinants of Infant Behavior, III.
Methuen, London, 1965.

13. Frijda, N.H.: Mimik und Pantomimik. In Kirchoff, R., ed., Handbuch der Psychologie, Vol. 5. 1964.

14. Gehlen, A.: Urmensch und Spatkultur. Bonn, 1956.

15. Hass, H.: Wir Menschen. Molken, Wien, 1968.

16. Koehler, O.: Das Lacheln als angeborene Ausdrucksbewegung.
Z. Menschl. Vererb., 32:390–398, 1954.

17. Konishi, M.: The role of auditory feedback in the vocal behavior
in the domestic fowl. Z. Tierpsychol., 20:349–367, 1963.

18. _____: Effects of deafening on song development in two
species of juncos. Condor, 66:85–102, 1964.

19. _____: Effects of deafening on the song development of
American robins and black-headed grosbeaks. Z. Tierpsychol., 22:584–599, 1965.

20. Lorenz, K.: Evolution and Modification of Behavior. University
of Chicago Press, Chicago, 1965.

21. Montagu, M.F.A.: Introduction to M.F. Ashley Montagu. Culture
and the Evolution of Man. Oxford University Press,
New York, 1962.

Environmental Communication

Edward T. Hall

ABSTRACT. *During a study of inter-ethnic encounters it was discovered that behavior of blacks and whites varied in the way in which space was handled. Territoriality was much more evident in the black neighborhoods, and territorial boundaries were closely related to group boundaries. Within the black territory there was apparently much more visiting back and forth and much less concept of what the whites call "trespassing". Indeed, the term trespass was virtually meaningless to our black subjects, whose territory is a group concern rather than a private or personal matter. Within black communities block clubs are apparently an urban adaptation of rural social organization with a well defined territorial context, patterns for raising the young and social controls that are shared by the mature adults. In the black community we found viable social groups that were extraordinarily effective and cohesive. However, these groups could not withstand the assaults of dislocation and relocation that accompany urban renewal. To our knowledge they have not reconstituted in the high rise public housing projects where architecture, paternalism and bureaucracy combine to destroy initiative as well as to foster dependence.*

If housing projects are to be designed in terms of black culture, they should be congruent with the informal, social, and territorial realities of that culture. Public housing for blacks should be planned to organize and not disrupt or separate functions. Overall distances should be held to a minimum and massive scale should be avoided, for there is something about the intimacy of black culture that is anti-

---

* This project was made possible by a grant from the National Institutes of Mental Health and has since been supported by the Council for Intersocietal Studies at Northwestern University.

thetical to large anonymous masses. In addition, there should be functions for the group to perform, alleys to be paved, yards to be kept up, lots to be cleaned up, houses to decorate, children to correct and be involved with. Otherwise group cohesiveness does not emerge. In the absence of group support and involvement of the type indicated, marginal individuals seem to lead extraordinarily fragmented, precarious lives in which the territorial alternatives may not include even venturing across the street. In their present form, high rise apartments enhance fragmentation of social relationships and, therefore, they can be said to be dysfunctional for many blacks. An added complication is the aftermath of the experience of being uprooted and displaced by urban renewal plus the fact that the housing is almost without exception designed, built, and administered by a white establishment including unions that are, for the most part, anti-Negro.

The following is a brief report on the relationship of informal culture patterns to architectural spaces in the context of the contrasting cultures of the blacks and whites in the United States.

The black population referred to in this presentation does not include upper middle class professionals. Also, just as for any generalization one might make about any group, it is not expected that the generalizations developed from the data will be universally applicable for the groups in question. Nor is it the intention or purpose of this paper to discuss or examine the etiology of the behavior that was observed or to suggest that one pattern is, in itself, more or less evolved or advanced or functional than another.

There is a point to emphasize however, namely, that there does exist in the world of men a kind of persistent, unconscious cultural imperialism whereby the members of any given group will in one way or another tend to try to get others to not only live their way, but to judge them accordingly. Man can no longer afford the luxury of valuing cultures on a hierarchical scale; instead he must begin the more difficult task of regarding them as simply quite different. Because not until then and only then can he get on with discovering what the differences really mean so that the appropriate adjustments can be made.

In the past, whites in the United States have designed the urban spaces in which blacks live and, with few exceptions, they continue to do so. The high rise apartment appears to reflect white family structure, and when it needs to be built for other groups it should be adapted to indigenous cultural needs. Space or distance can inherently be treated in terms of sensory inputs on the one hand, and position in a social system, activity and affect on the other [8]. Because space represents a kind of common currency and is often readily perceived, there is a tendency on the part of the layman and specialists alike to oversimplify. For example, a lot has been said and written on both sides concerning high rise public housing in Chicago. There are those who argue for the high rise and an equal number who condemn it just as strongly. Unfortunately, the question is usually seen almost solely in terms of density, and yet density turns into a chimera as soon as it is examined closely [8]. The fact is that density cannot be taken out of its context or even adequately considered apart from such things as social organization, child raising techniques, the enculturation devices used by a group, discipline (internal and external), informal organization, sensitivity to materials, need for screening of the various senses and the significance of the buildings themselves as a communication to the people who live in them.

Blacks living in public housing, such as the high rise apartments in Taylor Homes in Chicago, refer to these as the "Congo Hilton" and accuse whites of filing blacks away behind cement walls and stacking them up as though they were some sort of commodity. Negative feelings toward the apartments are expressed in many ways, most of them damaging to the buildings. The emotions generated would seem, at first, to be out of proportion to the actual faults in design. However, as is often the case when one group imposes environmental design decisions on another, behavior patterns are disrupted with apparently disastrous consequences.*

Defects in high rise apartments at first appear to be either mechanical or due to lack of what might be called common sense. Abrams, one of the leaders in the field of urban affairs, frequently cautions his readers and audiences that the application of "common sense" would have prevented many of the mistakes that people complain about in urban design [1]. But it is, apparently, not that simple. For example, common sense dictates that if one were to construct a building sixteen stories high and house people with children near the top, toilet facilities should then be placed near the playground so that children need not return to their own apartment. However, when we checked with high rise occupants, our subjects informed us that they did not want public toilets at ground level because this would provide a hiding place for muggers and perverts.

Why the vociferous rejection of the high rise? Untangling the skeins of this particular fabric involves attention to unstated assumptions (a sort of contextual analysis) on both sides. The whites see surface order in the buildings paid for by taxpayer's dollars. The blacks see edifices designed and built by a white power structure in which they do not participate and they sense that something is basically wrong: the edifices are affecting them in ways that they are not sure of. If one can forget for a moment the scars and sores of

---

* Only one low cost high rise apartment building has been erected in Chicago in the last few years. These comments are directed more to future planners, lest they forget the Chicago lesson.

past injustices and look at black social organization in contrast to
white social organization and, in particular, how social controls are
maintained and how children are raised and disciplined, some of the
pieces of this particular jigsaw puzzle begin to fall into place.
To comprehend what follows necessitates abandoning the notion that
blacks have no culture of their own but a stripped down sub-standard
version of the dominant white group. The culture of ethnicity is
complicated because there are numerous regional, ethnic, and class
differences, the details of which have been poorly documented even
for the dominant group.

As a rule, when people think of culture they think of technical
culture (the part that people can talk about and describe), and while
it is true that much of the more obvious features of black culture
have either been imposed on them or borrowed by them, sometimes self-
consciously, there is a deep, rich, highly regular informal substrate,
the structure of which lies below the general level of awareness.
What is most interesting about informal culture is that not only many
social scientists but the people themselves fail to see the regulari-
ties and rules governing informal behavior.*

The relation of informal culture to technical culture is similar
to that of the spoken language to written language, or more appropriately, any spoken language before it is reduced to writing. For example, native speakers of Arabic popularly believe that colloquial
Arabic, which is used for everyday business, has no structure and is
not properly a language! Similarly, many people, including some anthropologists, do not think that the vast category of behavior cate-
gorized as informal can be properly designated as culture [6,8]. For
this reason it is widely believed that black culture in the United
States is virtually nonexistent. Yet, investigation of informal behavior on practically any level has consistently revealed orderliness,
patterns, and regularity. There is also a logical inconsistency here
in the attitude of the dominant group, because it is known that se-
paratism in time and space sets in motion a series of subtle changes
in individuals as well as in groups analogous to genetic drift. No
one can deny that the blacks have been kept apart. One would expect
to find, and in fact does find, informal differences in social organization, language (on the syntactic as well as the phonological level
[12]) and in the way in which the division of the sexes functions--
how masculinity and femininity are expressed--in the handling of time,
space, materials, and music.** One of these differences will be
briefly described for its relevance both to urban renewal as well as
to black-white relations.

----

* The terms "informal culture" and "technical culture" are technically defined in The Silent Language and The Hidden Dimension [6,8].

** A more detailed report is in preparation; also see [3].

A basic social institution peculiarly adapted to black culture
is the block club as we found it in Chicago on the South and West
Sides. Block clubs, as first described by our subject (one of my
assistants), normally included an area two blocks long on a single
side of the street.* Block clubs constitute an important and vital
part of black community life. When they are functioning properly,
the community can be organized to clean up a vacant lot, give parties,
take up a collection to buy a jeep with a snow plow, pave alleys,
bring pressure to bear to get lighting in alleys, plant grass, prevent a landlord from overcrowding tenants, keep delivery trucks off
the street, cut down on noise, sponsor Christmas lighting programs,
and even run ads in the press inviting the public to pay $1.00 ad-
mission to "see a real slum" as a means of pressuring a landlord into
improving the lot of his tenants.** If a particular family on the
block does not conform to the standards of the block (after being
warned), pressure will be exerted on them to move. However, one of
the most important functions of block clubs may be to keep the young
from getting out of hand. In this particular respect, black culture
and white culture differ radically. White suburban culture, depending as it does on internalized controls for those controls that are
present, only permits the immediate family, usually the parents, to
correct a child. Like the Arabs, black adults, when they are in their
own neighborhood, are involved and are apparently expected to play an
active role in encouraging good behavior as well as disciplining children who do wrong. In discussing this with a black colleague, Professor Donald Henderson, I learned that the pattern of group responsibility can extend to an entire rural community. It appears, for instance,
that negative reactions by blacks to the Moynihan report*** were trace-
able, at least in part, to his use of a North European type model for
the family which he projected onto black society. Given the folk institution just described, where affection, responsibility, and control
over the young is shared by a large group of adults, the presence or
absence of a single male in the household is not nearly so crucial as
when all of the above is concentrated in the hands of one or two parents, as with whites. It is suggested that the informal communal en-
clave with a patriarch first developed in rural communities. This
same organization was later transferred to the city where it managed
to remain viable on blocks with separate houses and was even able to

---

*   Since our initial interviews, other patterns have emerged. In
one instance, an integrated blue collar mews on the North Side of
Chicago was organized into a block club by a young black male.

**   Ruth Moore, Chicago's urban affairs reporter, describes a block
club on the South Side of Chicago which forced a landlord to spend
$7000 to restore an apartment to its former condition after he had
begun to cut it up into smaller units [Chicago Sun-Times, July 13,
1966].

*** Moynihan, D.P.: The Negro Family: The Case for National Action.
Office of Policy Planning & Research, Dept. of Labor. Washington, D.C.,
U.S. Government Printing Office, 1965.

adapt to the row-houses and low rise apartments centered on a court
or mews. But the high rise apartment, plus over-management, has so
far proved to be too much for this institution of group responsibility to cope with. The effect has been to engender feelings of dif-
fused frustration and hopelessness--diffused because the people are
not generally aware of the specifics of their difficulty and are unable to formulate the real source of their trouble. In any case, if
there is little or no group support or if the fabric of a community
has been rent apart and destroyed by dislocation, social controls
no longer function.

There are those who will argue that white landlords would wel-
come the block clubs because they upgrade the neighborhood. This
is only partially true, for, as cited earlier, the block club works
as hard to keep landlords in line as it does tenants. The club or-
ganizer--assuming the country patriarch's role--is much more apt to
become the target of the landlord's wrath and is quite likely to find
himself out on the street branded as a troublemaker. Given the highly
vulnerable position of the block club organizer, those that have not
had to cope with attacks from white landlords seem to have greater
chances of survival. The white community is generally naive concerning the nature and extent of black social organization and leadership
on the grass roots level. In general, considering how little is known
about block club organizers, it seems fair to assume that, instead of
having been considered sources of stability and resourcefulness in
the black community, they have been viewed and treated as threats to
landlords who ran afoul of block club efforts to upgrade the community. There is no comparable role in white culture.

Time as well as space is featured in social control. The current study suggests three areas of geographic control in which behavior is likely to change as one moves from zone to zone: 1) within
the house where, under ideal circumstances, parents continue to maintain control over even young adults; 2) outside the house but within
the block which permits more leeway for young adults but maintains responsibility for children; 3) off the block or away from the block
but within the area where one can, if one is so inclined, be much more
free. A crucial point is that territories are circumscribed and
clearly demarked, and that control over the individual's behavior,
if it exists, passes from family and local groups to territorial gangs.*
Given this orderly progression, imagine what occurs when strangers
from entirely different parts of the city, some of them manifestly
anti-social, are jumbled together in a high rise apartment by a paternalistic bureaucracy which provides no responsibility or opportunity
for the exercise of initiative over the care and maintenance of either
grounds or property and where space (distance from the ground) is so
designed as to discourage, if not actually prevent, group supervision

---

* There has been independent corroboration of territorial contrast
between blacks and whites by Erickson [3] and Suttles [13].

of children. Apparently the loss of block club organization is one
of a number of factors contributing to the unbridled growth of youthful gangs, which are also territorial in character.*

Whether the high rise apartment would function any differently
if the people who occupied them were moved in, block by block, as
complete units is impossible to tell. Group occupation has occurred
spontaneously in other countries, in Brazil for example, where several
floors of apartments have been taken by large families of several
households.

It should be stressed that there is nothing inherently good or
bad about high rise apartments nor is there any universal index of
crowding or density [7,8]. For example in Hong Kong public housing
densities run several times that in the United States with apparently
little or no deleterious effect on the inhabitants. The explanation
lies in the fact that not only are the Chinese conditioned to high
density, but they are also highly disciplined in the family context
and have a remarkably strong and stable family. As a consequence they
do not have the same kinds of problems with their children which we
find even in our suburbs.** A most important point is that there does
seem to be a correlation between either discipline or homogeneity and
successful adaptation to crowded living. If a society is to survive
crowding beyond a certain point, it must develop effective social controls. The Northern European pattern has been one of internalization
of controls. Black institutions seem to emphasize group pressure,
centering around a single strong male, but he must have a turf in
which he can function.

The renovation and renewal of separate dwelling units in apartments in New York City has provided us with additional insights into

---

* Some of our subjects mentioned that even though they were black,
they would not go into certain other black territories simply because
they did not belong and if found there, they were likely to be robbed
and beaten.

** By European standards, Hong Kong densities are high. (Ten times
the maximum density permitted by the London County Council for Greater
London). The Hong Kong Housing Authority thinks nothing of densities
as high as 2,000 persons per acre in public housing projects running
up to sixteen stories. Apartments for six persons have 210 sq. feet.
They have a combination living room-bedroom, with a small kitchen and
a balcony. An important feature of these housing projects not found
in our own public housing is a nursery on each floor with school and
recreation rooms built into the middle of the apartment complex. The
authors of the Council of London Plan advocated three zones: 200 per
acre in the center, 136 in the middle, and 100 or less in the outer
ring. The 200 persons per acre was the maximum for the city of London
[10, p.30].

man's use of space. Position in the overall social hierarchy is an
important factor in patterns about to be described. The evidence so
far indicates that individuals occupying positions at or near the
bottom of the social scale live, function and move in extremely limited
areas. One black family, picked at random in a New York renewal project, was disoriented by a move across the street. It should be noted
that the center of the street itself is likely to be a boundary in
black urban culture. One of the women who was relocated with her family had known only her immediate neighbors on either side and some
storekeepers at the end of the block. For her, the move across the
street to a refurbished apartment was almost as extreme as if she had
been moved from one side of the city to the other. Her low status in
the overall system made her doubly vulnerable.*

    The refurbishing of older buildings provides confirmation of
Aries' hypothesis of the relationship between what I have termed
fixed-feature space and organization of the family. According to
Aries, rooms had no specialized function in European houses until the
18th century [2]. There was little privacy for families as we know
it today, no specialized spaces for different activities; no dining
room, living room, or bedroom. Rooms opened into each other without
hallways. With the introduction of corridors and hallways and the
separation of rooms, it then became possible to define functions in
spatial terms so that one had a bedroom, dining room, living room,
etc. The early railroad flat which we still find in many slum areas
was built on a pre-18th century European plan. Remodeled apartments,
however, either by accident or because they reflect mid-20th century
design, are equipped with hallways. This apparently insignificant
difference is, is some instances at least, a crucial element in the
success of the inhabitants' coping with an extraordinarily complex
world. Occupants who were moved from the railroad type apartment to
a remodeled version with a center hall noted improvements in study
habits, discipline and, in one instance, the beginning of a remission
of a serious speech disorder. The crucial difference was the screening provided by individual rooms opening onto a hall which allowed
privacy. Our evidence at this point is tentative, but it is consistent with what is known of the influence of architecture on the entire
process by which human beings alternately interact with each other
and require screening or separateness at other times. Stated differently, man seems to require both kinds of spaces--those for interaction and those for privacy--at different times of the daily and weekly
cycle [8].

---

* A check on the situational dialects at her command indicated that
her inventory was extremely limited. Situational dialects vary in
complexity and richness ranging from the language used when you take
a bus or buy a railroad ticket to the vernacular of physicians, law-
yers and college professors--they provide an index not only of one's
position in a given social system but where one can go. Failure to
master any given situational dialect immediately marks one as an outsider.

To continue, however, with the notion that individuals who occupy positions that are extremely marginal in the society have a rather limited area in which they feel comfortable: We noted that, in the public housing projects in Chicago, there was a great deal of hesitancy on the part of women from one building to visit a community center, or become involved in community centers in nearby buildings. Like the woman who seldom, if ever, crossed the street and knew only the neighbors on either side, these women were not venturesome and hesitated to enter what was to them another group's territory. In terms of planning this means that the more marginal the group and the lower its position on the social scale is, the more vulnerable it becomes, with concomitant dependence on administrative decisions expressed in architectural form.*

The experience of the Minneapolis Rehabilitation Center also supports our view that marginal people are more at the mercy of structural space than those who rank higher, for they discovered at the Center that one of the most basic and important skills to be learned by inner city blacks was how to master the public transportation system. Mastery of bus and subway systems is seldom easy; and if it proves difficult for old time residents with college degrees, ponder for a moment the forbidding and mystifying nature of the city to those who are deeply territorial as well as inexperienced in city ways.

This report has focused on the micro-structures of social events and their relationship to the man-made spaces in which these events are to take place. It is not presented as definitive in any way, but indicative of patterns as they were observed in context over the past five years in the course of research on inter-ethnic encounters. On higher organizational levels, Fried et al. have provided us with excellent examples of how it is possible for city planners and the bureaucracies of urban renewal inadvertently to destroy the very fabric of life [4,5]. Moynihan and Glazer, in a different context, have also described the ways in which the major ethnic groups in New York respond to space by either moving or resistantly staying put in the neighborhoods of their childhoods [11].

REFERENCES

1. Abrams, C.: The City is the Frontier. Harper and Row, New York, 1965.
2. Aries, P.: Centuries of Childhood. Alfred A. Knopf, New York, 1962.

---

* This has also been suggested by Lawton [9]. There is an exacerbating circumstance that tends to maintain or, rather, support the patterns of limited movement of poor people--the marked territoriality of the inner city which is dominated, in Chicago at least, by youthful "gangs" [13]. It is simply not safe to venture outside the "area".

3. Erickson, F.D.: Discussion Behavior in the Black Ghetto and in
        White Suburbia: A Comparison of Language Style and In-
        quiry Style. Northwestern University, Evanston, Ph.D.
        Thesis. Unpublished.
4. Fried, M.: Grieving for a lost home. In Duhl, L.J., ed., The
        Urban Condition. Basic Books, New York, 1963.
5. _____ and Gleicher, P.: Some sources of residential satis-
        faction in an urban slum. J. Amer. Inst. Planners,
        27, 1961.
6. Hall, E.T.: The Silent Language. Doubleday and Company, Inc.,
        New York, 1959.
7. _____: Human adaptability to high density. Ekistics,
        20:119, 1965.
8. _____: The Hidden Dimension. Doubleday and Company, Inc.,
        New York, 1966.
9. Lawton, M.P.: Ecology and aging. In Pastalan, L.A. and Carson,
        D.H., eds., Spatial Behavior of Older People. The
        University of Michigan - Wayne State University Press,
        Ann Arbor, 1970.
10. London County Council: London plan, first review. Administra-
        tive County of London Development Plan, County Planning
        Report, County Council Publication No. 4065, London,
        England, 1960.
11. Moynihan, D.P. and Glazer, N.: Beyond the Melting Pot. The MIT
        Press and the Harvard University Press, Cambridge, 1963.
12. Stewart, W.: Non-Standard Speech and the Teaching of English.
        Center for Applied Linguistics, Washington, D.C., 1965.
13. Suttles, G.: The Social Order of the Slum. University of Chi-
        cago Press, Chicago, 1968.

Discussion of Session IV:
Orientation and Communication

PANEL: W. A. Mason (Chairman), I. Eibl·Eibesfeldt,
J. M. Fitch, E. T. Hall, P. Leyhausen,
D. Lowenthal

Mason (Chairman):

I would like to open the session with Fitch's comments.

Fitch:

I regret that there are so few architects or urban designers in
the audience here today for, after all, we are the specialists to
whom the organization of space in the modern world is entrusted. I
have to confess that our intervention in these matters is, all too
often, every bit as disastrous as Hall has this morning indicated.
We tend to intervene fearlessly in all sorts of complicated situations.
And it becomes increasingly clear that, ironically, the greater our
expertise and the larger the scale of our operations, the more hazardous our interventions seem to become. We have very simplistic ideas
of how people behave in space: the consequences of this ignorance
are all too evident. In this sense, all the papers we have heard have
relevance for architects and urbanists. Today's papers have had a
more direct bearing on the subject - Hall's being one of the most suggestive.

I have been interested to note that two of our colleagues who
spoke at some length about the social consequences of certain types
of spatial organizations neglected to tell us much about the environmental conditions which obtained in those spaces during their observations. This tendency to handle space in abstract terms seems to
me to be a characteristic failing on the part of all of us. Yesterday
morning, Esser observed that scientists too often tended to regard
space as a kind of vacuum in which nothing happened. I share his mis-
givings.

257

But architects and planners have another kind of almost endemic conceptual weakness – that is, they tend to regard space as a purely visual construct. Intellectually, of course, they may know better; but the consequence of this basic attitude is that the environment is largely thought of from a visual point of view and its organization, therefore, is regarded as being largely a problem in visual aesthetics. All the other environmental attributes of architectural space – thermal, sonic, olfactory, tactile, etc. – are insufficiently understood or attended to. The result is a high degree of environmental malfunction in even some of our most prestigious new buildings.

Thus the appearance of men from the life sciences in our field is a very encouraging development. The psychologists, for example, are giving us a new understanding of the behavior of people in our buildings and cities. Their emphasis on the role of perception, sensory deprivation and stimulation in human experience and development has obvious significance for environmental designers. Yet even among psychologists, I find a tendency to divorce such phenomena from the environmental matrix in which they necessarily occur. Thus we hear a lot of talk about perception – and hardly any mention of the metabolic base on which all perception obviously rests. Clearly any environment has to satisfy the metabolic requirements of the animal before there can be any perception at all. Thus we will hear a fascinating paper on the behavior of young men in enclosed spaces – presumably in submarines – over long periods of time. But the text contains little or nothing about the environmental conditions under which the tests were run – temperature, air movement, odors, noise and illumination levels, etc. – let alone how behavior might have been modified by the manipulation of such environmental components. This last is the area of primary concern to architects.

As architects, we have already developed certain contacts with physiologists – at least with those specialists who deal with thermal stress, psycho-optics, acoustics and other areas which must furnish the norms for architectural technology. But here we meet another set of obstacles: many of these specialists know little about related fields, even those immediately adjacent to their own, and display little interest in any effort to integrate their data into one experiential whole. This tendency reaches its most acute form with the engineers who operate on the narrowest criteria of economy and efficiency. Though heating and ventilating engineers pay lip service to concepts of comfort and wellbeing, they usually think in terms of b.t.u.'s and cu. ft. per min. Similar blind spots occur in the vision of illuminating and acoustical engineers. Confronted with this kind of disparate and recondite assistance, it is small wonder that the architect often falls between the stools even when he tries to broaden his understanding of experiential reality.

From this point of view a Symposium like this is very stimulating, for it suggests the possibility of extrapolating from such fields as

ethology, ecology and animal behavior certain guiding principles for
the design of all animal environments including the human. What we
require in architecture and urbanism - if we are not endlessly to re-
peat the kind of errors of which Hall has accused us - is some kind
of synoptic model which will encompass and integrate all these kinds
of knowledge. Thus we could come to learn that when we raise a roof
or pave a block or furnish a room we must think not only in terms of
structural stability or heat gain or visual effect but in terms of the
total experiential consequences of our acts for the people who must inhabit our buildings. Any honest assessment of the profession would
have to recognize that we have scarcely scratched the surface of this
problem. We have a great deal to learn from meetings such as this.

Lowenthal:

There are so many delectable items to discuss, one hardly knows
where to begin. One kind of presentation in this session has emphasized interspecific similarities in which biological inheritance is
dominant. The other kind, of which Hall's paper is the best example,
emphasizes social and other differences among human beings and suggests
that cultural inheritance has played a principal role in these differences.

Thus a demonstration of homogeneity among human beings implies
or suggests one kind of inheritance, while a demonstration of difference seems to suggest another kind. Do these distinctions stand up
to analysis in depth? For example, with specific reference to reactions to high-rise buildings mentioned by Hall, I kept thinking: Of
course, he is quite right, high-risers are terrible for everyone, and
in England and in other countries this is generally recognized. But
is this a common characteristic affecting the whole human race? Or
ought it to be one which, when given the proper recognition as with
Hall, would affect the whole human race? At a lower level of generalization, are high-risers poor for living because they involve dislocation of existing populations in the community, or because "urban renewal means urban removal?"

At a level of still greater particularity, are high-risers worse
for black people than for others? If so, is this because of the ghetto
circumstances with which they have been afflicted, or because of antecedent cultural characteristics, or, finally, because of inherited
traits? And if culture can be demonstrated to be culturally inherited,
how does one explain cultural resemblances with black communities elsewhere in the world? And finally, how far can we be sure that responses, such as those elicited by Hall, reflect reality apart from
confrontation politics?

We ought constantly to remind ourselves, in assessing reactions
to spatial arrangements, that these reactions are never simple, can
never be perceived merely at face value; we need to take into account

the nature of the group, its special historical circumstances, the context of the interviews or assessments themselves, the context of the day-to-day situations in which people face themselves.

Mason:

I would like to ask Hall a question: I know that in your books you have drawn rather heavily on animal research on territorial behavior and on the findings of the ethologists. I wonder if you would care to comment on the general question of the relevance of animal research to some of the more complex aspects of human behavior. Do you feel that it could or should be increased, or do you have any other comments to address to us on this question?

Hall:

The reason I am here is that I believe that the more we learn about animals the more we will know about man. If there was ever a forgotten basic fact, it is that man is first, last, and always an animal, a biological organism. His cultural phase is extraordinarily recent, given the total past of all living things. It is about the thickness of a postage stamp sitting on top of Mt. Fujiyama. Just because we talk and write about that part of man's past commonly included in history does not mean that this is the whole picture; yet we tend to treat it as the whole picture.

In addition, we in the United States have a feeling that technology solves everything. We look to technology when we should be studying nature. The study of animals provides us with obvious shortcuts to studying man; the generations are shorter, the situations are simpler. Animals simply do not confound you so much; men are much more complicated to study. I learn more about <u>man</u> here, than by going to most anthropological meetings. My message to this audience is: Please keep the data coming.

Question from floor:

I want to question Dr. Hall as to whether or not there is any evidence to indicate if in the long run, political or social organizations might be superseding the block-club functional organization in terms of doing things together.

Hall:

They may be. But politics, as I see it, works on much higher organizational levels. At the present time it does not appear to be organized primarily as a territorial type thing. If politics were purely territorial it would work in a very different way than it does now when ideological, economic, historical, and power considerations are paramount.

Leyhausen (from the floor):

If I understood correctly, you said that, seemingly, there is
no so-to-speak biological limit to density as such; once the individuals are adjusted to high densities, they get along fine. Now, I
should like to ask you whether you think this <u>really</u> follows from
your observations, because I could well imagine that other factors,
such as economic ones, are so conducive to bringing people together
in high density, that these factors override the biological limit
which may be there all the same. It does not follow that these people
do not, in some way or other, suffer from this density, although they
are <u>seemingly</u> happy there. It may even happen that <u>the individual</u> becomes addicted to living in crowds, and, again, it could perhaps be
very difficult to judge the effect this has on the individual; and
the effect it has on the species in the long run. And this may be an
entirely different question with an entirely different answer.

Hall:

I agree heartily with this statement, I did not want to give the
impression that there is no biological limit. There is need for solid
studies of the adrenal cortex in human beings subjected to a variety
of conditions. Data for these studies should not be difficult to obtain from autopsies. Man is in danger not only because he is an extraordinarily tough organism, but also because culture does addict people.
Man will subject himself to all sorts of pressures, which is one of
the pitfalls of taking a strictly cultural view of things, and is another reason why animal studies are so important to man.

Question from floor:

I would like to ask Eibesfeldt whether there is any significance
to the human hand covering the yawn. I have had the experience of
seeing the yawn as a primate threat. Does the hand cover the yawn in
any culture other than our own? Is it something more than politeness?
Is it an attempt to disguise what might be interpreted as a threat?
What happens in primate situations?

Eibl-Eibesfeldt:

As far as ethnologists report, the hiding of the yawn is not
found in all cultures. Karl von Steiner mentions that Brazilian Indians yawned uninhibitedly in the evenings, and, once one started,
the others followed suit, and soon all went to sleep. Therefore, one
must not be so quick to consider it a threat. It is *ansteckend*, i.e.,
infectious. It may be that we hide a yawn for these reasons: either
in order not to show that we are tired, or not to show that someone
else tires us. But, yawning may also have a function of making people
become sleepy together. It may well be that when you are in a small
society, it is good to go to sleep at the same time.

McBride:

I find the papers extremely interesting and informative. There
is one point I would like to make, and I keep repeating: Behavior
is <u>organized</u> in certain ways. I do not see it organized into units
called genetic and units called non-genetic. Yesterday morning I
described aggressiveness as being in units, behaviorally organized
into interactions and into roles.

I do not think there is any geneticist who doubts that behavior
is organized genetically, that there are some genetic components here.
I have no more doubts about this in man than I have in any other species; no more doubts than I would have about morphology. After all,
morphology is only the behavior of the cells that move, orient, divide, attract, repel, and make different structures morphologically.

But behavior is always expressed in a social context. And perhaps I should state what I mean here. When a sow gives birth to a
litter, one will see the following morning that the sow stands up.
Now she is an enormous monster compared to the piglets, she is a hundred times larger than they are. She gets up by a very complicated
ritual, in which she is giving signals all the time. The effect of
these is to move the piglets to stand at the side and huddle together
about one to one and a half meters away from her. Now, every now and
then a piglet does not have its information properly coded, and moves
towards her. At first she pushes the strayer back, later she grabs
it - one thinks she has swallowed it - she gives it half a dozen violent shakes, and throws it back into its group. So, some behavior
here is first expressed and then supplemented in the appropriate context in which it is expressed. It is then built into this context
into specific patterns.

I think the smile is a very intriguing piece of behavior. We
once did some experimental work on it, where we exposed individuals
to a context where a smile was not asked for and in which they were
smiled at, and 39 out of 40 gave us one back. The one who did not
smile responded just as strongly as the others; we had him connected
to a galvanic stimulus response machine. So there is obviously a
very powerful tendency to respond by smiling.

But, when you put this into a social context, there are control
mechanisms. I lived in Bristol for four months last year, and for a
time tried riding a public transport. I always sat so I faced people,
and I threw smiles at everyone who sat on the seats opposite me. I
was not arrested, but most refused to return this smile. In other
words, the context was not appropriate. I soon learned when it was.
If the bus gave a lurch, then I could get a smile back. If the bus-
conductor, a typical English clippie, with a lot of sense of humor,
was bouncing around in the bus, then, of course, if I threw a smile,
I would always get it back. So this very powerful tendency to respond

to a smile is under a large number of social controls. If you see
a pretty girl walking down a street and you throw a smile at her, you
will find out what I mean.

Mason:

I think the issue is a very difficult one for us. Of course,
it is not the question of innate versus learned behavior, it is a
question of units, and what we are going to measure, and whether
there are such things as natural units of behavior, or whether these
are all human inventions. We know we do invent them all the time,
and sometimes we are mistaken in this and the units turn out to be
very reliable, or very easy to measure, or diagnostic; and sometimes
we are lucky. I suspect that this is an issue that we are going to
be coming back to for a great many years in the future.

Carson:

First, I have something to say concerning the work of Hall. It
reminds me of a line from Edith Sitwell:

> "The hard and braying light
> Zebra'd black and white!"

I will leave you to interpret that your own way.

Second, I find McBride slipping into something that another person can question him slipping on. This "nature-nurture" business has
always impressed me as being a pseudo-argument, because what we have
here is a total system. We have the same problem in basic vs. applied
research. All research is really applied at some level. We get one
person looking at a set, a family of straight lines with certain
slopes, saying: "Look at those slopes!" Another person says: "That
is trivial. Look at the intersects!" This is the way we view our
problems. Perhaps if we stood back a little and looked at the entire
set of graphs, we might begin to make some better sense.

McBride:

I thought that is what I said.

Mason:

Do we have any further comment from the audience?

Question from the floor:

Dr. Eibl-Eibesfeldt, you gave us the smile; what other similar
gestures, either sound or facial, or such as the shoulder-shrug or
handshake have you looked into, and could you mention them?

Eibl-Eibesfeldt:

Yes, for example, flirting, ambivalent behavior of turning toward or turning away occurs cross-culturally. Anger, too, is expressed similarly cross-culturally (stamping feet, frown). Concerning "yes" and "no", there are cultural differences to be found in
Europe. Papuans nod in approval and shake their head when saying
"no". So do many people all over the world. Italians, Greeks, Ru-
manians are said to do it just in reverse. I have film-clips, taken
recently in Greece, which show, however, that these statements are
not quite correct. Greeks nod in approval as we do. For "no" they
use a gesture which we too use for refusal--they throw their heads
back and close their eyes. And if they are very vehement they raise
their hands as we Germans do when we say *"Um Gottes willen!"*, and
toss their heads. Either the shaking movement or the latter gesture,
which is originally one of social refusal, can be used as a gesture
for "no" by cultural agreement. How it comes about that one culture
uses this "no" and another culture that "no", I do not know. There
is a parallel for the "yes". The Samoans, like us, use the eye-flash
in a friendly social context, but in addition as a very friendly "yes".

Question from floor:

How common is the handshake?

Eibl-Eibesfeldt:

The handshake appears in different forms. Papuans, for example,
have a handshake quite similar to ours. The gestures of assurance
in wild-living chimpanzees also consist of stretching out the hand
to let it be touched by the other. The human gesture is a similar
gesture of reassurance, but it also involves a measuring of the opponent and display. As you know, the handshake can be very uncomfortable with some people. In principle, you find contact greeting of
that sort trans-culturally, although with variations in the way people grasp each other.

Question from the floor:

Chimpanzees display a hand to thigh gesture, and that is described
in Genesis.*

Eibl-Eibesfeldt:

Yes, I have not looked for that. People do pat each other. In
Papua, for example, you are greeted with an embrace, patting, and
kissing on the cheek.

---

* This may refer to God's blessing of Jacob, Genesis, 32:25-32 [Editor]

The kiss is quite interesting. Here is an instance which shows how little one can rely on the literature. There you find that the kiss is absent in Polynesians and Papuans, in Indonesians, and in people who are nose-rubbing. I did not visit all of them, but I visited Papuan tribes who still live in the Stone Age, also the Balinese, Samoans, and the Masai, etc., all of whom are nose-rubbing. I did not see kissing in a sexual context. But, if you look at mothers handling their babies and other children, you will find that they will eventually hug and kiss them. And you will find certain greeting rituals involving kissing in Papuans. For instance, a father will greet his son after a long absence with a kiss on the cheek. So, the kiss is certainly present, one cannot say that it is absent. I looked for it, not believing in its absence, because we know that chimpanzees do it, and that it is a ritual derived from mutual feeling.

Leyhausen (from the floor):

I should like to say, in regards to the two gestures of negation and refusal, that those are very old instinctive acts which are present in all mammals. The head-up is originally a reaction to bad smell; the other one, the head-shake, may involve smell, but also involves taste, it reacts to something which is already in the mouth or which has been touched. Since both patterns are presumably present in all mammals, it is, of course, possible for social and other ways of ritualization to select either one or the other, and evolve into a standardized signal. There is nothing really difficult about understanding the fact that different cultures either restrict or further one pattern or the other. Both are available, and if we look at it closely, we find that we also use *ananouein*, as the old Greeks called it, for a certain kind of refusal--for instance, if we refuse to speak to a person whom we do not know. In modern man this gesture is therefore available, only its social ritualization is different from the ordinary negation.

Blaut (from the floor):

I am moved to comment on Fitch's comments, pertaining to the fact that we need some clarification of our concept of space here. In the work that David Stea and I are doing with the spatial concepts of young children, we find that the more we try to segregate the categories of spatial behavior, the less distinct the difference seems to be; there seems to be a continuum.

Ideas in territoriality recently tend to get reified, as though territoriality were a different conceptual category from ideas of property applied to small objects; as though possession of territory is entirely different from possession of resources in general. As a geographer I know that in the past 200 years we have been caught up in a snarl, half of our field being devoted to man in space, and the other half to the study of man and his environment. Recently, the halves have found it very difficult to communicate, although it looks more and more as though they are talking about the same thing. I am just wondering how certain problems might be solved, for example: territorial problems as being possibly a subset of problems involving simple control over units of resources, either well defined as units or simply quantities of resources. As for distance problems, one useful point might be to consider von Cranach's work as establishing a kind of unit; distance between ego and situation. A distance less than this would be kind of non-spatial behavior, or kind of grasping behavior, behavior with small objects. I merely want to reinforce Fitch's point that we have to be very careful that, when we talk of behavior of animals and man in space, we are not imagining that we are dealing with a totally different sphere of activity, which would imply that, at least, we search for new and different laws. Possibly some of the laws are already around us, from observations of other forms of behavior with small and near objects.

Mason:

If there are no further questions or comments I declare this session adjourned. Thank you very much.

Space Use and the Social Community in Animals and Men

Vero C. Wynne-Edwards

Seven years ago I put forward the hypothesis that social behavior plays an essential part in the natural regulation of animal numbers [7]; some of you are I know familiar with the general outline of the hypothesis.

It has two main foundations. The first is the demonstration, over a long period of years, that many of the higher animals, especially in the vertebrates and arthropods, are able to regulate their own numbers. They do this either by controlling the recruitment into the population, which comes from reproduction and immigration, or by controlling the losses, due to mortality and emigration; or, still more often, by combining both these processes. The conclusion reached by Darwin [1], that animals are always striving to increase in numbers, but are held in check by outside forces such as predation, disease, starvation and climatic factors, has turned out not to be the whole story. It is true that, during the history of most animal populations, there come periods when one or another of Darwin's checks takes a heavy toll; but, when that happens, the survivors normally compensate for it, most often by breeding at a higher rate. In that way they can often quickly restore their numbers to the previous level. If we design an experiment to exclude all external sources of mortality – that is to say, all Darwin's checks – we find that a completely isolated laboratory population almost always builds up to a ceiling density, and then stays at that ceiling as long as we keep the environment constant. In wild populations the same can occur, as long as the rate of uncontrollable mortality is not abnormally high.

The second foundation of the hypothesis is that animals dependent on natural food resources, whether these resources are animal or vegetable, can get a bigger yield, a better crop of food, if the resource

267

is efficiently managed. In many situations over-exploitation leads
to a progressive depletion of food resources. If herbivores over-
graze their pastures or predators consume too many of their prey,
the resource may not be able to produce as big a crop the following
year. We have gained insight into the management of recurrent natural resources in the last 30 years, for example with fish and game,
and we know that it is essential to limit the size of the annual crop
if the stock is to survive; we issue licenses and make regulations in
order to prevent over-exploitation.

In nature there are many devices that have evolved for the very
same purpose. The best-known of all, as you are aware, is to parcel
out the ground where the food is found into a mosaic of territories
owned by the consumers. Then, provided the average territory size
is large enough, population density can be held down to a level at
which no harm can possibly be done to the food resources: on the
contrary, a theoretically perfect territorial system shares out the
maximum sustainable yield of food among the largest possible number
of consumers.

I have, for obvious reasons, simplified these two foundation
premises, first the discovery of self-regulation or homeostasis, and
second the need to regulate food-demand; in fact they have been considerably over-simplified, though not to the point of distorting in
any way the essential principles they contain.

The density-limiting devices found in nature fall into two types.
Some of them require the individual to obtain a property qualification, such as a territory or a recognized breeding or resting place,
which serves as his license to use the habitat and enjoy the right
to feed in it. The other devices admit to the establishment only
those individuals that achieve a sufficiently high personal rank among
their fellows and rivals. Both kinds of device can be dove-tailed together, as when personal dominance is essential to the winning of property. Both have the effect of excluding surplus individuals and forcing them to become outcasts or emigrants; Watson has given us an il-
lustration of this in the red grouse [6]. Between them they provide
a safety-valve for relieving pressure on food resources.

Another set of devices, overlapping the ones I have just described, control the reproductive input to the population. They either restrict the opportunity of breeding only to those individuals
that are qualified by rank or property possession, or they bring
density-dependent pressure to bear which reduces individual fertility
and breeding success.

With all these various homeostatic adaptations working in uni-
son, it is not difficult to see that competitive pressures on the
population can influence both its outcome and its losses; given a
little time, the population can adjust its density either upwards

or downwards with equal facility.

The most interesting conclusion from the hypothesis concerns
the role of social behavior in population control; it arises from
the observation that these devices are in their nature artificial.
What is ultimately being held in check is the demand for food, in
order to ensure that the food resources are properly conserved.
The right to feed is the primary object of competition between the
rival members of a population; but in fact the members are side-
tracked into competing only for token substitutes, like territories
and personal status; they do not fight for the food itself. They
contest for conventional rewards, and these, once they have been won,
confer the right to feed on the successful competitors; those that
are unsuccessful forfeit their rights. Sometimes the same competition confers also the right to breed, but in other cases this right
is separately contested.

Because the rewards sought are only conventional tokens, which
confer rights to the things that really matter, namely feeding and
breeding, the competiton itself becomes conventionalized. Stags roar,
antelopes butt and wrestle, skylarks sing and peacocks display their
finery, but little or no blood is shed in the process. The bitter-
ness of the struggle for existence has been sublimated and ritualized;
the outcome is still as vital as ever, rewarding the successful with
the right to a full life, and condemning the losers to barrenness and
often to premature death.

My conclusion is that this transformation of the bitter struggle
for existence into a ritualized contest, with rules to protect the
contestants from both getting mortally hurt, is the central characteristic of sociality. Social codes bind the members of the group together; they regulate admission to membership through conventional competition, and they govern the competition rules. Members that have
been admitted enjoy the privilege of using the habitat and its resources, and in due season the right to breed. Those that are not
admitted are kept out. <u>This I infer to be the inner biological function of social life</u>.

The rudiments of social life can be traced right down to the
primitive invertebrates and the Protozoa. It is a typical feature
of the animal world and has been evolving progressively for roughly
a thousand million years. In the most advanced animals it has reached
the greatest complexity. I may remind you that sociality does not depend primarily on whether a particular kind of animal is gregarious or
solitary in its habits. Different social organizations demand different patterns of individual dispersion. Sometimes the individuals are
spaced out, singly or in pairs or family groups, sometimes they are
clumped into flocks, herds or shoals. Space patterns often change
with the time of day, the season of the year, or the stage of the
life-cycle. Even when the individuals are aggregated they may still

keep each other at arm's length, as in a school of fish or a flock
of birds resting on the ground. Communication has to be maintained
in a social group, by sight, sound, odor or some other signalling medium, but there is nothing inherently more social in a gregarious way
of life than there is in a solitary one. Leyhausen has made this abun-
dantly clear by his studies of the rich and varied social life of cats
[5].

You should have no delusions about the competitive nature of social life. Nothing is more typically social than a hierarchy of individuals, all known to one another, in which each holds an accepted
rank and is accorded the privileges and penalties that go with it.
At the same time they are a close-knit group and will often unite to
exclude outcasts and repel strangers.

If the interpretation I have given is a true one, there are a
number of deductions to be made about the use of space. In my contribution here I do not propose to say any more about the use of
space by individuals or about the forms of wanted property for which
they compete such as territories and established sites. Many of these
aspects have been discussed in the contributions of previous speakers.
I want instead to consider the use of space at a higher organizational
level, and review the space requirements of societies as a whole.

Man no longer retains any natural adaptations that are effective
in controlling population growth; but they appear to have remained
functional in all the stone-age peoples that survived into modern
times. They operated through mechanisms of behavior and did not, for
example, directly affect reproductive physiology as they do in many
animals. Family limitation was achieved by rules concerning the de-
ferment of marriage, abstention from sexual intercourse for long periods after childbirth, and by socially ordained abortion and infanticide. These practices were all quickly abandoned with the dawn of civilization, with the establishment of settled agriculture and the rise
of villages and towns. Uncontrolled growth of world population probably began only at that time.

Modern man is thus an anomaly among the higher animals in not
having any established machinery for population homeostasis. In a
typical vertebrate species, each local population is engaged in se-
curing its own future by preserving a careful balance between population density on the one hand and food resources on the other; in this
way it prevents the habitat from being plundered and despoiled.

The local group is socially integrated, and its social code
nearly always comes to contain accepted customs involving the local
geography. There may be customary places for assembling to retire
or sleep, or arenas for communal displays, or special localities for
breeding. There are often traditional boundaries between the ranges
of one socially-bonded group and the next, across which the individual

must learn not to stray. There may equally be customs about the
places where food is to be sought at particular seasons. In northern
Scotland, for instance, the red deer feed in summer on the open tundra
of the hills, leaving the browsing in the sheltered glens and woods
for winter when snow and exposure drive them off the higher ground.
Different herds have different customary movement patterns, depending
on details of the local terrain.

Traditions have to be learnt by each new generation from its pre-
decessor. Holding to them is part of the formula for survival of the
group itself. They insure against misuse of the habitat; and this
puts a big premium on making each local group perpetuate itself on
its own ground, so that it will continue to reap the rewards of its
own good husbandry. Every locality is unique in its topography, and
homeostatic principles have consequently to be translated into practice on the actual ground. When this has been successfully worked
out, local practice can be handed down in the form of established traditions.

Tradition has evolved as a medium of heredity in matters concerning the detailed use of space, because it can be adapted to the infinite variety of local conditions, and adjusted to secular changes; it
can be learnt by a newly arrived individual. All this would be impossible for the far less flexible genetic system.

In the long run there is an advantage in having the gene-pool
similarly adapted, at least on a broad regional scale, and if this is
to be achieved gene-pools must not be continually swamped by genetic
interchange between widely distant groups. The inheritance of traditions and the inheritance of genes thus reinforce each other in con-
ferring a great advantage in the long run on the stock that perpetu-
ates itself on its own ground.

What emerges from this discussion is the importance assumed by
citizenship and nationality (to borrow human terms) among animals;
they impel the individual to stay faithful to its own neighborhood
and breed within it. I am not suggesting that population homeostasis
requires that all should invariably act in this way, or that it cannot
be made effective in any other circumstances. One thinks immediately
of the need for colonists and pioneers, to enter new regions where
traditions do not exist; I shall refer to them shortly. But once a
local group has become self-perpetuating without too much adulteration
from outside, the machinery for population control becomes much simpler
to maintain.

One of the most marvelous accomplishments of adaptation to be
found anywhere in the animal world is the power of precise long-dis-
tance navigation. It has evolved in parallel, as far as we know to
about an equal degree of infallibility, in every animal group that
performs long two-way migrations; that is to say in birds, bats, seals,

whales, marine turtles, fish and, the evidence suggests, in a few insects as well. All I think have evolved their extraordinary powers as a condition of achieving the freedom to wander; they never need to sacrifice the advantages of permanent citizenship because they are able to return at will to their own social and reproductive group. There must be some immense advantage to be gained where mechanisms of such fantastic complexity have evolved – mechanisms which, it seems reasonable to expect in most if not all cases, require the angular positions and movements of the sun and stars to be determined, and timed with exact precision, and the data to be fed into an automatic information store and computer evolved in the brain which reads out conscious instructions for action.

An example may help to drive the point home. It has been discovered in the last 10 years that immature Atlantic salmon from both Europe and North America visit the coastal waters of West Greenland in great numbers for the purpose of feeding. When the time comes, millions of these fish proceed to sort themselves out, each setting off on a journey to seek that one among hundreds of far distant rivers which is its own, and finally the one among thousands of tributary streams. The mere need to regain a suitable habitat for spawning is not a sufficient explanation for such an accomplishment, nor for the long train of evolutionary development behind the perfection of sensory powers, and of memory, it entails. By these powers a mature fish steers its way back, sometimes thousands of miles, to the place it grew up in, and left one to three years earlier. It seems reasonable to conclude that some more compelling advantage has been the cause of the continuous selection pressure required to bring navigational performance to such a pitch. What I hope to point out in this paper is that citizenship and nationality, and their animal counterparts, confer such an advantage.

It is common to find that the adaptations of living organisms have struck a compromise between opposing values. Any species whose members were rigidly confined in their activities to their own immediate neighborhood would lose ground every time there was some minor disaster in local conditions, and not be able to regain it; in the end the species would die out altogether and become extinct. Populations must produce pioneers able to recolonize lost ground, and gain a foothold in new places when the chance arises. Pioneers have of course to leave their local traditions behind; to be successful they must carry with them an innate capability for constructing new ones, along with all the other paraphernalia of social life. Experimental banding and tagging of individual animals has shown us that in the vertebrates generally, just as in man, it is the young adults attaining maturity for the first time that have the strongest tendency to move away from their home neighborhood. Once they become established in a new locality they generally stay on, absorbed into an alien social group with which they spend the rest of their lives.

Pioneers do not, of course, always find vacant ground to colonize. Many, and probably as a rule the majority, perish. Suitable habitats tend to be fully occupied already, and the previously established individuals automatically have a superior social status. Much the same may apply to local recruits as well, so that in some of the longer-lived species, like fur-seals and European storks, even the young adults that do win a place in the community may have to wait for years before they achieve the second step and gain possession of one of the traditional breeding sites. In the birds that do not live so long on the other hand the territorial pattern is not permanent; each year after the breeding season the slate is washed clean, as it were, and many new recruits succeed in finding an immediate place.

Sometimes there is a clear distinction between recruits that take up permanent residence in their native locality, and pioneers that break clean away to try elsewhere. Emigrants are often simply outcasts, forming an unwanted surplus at the point of departure; but there are a few species at any rate, such as the migratory locusts, which have evolved the practice of producing pioneers as a specially equipped expeditionary force.

Even among the stay-at-homes there are marked differences in the scale on which mixing takes place in different species. This is clearly shown among birds, which have been banded in larger numbers than animals of any other class. Some are extremely sedentary, like the red grouse; four out of five grouse, if they succeed in becoming established at all, do so within a mile of where they were reared as chicks [2, p.323]. Other birds are less restricted; the population biology of the rook is also under study near Aberdeen, and here there tends to be an interspersion of young adults over several hundred square miles.

This implies differences in scale in different species in what constitutes a local group; but it does not alter the general rule that the foundation stock stays close to home, and that populations really do perpetuate themselves on their own ground. Recruits that emigrate into distant communities learn new local traditions when they get there. At that age they are still juniors, subordinate to the majority in the group they join and their innate response is to conform with custom as they find it.

If panmixis on a global scale is undesirable and there is selection pressure against it, we should expect that adaptations would have arisen to discriminate against individuals that move too far from home. It seems likely enough that this has happened in man. Customs change fast nowadays, but in rural communities it is still not surprising to find that strangers are regarded with suspicion if not with open hostility. In a neighborhood where every face is known the newcomer is immediately identified. He may in addition reveal whether he comes from near or far by the way he is dressed and by his speech. In times gone by the wearing of distinctive local traditional clothing and ornaments was very general, for example in different tribes of Eskimos and Indians, in the small feudal states of Europe (not forgetting the clans of Scotland), and in the innumerable peoples of Asia and Africa. With our intensely developed ability to distinguish individual faces we are quick to detect foreign features; and in primitive times nationality was sometimes imprinted beyond concealment by marking the adults of both sexes with tribal cicatrices, tatoo patterns or conspicuous mutilations.

Speech tends to be just as localized among long-settled peoples. The stranger's dialect will show that he is an outsider, even if it does not prevent him from being understood. Within periods of the order of a thousand years, more or less, it is easily possible for dialects to grow into languages, no longer mutually intelligible. It becomes then more difficult for a newcomer to establish himself when he has to cope with a foreign tongue. The development of spoken language is the most distinctive feature of man, and it is most apparent that, under natural selection, languages have tended to proliferate.

The progress of civilization has brought many changes to the ancient spatial structure of the local populations of mankind. Two or three centuries ago it was of course much less fluid than it is now, even in the countries of western Europe and North America. There was a strong tendency to marry within one's native community, although in the more progressive areas there has always been a greater tendency toward exogamy due to the larger numbers of men whose occupations took them far afield, such as traders, craftsmen, soldiers and sailors. There are still some pockets in England, and still more in Scotland, where distinctive local surnames greatly outnumber the Smiths and the Joneses. Not very long ago the average young country-bred adult had no more than a hundred potential mates to choose from, if that. Mendelian interchange on this sort of scale is quite usual in many species of warm-blooded vertebrates.

The volume of gene-flow between neighboring populations of the same species must depend partly on whether or not geographical barriers tend to interfere with it and increase isolation. There is plenty of evidence too that gene-flow is faster in some species than it is in others. Looking again at the peoples of western Europe, it is not difficult to detect at least the typical physical differences between what were once major racial groups, as between Scandinavians and Mediterranean people or between Celts and Slavs. But physical features are at best an uncertain means of distinguishing members of one nation from those of another. Culture, on the other hand, is much more reliable, especially if we include under the term culture our languages and dialects, laws and customs, arts and techniques, beliefs and loyalties – all the things in fact that characterize a society. We can take culture to comprise our whole tradition, all

that we learn in childhood at home and in school, all that is similarly acquired by other members of our culture group, and what we pass on
to the next generation in the wisdom of our riper years. Social culture in Europe and elsewhere is nowadays more conservative and localized than the genetic constitution that underlies it. Gene-flow can
percolate quite rapidly in the civilized world beneath the firmer cultural crust, which tends to preserve intact each local way of life.
All this helps to emphasize once more that the inheritance of traditions and the inheritance of genes are mutually independent and separate.

Individuals coming into a local group from outside, if they are
young and adaptable, are disposed to accept the culture they find,
and within a generation may be completely assimilated. It is equally
characteristic to get the wanderlust out of one's system fairly early
in adult life and settle down permanently in the home of one's choice.
In fact we readily become clannish about our own community, and com-
placent about its attractions.

The important condition for assimilating newcomers is that they
should arrive singly or in small groups. Human history contains many
examples of a completely different process, wholesale invasion and
conquest, where not only genes but cultures are transplanted as well.
There is no good evidence either way to suggest whether this second
process is confined to human beings, or whether supersedence of one
social system by another more vigorous one could occur in other animals as well.

I am not by any means the first to emphasize the mosaic or cellular structure of populations, and the important part it plays in evolution. A generation ago it was clearly expounded by the distinguished
Scottish anatomist, Sir Arthur Keith in what he called his group theory
of the evolution of man [3,4]. His thesis was that right down to the
dawn of civilization the habitable earth had formed a mosaic of home
areas each belonging to an isolated local community, and that such a
grouping had favored rapid evolutionary change. He knew, and it has
since been fully confirmed, that some of the non-human primates show
the same mosaic pattern. Presumably then it had already been in existence when man's immediate ancestors began to spread. "The area
of distribution", he wrote, "was extended by older successful groups
giving off broods which formed new groups or communities. The size
of a local group depended on the natural fertility of its territory;
in primitve peoples which still retain the original mosaic form a local group varies from 50 to 150 individuals - men, women and children.
Such local, interbreeding, competitive groups I shall speak of (he
says) as 'evolutionary units'; they represent the original teams which
were involved in the intergroup struggle for survival." "Far from
speech tending to break down the barriers between local groups, it
had an opposite effect, for we know that speech changes quickly when
primitive peoples become separated."

In the later stages of human evolution the tendency has, he said,
"always been towards the production of larger and more powerful evolutionary units;" but his own conclusion was that evolutionary change
proceeds fastest when the competing units are small and of great number. His enquiries left him in no doubt that every one of the units,
whether a local community, a tribe or a nation, "inhabited and claimed
the sole ownership of a demarcated tract of country; all were bound to
their homeland by a strong affection; and life was willingly sacrificed
to maintain its integrity." He "came to regard the territorial sense -
a conscious ownership of the homeland, one charged with a deep emotion
- as a highly important factor in human evolution. Every such territory," he wrote, "served as an evolutionary cradle" [4, pp.3-5].

Let me return to my own theme. From the earliest times, cultures
have profoundly affected the fortunes of the people that practiced
them. Some have led to enlightenment and progress, some have held
back their adherents in barbarity and ignorance. Pastoral and agricultural practices have tended to supersede hunting and gathering,
and in more modern times the industrialized cultures have dominated
the agrarian ones. People can forsake one culture for another and
this reminds us again of the essential independence of cultural and
genetic inheritance; people of a single genetic stock, in fact, are
capable of adopting any one of a number of different cultures.

A social system, and the culture that is part of it, is a tribal
rather than an individual attribute. It takes a group of people, or
animals for that matter, to make up a society, and they do not all
play the same role within it. Typically it takes account of the age-
structure represented in the component members. Human tribal societies prescribe conspicuously different roles for the young, the adults
in the prime of life, and the older generation, rich in experience.
Perhaps to avoid confusion about the class to which a person belongs,
each of us undergoes a physical metamorphosis at puberty when we change
from juvenile to adult, and again between the second and third stages
when our hair turns grey and in some races the men go bald. It takes
members of all three age classes to make up a human society fully capable of exploiting its cultural heritage. We need also people of
varying abilities and character, people who can specialize according
to their skills, as scientists, preachers, artisans or administrators,
people who will do what they are told and people who can tell us what
to do.

I want to make it clear that a society is an organic entity in
its own right; and especially that it has its own traditions, distinguishing it from other conspecific societies. Its biological function
is to promote the welfare and survival of the stock that comprises it.
Its culture is the property of the society as a whole, the common heritage of all individuals regardless of the parts they have to play in it
or the genetic variance that exists among them. At the tribal stage of
evolution any major change in cultural practice involves the whole

tribe; they either adopt the innovation or they hive off into separate groups each adhering to its own way of life.

Accepting the fact that at any stage of evolution not all the cultures found are equally promising and viable, it follows that cultures are subject to natural selection. The more successful ones survive and spread. This happens in spite of the fact that they are transmitted from generation to generation primarily by tradition and not by gene inheritance. The yardstick of fitness between one culture and another applies to each cultural group as a whole, and ignores the personal differences in fitness that exist among the individuals that comprise each group.

There is no difficulty in understanding here how two kinds of selection can proceed together at different levels, the first a selection between individuals which will determine the frequency of genes in the gene-pool, and overlying this a second level of selection between culture groups, differing primarily in their traditions and only secondarily in the constitution of their gene-pools. It is the independence in the methods of inheritance of the variance at the two levels, genetic at the individual level and traditional at the culture level, that enables one to see so clearly in this special case that two selective processes can exist simultaneously.

In more primitive times, and among non-human animal species, the interchange of members between different local groups and the spread of cultural changes by communication and conversion from old ways to new, was far more restricted than has been usual among human peoples within the span of history. Some animal traditions are known to us, relating the use of particular breeding places by certain colonial birds and seals for example, which go back a thousand years and more. Gene flow between neighboring stocks has been sufficiently slow to allow observable genetic differences to develop within time periods of that order of magnitude. In some animals therefore it may have been more nearly possible for gene-transmitted and tradition-transmitted inheritance to keep in step with each other than it has been in man, especially if we are thinking of the last hundred centuries of our swift-moving cultural evolution.

I have as you will have noticed been using 'culture' and 'social system' as interchangeable, synonymous terms. Culture is strictly appropriate only to mankind, though the social systems of animals provide an exact homologue. A particular culture or social system does presuppose an appropriate genetic background, because it depends on the innate physical, mental and behavioral capabilities and limitations of the individuals that practice it. There is always an innate component of social behavior, just as there is always also an acquired and traditional one. In the more primitive animals the innate component tends to get larger and the learned component smaller than in man.

One of the most essential social responses is a willingness to comply with the social system and its conventions; above all not to seek self-advantage at the expense of the group. Altruism in some form or other extends far down the scale in the animal kingdom as an ingredient of social behavior; population homeostasis is scarcely possible without it. Altruism can be largely or even entirely gene-controlled, and it is almost always automatic and involuntary. Among vertebrates particularly, the endocrine system responds to social pressures, with the result that it is common for particular individuals to be inhibited from sexual maturation in the interests of population control, or to die because they have been socially identified as surplus to the capacity of the habitat. This is an innate form of altruism, a suppression of personal advantage for the welfare of the stock. Behavioral altruisms also exist, for example in food-sharing, or in the feeding of young born to other parents.

Group selection can operate just as readily on gene-pools as it can on traditional cultures; but there has to be a system of self-perpetuating local groups to provide the raw material. It results in the elimination of some groups, while others continue to survive. In the evolution of social organizations it must discriminate against those that fail to control population density and either curb recruitment too strongly or else let numbers grow so great that the habitat is plundered and destroyed. As long as the local groups are small and numerous they are individually expendable, and group selection need not threaten the survival of the species over vast areas at any one time. Automatically it will overtake and suppress selection for individual advantage whenever this advantage tends in the long run to undermine the fitness of the group. In that way it can select to provide genetic safeguards for altruism, and thus protect the group against short-term selfish advantage to the individual; I have in mind for instance an increase in an individual's reproductive rate or increasing its life-span.

Man is unique in the extent to which he exercises a conscious choice between taking a selfish or a public-spirited action. It is part of the pattern of versatility and freedom to make decisions which is such an important characteristic of our species. It allows man to take short cuts to social advantage, for instance by permitting the individualist to act on his own judgment against the majority and come up with something new that turns out to benefit the society as a whole. In animals, toeing the line in the behavior code is always far more automatic, often completely so; and in those circumstances social progress can only proceed by the immensely slow and cumbrous process of group selection.

Mankind abandoned the ancestral methods of achieving population homeostasis long ago, as part of the price of developing civilization. World population is tending more and more to become a single exploding group, plundering resources on a global scale. The future of our ci-

vilization has got to rely now entirely on our own decision making
- on finding the means of preventing group selection from taking its
predictable course.

There are evolutionists who still deny the possibility of group
selection. They believe it is possible to explain the evolution of
all adaptations by the single process of selecting for fitness among
individuals. I hope I have made my view clear, that the social group
is an organic entity with properties of its own, properties that
could not be vested in separate and independent individuals. I am
thinking of the existence within it of hierarchies of individuals,
of the customs that dictate the collective behavior and social inter-
relationships of its members, and secure its collective rights. I
have attempted to show that groups with such characters exist, especially in the higher vertebrates and arthropods. If there are many
groups within the geographical area of a single species and they differ as they must in survival potential, nothing can prevent selection
from occurring between them. The view sometimes expressed that there
is no mechanism by which group selection could take place ignores the
particulate structure of self-perpetuating groups, which ecologists
have shown to exist. Even in such a difficult environment as that
of the plankton, drifting along in ocean currents, the evidence begins to show that some of the crustacean species are broken at least
into broad area groups, morphologically distinguishable.

It is because group selection depends so greatly on a pattern
of space use that I have ventured to introduce it into this symposium.
It has I believe played a leading part in evolution, not only in the
development of social organization and human cultural practices, but
of physiological and genetic mechanisms as well. It has the important
property of being able to select for adaptations that can only prove
their worth in the long term, involving so many generations that the
genes of any one individual and his family have become completely dispersed within the common pool. It can select for traditions which are
the equal property of every member of a group, and have a large non-
genetic component of inheritance which cannot be selected for through
the fitness of the individual. Traditions likewise outlast the span
of individual life, and influence the survival of the stock as a whole.
But perhaps the most valuable function of group selection has been to
find means of protecting the stock against the sabotage of short-term
individual advantage.

REFERENCES

1. Darwin, C.: The Origin of Species. J. Murray, London, 1859.
         (Cited from 6th Edition, 1872).
2. Jenkins, D., Watson, A. and Miller, G.R.: Population studies
         on red grouse (Lagopus lagopus scoticus) in north-east
         Scotland. J. Anim. Ecol., 32:317-376, 1963.

3. Keith, A.: On certain factors concerned in the evolution of
             human races. J. Roy. Anthrop. Inst., 46:10-34, 1916.
4. _____ : A New Theory of Human Evolution. Watts, London,
             1948.
5. Leyhausen, P.: The communal organisation of solitary animals.
             Symp. Zool. Soc. Lond., 14:249-263, 1965.
6. Watson, A.: The links between territorial behavior, intraspeci-
             fic strife, population density, and the environment.
             [This Volume].
7. Wynne-Edwards, V.C.: Animal Dispersion in Relation to Social
             Behaviour. Oliver & Boyd, Edinburgh, 1962.

Spatial Parameters in Naturalistic Social Research

Robert Sommer

Man-environment relations is such a broad field that a researcher has to choose his audience as well as his problem area. Over the years, I have had three different audiences in mind, which has meant writing three different kinds of articles. The first contained various social scientists. Interestingly, sociologists have been far more receptive to studies of spatial behavior than have psychologists who tend to think in terms of psychological rather than physical spaces. Anthropologists were interested in the work from the standpoint of non-verbal communication. Because I want to change the world, I also aimed at architects, landscape people and others concerned with the design of the physical environment, and space managers such as hospital administrators, student housing directors, school principals and air terminal managers who are directly responsible for the furnishing, allocation, and utilization of institutional spaces. It is noteworthy that animal biologists and ecologists, whom I have never tried to reach directly, are the people to whom I am most indebted for my theoretical orientation and concepts.

Two processes that have interested me are dominance-subordination behavior and territoriality. I would like to make it clear that, when I use the term "territoriality" in my research, there is no implication that the behavior described is innate rather than learned or that the underlying mechanisms in studies with humans are similar to those in studies with other species. Following Hediger, I used the term to represent an area which "is first rendered distinctive by its owner in a particular way and, secondly, is defended by the owner." (7) The major components of this definition are personalization and defense.

Both dominance-subordination behaviors and territoriality limit

aggression, because an individual either refrains from going where
he is likely to be involved in disputes or, based on his knowledge
of who is above and below him, engages in ritualized dominance-
subordination behavior rather than in actual combat. The complementary relationship between territoriality and dominance behavior
is expressed in Victor Hugo's declaration "Every man a property
owner, not one a master." The implication is that when everyone
possesses an individual territory, the reasons for one man to dominate another will disappear. Unlike most forms of social organization which tend to weaken or disappear in captivity, dominance relationships in captivity are often strengthened or even created
where none existed previously (12). Examining the records of all
aggressive acts between mental patients, Esser et al were able to
discern territorial behavior and a relatively stable dominance hierarchy (3). Altman and Haythorn, who studied pairs of sailors in confinement, found that the individuals gradually withdrew from one
another or "cocooned," so that each person rigidly respected the zone
of personal space around his neighbor (1). Pairs which were incompatible in terms of dominance, with both sailors either very high or
very low in dominance so that no easy accommodation was possible,
adhered more rigorously to preferences for a particular bed, table
or chair. If we accept the authors' operational definition of territory (the consistent use of particular beds, chairs, and table
areas), there is an interesting parallel to the animal studies,
where both territoriality and dominance behavior are ways of maintaining a social order, and where, when one system cannot function,
the other takes over. With pairs incompatible in dominance, such as
two highly dominant individuals, no stable order can be found, so
aggression is limited by strict adherence to territorial rights.

Apart from societies with clear caste lines and military organizations (which do not really qualify as societies, although one can
find microcosms of societies within them), the clearest dominance
orders are found in closed communities with restricted movement and
limited space. Within prison society, for example, certain cells as
well as lower bunks and soft jobs are regarded as more desirable than
others and become sources of contention within the inmate society.
When the convict order becomes stabilized to the point where each person knows his place (both socially and spatially), dissention ends.
In American prisons, the constant turnover among inmates, particularly the addition of fresh fish of unknown rank, produces an atmosphere
of constant tension that requires continuous venting in profanity and
aggressive fantasies. Turnover among guards also produces the same
probing for strength and weakness that occurs with a new fish. All
residents of the cell block, convicts and guards alike, must wait for
the new man (guard or convict) to learn how things really happen as
distinct from the regulations.

Because social and spatial orders serve similar functions, it
is not surprising to find spatial correlates of status levels and,

conversely, social correlates of spatial positions. In the barnyard, the top chickens have the greatest freedom of space and can walk anywhere, while lower birds are restricted to small areas and can be pecked by other birds wherever they go (10). In human society, the social elite possess more space in the form of larger home sites, more rooms per house and vacation homes. In addition, they have greater spatial mobility and more opportunities to escape when they become tense, uncomfortable, or bored. An institutionalized status hierarchy, such as that found in corporations or universities, generally possess rather complex spatial norms. There are many places where a factory supervisor cannot go without the workers feeling he is spying on them. Officers keep out of the enlisted men's quarters except on inspection. School administrators stay out of the classrooms unless there is some emergency or the teacher asks them to visit. There have been a number of studies on the connection between status and location. Typically, the two are confounded in that prestigious individuals occupy the best places. Space assignment policies in complex organizations not only indicate the role that people are expected to play, but also make it difficult for people in other locations to exercise leadership. In housing projects for non-married commissioned officers at several British Army stations, a difference of more than one step in rank decreased contact between neighbors. This trend was sufficiently marked to warrant the recommendation against mixing ranks since this practice appeared to discourage friendships from springing up between close neighbors (9). Recently, we finished a study of several academic office buildings. High status faculty were the best known men in the building, even though they were in their offices least often, and this was true even when the length of stay at the university was taken into account. There was strong segregation by rank in informal interaction. Tenured faculty took their coffee breaks with other tenured faculty, while non-tenured faculty drank their coffee with non-tenure people (4).

More use is being made of territorial mechanisms to keep down density in public areas in the face of increasing population pressures. Some years ago, most state parks were open to as many campers as could squeeze in. As in New York subways during the rush hour, there was always room for one more. The resulting crowding not only annoyed many campers, but also posed a threat to the parks where a delicate balance existed between natural elements such as trees, grass, flowers, and visitors. A surplus of people would drive away some animals, domesticate others, attract scavengers, pollute the streams and ruin the meadows and flowers. Crowded campgrounds also presented health, safety, crime and refuse disposal problems.

One solution has been to divide the campgrounds into a finite number of territories based on expert opinion as to the optimal population density for the specific park. This system has kept campground occupancy to a desired level, but produced many complaints

about the unpredictability of the system. People did not know
whether they could obtain a camping spot until it was too late to
go elsewhere. This led to a further solidification of territoriality with the introduction in California of a computerized reservation system for camping places. A family writes several months in
advance to reserve a spot in a particular park. With this system,
there is less waste motion at the campgrounds and fewer possibilities
of dispute as to who gets which spot and how long a family can stay,
since this is programmed beforehand. The system works well when the
number of applicants coincides with the number of available places,
but, during the summer months and the holidays, it requires procedures for selecting a chosen few. This brings forth dominance
considerations, which tend in the long run to become class oriented.
Those families who can plan their vacations six months in advance,
obtain and fill out the necessary application forms and return them
with the reservation fee, will secure the best places. In a free
market situation, the division of space becomes strongly intertwined
with the existing dominance order. Not only does space allocation
indicate status, it also reinforces it.

Let me describe our studies of small group ecology, or the
way people in face-to-face groups arrange themselves. The first
study, which took place in an old folks ward in a state hospital,
showed that the side-by-side placement of chairs along the walls of
the room severely hindered social intercourse (13). This launched
us upon a quest to learn how people arranged themselves when they
wanted to interact under natural conditions. I have spent many hours
in cafeterias and lounges diagramming how people sat or stood when
they talked together. It became very clear that at rectangular
tables or small square tables people preferred to sit corner-to-
corner when they conversed. Going somewhat deeper, they wanted eye
contact but not so direct that they could not escape. It was interesting that people rarely looked directly at one another. Later
studies made it very clear that a desire for eye contact (but not a
direct gaze) was an important factor in how people spaced themselves.
We then switched to an experimental approach and asked pairs of
people to enter a room and discuss topics, and we recorded how they
sat. Again we found a strong preference for sitting corner-to-corner
rather than directly across or side-by-side (14).

In groups with leaders, the leader tended to select a head position at a rectangular table, and other people arranged themselves so
that they could see him. Visual contact with the leader seemed more
important to others at the table than physical proximity. A similar
finding was obtained by Strodtbeck and Hook who recorded the seating
arrangements in experimental jury sessions which were not actual
court cases (16). The jurors' first task was to elect a foreman,
and there was a striking trend for the person seated at one of the
head positions to be elected foreman. It was also found that the
initial choice of seats was not random. People of higher status--

proprietors and managers--selected head chairs more than would have
been expected by chance. In electing a foreman, it appeared that the
jurors looked at both occupants of the head chairs and selected the
one with the higher status. It was also found that people in the
head chair participated in the discussion more than people at other
positions, and that others at the table rated the head people to
have made the most significant contributions to the deliberations.

I have been interested in individual distance as it relates
to the personalities of the people involved, what they are doing,
and the external situation. I have left the question of cultural
differences in individual distance to Hall (6). Only a beginning
has been made in studies of the way personality factors relate to
spacing. It seems clear now that introverts sit and stand further
away from other people than do extroverts. Antipathy between people
or anxiety on the part of one about what the other may do will also
tend to keep them apart. A perceived stigma will keep others at a
distance also. Kleck found that people stayed further away from
someone who is described as an epileptic than from the same person
when he was described as simply another student (8).

The functional requirements of different task sets also has an
effect on spacing. Studies of cooperative activity show that people
sit side-by-side to enable them to share materials, but when they
are competing, they like to sit across from one another. They report that the eye contact, when they sit directly across from one
another, helps to stimulate competition. People engaged in separate
tasks--coacting as it were--tend to sit in some catty-corner arrangement where distraction from eye contact is minimal (11). The situation in which people find themselves also has an effect on spacing.
When room density is high people will sit closer together so that
others cannot come between them. A high noise level also tends to
bring people together. There is the curious but understandable finding that conversational distance varies inversely with room size.
In small rooms, people sit at some distance, probably back against
the walls, but in large rooms they move their chairs relatively close
together.

Over the last few years, we have undertaken a series of individual distance studies in college library study halls (15). We
chose this location, because a study hall is a place where students
try to avoid one another--apart from the occasional study date which
we treated separately. We used an ecological model of invasion and
succession and found particularly helpful the concepts developed in
bird spatial studies by Crook (2). We arrived when the study hall
first opened and observed it as it filled up. The first students
in the room arranged themselves one to a table at an end chair.
When room density reached one per table, the next person sat down
at the opposite corner of the table. Long tables made it easier for
the students to ignore one another at low room densities. At small

four-chair rectangular tables, with two chairs to a side, we found
that sexual segregation was apparent. A girl would be much more
likely to sit down at a small table where there was another girl
than if there were a boy there. Yet at long rectangular tables,
with six chairs to a side, this pattern of sexual segregation was
absent. If there were a girl at the far end of the table, the next
occupant was as likely to be a boy as a girl.

In the library study hall, I noticed that readers sometimes
maintained their privacy through offensive displays and other times
through defensive gestures. Offensive displays are based on the
idea the best defense is a good offense and include both threat positions and postures. Position refers to a person's location in the
room--sitting in a corner location conveys a different meaning to a
newcomer than sitting in the center of the room. While position
refers to a person's location with respect to external coordinates,
posture describes his particular stance--whether he spreads out his
belongings "as if he owned the place," or pulls himself in to take
up as little room as possible. Gesture can also be used to defend
a given area, a person indicating by his expression that he is receptive for contact or prefers to be by himself. Biologists speak
of agonistic displays which keep other species-members away through
threat gestures. These serve to reduce overt physical contact by
substituting rituals of approach, display, struggle and retreat.
A given area can be defended by any combination of position, posture
and gesture. Avoidance works best in a room with many corners, al-
coves and side areas hidden from view. Offensive display is most
effective when a person can use features of the landscape to reinforce his dominance and control access. Overt aggressive reactions
to the approach of a newcomer, such as profanity, insults, or physical assault, rarely occur in a library where norms for individual
privacy are well established. We conducted several questionnaire
studies, later followed by experimental studies, to learn how offensive display and avoidance each achieves privacy though by different
routes. The first study used a three-page questionnaire, each page
showing a rectangular table with three, four or five chairs per side.
Some students were given the avoidance instructions, although the
word itself was not used:

> If you wanted to sit as far as possible from the
> distraction of other people, where would you sit?

Twenty-one students from the same class were shown the same
diagrams and given the offensive display instructions without the
phrase being used:

> If you wanted to have the table to yourself,
> where would you sit to discourage anyone else from
> occupying it?

Even though both groups of students were asked to arrange themselves to gain privacy, the two tactics produced very different results. Those students who wanted to sit by themselves as far as
possible from other people overwhelmingly chose the end chair. Those
students who wanted to keep others away from the table almost unani-
mously chose the middle table. When I sent an account of these findings to Fitch, his first question concerned the location of the door.
The diagrams had shown a table and chairs floating in space with no
indication of where the door, other tables, or even the walls were
located. One hypothesis that came to mind was that someone attempting an offensive display would be likely to face the door. It also
seemed that the back of the room would be more heavily used by people
in retreat. To explore these possibilities, another set of diagrams
was drawn, each one showing a full room containing two rows of rectangular tables, aisles, and walls. Four sets of instructions, involving both retreat and active defense conditions as well as high
and low densities, were used with these diagrams.

Hypothesis 1. During the retreat conditions, people will gravi-
tate to the end (wall) chair; in active defense they will make greater use of the center and aisle chairs. This hypothesis was strongly
supported by the data. With the retreat instructions, 76% of the
students chose a wall chair compared to 38% during the active defense
conditions.

Hypothesis 2. Students in retreat will face away from the door
while facing toward the door during active defense. The results
show a general preference in all conditions to sit with one's back
to the door--60% of the total sample facing away from the door compared to 40% facing it. There was still a significant trend in the
predicted direction, since 44% of the active defenders faced the
door compared to 36% of those in retreat. It seems likely that the
preference for facing away from the door is related to the situation
being described as a library study hall. I do not suggest that this
trend would occur in other public areas.

There was also a strong preference for chairs toward the rear
of the room, only 21% selected chairs at the front. Further analysis showed the occupancy of the rear chairs was highest in the retreat conditions under high room density. There was also a marked
preference for smaller four-chair tables when they were paired with
eight-chair tables and also for tables which were placed against the
walls when they were paired with tables containing aisles on all
four sides.

Overall, it did not make much difference whether the students
were told that room density was going to be high or low. However,
density interacted with several of the other conditions and had more
influence with the retreat instructions than with the active defense
instructions. When students were told that room density would be

high but they should try to sit far from other people, there was
greater use of the rear half of the room, tables against the wall
and chairs closest to the wall. It appears that the attribution of
high room density increases the amount of physical retreat by those
people who want to retreat, but has little effect on those who want
to employ active defense.

At this point, we decided to alter the situation experimentally
by violating the spatial norms of the library. In one study, conducted by Nancy Russo, the subjects were all female students sitting
alone with at least one book in front of them and empty chairs on
either side and across (5). In other words, the subject was sur-
rounded by empty chairs, which indicated something about her preference for solitude as well as making an invasion relatively easy.
The second girl to meet these criteria each session and who was
visible to Mrs. Russo served as a control. Each control subject was
observed from a distance and no invasion was attempted. There were
five different approaches used--sometimes Mrs. Russo would sit along
side the subject, other times directly across from her, etc. All of
these were violations of the typical but unverbalized seating norms
in the library, which required a newcomer to sit a considerable distance from those already seated, unless the room were crowded.

Occupying an adjacent chair and moving it closer to the subject
produced the quickest departures, while there was a slight but still
significant distance between the other invasion locations--sitting
across from her or sitting across and one seat over--and the control
condition of the subject whose space was not invaded. There were
also wide individual differences in the way the subjects reacted--
there was no single reaction to someone sitting too close. There
are defensive gestures, such as putting one's hand up to the side
of the head, averting one's eyes and placing one's elbow out as a
barrier against the invader, a shift in posture such as moving over
halfway in one's chair, or hunching oneself over one's books, as
well as attempts to move one's chair away from the invader. If
these fail or are ignored by the invader, or if he shifts position
too, the subject eventually takes to flight. Crook measured the
spacing of birds in three ways--arrival distance or how far from
several birds a newcomer will land, settled distance or the resultant distance after adjustments have occurred, and distance after
departure or how far apart birds remain after intermediate birds
have left (2). When Mrs. Russo moved her chair if the subject did,
i.e., maintained the arrival distance at about six inches and did
not permit the subject to achieve a comfortable settled distance,
a preponderance of flight reactions occurred. There was a dearth
of direct verbal responses to the invasions. Only two of the 80
students asked her to move over. This provides support for Hall's
view that "we treat space somewhat as we treat sex. It is there,
but we don't talk about it." (6)

We have attempted these invasion techniques in other settings too. It is paradoxical but perhaps not illogical that the best way to study invasions of privacy is to stage them deliberately. I feel apologetic about the breeches of good manners that occurred--standing and sitting too close to other people. From the standpoint of the ethics of such research, it can be said that the most serious effect of our invasions sequences was mild annoyance of the kind common to many social situations. I also believe that there is a practical payoff from this research in the form of designed physical environments that will facilitate privacy--give each student a private place of his own--or in other situations, to bring people together. A library which is intended to be sociofugal space, where interaction is discouraged, requires knowledge of how to arrange people to minimize unwanted contact. One possibility is to use the rank order of preferred arrangement by interacting groups as arrangements to be avoided in sociofugal space. On this basis, corner seating would be less satisfactory in a library reading room than opposite or distant seating. An Emily Post or Amy Vanderbilt may know these principles intuitively, and diplomatic protocol may codify them, but there is need to make them explicit and subject them to empirical test. To increasingly greater extent we find ourselves being arranged by impersonal environments in lecture halls, airports, waiting rooms, and lobbies. Many aspects of these settings have been designed for ease of maintenance and efficient cleaning with little cognizance to their social functions. The study of small group ecology is important, not only from the standpoint of developing an adequate theory of human society that takes into account the context of social relationships, but also from the practical standpoint of designing and maintaining functional spaces where human relationships can develop.

REFERENCES

1. Altman, I. and Haythorn, W.W.: The ecology of isolated groups. Behav. Sci., 12:169-182, 1967

2. Crook, J.H.: The basis of flock organization in birds. In Thorpe, W.H. and Zangwill, O.L., eds., Current Problems in Animal Behavior. Cambridge University Press, Cambridge, 1961.

3. Esser, A.H., et al.: Territoriality of patients on research ward. In Wortis, J., ed., Recent Advances in Biological Psychiatry, Vol.8, Plenum Press, New York, 1965.

4. Estabrook, M.E.: The Ecology of an Academic Office Building. University of California, Davis, unpublished M.A. thesis, 1968.

5. Felipe, N. and Sommer, R.: Invasions of personal space. Soc. Prob., 14:206-214, 1966.

6. Hall, E.T.: The Silent Language. Doubleday, Garden City, 1959.

7. Hediger, H.: Wild Animals in Captivity. Butterworths, London, 1950.

8. Kleck, R.: Physical stigma and task oriented interactions. Hum. Relations, 22:51-60, 1969.

9. Madge, J. and Madge, J.: Survey of New Army Married Quarters. Ministry of Public Buildings and Works, London, 1965.

10. McBride, G., James J.W. and Shoffner, R.N.: Social forces determining spacing and head orientation in flock of domestic hens. Nature, 197:1272-1273, 1963.

11. Norum, G., Russo, N. and Sommer, R.: Seating patterns and group task. Psychol. in the Schools, 4:276-280, 1967.

12. Scott, J.P.: Animal Behavior. University of Chicago Press, Chicago, 1958.

13. Sommer, R. and Ross, H.F.: Social interaction on a geriatrics ward. Int. J. Soc. Psychiat., 4:128-133, 1958.

14. _____: Studies in personal space. Sociometry, 22:247-260, 1959.

15. _____: Sociofugal space. Amer. J. Sociol. 72:654-660, 1967.

16. Strodtbeck, F.L. and Hook, L.H.: The social dimensions of a twelve-man jury table. Sociometry, 24:397-415, 1961.

Ecological Aspects of Interpersonal Functioning

Irwin Altman

For several years, my colleagues and I have been studying the
"social penetration process", a term we use to encompass the events
which take place as people develop and dissolve social bonds with
others. We have addressed ourselves to such questions as: What is
the behavioral course of development of an interpersonal relationship?
Do the processes of self-disclosure, psychological accessibility and
openness between people follow a systematic developmental history?
How do such factors as personality, inter-personal compatibility, and
environmental pressures slow down or accelerate the process?

It is our hypothesis that the growth of an interpersonal bond
follows a systematic behavioral flow from strangership to acquaintance-
ship to friendship to deep-seated emotional bonds. This historical
development involves, loosely speaking, gradually increasing and systematic penetration toward the core of their respective personalities by
social actors. As a social relationship develops, there appears to be
exchange, including eye contact, facial expressions, head and body positions, movements, gestures, etc. But individuals also do not deal
with one another in an environmental vacuum. Their exchanges occur
within a physical environment and involve active use of that environment to cope with and structure their social relationships. Environment within this framework is viewed in both an independent and dependent variable sense--it affects, constrains, and serves as a determinant of behavior; as when groups are socially and physically isolated
from the world for several days vs. not being so confined. And it is a

* From Bureau of Medicine and Surgery, Navy Department, Research Task
MF 022.01.03-002. The opinions and statements contained herein are the
private ones of the author and are not to be construed as official or
reflecting the views of the Navy Department or the Naval Service at
large.

medium of response and communication, as when socially isolated group members exhibit systematic patterns of use of chairs, beds and areas in their environment. But this third level of exchange--use of environmental props--is not all that occurs in interpersonal relationships as people build or remove themselves from ties with others or as they adapt, cope, and strive to adjust to a situation and to one another. They also think, feel and experience at subjective covert levels or, in more formal terms, they evaluate their experiences, build cognitive models and expectations about one another, and forecast likely future responses by themselves and others.

All these levels of response--verbal, non-verbal, use of the environment and subjective processes--occur simultaneously as a coherent "system". Therefore, ideally, one should study these different levels of exchange as a unitary complex behavior pattern, with equivalency of functioning across response modes, complex feedback mechanisms, etc. But, as we all know too well, this ideal is not easily at hand, for every small facet of a problem comes to have its own enormous conceptual complexity and unique requirements for technologies and research tools; all of which makes it very difficult to do or think about everything at once. Our own frailities in these matters led to a series of studies of the social penetration process which emphasized the verbal and subjective covert facets of the phenomena, somewhat at the expense of environmental prop behaviors and completely to the neglect of self-marker behaviors. But we have made some progress in these latter areas and wish to share some of this research with you in support of the following propositions:

1. The active use of space and of the environment by group members is simultaneous with and complements other modes of interaction and reflects the social-emotional or interpersonal status of the group.

2. Groups use their physical environment in an active, adaptive, coping fashion as they strive for viable and/or optimum levels of interpersonal functionings. Thus, they are not only "affected by" the environment, but also "act upon it".

3. Active use of the environment in the management of interpersonal relationships may be anticipatory or reactive, i.e., prearranging or prestructuring the environment to create certain interaction settings or use of the environment in reaction to developing events.

In light of the extensive work on the use of space by animals reported elsewhere in this Symposium, these basic propositions may appear unsophisticated and analogous to well-established subhuman modes of functioning. But relatively little research has been conducted on the human use of the environment and even less has focused on use of the environment in the management of developing interpersonal relationships. I will therefore review several studies conducted in our laboratory which tap aspects of the themes cited above and also discuss

some plans for new work. The first set of studies (two completed,
one in process) was done in the context of socially isolated situations, where pairs of men were confined in small spaces for several
days with little outside contact. (Their environment and social
tasks are illustrated in Figures 1 and 2). The second set of studies
was of a more limited nature, being laboratory experiments concerned
with specific aspects of the social penetration process.

SOCIAL ISOLATION STUDIES

In one study, a variety of data involving individual and team
performance, stress reactions and emotional symptomatology, social
interaction and use of space and the environment were obtained from
pairs of men socially isolated for ten days [1,2,3,13,14,15]. The
groups were organized to create hypothetically compatible and incompatible pairs on four social need characteristics: dominance, achievement, affiliation and dogmatism. A matched series of control groups
followed the same work schedule but were not confined for meals or
sleeping. As predicted, isolates in general, and incompatible isolates in particular, (especially those incompatible on need dominance
and need achievement), showed more subjective stress reactions, emotional symptomatology and interpersonal conflict, as well as some ta-
pering off in performance effectiveness on team tasks. These data
also mesh quite nicely with behaviors of interest here--mutual self-
disclosure, social interaction and use of the physical environment.
Mutual self-disclosure, a verbal aspect of the social penetration process, was measured by responses to a questionnaire administered at the
end of isolation regarding how much had been disclosed about the self
to one's partner. The data indicated little differences in opening up
to others as a function of compatibility, which illustrates the over-
riding effects of being totally restricted to the company of another
person. Isolates reported disclosing much more to their partners than
did controls, especially in intimate topical areas and, in some respects, had a level of openness similar to that achieved with a close
friend. Thus, the environmental milieu clearly led to an accelerated
social penetration process and "acted upon" the group in an independent
variable sense. With this increased knowledge of one another, it is
interesting to see how compatible and incompatible group members coped
with one another in terms of actual social interaction processes and
active use of their physical environment. Here we come closer to the
theme of this presentation.

Several facets of use of the environment were measured. Systematic observations were made of which of two chairs men sat in, which
bed they used and in which corners of the room they were located. An
index of "territorial behavior" was developed to reflect degree of exclusive use of objects and areas by group members. Simultaneous observation was made of how often men did things together (talking, playing
cards), alone (reading, writing) or were in bed asleep. The results
indicated that different forms of incompatibility were associated with

Fig. 1: Isolation environment; sailors in a 12x12 ft. room, being watched through one-way glass

different modes of using the environment. Consider first those pairs
incompatible on need for dominance. Such groups consisted of men
both high on desire to control and dominate others, whereas compatible
groups were composed such that one man wished to dominate and the
other desired to be dominated. The characteristic mode of interpersonal adaptation by incompatible dominance groups was to be quite territorial in use of their mutual environment and to be highly socially
interactive. These were volatile groups in which men had great difficulty in managing the situation (both groups who could not complete
the isolation period came from these conditions). They gradually
came to divide up the room and have their own territories, as reflected in their exclusive use of chairs, beds and sides of the table, but
still dealt with one another in a very active, perhaps competitive
way. In many respects, they never accommodated to one another and never achieved a working consensus, with quite stormy and perhaps inadequately resolved adaptation and coping. A very different pattern was
shown by those incompatible on need affiliation, where one man was
highly affiliative and desirous of social relationships with others
and the other man was not so inclined. These groups gradually became
quite territorial, as did the incompatible dominance dyads, but they
withdrew from one another socially. This was a "quiet" form of incompatibility, with the members staying in their own places and having
little to do with one another. These groups also showed little subjective stress and symptomatology, indicating that they had achieved
some working consensus as a group, if not by liking or compatibility,
at least one which permitted them to cope with isolation, to be viable
and adapted to one another and to the environment. Incidentally, no
comparable differences occurred for control groups, who were in a
much less restricted environment.

Thus, this study demonstrates how interpersonal adaptation and
adjustment occurs at several levels of behavioral functioning, and as
an integrated set of behaviors involving use of the environment, social interaction, subjective social-emotional states and overt behaviors. Furthermore, the study demonstrates how interpersonal relationships are not only affected by an environmental milieu such as isolation, but also how the physical environment is actively used to manage
social relationships in accord with interpersonal compatibility.

In the next study, we turned to a more detailed analysis of the
role of a socially isolated environment on adaptation processes, and
examined interpersonal coping processes across a range of isolation
conditions. Thus, we became more actively interested in the environment both as determinant and as response vehicle. Three aspects of
the environment were varied in a 2x2x2 factorial design--availability
of privacy, expected length of social isolation and degree of stimulation from the outside world. We again worked with two-man sailor
teams, although this time men were randomly assigned to groups, not
pre-selected on the basis of interpersonal compatibility. Two degrees
of "privacy" were established (although we must admit this to be a

rather complex concept). Half the groups spent the complete eight-
day isolation period living and working in the same room (no privacy);
the other groups had a two-compartment chamber with each man living
in a separate area (privacy). In the privacy arrangement the rooms
were connected by a door which opened from either side, so that men
could spend as much or as little time together in either area as they
desired. Stimulation and outside contact was also varied at two levels: a "stimulation" condition was created by having a mission control center give verbal instructions for tasks and request periodic
room temperature and food supply reports. The center also transmitted short musical excerpts, a question-and-answer program of general
interest and documentary news clips. In a "no stimulation" condition,
subjects rarely heard a human voice, all instructions were given by a
buzzer code system, no reports about their status were requested and
no entertainment was provided. The third variable involved manipulation of expectations about length of the isolation period, with some
groups expecting to be isolated for four days and others expecting a
20-day stay. The actual period of the experiment in all cases was
eight days. Those in the four-day condition were not released but were
left in the situation, creating great uncertainty for them. (Incidentally, they did know when four days had passed and that extension
of the mission was a possibility). These various conditions, in combination, yielded eight isolation conditions ranging from a short four-
day, private, stimulated environment to a 20-day, non-stimulated, non-
private environment. The question is, then, how do variations in the
physical environment, as reflected in these variables, result in different individual and group adaptation and coping processes of the
environment?

First, we found that a relatively large proportion of groups
(53%) were unable to complete the isolation period and aborted. This
was somewhat more prevalent for 20-day groups in the first few days
and for four-day groups after the fourth day; and somewhat higher for
the privacy vs. no-privacy groups. Those in the 20-day privacy groups
and in the 20-day no-stimulation groups had higher abort rates than
others, attesting to the impact of these conditions on adaptation to
isolation.

What is interesting from the point of view of this paper is that
aborters had a characteristic syndrome of behavior which cut across
several levels of functioning. They reported more feelings of stress
and anxiety [20], performed less effectively on team tasks, had perceptual changes involving greater stimulus boundedness and lower ideational activity and imaginative capacity [19]. Most important, they
showed a characteristic pattern of territorial behavior, social activity and bed usage as they approached their abort day. Aborters,
typically, showed lower territorial behavior early in isolation, compared with completers, and higher territorial behavior later. They
were initially lower in exclusive use of environmental objects and
areas and then rose sharply over days, whereas completers either re-

mained level or declined during the first four days. Furthermore, aborter groups spent <u>less</u> time in social interaction early in isolation compared with completer groups, but <u>increased</u> above completers as they approached their abort day. Thus, aborters were under-territorial and under-socially active early and over-territorial and socially hyperactive as they moved toward aborting from the situation. Piecing these data together with other aspects of their behavior and with data from the earlier study led us to propose tentatively the hypothesis that aborter groups had "misread" the demands of the situation and had not gone about the business of adapting to their environment and to one another in terms of group formation processes. They did not effectively form a group or attune themselves to one another and to the demands of social isolation sufficiently early in the experience. It should be noted that the territorial behavior pattern described above was most evident in 20-day abort and in private abort groups, while the social activity patterns appeared most strongly in private abort groups, precisely the conditions where most subjective stress was experienced.

In thinking about these data and those of the earlier study, we came to see them form a pattern that reflected similar modes of adaptation by compatible and successful groups vs. incompatible and aborter groups. Those incompatible on need dominance and need affiliation and aborters <u>both</u> showed similar developmental patterns of territorial behavior--they were very low at first and then very high later, whereas compatible and completer groups started high and eventually declined. If one views territorial behavior as an adaptive response, important to individual and group integrity and identity, especially in an isolated and confined situation, then the manifestation of such behavior early in a relationship could be taken as a sign that the group members had begun behaving so as to create a viable relationship with one another. Once successful in the business of group formation, territorial behavior of the type studied here may no longer be as essential to maintain. The data from both studies fit this post hoc hypothesis that the incompatible and aborter groups only began the process of accommodation later in the isolation experience, perhaps too late for group viability purposes. It might be speculated that if incompatible groups had established stronger territorial behaviors early in their experience, they might have had more viable group experiences. In not so doing, the incongruence of their social need properties may have become strikingly salient and no longer amenable to accommodation.

As discussed, aborters spent less time in social interaction compared with completers early in isolation. It is probable that much of the early interaction by completers revolved around the isolation situation and its management, their roles and relationships vis a vis one another, etc., all of which is part of a group formation process. The aborters engaged in this process much less so at first and more so later. We plan to do content analyses of freely occurring verbal

behavior to test the hypothesis that much of the later heightened social activity by aborters was not directed at group adaptation to isolation, but to the matter of when to abort, how to do it, and the implications of so doing.

At still other levels of functioning, the data are not incon-
sistent with the theme that completer group members attuned themselves
to one another more effectively than aborters. Use of their beds, in
terms of actual "time in bed" (a possible indicator of withdrawal) and
frequency of "on-off-bed" (a possible indicator of restlessness) were
measured on a 24-hour basis, in addition to the samples collected in
connection with social activity measures. The data indicated increasing restlessness by aborters, especially in the four-day condition, as
they approached their abort day, and generally higher levels of restlessness than completers. Completers gave a picture of paced and
steady bed behavior in the sense of low and level movements in and
out of bed throughout the isolation period. With respect to time in
bed, the data were less definitive but suggested a general trend for
aborters to spend more time in bed and to withdraw from one another.
When both types of bed usage data were pieced together, there emerged
several syndromes of bed oriented behavior by aborters. Those in the
20-day conditions who aborted appeared to show a withdrawal syndrome
--they went to bed and seemingly tried to "sleep the situation away",
with the consequence that they spent little time together early in the
situation and did not establish viable group functioning. The four-
day aborters had a different bed usage syndrome--they moved in and out
of the bed a great deal and were quite restless. While they interacted
a fair amount, one had the impression that it was not directed at adaptation to the situation, but was diffuse and sandwiched in between a
great deal of restless activity.

To move a bit closer to the attuning of members to one another
in aborter and completer groups, time in bed scores were correlated
for men within a dyad, as were on-off bed scores per 24-hour period.
The results were very clear. Successful groups had members whose bed
usage behavior was highly correlated. The level of restlessness for
completers was very similar for men in the same group, as was their
time in bed. The aborter group member behavior on these measures
showed either no correlation or negative correlations. That is,
amount of time on-off bed and time in bed by one man was not related
to that of the other man. Thus, they were not synchronized in terms
of these very simple ecological measures, findings which blend in with
their social activity patterns and territorial behaviors. They just
never "got going" as a team, except too late and then perhaps only for
the purpose of leaving the situation. As one final piece of documentation of this absence of an adaptive/coping syndrome by aborter groups,
it should be noted that they also performed least effectively as a
team on a periodically scheduled task, especially in the most difficult
and stressful 20-day private condition.

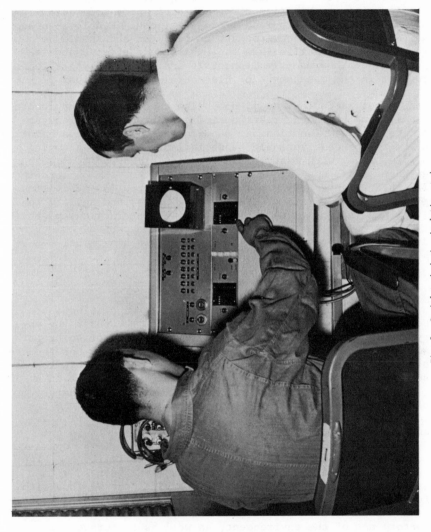

Fig. 2: Social task during isolation study

From these studies we see some of the elements of a behavioral syndrome, involving use of the environment which reflects the adaptive/non-adaptive nature of group formation and functioning. Furthermore, the data from these two social isolation studies illustrate how, although somewhat imperfectly, different levels of organismic functioning can be pieced together to yield an "ecological" viewpoint of human social behavior, i.e., subjective stress, use of space and the environment, task performance, interpersonal exchange, etc. Finally, these data illustrate how the man-environment complex can and should be viewed from a dual perspective--how the environment affects and impinges upon man, and how man simultaneously and inseparably acts upon the environment in the management of his social relationships.

Another group isolation study, now being conducted in our laboratories by Smith and Haythorn, takes a similarly broad ecological approach to interpersonal functioning. Environmental conditions being varied in the independent variable sense include degree of crowding and group size, along with interpersonal compatibility of team members. On the dependent side, use of the environment in the form of territorial behavior, bed oriented behavior, social and recreation activities are being observed, in addition to subjective stress and anxiety reactions, team and individual performance, social interaction and physiological indicators of stress. A new and unique aspect of this study, neglected in the earlier studies, is an interest in non-verbal behaviors such as use of the body, face, hands, etc..

GROUP INTERACTION STUDIES

With regard to active use of the environment, we distinguished earlier between anticipatory and reactive types of response. By anticipatory use of the environment we mean the pre-interaction or early stage of interaction arrangement of the environment, which has the effect of setting limits on and pre-structuring, to some extent, the nature of subsequent interaction. The arrangement of furniture in a living room, office or classroom, clearly has an impact on the nature of social interaction. But, as isolation studies demonstrate, the environment is also used in a "reactive" sense, as an interaction develops, and simultaneous with other modes of response. It is not easy to separate these orientations to the environment in an operational sense. In one respect the early high territoriality and high social activity of successful isolation groups might be seen either as reactive or as anticipatory use of their environment to cope with their situation, while their later behavior and that of the unsuccessful groups was clearly more reactive in character. To begin looking at anticipatory use of the environment, as well as to pursue the themes of multi-level processes occurring in social penetration, we conducted a series of laboratory experiments. The primary purpose of these studies was to examine verbal aspects of the social penetration process, but data were also collected relevant to the present discussion.

In the first experiment, Navy subjects talked with another man
about themselves over an intercom system (the other man was an experi-
menter confederate) [18,6]. The subjects believed they had been selected to take part in a future undersea exploration project and would
be teamed alone with the other man for either a long period of time
(six months) or for a short period (three weeks), after which they
could select another teammate to fill out a six-month tour. The purpose of the conversation was to allow team members to get to know one
another as much as they desired prior to the mission. To do this,
they were given sets of statements about various aspects of themselves
which had been scaled previously for intimacy of content. They were
free to select from this material and, therefore, could talk about
very personal or very superficial topics, could talk as long or as
little as they desired per item, and could select as many or as few
things to talk about as they wished. The confederate also talked
about himself, discussing the same topic as the subject and following
him each time. The confederate had pre-set responses to each item and,
by the content and tone of his remarks, created one of four interpersonal reward/cost or compatibility conditions: 1. <u>continuous positive.</u> The confederate approved and agreed with the subject's self-
description throughout four 45-minute interaction periods and tried
to indicate compatibility with the subject; 2. <u>later positive.</u> The
confederate initially reacted negatively to the subject's self-disclosure, but then switched to a favorable reaction (a bad first impression which was reversed); 3. <u>continuous negative.</u> The confederate
responded negatively to the subject and was incompatible during the
entire three hour session; 4. <u>later negative.</u> The confederate initially acted positively, but then switched and was unfavorable through
most of the session (a good first impression which proved to be incorrect).

As social penetration theory would predict, the more positive interpersonal experience, the more open were subjects to their teammates.
Those in the positive conditions generally spoke about more facets of
themselves, talked longer and about more intimate things compared with
those in unfavorable conditions. This was especially true of the continuous positive condition and somewhat less so for the later positive
condition. Consistent with the theme of this presentation, we were interested in going beyond verbal behavior and seeing how subjects would
use their environment in an <u>anticipatory</u> fashion to cope with a relationship which had been established during the three hour conversation.
After the discussion, subjects were asked to indicate their preference
for three types of architectural plans of their two-compartment, undersea capsule, i.e., which they thought would be best for their team.
One plan was a "separate territorial" arrangement, in which each man's
bed and equipment was in a separate compartment connected by a door.
The second plan was a "joint territorial" arrangement, in which men
lived together in one room and worked in the other room, with a lay-
out of furniture and equipment clearly indicating which side of the
room belonged to each man. The third arrangement was a "joint random"

plan, with the men living in one room but with the furniture, equipment and facilities of both men intermingled. Here neither man had
an area of the room clearly demarcated as his own.

Hardly any subjects preferred the joint random arrangement, perhaps not surprising since most people probably desire living areas
identified as their own. Those who experienced a positive relationship with the confederate chose to live in the joint territorial arrangement, while those in the incompatible situation wanted to live
apart. However, the live-together design preference held only for
those who had a continuously positive experience, suggesting that any
degree of negative relationship, regardless of how much or how little,
was associated with a preference not to live together. This is especially interesting in view of the additional fact that the later positive subjects reported "liking" the confederate as much as the continuous positive ones, yet were unwilling to translate this into a
sharing of the environment in a relatively intimate way. Thus, subjects seemed to have integrated their conversational experiences into
a general affective judgment about the other person and then projected
this upon the environment in an anticipatory way which they felt would
assist or be in accord with the demands of the situation. Thus, continuously "good" experiences yielded a profile of verbal openness, a
positive affective state and a willingness to embed the relationship
in an intimate environment. Predominantly favorable experiences
yielded a somewhat less unrestricted interpersonal coping response.
There was verbal accessibility of the self to the other person, as
well as a positive affective feeling, but there was also some reluc-
tance to embed the relationship in a close environment. Perhaps the
early negative experience made the multi-faceted commitment to the
other person less reasonable.

These results focus only on that part of the study which dealt
with anticipatory use of the environment in the dependent variable
sense. Recall that subjects also had different expectations about
how committed they were to the other man--six months vs. three weeks--
which represents an independent variation in their restriction to the
environment with the other person. Everything described above regarding architectural design preferences held only for the short-term condition, with no differences where they perceived a long-term tie and
commitment to their partner. We have just replicated these findings
in another study and are convinced of their reliability. It may be
that it was easier to commit to or withdraw from another man in a
short-term situation, but that a long-term one created certain ambiva-
lences--liking another man and wanting to be close to him, but recognizing privacy needs during a six-month period vs. not liking another
man and desiring to be physically separated, but also realizing him to
be the only source of human stimulation. We do not yet have data to
untangle this web of possibilities, but the results illustrate again
how the environment, in a broad sense, is both a determinant of behavior and a mode of behavior. In accord with the other facet of our

ecologically oriented thesis, we are trying to see how different levels of functioning--verbal, affective and environmental--may explain the curious reaction to the long-term situation. It is too early to be firm, but it appears that long-commitment subjects, who chose separate territorial arrangements and who were in negative compatibility conditions, tended to have a verbal behavior pattern of openness to the other man, while those who chose to live together had a reticent verbal pattern, suggesting different strategies for dealing with a difficult situation. One strategy was to stay away from the other man but to talk a lot; another strategy was to stay in close physical proximity but to withdraw verbally.

Page corroborated these general findings in a study using a similar paradigm involving college students, who indicated architectural design preferences for two and three-man rooms following a roughly comparable period of discussion [16]. In this study, architectural plans were developed which systematically differentiated between alone and together arrangements for living and study functions. Thus, there were four combinations of room layouts: study together-live together, study apart-live together, study together-live apart and study apart-live apart. In general, most subjects desired joint living roommate arrangements in two-man groups and separate living arrangements in three-man groups. However, they were distinguished in terms of differential preferences for study arrangements as a function of compatibility. Those in positive interpersonal conditions preferred plans involving joint study arrangements, those in negative groups desired separate study plans. Again, any degree of negative experience, however temporary, led to preferences to remain apart, in spite of general verbal openness and positive affective feelings toward the other person.

DISCUSSION

We have described a series of empirical studies which bear on our general thesis concerning an ecological approach to interpersonal relationships. Admittedly, these studies are rather crude and have not intensively followed a single line of investigation. But they reinforce us to pursue the matter further and to search for a holistic approach to human social behavior. Human interpersonal functioning, to reiterate our earlier theme, occurs as a "system" with many levels or modes of behavior. A person does more than speak with another person--he has subjective covert feelings, he moves about in space and uses his body to communicate. While any single piece of research necessarily emphasizes only a few facets of behavior, we must not forget, in practice as well as in dicta, that man is a multi-modal, multi-faceted organism. To be sure, the research reported here has paid the price of superficiality for the presumed gain of breadth of examination, but that is a personal preference and is hopefully not a permanent state of affairs. The problem with seeking a multi-level approach to interpersonal behavior is that a vast array of knowledge collected in disparate fields and a vast technology appropriate to each field must be

integrated and learned. Even in the area of "man's use of space" we
are rapidly accumulating a large body of information concerning per-
sonal-social distance, territorial behavior, seating habits, positions,
and arrangements, use of various areas [17,4,10]. There is also a
vast array of research and thinking regarding the use of "self-markers"
or non-verbal communication (body positions, gestures, facial expressions and general use of the body) which is relevant to the development
and dissolution of interpersonal relationships [7,11]. Incidentally,
none of the studies reported here have as yet focused on this non-
verbal level of functioning. In many respects, our own perspective
is still too narrow and violates the principle of the "wholeness" of
man, although we plan to undertake such studies in the future.

At a less philosophical level, and more pointed to man's relationship with his physical environment as he engages in interpersonal relationships with others, we see our research as demonstrating the two-
way relationship between man and his environment--it acts upon him and
he acts upon it. Neither is more important, but, until recently, social psychologists concerned with interpersonal relationships seemed
to focus more upon the environment as determinant. Our isolation work,
and that of many others in other areas, clearly indicates the role of
the physical environment as an important press on interpersonal behavior. But a theme developed here is that we must continue the study of
man's shaping and use of the environment as he copes with it and with
other people. In many respects, this issue is merely a revival of the
older philosophical views of man as a "responder to" vs. man as a self-
propelled "active-on organism" [8], e.g., the Lockean vs. the Leibnitz-
ian viewpoint, or the behavioristic vs. the existential tradition.

Within the active use of the environment aspect of the issue, our
data also lead us to see some value in the heuristic distinction between use of the environment in a reactive vs. anticipatory fashion,
which may be analogous to the difference between anticipatory marking
of a territory by an animal and subsequent defensive responses to intruders. Admittedly, this distinction is not always easy to make, especially during the initial stages of social interaction, where actors
are reacting to immediately occurring events and also pre-structuring
future interactions by use of their environment. But if human use of
space and environment has a significant anticipatory component to it,
and we think it does, then studying reactive use of the environment is
too restricted, and vice-versa.

The goals set forth in this paper are obviously not easy to
achieve. But a multi-level approach to social behavior and the recognition of man's mutual relationship with his environment has research
importance, for it seems to be the only way to approach our personal
aspiration of understanding "whole man" and his interpersonal bonds
with other "whole men".

REFERENCES

1. Altman, I. and Haythorn, W.W.: Interpersonal exchange in isola-
        tion. Sociometry, 23:411-426, 1965.
2. _____ and _____: The ecology of isolated groups.
        Behav. Sci., 12:169-182, 1967.
3. _____ and _____: Effects of social isolation and
        group composition on performance. Hum. Relations,
        20:313-340, 1967.
4. _____ and Lett, E.E.: The ecology of interpersonal relation-
        ships: A classification system and conceptual model. In
        McGrath, J.E., ed., Social and Psychological Factors in
        Stress. Holt, Rinehart and Winston, New York, in press.
5. _____ and Taylor, D.A.: Disclosure as a measure of social
        penetration. Paper presented at a symposium on Self-
        disclosure and the Inter-personal Relationship. American
        Psychological Association, San Francisco, California,
        September, 1968.
6. _____, _____ and Sorrentino, R.: Ecological impli-
        cations of inter-personal compatibility and incompatibil-
        ity. 1968, mimeo.
7. Argyle, M. and Kendon, A.: The experimental analysis of social
        performance. In Berkowitz, L., ed., Advances in Experi-
        mental Social Psychology. Academic Press, New York, 1967.
8. Coan, R.W.: Dimensions of psychological theory. Amer. Psychol.,
        23:715-723, 1968.
9. Cole, J., Machir, D., Altman, I., Haythorn, W.W. and Wagner, C.M.:
        Perceptual changes in social isolation. J. Clin. Psychol.,
        23:330-333, 1967.
10. Craik, K.: Environmental psychology. In Newcomb, T. and Farbin, T.,
        eds., New Directions in Psychology. Holt, Rinehart and
        Winston, New York, in press.
11. Ekman, P. and Friesen, W.V.: Origin, usage and coding: The basis
        for five categories of nonverbal behavior. Paper pre-
        sented at symposium: Communication Theory and Linguistic
        Models in the Social Sciences. Torquato Di Tella Insti-
        tute, Buenos Aires, Argentina, October, 1967.
12. Hall, E.T.: The Hidden Dimension. Doubleday, New York, 1966.
13. Haythorn, W.W. and Altman, I.: Personality factors in isolated
        environments. In Appley, M. and Trumbull, R., eds.,
        Psychological Stress. Appleton-Century-Crofts, New York,
        1967.
14. _____ and _____: Together in isolation. Transaction,
        4:18-22, 1967.
15. _____, _____ and Myers, T.I.: Emotional symptoma-
        tology and subjective stress in isolated pairs of men.
        J. Exp. Res. Personality, 1:290-306, 1966.
16. Page, J.: Social Penetration Processes: The Effects of Interper-
        sonal Reward and Cost Factors on the Stability of Dyadic
        Relationships. The American University, Washington, D.C.,
        Doctoral Dissertation, 1968, unpublished.

17. Sommer, R.: Small group ecology. <u>Psychol. Bull.</u>, 67:145-152,
        1967.
18. Taylor, D.A., Altman, I. and Sorrentino, R.: Interpersonal ex-
        change as a function of rewards and costs and situational
        factors: Expectancy confirmation-disconfirmation. <u>J. Exp.</u>
        <u>Soc. Psychol.</u>, 5:324-339, 1969.
19. _____, _____, Wheeler, L. and Kushner, E.: Personality
        factors related to response to social isolation and con-
        finement. <u>J. Consult. Clin. Psychol.</u>, 33:411-419, 1969.
20. _____, Wheeler, L. and Altman, I.: Stress reactions in
        socially isolated groups. <u>J. Personality Soc. Psychol.</u>,
        9:369-376, 1968.

Prepared Contributions for Discussion of Session V: Communal Behavior and the Environment

SIGNIFICANCE OF THE IPSEFACT: IN ECOLOGY, ETHOLOGY,
PARASITOLOGY, SOCIOLOGY, AND ANTHROPOLOGY

J. R. Audy

The ipsefact ("made by oneself," my term for "specific artifact"
(1;2, p.23)) of an individual, colony, population, or species of an
animal is the manifold unit of environment that it has modified
chemically or physically by its own behavior. Ipsefact may also
loosely refer to a single item so modified, such as a nest, a scent-
mark, or exhaled CO_2. Ipsefacts may be long-lasting or ephemeral,
elaborate or simple, regularly or unevenly distributed, unique to an
individual or partly shared. An ipsefact is specifically a product
of behavior and not merely something used or lived with. The term
is needed to refer to, and to think in terms of, units of modified
environment, whether as bricks of the ecosystem, or as specific sets
of factors to which other organisms will adapt and evolve a relationship, or as "crystallized behavior," or as a manufactured microhabi-
tat--just as, for other purposes of discussion and thinking, it may
be necessary to use one of several terms that overlap with each other
and with ipsefact but do not coincide (for example, home range, territory, Umwelt, or E. T. Hall's extensions.(3))

The living unit or animal is what Pavlovsky calls "organism-as-
habitat," (4) but to this we should add its carcass to make one
space-time unit, plus a second unit, its ipsefact, formed and con-
tributed to the ecosystem by the animal, usually in a highly characteristic way. The two units provide many more or less specific
"potential" niches which other organisms will adopt, followed by
niche-adaptation and niche-differentiation; this is the process of
developing the various forms of symbiosis, including parasitism in
the host or commensalism in its ipsefact. Recognition of the ipsefact improves our understanding of symbiosis (for example, a gall or
cecidium is a special type of domiciliary ipsefact formed by a host
in response to a specific chemical ipsefact produced by the parasite).

The larger and more structurally and behaviorally complex an organism, and the more elaborate its ipsefact, the more it will create potential niches that become adopted, adapted to, and differentiated by other organisms. This is one of the chief ways in which ecosystems evolve in complexity.

The behavior that produces an ipsefact is genetically controlled in animals and largely culturally controlled (hence also considerably inherited) in man. Ipsefacts may therefore be used as indicators of phylogeny (for example, evolution of termitaria), cultural evolution, or even individual derangement (for example, nest-making or schizophrenic art). Ipsefacts are to varying degrees parts of the extended organism, for example, when sexual selection is concentrated on the ipsefact, as on the bowers of male bowerbirds. Thus selection may become transferred from morphological characters of the bird to its ipsefact, the decorated bower.

Human ipsefacts have several peculiarities. One is the extension or prosthesis, including the artificial limb and, less obviously, the automobile, crane, factory, and computer. Another is man's dependence on "skilled workers" to build the human nests, burrow-systems, and runways that make his ipsefact, rather than on his own teeth and claws, as in animals. Demands set by people and fashions adopted by builders are decided by complex and ever-changing social, economic, and technical factors. These are frequently whimsical and may be unconcerned with human welfare. Changing societies inherit outmoded but solid urban ipsefacts; and the microhabitats may be unsuited to human efficiency, especially since there is constant feedback between ipsefact and man. Personally modifying one's own habitat is an act of creation that makes some ipsefacts parts of one's personality; loss of an ipsefact may be as serious as loss of a prosthesis or a loved one. Also, a human group does not function meaningfully unless it achieves some "group identity," being socially integrated by shared activities and the group possessions comprising the collective and individual ipsefacts. Parts of man's ipsefacts may achieve symbolic importance out of all proportion to their size, complexity, or relevance to the functioning of the urban ecosystem. Finally, man alone among animals is tending to replace internally coherent natural ecosystems with collective ipsefacts-- the urban and rural human ecosystems. These lack the long-standing internal genetic adaptation and structure that make for stability and self-sufficiency.

REFERENCES

1. Audy, J.R.: The environment in human ecology: Artifacts --
            the significance of modified environment. In Environ-
            mental Determinants of Community Well-Being. World
            Health Organization, Sci. Pub. No. 123, 1965.
2. _____: Red Mites and Typhus. Heath Clark Lectures.
            University of London (1965). Oxford University Press,
            New York, 1968.

3. Hall, E.T.: <u>The Hidden Dimension</u>. Doubleday, New York, 1966.
4. Pavlovsky, E.N.: Organism kak sreda obitaniya. Priroda 1.
                 (Also in Pavlocsky's textbook, <u>Laboratornyi Praktitum</u>
                 <u>Meditsinskaya Parasitologii</u>, Medgiz, Leningrad, 1959)
                 ("Organisms as habitat"). 1934.

COMMUNITY CONTROL OVER SPACE AND POPULATION

G. Morgan

"Unlike man, most animals maintain fairly constant population levels" - So runs the subtitle of an article by V. C. Wynne-Edwards, who concluded "Primitive man, . . . had evolved a system for restricting his numbers by tribal traditions and taboos . . . These customs, consciously or not, kept the population density nicely balanced against the feeding capacity of the hunting range. Then, some 8,000 to 10,000 years ago the agricultural revolution removed that limitation . . . The old checks on population growth were gradually discarded and forgotten. The rate of reproduction became a matter of individual choice rather than of tribal or community control." (5)

Such references to effective population controls having existed among human societies is the exception rather than the rule in current literature. However, extensive and detailed documentation on the subject has been available since the early twenties, proving that most human societies until a few centuries ago had strong controls over population growth. The prominent English sociologist A. M. Carr-Saunders, in his book <u>Population Problems</u>, massed detailed evidence of population controls prevailing until a few hundred years ago widely over the world. (1) The uncontrolled population growth at the time of Malthus and since the second world war seemed to prove Carr-Saunders wrong in his assumption that human populations tended to reach an optimum balance with their resources. Consequently Carr-Saunders' work has been relegated to the realm of <u>theory</u>, and his factual determinations have been forgotten.

He pointed out and illustrated the role of <u>misery</u> and <u>demoralization</u> causing the breakdown of standards such as population control; for uncontrolled drives tend to take over when the larger social order of family and community break down. I think that a factor related to this must be given particular attention: past societies with effective population controls existed each with its limited boundaries of space, each with its <u>economy</u>, which included not only natural resources but the population that had to be related to them. Each society, community and family had the memory or traditional experience of famine, with the need to relate population to limited resources. This is the basic response to population problems that society on a world scale is now having to make. Reduction of mortality from infections, diseases and improved food production and

distribution have stimulated the world-wide population increase,
but the loss of the community's responsibility for its own economy
and population has largely eliminated past social controls over
population.   Can we still have the benefit of local controls while
living in the larger world order?

A close examination of the process that caused the breakdown
of the local economy and controls of the past suggests an important
part of the answer to this question.   According to the <u>Newsletter</u>
of the Institute of Ethnic Affairs (Washington, D.C., Nov. 1948):

"A world-wide urgent problem is that of the rural local com-
munity--the village community--in the modern world.

Can it become once more, what it was for aeons, the richly
nourishing home of its members . . . while also uniting its members
with the nation and the world?

Dutch administrators and scholars have thought long and deeply
upon this question.   They generally conclude that when money economy
enters the village community, the genius of the community starts to
die.   The complexly organic unity falls apart, intra-village rivalry
takes the place of mutual aid, social value perishes."

Capitalist economy displaces the local economy largely because
of a little recognized characteristic of the conventional monetary
system: our money serves both as a medium of exchange and as a
store of wealth.   In the latter case:

"Money in its role as a store of wealth stands as a barrier
to full production, that is, unemployment is caused by money."(3)

But there have been effective monetary systems that have had
fundamentally different characteristics and effects; such a monetary
system prevailed for more than two hundred years in Medieval Europe.
This was a time of rapid technological advance, commercial prosperity,
full employment and of prosperous small cities predominantly less
than eight thousand in population.   Carr-Saunders gives detailed documented accounts of the way population controls worked during this
era among people of town and country.   There was not unemployment in
the midst of wealth, and so there was not the demoralization and
division of the community that leads to breakdown of morale.   And
the monetary system strengthened rather than destroyed the local
and regional economy, while stimulating trade between regions.

The distinctive feature of the monetary system during this
crucial period of European history was the "seigniorage" tax on
money, making it unfeasible to use money as a store of wealth.
After this tax was discontinued, economic depression and unemployment set in over Europe, and the ensuing misery led to the peasants

rebellions in Germany and England, widespread breakdown of the
traditional small communities, the displacement of rural people to
the cities, and simultaneously the breakdown of the traditional
population controls (2).

Recent experimental use of such a taxed currency in communities has similarly achieved full employment out of drastic unemployment. I suggest that today, as in similar times in Greece,
Rome and England, money scarcity and consequent unemployment in the
smaller communities away from the metropolis forces the migration
into our large cities. (4)

REFERENCES

1. Carr-Saunders, A.M.: Population Problems. Clarenden Press,
          Oxford, 1922.

2. Dahlberg, A.O.: Money in Motion. John DeGraff, Tuckahoe,
          New York, 1962.
3. Dillard, D.: The theory of monetary economy. In Kurahara (ed),
          Post Keynesian Economics, Rutgers U. Press, New
          Brunswick, 1951.
4. Morgan, G.: The Community Need for an Economy. Community
          Service, Inc., Yellow Springs, Ohio. [n.d.]
5. Wynne-Edwards, V.C.: Population controls in animals. Sci.
          Amer. 211: 68-74, 1964.

Discussion of Session V:
Communal Behavior and
the Environment

PANEL: D. Lowenthal (Chairman), J. B. Calhoun,
K. H. Craik, J. M. Fitch, U. Olin,
R. G. Studer, et al.

Lowenthal (Chairman):

The special theme of this session, the extension of insights
and concepts from the realm of animal studies to the world of man,
has elsewhere elicited some criticism as a simplistic overreaction
to anthropomorphism. "Scarcely had ethologists finished shaking
their fingers at sentimentalists who spoke of animals as though they
were men," writes one critic, "when they themselves set to work to
prove that men were animals. Zoomorphism became rife." [2] And
zoomorphologists tend to cast a bleak eye on man; whenever humans
are shown to differ from animals, the results are viewed as ecologically deplorable. Thus man, unlike animals, has no built-in mechanism to prevent his population from rising to the level of starvation, as Wynne-Edwards has just reminded us; and man's degradation
of the environment is not corrigible by ordinary ecological constraints.

The papers and discussions of these past few days amply demonstrate, however, that we have little to fear from zoomorphism. In
the first place, all human observers remain inevitably anthropomor-
phic, however great their dedication to other species may be. When
Lorenz writes that the loud laughter "of two reunited human beings
must inevitably remind an objective behavior investigator of the
triumph ceremony of greylag geese," [5] it is clear that he is interpreting greylag geese in human terms. We inevitably view all
life from a human point of view.

In the second place, whenever observers of human societies and
cultures are tempted to generalize excessively from animal analogies,
they will be speedily and definitively corrected. Ethologists have

312

not hesitated, here, to underscore critical distinctions between
man and other species in terms of types of inheritance (genetic and
cultural), degrees of imprinting, and so forth. Let us hope that
anthropologists and historians will supply similar corrections when
social psychologists and social scientists speculate about the universality of human behavior with inadequate understanding of group
differences and cultural inheritance.

So much for the risks of comparison. The virtues of comparison illustrated in this session are manifold. To begin with, men
are animals, not only in terms of their physical nature, but of many
aspects of individual and group behavior and needs, of culture, and
of social organization. Secondly, an understanding of man's development from pre-human conditions is essential if we are to know what
man is like today. Evolutionary change must be examined both in
physiological and in psychological terms. Consider the transition
from hunting and gathering through agriculture to technological civilization: how far have genetic inheritance and sociocultural form
kept up with these ecological and economic transformation? How significant is the role of atavism and memory in contemporary behavior?
To what extent is man physiologically adapted to cope with change
from generation to generation, even from decade to decade? Historical demography illumines one such transformation: only within the
past half-century has increasing length of life made the three-gener-
ation family the rule rather than the exception in Western Europe
and North America. In the past, as in the rest of the world to this
day, people rarely knew their grandparents; and grandparents rarely
survived into a world so utterly unlike that in which they grew up,
for which they were educated, and to which they had adjusted. In
this sense, at least, the generation gap is a relatively new and
wholly unsolved problem [4].

It is the speculative analogies between animal and human life,
rather than any precise similarities, that yield the most fruitful
benefits. These past few days we have all been stirred again and
again to wonder, to consider exceptions, to inquire whether comparisons were real or symbolic, to make extensions and linkages with our
own research. Consider a theme common to all three papers in this
session: the way social structure alters the perception and use of
space and, more specifically, the relations between density and
crowding and territoriality and dominance. The historical evidence
is abundant, but raises questions as to the universality of the patterns, and sometimes suggests alternative explanations. Hierarchical organization in animal species permits closer packing than an
egalitarian system, as Sommer reminds us. And the historian recalls
the post-medieval European transition from a densely-structured,
avowedly hierarchical society where rank was seldom in doubt, to a
demand for privacy along with an uneasy acceptance of egalitarian
principles, where doubts about rank reinforced distance between master and servant.

Prior to the 18th century, ladies and maids not only traveled
in the same coaches but shared the same table, even the same bed
and chamber-pot, a degree of propinquity comfortable because status
between them was as clear as peck-order in a hencoop.

Altman's experimental work with enlisted naval personnel, simu-
lating conditions on submarines and spacecraft, shows that a clear
sense of rank and dominance is essential for any prolonged experience
of isolation and crowding. The risks of competition are grave, even
among highly motivated scientists; emerging after several months of
voluntary confinement, a group of Russian scientists have warned that
men living at close quarters must not play competitive games because
of the traumas of victory and defeat.

Sommer noted that a stratified society reduces the likelihood
of conflict; people who know their places can coexist peaceably even
in confined areas. Does this proposition hold true, however, where
the hierarchical order is not accepted at all levels of the hierarchy? Few slaves, for example, believe slavery benefits, and they
subvert or seek to overthrow the system whenever they can. Hierarchical structures are socially and individually beneficent only when
there is general social consensus.

Spacing and social stratification among animals and humans alike
depend on the extent to which groups use up available resources.
Americans are colonizers by tradition, and the frontier spirit is
still our heritage; we brook few restraints on elbow room, on freedom
to move about. As a people imbued with egalitarian principles, we
seem to require more space, both physical and social, than those pre-
disposed to a stratified order. Yet even Americans unhesitatingly
socialize on a hierarchical basis. This is well brought out in Sommer's description of academic coffee groups. The tendency to association by rank is, as one might expect, even greater in English universities. A colleague who recently took up a professional chair at
Cambridge discovered no fewer than five separate tea cliques in his
department, adherence depending on departmental status, college membership, university background and seniority. To promote unity the
chairman persuaded everyone to drink tea together, but the conversational groups in the joint tea-room remain as stratified as before.

Territorial location as a force in social life may retain symbolic value long after it has lost practical significance. Vassar
College was formerly an exclusive women's college where admission
was closely allied to birth and social status, but is now strictly
on the basis of merit. Yet elite graduates continue to register
their daughters at birth. This does not enchance their chances for
admission, but for those who do get in, priority of registration is
said to govern choice of dormitory rooms.

The primacy of group over individual values, so well documented by Wynne-Edwards for animal species and earlier shown by Carr-Saunders to be characteristic of primitive man, is a homeostatic instinct lost by more advanced human groups. Yet, Wynne-Edwards points out, all viable social groups <u>need</u> leaders and followers, "people who can do what they are told, and people who can tell us what to do." Such a society was taken for granted throughout the Middle Ages; it is documented as a philosophy and an ecological system in A.O. Lovejoy's <u>Great Chain of Being</u> [6]. The scientific discoveries and social changes of the Renaissance caused that stratified order to crumble, leaving in its wake a sense of desolation at the overthrow of established values best expressed in Donne's famous poem, at once a lament for the older physical verities and for the stratified order of his childhood. Relations between master and servant, father and son, teacher and pupil were now things forgot;

> None confess that this world's spent
> When in the planets and the firmament
> They seek so many new
> 'Tis all in pieces, all coherence gone
> All just supply and all relation

These and other nostalgic relics of stratified society infuse our historical understanding. Egalitarian precepts notwithstanding, there remains a deep conviction that the hierarchical order is appropriate, natural, innate.

Group survival and homeostasis as opposed to individual motivation are exemplified within certain religious sects that stress communal values. Among the Hutterites and Mennonites, for example, group discipline submerges virtually all individuality and private ambition. As a consequence, these groups have exhibited the world's highest rates of natural increase. Instead of promoting territorial aggrandizement, however, this unparalleled increase arouses the hostility of fearful neighbors, leading to persecution and often to territorial restriction. Such an increase is not even evidence of true ecological success. Homeostasis would not involve enormous population increase but a leveling off, as with animal species in equilibrium with their resources. Among Mennonites and Hutterites, moreover, group loyalty and the submergence of individuality inevitably leads to a loss of inventiveness, and of ability to meet new problems or perils that natural or social change might occasion. As Bates remarks of small societies in general, the pressures for conformity needed to ensure community stability and survival are often stultifying [1].

The opposition of group to individual values, and the need for homeostatic equilibrium such as Wynne-Edwards describes, is eloquently stated by Hardin. Following the argument employed by William Lloyd in 1833, Hardin notes that each rational herdsman who shares a grazing common with others will rationally seek to maximize his own gain.

Overgrazing becomes inevitable, even when the common is grazed to
its carrying capacity, because the fractional cost to any individual
of adding one more animal is less than his gain; the gain is his
alone, the loss is shared among all his fellows:

> "The rational herdsman concludes that the only sensible
> course for him to pursue is to add another animal to
> his herd. And another; and another..." "But this is
> the conclusion reached by each and every rational herds-
> man sharing a commons. The rein is the tragedy. Each
> man is locked into a system that compels him to increase
> his herd without limit - in a world that is limited.
> Ruin is the destination toward which all men rush, each
> pursuing his own best interest in a society that believes
> in the freedom of the commons. Freedom in a commons
> brings ruin to all." [3, p.1244]

We have solved this problem by abolishing the commons in favor
of private property, under which self-interest usually persuades
each landowner to maintain his terrain in the best ecological health,
assuring him the highest long-term benefits. But private property
is helpless when the problem is pollution:

> "Here it is not a question of taking something out of
> the commons, but of putting something in - sewage, or
> chemical, radioactive, and heat wastes into water;
> noxious and dangerous fumes into the air; and distract-
> ing and unpleasant advertising signs into the line of
> sight. The calculations of utility are much the same
> as before. The rational man finds that his share of
> the cost of the wastes he discharges into the commons
> is less than the cost of purifying his wastes before
> releasing them. Since this is true for everyone, we
> are locked into a system of 'fouling our own nest', so
> long as we behave only as independent, rational, free-
> enterprisers. The tragedy of the commons as a food-
> basket is averted by private property..." "But the
> air and waters surrounding us cannot readily be fenced,
> and so the tragedy of the commons as a cesspool must
> be prevented by different means, by coercive laws, or
> taxing devices." [3, p.1245]

Unlike Wynne-Edwards, Hardin discounts altruism or conscience
as pathogenic, and assumes social coercion is essential. But people
only willingly relinquish freedom, as I mentioned before, when they
believe the social consensus is ultimately fair and also that it en-
sures their well-being. What Wynne-Edwards describes as "willingness"
to comply with the social system" may apply in small groups that have
built up durable systems of social relations and values over many
generations. But, it is conspicuously absent in modern mass societies

with freedom of migration.

Stress under crowding is something man, unlike other species, can avoid by creating a multiplicity of occupational niches. At any given time and for any given purpose, we interact only with select individuals, ignoring all other people we may chance to meet. Typically, we move from the small world of our home to the small world of our office or workplace, seeing many people en route with whom we do not interact in any meaningful way.

Let us explore the significance of this behavior in the light of the insights provided by Fischer and by Wynne-Edwards. Is it possible or plausible that interactions with strangers do not provoke anxiety? Are we able to move in free anonymity in our great cities? What environmental role do we assign to those whom we see – or sometimes bump against – without knowing as individuals or caring to place in our social network? Since we tolerate slum conditions on trips between home and office, we seem to identify folk met en route as non-people, just as Sommer's college students viewed janitors. To us they are almost members of another species. This perspective ultimately extends to all non-intimate urban relationships. We end up by divesting ourselves of responsibility for whatever happens to these non-persons even if they live in the same building: witness the Kitty Genovese affair. Failure to come to her aid has been condemned as apathy or irresponsibility, but it would in fact be impossible for any individual in his private capacity to take on all individuals encountered – much less seen or heard – in the urban milieu. Just as we must screen out the vast majority of sensory inputs we receive in order to make sense of the vital fraction that we need to live with, so we must slough off non-intimate relationships in order to give intimacy the attention and energy it requires.

Relational overload is a root cause of the "indifference" that seems so shocking to the poor, the black and the young, whose deprivations or inexperience do not enable them to make (or reward them for) ready distinctions between structured and essential, and unstructured or accidental, environmental interactions. To combat the distinction (which usually operates to their disadvantage), they sensibly emphasize "confrontation" – that is, direct physical and emotional involvement, bringing themselves to our attention as individuals so that we can no longer lose sight of them as categories. And it is by evoking our hostility, even more effectively than by winning our sympathy, that they succeed in shattering our ability to differentiate familiar from unfamiliar places and faces. At the extreme, they may make our trips through space and through time more hazardous than those described by Fischer for animals, requiring us to be always on our conscious guard against assaults at whose motivations we cannot guess.

Imagine a person afraid of being mugged on a city street. If the street is empty, he will take such precautions as keeping under cover, moving rapidly, avoiding long stretches of open space, suggesting that the presence of other people is desirable, either as a deterrent to would-be assailants or, perhaps, because he imagines they might come to his aid in the event of attack. If the street is thronged and he _is_ attacked, he will be shocked if others fail to come to his aid. Yet he himself ordinarily regards others on the street as non-people. The need to transform them into people in times of crisis, and the ensuing doubt as to how really to regard them at all, is part of the schizophrenia that characterizes urban life in the absence of strong neighborhood and community ties.

REFERENCES

1. Bates, M.: Crowded people. Natur. Hist., October, 1968.
2. Ellis, M.F.: The naked ape crisis. New Yorker, March 23, 1968.
3. Hardin, G.: The tragedy of the commons. Science, 162:1243-
        1248, 1968.
4. Laslett, P.: The World We Have Lost. Scribner, New York, 1966.
5. Lorenz, K.: On Aggression. Harcourt, Brace and World, New
        York, 1966.
6. Lovejoy, A.O.: Great Chain of Being. Harper Row, New York,
        1960.

Olin:

Population pressure or crowding has been a recurring phenomenon in human history. At the moment it is commonly depicted as mankind's Number One problem.

As pointed out earlier during the Symposium, it is not primarily numbers as such that constitute a problem, but the effect of crowding on our behavior. Crowding or population pressure is, typically, the result of increases in the carrying capacity of our environment, brought about by innovations in production methods. Through its direct and indirect effects, such changes are likely to lead to increased population growth. Direct effects include improvements in morbidity and mortality conditions. Indirect effects are largely the results of accompanying changes in the system of social organization. The latter appear, typically, to be the result of an intensification of the social competition, which, among other things, improves the chances of advancement of some, hits hard those incapable of adjustment, and, in general, tends to increase expectations.

As a result, and simultaneous with increases in the gross national product, various population groups gradually find themselves only partly or marginally integrated into the social machinery. This, in turn, leads to nervous stress and tension, roughly proportional to the lack of participation in the social game. Such a state of af-

fairs appears to an increasing extent to characterize the developing
countries, all of which experience rapid economic and social change
along the lines indicated.

What does this mean in terms of behavior? It would seem to indicate that growing segments of the population may be expected to
display a behavior pattern that is consonant with chronic stress and
nervous tension. In individual behavior we know that this tends to
lead to a simplified or primitive reaction pattern, characterized
by increased motor activity as a means of release of tension. If
large groups of a population are known to live under conditions of
chronic stress, there would seem to be reason to believe that the
same thing is likely to happen on a large scale. This type of reaction may therefore be assumed to be the underlying reason for the
growing incidence of social unrest, accompanied by violence, that
seems to be occurring the world over. As the pace of industrial-
urban development increases, the potential for violent social disturbances appears likely to increase. This is particularly true in
the developing countries, although the problem is certainly not limited to these.

If this hypothesis is correct, the risk of violent social disruption would seem to constitute an environmental problem which de-
serves far more attention than has been paid so far. Personally, I
can think of only one way of coping with it, and that is through the
creation of meaningful employment for the increasing flow of rural-
urban migrants. Within this group, the educated young men would seem
to deserve primary attention by virtue of their potential for future
leadership - for better or for worse, depending on the conditions
with which they are confronted. This problem would seem to be no
less challenging and important than that of family planning.

As the question has been raised by Wynne-Edwards during this
session, I would in conclusion also like to add that I consider my
interpretation of the pattern and function of social competition under population pressure to be in line with his hypothesis of social
competition as the behavioral mechanism responsible for "internal"
population control in the animal kingdom in general. My main in-
spiration in arriving at this interpretation has been his major work
[2], and I hope some day to be able to persuade him of the validity
of this extension of his ideas. In brief, the main differences between animal and human behavior would appear to stem from the human
ability to radically and continuously alter environmental conditions,
thereby often preventing the creation of stable social conditions.
What appears to happen is that mechanisms responsible for maintaining relative or dynamic stability in numbers do not have time to
fully assert themselves, until further adjustments to new environmental changes become called for, and so forth and so on. This
would not seem to preclude the hypothesis that, in principle, similar regulatory mechanisms exist. In fact, there are strong arguments

favoring such a hypothesis [1].

REFERENCES

1. Olin, U.: Feedback mechanisms in human populations. Presented
              at the Symposium on Population Control, Annual Meeting
              of the American Association for the Advancement of
              Science, Washington, D.C., 1966.
2. Wynne-Edwards, V.C.: Animal Dispersion in Relation to Social
              Behaviour. Oliver & Boyd, Edinburgh, 1962.

Craik:

     Zoological methods and concepts have contributed importantly
to the identification of spatial attributes of human behavior. In
seeking to understand organisms capable of sitting and talking, the
student of human behavior is usefully reminded that the spatial aspects of persons' activities can be directly observed, tracked, and
recorded relatively unobtrusively in the field [3]. Unlike the ecological studies of sociology and geography, but like those of zoology, the research reported by Altman and Sommer deals with the spatial
and temporal distribution of the ongoing activities of individual organisms, alone or in groups. The data yielded by observational
studies can be analyzed in terms of the spatial properties of activities, the behavioral character of places, and the locational behavior
of individuals [6].

     A varied, and still growing, taxonomy of locational behaviors
of the individual is emerging. His range refers to the areal extent
of his activities or the likelihood of his being at a given location,
while his exclusive range refers to that portion which does not overlap with the range of other individuals. In these definitions, 'location at' can entail 'use of.' If the individual shows certain behaviors with reference to an exclusive range, such as personalizing
or defending it, the exclusive range is considered his territory.
In addition, relative locational behaviors can be studied. In Chapin
and Hightower's research, the locations of a household's out-of-the
house activities (e.g., socializing, shopping, working) are considered in reference to the location of the home [4,5]. In the research
by Hall [9,10], Sommer [13], Little [11] and others on mutual locational behaviors, the reference points are other persons.

     But, because human organisms can talk, mediate their behavior
by complex cognitive processes, and guide their actions in reference
to social concepts and norms, research on human spatial behavior need
not, and must not, be limited to observational study. The reports by
Altman and Sommer describe strategically apt combinations of observational study and direct inquiry (e.g., interviews, questionnaires).
From this cognitive and social perspective, additional aspects of
human spatial behavior also come into view. Roos' concept of juris-

diction refers to the establishment of temporary territories within
the context of social structure and norms [12]. For example, a
professor's office is his territory most of the time, but the jani-
tor's territory some of the time. Each has jurisdiction, or temporary territorial rights. In Altman's study, to whom do those now
famous red and green chairs belong? Within the context of their
confinement, the sailors did or did not establish territory, but
they surely recognized that within a wider framework they merely
had jurisdiction. Reservation of campground sites, noted by Sommer,
is another instance of jurisdiction. The notion of license, used by
Wynne-Edwards in analyzing animal behavior, holds literally at the
human level.

That the men in Altman's study indubitably possessed concepts,
beliefs, attitudes and dispositions about jurisdiction and territory
is important, and suggests an additional area for research. To illustrate only one approach here, the developmental approach, Adelson
and O'Neil, in a study of the growth of political ideas, traced the
development of the sense of community in 11-, 13-, 15-, and 18-year
olds, using the notion of a hypothetical island, purchased by 1000
men and women who settle there and must devise their laws and modes
of government [1]. A series of questions dealt with the concept of
eminent domain: the island's Council decides to construct a road
across it, but one person refuses to sell his land. Initially, there
was no developmental trend among the age groups, who supported neither the landowner nor the community strongly, but as persuasion
fails and the landowner resorts to a shotgun, the youngsters, especially the older ones, shifted in favor of governmental coercion.

As the complex nature of human territorial behavior becomes
more precisely delineated, the relation between dominance and territoriality, in non-confined as well as confined situations, can be
more fruitfully appraised. Dominance, as a disposition toward leadership, interpersonal initiative, and social ascendancy, is one of
the best measured personality traits [2,7]. Once adequate measures
of individual differences in varieties of territorial behavior also
become available, determination of their relationship to dominance
will be a straightforward undertaking. In Altman's situation, where
the establishment of territory appears to be an adaptive response to
group needs, the trait of social intelligence or social insight [8]
may be as relevant as dominance, while the acquisition of differential amounts of territory in a territory-establishing situation may
be particularly related to dominance.

I would like to turn briefly to more general consideration of
this excellent international symposium on the use of space in animals
and men.

The advent of massive urban renewal programs, the creation of
entire new communities, the construction of continent-wide transpor-

tation systems, and the management of vast tracts of wilderness
areas, park lands, and watershed districts indicate the extent to
which the form and processes of the contemporary physical environment are becoming increasingly man-influenced. Indeed, barring actual catastrophe in other realms, the next 50 years may come to be
known as the age of the physical environment.

Because variables of human behavior are intermixed throughout
the full cycle of environmental policy-making, planning, design,
management, and maintenance, the sciences and professions dealing
directly with the physical environment, such as architecture, city
and regional planning, landscape architecture, transportation planning, geography, and natural resources management, are coming to an
acute recognition of the behavioral implications of their endeavors.

The rapidly developing new fields of environmental behavioral
science, e.g., environmental psychology, behavioral geography, environmental sociology, through seeking to advance knowledge of the
interplay between human behavior and the everyday physical environment, will inevitably contribute to a realization of the humanistic
goal of a better physical environment, by clarifying implicit behavioral assumptions embedded within professional practice, overcoming
social and administrative distances between professionals and user-
clients, and conducting follow-up evaluations of the behavioral consequences of planning and design decisions [6]. Surely the vision
of an everyday physical environment which truly reflects the values,
activity patterns, and aspirations of its society through the constant, sensible, effective monitoring of its performance and behavioral impact would appear to be a modest goal, even in light of
steadily increasing social and technological complexity.

Yet, the intricacy and scope of research possibilities uncovered
by analysis of the spatial aspects of human experience and behavior,
which is only one of several fundamental topics in environmental behavioral science, remain impressive and sobering. Even with a gen-
erously financed, large-scale crash program of investigation, the
magnitude of methodological and empirical groundwork required to establish the basis for a mature branch of research makes it imperative
to think in terms of decades rather than months or years, and makes
it incumbent upon environmental behavior scientists to be humble in
their advice and realistic for environmental policy-makers, planners
and designers to be patient in their expectations. While it will be
greatly beneficial and enlivening to the basic research enterprise
if the professions exert strong and steady pressure upon environmental behavioral science to carry on research appropriate to their
needs, there will necessarily be inherent sequential constraints upon the timing, direction, and ordering of the new field's development.
To be sure, substantial immediate and continuing benefits to practice will accrue, but the points of contact between research and
practice must inevitably be intermittent rather than constant. Fur-

thermore, consideration of how behavioral research findings can best be incorporated into the processes of environmental policy-making, planning, and design itself warrants imaginative systematic experimentation.

REFERENCES

1. Adelson, J. and O'Neil, R.P.: Growth of political ideas in adolescence: The sense of community. J. Personality Soc. Psychol., 4:295-306, 1966.
2. Allport, G.A. and Allport, F.H.: A-S Reaction Scale: A Scale for Measuring Ascendance-Submission in Personality. Houghton Mifflin, Boston, 1939.
3. Barker, R.G.: Explorations in ecological psychology. Amer. Psychol., 20:1-14, 1965.
4. Chapin, Jr., F.S.: Activity systems and urban structure: A working schema. J. Amer. Inst. Planners, 34:11-18, 1968.
5. _____ and Hightower, H.C.: Household Activity Systems -- A Pilot Investigation. Center for Urban and Regional Studies, Chapel Hill, North Carolina, 1966.
6. Craik, K.H.: Environmental psychology. In Craik, K.H. et al., eds., New Directions in Psychology, IV. Holt, Rinehart and Winston, New York, 1970.
7. Gough, H.G.: Manual for the Chapin Social Insight Test. Consulting Psychologists Press, Palo Alto, California, 1968.
8. _____: Manual for the Chapin Social Insight Test. Consulting Psychologists Press, Palo Alto, California, 1964.
9. Hall, E.T.: A system for the notation of proxemic behavior. Amer. Anthropol., 65:1003-1027, 1963.
10. _____: The Hidden Dimension. Doubleday, Garden City, New York, 1966.
11. Little, K.B.: Personal space. J. Exp. Soc. Psychol., 1:237-247, 1965.
12. Roos, P.D.: Jurisdiction: An ecological concept. Hum. Relations, 21:75-84, 1968.
13. Sommer, R.: Small group ecology. Psychol. Bull., 67:145-152, 1967.

Fitch:

One of our colleagues, yesterday, pointed out that crowding and density tended to be used as pejorative terms, as though there were no positive factors connected with these situations and conditions. The history of cities fully confirms his position; because the city is always characterized by very dense structure and by high conjective use of space. And this fact must unquestionably be related to

the special climate which cities create, which exists nowhere else,
which must be the pre-condition for social invention and innovation.
From this point of view, the city and all the buildings that make
it up should be regarded not as a container of civilization, but the
actual generator. This, of course, is implicit in words of various
etymology; city, civilization, civil, civilized, or urban, urbane,
urbanity - all of these reveal the fact that this has been generally
understood.

We try to examine this problem of urban density and habitat;
it seems to be apparent that two factors are involved; one is size,
the other is density. Both of these relate to the appearance of
this special climate that cities - and no other forms of settlement
- reveal. I suppose that, in a sense, we might use the term of
physics, there is a critical mass involved here. Below a given
size and density the profit does not begin, it is not self-generat-
ing. Only above this level does the special climate appear. If we
look at this problem in historical terms, it seems to me that both
size and density have varied with developments in technology. In
terms of size, Periclean Athens or Michaelangelo's Florence were
actually not any larger than Chattanooga, Tennessee, whereas Detroit
has for decades been much larger than Imperial Rome; and yet, I
would not be wholly subjective if I suggested that Florence functioned more efficiently than Chattanooga, and Rome, with all its
drawbacks, accomplished certain things that Detroit has not yet accomplished. It seems to me that size is clearly a civilized function of the city, but it is clearly variable. It is not possible
to say that there is an absolute size below which a human aggregation will not function as a city, or a cut-off point at which it is
bound to function as a city. Size seems to be a variable factor
and related to the general level of thought, and especially to that
of technology.

But, I think that density in the city can be argued as being
very much constant, because density is just another defining of spatial displacement of interpersonal relations. I, for one, do not
think that technology can ever modify this by a millimeter. My
blinking rate or the way I use my eyes, all these signs of recognition we have been told about will not operate unless they are perceived, and the space across which they can be perceived has very
little limits. So it seems to me that this question of density is
a permanent and constant factor in the development of the city.

Modern technology has had the ironic effect of making possible
an enormous increase in size of the city and an almost equivalent
decrease in density. This certainly has a definite effect upon the
quality of our life, and, in general terms, a negative effect. Obviously, overcrowding might have been difficult (as in medieval
Paris, Renaissance Florence) for the individual, and might have been
expensive for the maintenance of the individual in terms of contagion

and starvation; but there seems no doubt that it was socially desirable. The interjection of the uncritical adaptation of technical
means of communication and transport which characterizes a town like
Dallas seems not at all proven to be an absolutely positive effect.
On the contrary, if one goes to the few cities left on earth like
Venice, one immediately observes the benign effect of an urban density which is still based on pedestrian communication.

The implications of many papers which have been read here are
of great significance for architects and city planners. I only regret that there are few architects and planners in this audience.

Studer:

Underlying most if not all of the findings reported at this
symposium is their possible application to real human settings. Indeed such a proposition is never too far from our thoughts. Clearly
the data concerning population density could be critical to our very
survival as a species. Of equal importance, however, is the decision
about what we humans shall do while we are still here. Of fundamental concern are issues dealing with what sorts of behavioral topographies are relevant to our goals, and how these topographies can be
realized. How do the findings reported here relate to the problems
of organizing viable human systems?

The processes involved in applying findings in environment-behavior causality we call generally, environmental design. It is the
act of self-consciously designing or controlling environments to
realize specific human biological, behavioral and social outcomes.
My own research interests primarily involve the development of conceptual links between environmental research and environmental design. I would point out that the design and research functions (be
these experimental, naturalistic or other), while interconnected,
involve significantly contrasting methodological issues. A recurring terminal theme throughout these presentations was "...but this
is all very complicated". Comprehensive causal explanations of the
environment-behavior systems examined by these researchers are indeed complex. But allow me to observe that the ordering of man-made
environments producing somewhat predictable human outcomes is infinitely more complex. That is why we do it so badly. Behavioral
scientists, ecologists, and all relevant researchers must, if they
intend to help, become more aware of the issues related to environmental design. No doubt many of us have, during each of these presentations, experienced the momentary realization that "these data
are highly relevant to environmental decision-making and must be
systematically taken into account." During the next presentation,
the same response. But how does one connect these points of knowledge in a sea of ignorance?

The first point I want to make then is that we have no overall

conceptual framework for interrelating our knowledge of man-environment phenomena. The search for environment-behavior causality is
launched from disparate and conflicting epistemologies and assumed
paradigms. Limiting one's attention to a particular research issue
is essential to scientific progress. One must ask limited questions
and answer them thoroughly -- taking care not to move beyond the
facts. If we could, by some conceptual miracle, combine under a
single unifying metastructure all of the findings reported at this
symposium, the resulting information would be relevant to but a very
small portion of the issues facing environmental designers and managers. Why is this? The designer cannot select particular variables
to deal with, nor can he artifically impoverish the problem space.
He must deal with human systems as they come -- behavioral samples
which are both large and complex. All classes of environmental variables, e.g., luminous, sonic, olfactory, tactile, must be ordered because all sense modalities are affected. That is, each class of
variable must necessarily take a state, even though each will obviously exert a differential influence. The resulting environmental
configuration will, in the context of certain phylogenetic and onto-
genetic givens, produce a specific behavioral result. In most of
the investigations reported here the milieu was given. In most designed environments little is given, all must be ordered from scratch.
There are endless technical issues involved in ordering man-made environments. For example, how does one interpose and order energy-
matter systems between humans and the antithetical demands of extant
environmental states (e.g., gravity, climate)? How does one accommo-
date time-dependent response variability? There are of course numerous other technical issues too tedious to go into here.

     The class of problems encountered in moving from pre-defined
behavior to supporting environment, then, presupposes more comprehensive, continuous and interconnected resources than presently exist. Suffice to say that arranging environments with predictable
human outcomes is painfully difficult -- let us say impossible within present states of knowledge. On the other hand, man-made environments are required, and arrange them we must. These environments result in particular, often profound, behavioral, social and biological consequences. The very act of configuring designed environments
is an act of social or behavioral engineering! This is what we are
involved in and apparently we have no choice if we are to make physical decisions. The frustration of course is that our understanding
of environmental effects, our methods for realizing predictable environment-behavior ensembles, both of these areas of knowledge are
incomplete and relatively crude. The probability of success in realizing precisely well-fitting environments is certainly equivocal.

     Ostensibly we agree that behavior is the class of phenomena
which must be observed in order to assess environmental effect. It
is thus the generating criteria in defining and arranging environments. This fact has led me to adopt and attempt to explicate a

behavior-contingent approach to environmental design [1,2,3]. The
underlying argument is that we must decide what it is we want to do
as individual and collective humans, and then arrange our environment to maximize the probability that we will consummate these intentions.

I have become increasingly convinced, and thus agree with Sommer, that the traditional role of the physical designer requires
modification. We are becoming a planning culture. This is to the
good, but a corollary proposition is that affected populations must
have a major role in arranging their milieu. The role of the environmental designer and/or manager is to provide the means -- hard-
ware and software -- to enable them to do this. These technicians'
success is obviously constrained by limited intellectual, fiscal and
physical decisions and generate alternatives. They must also attend
to continuity with other affected environment-behavior systems. In
essence the environmental designer provides "power steering" toward
the realization of human intentions. On a larger scale this is perhaps identified as "participatory democracy". Be this as it may,
the more sophisticated our tools, the more careful we must be in selecting our goals.

The fact still remains, however, that we do not, as has so often been mentioned, know enough about what must be done environmen-
tally to precisely realize our human goals. Because of this ignorance and some of the complex conceptual issues which grow out of
it, we can only view the environmental design act (i.e., the self-
conscious effort to structure our environment) in a different way
than is traditional in the design community. There can be no "solution" per se, only an environmental hypothesis regarding what might
be the human effect. Beyond the fact that our tools and knowledge
are impoverished, the human problem changes before a physical solution can be realized. What is needed, it seems, is not simply more
empirical data to better understand man-environment interactions,
but a new epistemology of environmental design, one which recognizes
the uncertainty and state-changing requirements for man-environment
equilibrium. We would do well to realize that we are simply involved
in an experiment, an experiment in which the various actors are making decisions (via some sophisticated and systematic information-
processing, decision-making mechanism) to manipulate the man-made
environment toward some equilibrium state with respect to our individual and collective goals. We are involved in an on-going experiment to better our environmental lot. As a consequence (assuming
that we systematically monitor resultant human manifestations) we
learn more about the effects of environmental manipulations, thus
increasing our knowledge base for generating future hypotheses. It
is my conclusion that no designed environment should be contemplated
unless it is based upon this underlying conceptualization. If we
see "solutions" as experiments, many of the questions we contemplate
become either irrelevant or answerable in the day-to-day process of

interacting with our environment to attain our individual and collective goals.

REFERENCES

1. Studer, R.G.: On environmental programming. Architect. Assoc.
        J., 81:290-296, 1965.
2. _____: The dynamics of behavior-contingent physical
        systems. In Broadbent, G., ed., Design Methods In
        Architecture. Lund Humphries, London, 1969.
3. _____: The dynamics of behavior-contingent physical
        systems. Ekistics, 185-197, 1969.
4. _____: The organization of spatial stimuli. In Pasta-
        lan, L.A. and Carson, D.H., eds., Spatial Behavior of
        Older People. University of Michigan Press/Wayne State
        University Press, Ann Arbor, 1970.

Calhoun:

   Wynne-Edwards pointed out that there are two basic processes
for maintaining social stability while providing the opportunity
for change. The first is the genetic control over the character
and variability of individual behavior which permits patterns of
organization of groups and populations to develop in harmony with
the ecological setting in which the species has evolved. Change
in the pattern of social life proceeds slowly by natural selection.
Secondly, we have control by tradition and culture, whereby the
norms for behavior which determine patterns of social life may be
altered without waiting for genetic change. Historically, cultural
change has permitted only minor changes from one generation to the
next. However, the rate of cultural change has continually accelerated until we are now entering a time where cultural inheritance
no longer suffices. Margaret Mead remarked to me that the present
generation has introduced a code of life based not upon tradition,
but developed from their own experiences solely within the context
of their development. Furthermore, this comment of Mead's regarding the generation-gap suggests that we are also in the process of
proceeding to an intra-generation-gap in which there will be such
significant changes through time within a given generation that its
members lose contact with their former selves. This consideration
takes us to the focal issue of our times.: How do we preserve social continuity in the current era of radical change? Answering
this question requires focus on micro-space, that physical or conceptual space precipitating an alteration within value systems reflected by altered norms of behavior. Altman's experimental studies
of sailors in confined physical space provide one promising beginning. Study of adaptation to a sequence of confined physical spaces
may provide a guide to the processes for successful adaptation to a
sequence of differing conceptual spaces, where each such conceptual
space consists of the unique value system and related ideas guiding
that behavior most appropriate to a transient setting.

Space and the Strategy of Life *

John B. Calhoun

ABSTRACT. *Space has value to life as a continuum which contains resources and provides experiences. Effective utilization of resources has culminated in the evolution of both aggressive defense of area and the formation of groups which share the same range. To the extent that an individual is alone when he experiences some aspect of his environment, he incorporates that item into his personality. The presence of others within his extended ego boundary may generate anxiety and produce defensive antagonism. This process of developing an identity with surroundings initiates the formation of a second kind of space within which we spend our lives. The experience of things becomes transformed into concepts about them until evolution produces a conceptual space in which values are related to relationships between abstract ideas rather than to ways of behaving in relation to physical situations. The responsible choice among ideas forming one's conceptual space replaces the search for resources in physical space. Commitment to abstract values which guide action replaces aggressive defense of physical objects incorporated into one's ego. Compassion --the understanding support of others with differing values--replaces submission to aggressive action. Evolutionary progression tends to increase the time and energy devoted to conceptual space. Herein lies a.partial solution to the population dilemma. Increase in numbers must cease within the next century. Nevertheless, evolutionary progression may continue through enlargement of conceptual space. Promoting enlargement of conceptual space requires increasing diversity of physical and ideational resources, kinds of living units, and assemblies they form, while increasing the number and effectiveness of*

---

* Presented as a Frontiers of Science Lecture at the 1968 Annual Meeting of the AAAS, Dallas, Texas. The section on "The Breakdown of Social Control of Population Growth" has been brought up to date as of August 1970.

links between these diverse elements and assemblies. Promotion in this sense will replace conservation as we--with compassion--guide the destiny of Earth toward creative exploitation of conceptual space through responsible commitments.

INTRODUCTION

Many traditions mingle in my past. Each in some way contributes to my concern with space. One of these traditions involves the Scottish people.* Their history embraces the development of the clan system as an eminently successful means of adjusting to life in a trying terrain. This very success led to dismal failures as many strictures, from the statutes of Iona in 1600 to the Battle of Culloden in 1746, dissolved clan authority. I come from a long line of Calhouns often characterized by failure to maintain territorial prerogatives. Just before 1600, the Colquhoun clan was resoundingly massacred in Glen Fruin above Loch Lomond by the immediate ancestors of Rob Roy MacGregor. This local fracas was part and parcel of a more general tension accompanying the incipient population explosion which resulted in part from a decline in the authority of clan chiefs to control marriage. Even at this early date the impinging of population on available space stimulated 35,000 Scots to settle in northern Ireland during the first two decades of the 1600s. By a century later, the prolific Scots in northern Ireland were again in a population and space bind. The Calhouns were on the march again. Some few years of wandering later, a large part of the American branch of the clan, some 150 strong, found themselves crossing Long Cane Creek in South Carolina one fine day in 1760. In a typical Calhoun error in tactics, the men stacked their guns and went down to help extract a wagon mired as it was crossing the creek. While so engaged, a band of Cherokees massacred a third of their number. Of the survivors the more activist half remained and established the settlement of Abbeville. Out of this group stemmed "John C.", whose place in history depends upon your point of view. The other half of the survivors retreated back up into North Carolina to the protection of the earlier Scottish settlement of Waxhaw. I come from this cowardly branch of the Calhouns. They tended to produce teachers and preachers, to retreat into the world of ideas.

Whether this family history has any bearing on my specific scientific concern with the subject of space, I do not know. However, it exemplifies the central theme of my presentation, that there are two kinds of space, one physical and one conceptual. If we are to grapple successfully with the myriad crises and tensions accompanying the developing rapid increase in human numbers, both physical and conceptual space need to be considered.

----

* Irrespective of the relationship of Scottish history to the origin of my research interests, I have found its perusal stimulating in evolving insights about the influence of space on man [17,18,28,29,34].

My own strategy for avoiding the pressures of the present has been to escape by seeking only to understand the life and times of lower mammals [6,7,8]. During each such reclusion I keep stumbling on to principles which seem to have some bearing on the human situation also. And yet, my very immersion with these problems makes it difficult for me to recognize whether I have been just wandering in a sterile wilderness or am in fact approaching a frontier of science, a zone of tension and change between traditional systems of thought. You will clearly recognize that much of what I will say may be classified as poetry rather than normal science.* I say this without apology for it is my firm conviction that there is no science which did not have its earlier expression as an art form.

Tonight I am here as a replacement for a very kindred spirit whom I deeply respect, Professor Konrad Lorenz. His life and work exemplify the tension at the interface between art and science.** He flows easily across this boundary, now playing the role of artist and then again the role of scientist. Neither he nor I are either competent or temperamentally inclined to present an adequate summary of the great diversity of effort and thought which many investigators are now directing toward developing an understanding of the importance of space to the life of animals and man. The present symposium on this topic reflects the broad scope of this emerging field of science.

Let us now turn to some of the studies now underway at my laboratory. They will serve as a point of departure to related issues more particularly characterizing the human scene.

EXPERIMENTAL UNIVERSES

An experimental universe is a bounded physical space consisting of one or more similarly constructed cells (Figure 1). Each cell provides opportunity for the expression of many of the behaviors characteristic of the species for which the universe is intended as a place of habitation. The example shown here is of a four-cell universe designed for house mice. The floor is merely a large tray, 51 x 51 inches, covered to a depth of three inches with ground corn cobs. Partitions, slightly higher than the surface of the ground corn cobs, divide the floor space into four equal areas, each covering 640 square inches. Mice utilize these partitions as boundaries of territories. A chemical ring stand with its base covered by the

---

* Kuhn makes a particularly strong argument for the necessity of a more artistic form of expressing the formulations of the scientific revolutions which later permit a new field of normal science to emerge [26, p.172].

** Konrad Lorenz discusses the juncture of art and science in the development of new value systems, new ways of viewing life and functioning in it [27, p.286-299].

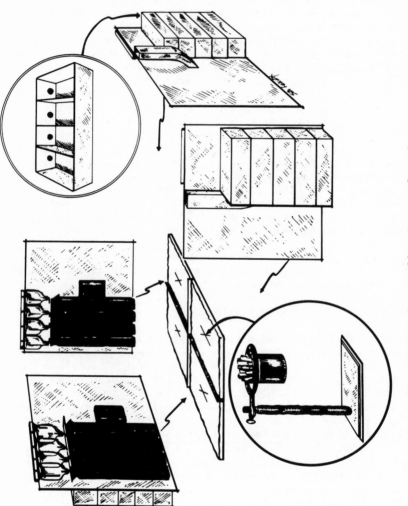

Figure 1: A four-cell universe for mice

ground corn cobs is placed in the center of the floor of each cell. Wire screen wrapped about the rod enables the mice to climb up and procure nesting material from the can suspended within the ring. In point of fact this structure becomes the focus of a number of kinds of activities. For example, during the hours of heightened activity it often serves as a temporary haven for subordinate mice. The four wall sections, shown displaced in the figure, are bolted together about the base to form the closed universe. Adjacent to the floor space of each cell, four vertical wire screen tunnels give the mice access to a battery of sixteen nesting compartments, four at each of four levels in each cell.

In each battery each of the four levels contains four nest compartments. This arrangement does make an efficient use of space. However, the prime function of this arrangement is to introduce the economic factor. The higher up a mouse lives in this apartment complex, the lower is its income because it must expend more energy during each round trip from its home to obtain such resources as food and water. Food is provided in a hopper in each cell located on the wall to the right of the tunnels. Obtaining food requires that the mouse run across the outer surfaces of the tunnels to the hopper and hang on it while it gnaws at the contained pellets of food. An outside accessory hopper enables the food surface to be covered with food at all times. Four 2500 cc bottles suspended above a platform above the tunnels provide an ample source of water.

This spatial arrangement will permit in excess of 250 mice per cell, in this case more than 1000 mice per four-cell universe before "standing room only" and lack of opportunity to gain access to resources places an upper limit on population level. Our present program is particularly focused on trying to understand the conditions which permit or prevent the population from arriving at the "standing room only" terminal stage.

THE BEHAVIORAL SINK

Among the studies now underway is one in which we are investigating the effect of group size on social withdrawal. Each group consists only of males introduced at weaning. The number of mice in the four groups are four, eight, sixteen, and thirty-two. Each group inhabits a four-cell universe. So far we do not know what the optimum size group is for this universe, although we suspect that it is more than eight, but less than sixteen. Above the optimum size group a strange pattern of eating is developing (Figure 2).

Each bar graph represents the percentage of the food consumed from the food hopper located at approximately the position shown in the diagrammatic cross section of the universe. It will be noted that as the group size gets larger, the deviation from equal usage of the four hoppers becomes more accentuated. From past experience

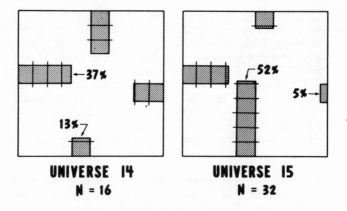

FIGURE 2 - BEHAVIORAL SINK DEVELOPMENT IN MICE

Diagrammatic representation of food consumption,
13 Sept.-12 Nov., 1968. Bar graphs indicate percentage of food consumed from each of the four
food hoppers in each universe.

with other similar type studies of rodents, I can predict with fair
assurance that this trend will continue to become more accentuated,
particularly in the larger group. The end state will be one in which
over 90% of food consumption takes place from one hopper and essentially none from at least two of the others. This will mean that most of
the mice eat only at this one hopper and all of them eat mostly there.

This end state represents the development of what I term the
"behavioral sink". However, the concept of the behavioral sink encompasses both the development of the end state and the consequences
of its continuance upon the contained individuals. For it to develop,
the physical environment must contain a few localized response-per-
mitting situations which require that any individual spend an appre-
ciable span of time at one of them in completing the appropriate response. Gnawing at food through the mesh of a food hopper represents
such a situation. When few animals are present, the usual circumstances will be that each individual will terminate most episodes of
eating without another mouse being present on the hopper. However,
as the group increases in size, the chances increase that while one
individual is still eating another will join him at the same hopper.
After a number of such coincidences of joint eating in close proximity,
each individual comes to associate the presence of another with the
reward of eating. This association becomes so strong in time that

the eating situation is redefined by the mice as requiring the presence of an associate. Most mice will return to that particular hopper and at those particular times of day previously characterized by the highest probability of finding other mice present. At the terminal stage of the process the aggregates at a particular hopper may be so large that most individuals experience some difficulty in completing any particular episode of eating. This derived heightened need for proximity to others becomes pathological. It becomes pathological because it increases the number of social contacts far beyond that which the overall density of the universe would otherwise evoke. I shall return shortly to this question of the relevance of the number of contacts per unit time.

Although this kind of environment was designed by intent to permit the development of the behavioral sink, the very confirmation of its anticipated development tells us how not to design an environment. It points to the detrimental consequences of a static environment, particularly ones where any of the kinds of response situations are highly restricted in number and place. On a theoretical basis, increasing uncertainty, enhancing the necessity for searching and demanding continual solution of new problems should prove beneficial as a basic strategy of environmental design. However, the cost, complexity, and magnitude of such studies have so far forced us to resort to crude simulations on paper as an interim strategy for readying ourselves for such critical studies in the future.

THE BREAKDOWN OF SOCIAL CONTROL OF POPULATION GROWTH

In 1963 Kessler, then of the Rockefeller Institute, began one of the most important experimental studies of population of recent years [24]. His universes were of approximately the same size as the four-cell one which I am now using. However, in order to study selection under crowded conditions, he initiated each of his two universes with 16 pairs of mice, four pairs each of four inbred strains. At the termination of his studies, one universe contained 800 and the other 1000 individuals. When I saw this terminal phase of his study, I concluded that this unusual attainment of very high density must have in some way been dependent upon the large number of initial colonizers. How this insight led to our current large-scale study requires a brief historical background. Before he initiated his study, Kessler asked my advice about an appropriate size for the habitat. I had then just completed an analysis of the minimum spatial requirements to be utilized in experimental studies of group behavior and population dynamics in a range of animals from mice to monkeys. For a colony of mice, this minimum lay between 80 and 100 square feet with considerable additional vertical structuring of retreat or nesting spaces. Due to the strictures of available laboratory space, Kessler was forced to reduce his experimental pens to one-fourth that which I had thought necessary. Moreover, his background as a physician left him unencumbered by presumed ecological truisms, whereas my thinking

had stemmed from an ecological model which says that ecologists "know"
how natural populations are initiated. That is, the population is
assumed to start from a very few survivors following some catastrophe.
Therefore, I was thinking in terms of introducing only one or two
pairs of animals into the "minimum" space.

Since Kessler wished to study the interrelationship between
crowding and natural selection utilizing coat-color gene markers,
his basic stock consisted of four inbred strains of house mice. To
reduce initial gene drift, he took recourse to two strategies. First
he established a hybrid stock of hybrids, H_3, in which $H_3 = H_1 \times H_2$,
and $H_1 = A \times B$, and $H_2 = C \times D$, in which A, B, C, and D were the inbred stocks. Second, he started his populations off with 16 pairs.
Thus he began with 32 to 64 times the density (one-fourth the space
and eight to sixteen times the number of colonizers) that my ecological evaluation deemed appropriate. The population eventually reached
"standing room only", less than three square inches per mouse. How
could this be reconciled with my earlier studies of population growth
and social behavior in experimental environments? In these earlier
experiments, the presumed "minimum" desirable space was exceeded and,
confirming the results of most other workers, an upper level of population was reached far below that attained by Kessler's study.

In order to evolve a more precise hypothesis, I tried to visu-
alize two pairs and 64 pairs of mice in separate "minimum" area environments, as follows: In the lower-colonizing-density situation,
each male would often roam about without encountering his associate
male companion. This solitary roaming permitted incorporation of
many objects into each individual's personal space. All of these
objects with which each mouse gained identity became part of its extended self. Each individual's body, by such measure, became larger.
Two individuals could thus collide even though their physical bodies
were some distance apart by one of them merely occupying or passing
through a space that the other had come to identify as part of himself. Therefore, when two individuals did approach each other, such
a collision at a distance would generate anxiety and precipitate intense fighting, culminating in relatively large territories for each
male. This intense territorial strife would reflect back on the female associates who would then experience initial difficulty in con-
ceiving and rearing litters. In contrast, in the case where there
were 16 males in the same amount of space, any colonizing male would
typically encounter another male during his periods of exploration.
Therefore, the number and spatial extent of objects incorporated
within any individual's extended identity would be much reduced. As
a consequence, the frequency and intensity of fighting would be markedly reduced and territories rarely established. With little stress
from male aggression impinging upon them, females would be subject
to very little inhibition of conception or maternal care. As a consequence, populations initiated with a high density of colonizers
should reach very high terminal densities approaching "standing room
only."

This line of reasoning led to a rather extreme hypothesis: "The greater the density of initial colonizers, the greater the terminal density". To explore this hypothesis, Gerald G. Wheeler and I developed a series of experiments in which both the amount of space and the number of colonizers were varied. Units of space (the "cells" shown in Figure 1) were varied in an ascending series of one, two, four, eight and sixteen cells to form closed physical "universes" of increasing size. Five universes of each size were to be colonized with one, two, four, eight and sixteen pairs of mice, respectively. All 25 universes were designed and constructed; however, a shortage of personnel dictated an initial constriction of effort. We decided to restrict our first effort to one universe of each size, each initiated with four pairs of mice (the midpoint number of colonizers of our original design).

Preceding the initiation of this study, Charles L. Bishop of our staff ran a pilot study of a one-cell universe with four pairs of colonizers. This population, in a space approximately one-fourth of that Kessler used, reached an upper level of 250 adult mice, exactly one-fourth of the "standing room only" level reached in Kessler's study. With this confirmation in hand, and considering the hypothesis stated above, we proceeded to a second level hypothesis relating to the five-universe study we then initiated: "The larger the physical space when there are several colonizing pairs, the smaller will be the absolute size of the population when the maximum number is attained." From the one-cell to the 16-cell universe, the predicted terminal population would be respectively, 250, 230, 205, 168, and 110; and in relative density (i.e., number of mice per cell) the series predicted would be 250, 115, 51, 21, 7. This hypothesis was presented in my AAAS Frontiers of Science Lecture in December 1968 at a time when the populations were in their earliest phases of development and so far confirmed the hypothesis.

This confirmation lay only in the initial history of these populations. Within the first two months after introduction, two of the males in the largest universe (16 cells) succumbed from the stress accompanying their intense fighting. Likewise, one soon died in the second largest universe (eight cells), and after a longer time, one also died in the middle-sized universe (four cells). In contrast, there were no deaths of colonizers for many months in the two smallest universes. In them fighting among colonizers was relatively subdued and was accompanied by an even more interesting phenomenon-- self-grooming became transformed into mutual grooming. That is, each individual's identity became fused with others. Such mutual grooming among colonizers was never observed in the two larger universes. Instead, the more classical picture of territoriality and hierarchies developed with the overflow of stressful situations affecting females to the extent of reducing conception and interfering with proper maternal behavior. In contrast, this feedback loop, which functions to inhibit population growth, hardly functioned during the establish-

ing phase of the two smaller universes. For example, the first surviving litters were born 25 days after colonization in the two smaller
universes, but not until 50 days in the two larger ones.

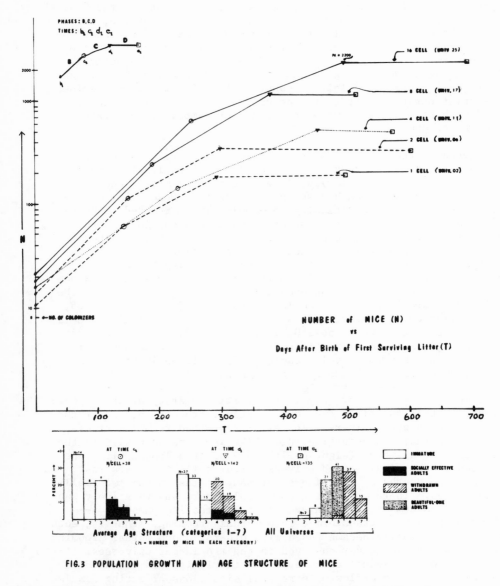

FIG.3 POPULATION GROWTH AND AGE STRUCTURE OF MICE

The remaining histories of these colonies (Figure 3) only partially substantiated the original hypothesis. It is obvious from
this figure of population growth that the larger universes culminated

in larger absolute populations than the smaller ones. At the upper
limit of population growth (at time d_1 on the curves) the number of
mice per cell from the smallest to the largest universe was respectively, 180, 175, 130, 142, 138. The middle-sized universe, the one
with four cells, had a history of unusual social disturbance which
seemed to stem from an exceedingly pathological aggressiveness of
the one territorial male among the colonizers. Both of the two initial phases of population growth in this four-cell universe exhibit
a marked reduction in the rate of increase in contrast to that holding in the other four. Therefore, if we ignore this universe and
focus only on the other four, it may be seen that the final density
(180 and 175) of the two smaller universes was 25% greater than that
of the final density (142 and 138) for the two larger ones. This is
the extent of the confirmation of the original hypothesis. However,
similarities in the histories of all universes have produced insights
that are of even greater significance.

To appreciate these new insights, mention must be made of changes
in the physical environment. In the original designing of the universes, Wheeler came up with the concept of "physiological" physical
space as opposed to "social" physical space. "Physiological" space
is that where ingestion of food and water takes place, and where the
animals retreat to rest and rear their young. "Social" space is that
where status interactions take place. In the original design, a water
source inserted into the back of each of the 16 nesting compartments
in each cell and a food hopper forming the false roof of each compartment confined these more basic survival behaviors of ingestion,
sleep, and reproduction to these retreat spaces. All external space
was left for more involved social interactions. However, since mice
tend to urinate and defecate near where they eat and drink, this design led to such a fouling of nests and high humidity in them that
the overhead food became extremely moistened and caked, making it less
accessible and desired by the mice. For this reason, the food and
water sources had to be shifted out from the retreat compartments to
the positions shown in Figure 1. This still left the floor as more
truly "social" space. We believe that this change in physical environmental structure increased the amount of stress experienced and
was instrumental in producing a reduction of maximum density in the
one-celled universe--180 in contrast to 250 obtained in the pilot
study. This change in environment was made in December 1968, five
months after colonization and during the writing of the original
draft of this paper. With this background we may now examine the
longer history of these populations.

All populations passed through four discrete phases:

Phase A: The establishing phase extending to the time
          of birth of the first surviving litter.

Phase B: Period of rapid population growth during which on
          the average the population doubles every 56 days.

Phase C: Period of reduced rate of population growth
          during which on the average the population
          doubles every 105 days.

Phase D: Period of stability, or slight decline (less
          than five percent) of population numbers.

A schematic representation of the last three phases is shown in the
upper left corner of Figure 3. Times c_1, d_1, and e_1 mark the ends
of Phases B, C, and D, respectively. In all cases, the end of Phase
D at e_1 might have extended beyond that shown. The one, two, four
and eight-celled universes were terminated at the e_1 times shown.
The 16-celled universe is being continued to determine if later periods of either rapid decrease or increase may occur. For each universe age cohorts were established for those born each ten days after
colonization and the number surviving each ten days thereafter calculated from the observed dates of birth and death (or survival to
termination of the colony). From these source data the growth curves
and age structures of the population at the critical times c_1, d_1,
and e_1 were calculated. The seven age categories represent meaningful biological-social periods of life:

Category Number	Category (cohort)	Span in Days From Birth
1	Preweaning	1 to 30
2	Juvenile	31 to 70
3	Subadult	71 to 130
4	Establishing Adult	131 to 210
5	Adult	211 to 320
6	Declining	321 to 450
7	Senescent	451 and over

The three age structure histograms in the lower part of Figure 3 represent averages of those for the five universes at the times indicated.

Over most of Phase B (rapid population growth), the social structure in each universe remained dominated by one or two colonizing
males, while successful production of litters was by both colonizing
females and subadults. These latter do contribute to population increase provided the ambient social structure is relatively stable with
regard to male territories. Practically all litters born during this
phase survived. Toward the end of this phase, males began entering
the Establishing Adult age category. This indicates that they have
reached an age when they can effectively contend with each other and
with the older colonizing males for territories and dominance status.
This Phase B terminated at time c_1 with an average of 38 mice per cell.
Of these, six to seven were in the Establishing Adult and Adult age
categories. However, the average territory covered approximately

one and one-half cells, which means each territory on the average
included 10 - 11 mice in socially active age categories. For reasons
not now well understood, the sex ratio in these five universes held
quite constant at 40 males to 60 females. Thus, the basic social
unit consists of one territorial male, three contesting but subordinate males and six effectively reproducing females. At the end of
Phase B, all universes were filled with such basic social units, which
on the average inhabited one and one-half cells. At time c_1, the
three younger age categories had insufficiently matured to offer any
serious competition to these older, socially established mice whose
relative numbers are indicated by heavy shading on the age structure
graph for time c_1.

During the Phase C period of inhibited population growth, these
younger mice born during Phase B successively shifted into the age
categories of Establishing Adult and Adult. As they moved into these
later ages, they began to contest with the territorial males since
there was essentially no vacant space to occupy as a territory. A
few were successful, but most, after initial striving, began to withdraw both physically and psychologically. These remarks apply particularly to males. Early in Phase C, when the territories of males
still included the nest compartments, these withdrawn rejected males
were forced out of the nest compartments to places of rest at the
periphery of the territories—out in the center of the floor space
or on the water or food platforms. Here they would cower except for
minimal movement necessary to obtain food and water. Some continued
through most of their lives as Solitary Withdrawns. However, most
of the withdrawn males assembled in large aggregates and so have been
termed Pooled Withdrawns. During most of Phase C, these withdrawn
males were characterized by masses of recent wounds. In only a few
instances were these wounds inflicted by territorial males. Periodically, each withdrawn male would burst into a brief flurry of violence in which he would attack one of his associated withdrawn males.
The one being attacked would rarely flee, but instead crouched and
allowed himself to be bitten. As Phase C proceeded, the extent of
territories diminished to an area within a radius of less than 12
inches from the base of the ring stands. As this reduction of male
territories took place, the older adult reproducing females became
excessively aggressive toward immature mice within the nest compartments and toward any adult of either sex being about the bases of the
tunnels leading up into the nest compartments. The age structure
graph for time d_1 at the end of Phase C is particularly instructive.
By this time, there were at most no more than 10 mice in each cell
in the Establishing Adult and Adult age categories (Nos. 4 and 5)
who retained even a modicum of normal behavior. They are shown as
heavy shading. The hatched portions of the bars for the four older
age categories represent the withdrawn mice, 32% of the 142 mice in
the average cell. These mice are no longer "mice" in the social
sense of contributing to the survival of the species. By this time
they have lost to a large extent even the capacity for the violent

type of aggression and the only sexual behavior is a rare episode of
over-intense copulation, apparently not involving intromission. Sixty
percent of the population, then standing at 14 times the optimum, consisted of those in the three immature age categories, whose fate became apparent only after Phase D began.

Successful rearing of young terminated early in Phase D. The
frequency of conception also became markedly reduced, being largely
confined to females born early in Phase C. Those mice which had
withdrawn during Phase C remained as inactive nonparticipants--but
even more so. Even their capacity for violent, nonfunctional aggression disappeared. Those 10 mice per cell who retained some modicum
of involvement in social activities during Phase C entered the ranks
of the withdrawn mice. No mice replaced them. By midpoint of Phase
D there were, for all practical purposes, no territorial males, no
contesting males and no reproducing females capable of caring for
young; the genetic and learned templates for guiding effective adult
behavior had been "washed out" among all who had ever exhibited behavioral competence of a reproductive or aggressive nature.

Such lack of competence also characterized the 53% of the population who had entered age categories 4 and 5, where normally such
behaviors would have at least been attempted. We have designated
such mice as the "Beautiful Ones." They neither fight nor "sex" nor
build nests, nor have they ever exhibited these behaviors during their
development to adulthood. They carry no wounds of battle; their pelage remains excellent due to frequent self-grooming. Essentially,
they remain as juveniles who age. Like juveniles, they retain the
capacity to remain in the nesting compartments during periods of resting. Dr. Julius Axelrod has assayed the enzyme which transforms nor-
adrenalin into adrenalin in this and other categories of mice of
Phase D. Unlike the mice who have contested, been rejected, and
withdrawn, these "Beautiful Ones" show no evidence of ever being
stressed. We can only suspect that some combination of the heightened
aggressiveness of adult females during their early development, in
conjunction with their experiencing a high rate of contact with other
mice, blocked the unfolding of that behavior whose expression is
guided by the genetic template. This very early blocking of sexual
and aggressive behaviors precludes the possibility of learning elab-
orating their expression.

When Mayer Spivack of the Department of Community Mental Health,
Harvard, viewed these populations during Phase D, he remarked that
they were "overliving". By this he meant that all purpose in continued living had been lost once the capacity to engage in those social behaviors requisite to the survival of the species had been suppressed or blocked. If the state of affairs characterizing Phase D
persists, the population will eventually completely die off with no
reinitiation by the last survivors. This issue is being explored by
Halsey Marsden of our staff. I will give a brief overview of his

studies: When the two-celled universe was terminated, all were au-
topsied except for eight males and 16 females (adult mice). At the
end of 60 days at this reduced density, territorial behavior had
failed to reappear and no pregnancies had resulted. (In contrast,
when the original population included 24 Establishing Adult and Adult
mice, the total number trebled from 123 to 350 in a similar time
period). Gradually, most of the females shifted their residence to
the same nest box, as if in an effort to recoup the former nesting
compartment density. The females were then placed in an identical
universe with eight sexually active males from the stock breeding
colony. Even with one sex now competent, only six females conceived
and only three of these produced litters. Since these litters were
all dropped in the compartment housing 13 of the 16 females, only
five pups were reared long enough to indicate that, had this study
not been then terminated, they would have been weaned. Furthermore,
Marsden has made a detailed study of most categories of males removed
from the mid-Phase D period. After intensive observation, 12 mice
most representative of each of six categories (territorial, solitary
withdrawn, younger pooled withdrawn, older pooled withdrawn, younger
beautiful ones, and older beautiful ones) were removed from their environment and each category introduced into its own four-celled universe. Invariably they failed to develop a status ranked social
group as might be expected for normal mice. Instead, the typical
situation was that of three socially active males and nine who essentially failed to become involved in any social interactions. When
competent females from the breeding stock were introduced, extremely
few pregnancies resulted; in some cases none. At most, only one or
two males in each group had retained the capacity for effective sexual behavior.

     We are now continuing the study of Universe 25, the 16-cell uni-
verse. There remain two possibilities: First, there will be no
further reproduction and the mice will gradually senesce and die,
until no more remain. Second, after two or three months more of living in a setting with no significant continuing aggression, the Beautiful Ones may recoup some of their blocked genetic templates to the
point that reproductive behavior, unaccompanied by aggression, may
be reinstated. The hunch that this possibility may materialize derives from a few observations by Marsden that isolation for two to
four months may lead to reinstatement of reproductive behavior. The
current absence of social involvement in Universe 25 indicates that
for all practical purposes each mouse is isolated from his fellows
despite their contiguity.

     In searching for the relevance of these studies to the human
scene, we must clarify how the present study differs from the natural
ecological situation. In a state of nature, available space in acceptable habitats rapidly becomes filled with effective social units
--groups of 10 or 12 adult mice. Thereafter, most excess young begin to migrate into less desirable marginal habitats where they are

exposed to predation. In our experimental habitats, the possibility
for emigration has been precluded, and predation, except for rare accidental deaths by observer action, has been excluded. Thus, the experimental populations continued to increase to more than 14 times
the upper optimum point of 10 adult mice per cell. Furthermore, the
static nature of the experimental habitats with localization of food
resources fostered development of the behavioral sink phenomenon.
Even though the maximum number of mice attained did not preclude mice
obtaining enough food, the behavioral sink process culminated in excessive eating in some places while other identical sources were
nearly ignored. Among the consequences was that the learned need for
proximity to other mice generalized to places of sleeping--to the extent that so many mice would aggregate in nesting compartments that
some would suffocate; this, despite the fact that 30% of all nesting
compartments at maximum density contained no mice, or only one or two.
Such behavioral sinks accentuated the heightened contact rate which
culminates in brevity and incompleteness of response and finally
blocks expression of behaviors to the point that "Beautiful Ones" are
produced. Such behavioral changes must also occur in nature in those
rare instances where predation fails to remove the excess population.
However, we must conclude that predation and other causes of death
normally suffice for natural selection to preserve behavioral repertoires consonant with life within small social groups. The basic
conclusion in these studies is that, where density increases beyond
the limit of group size and rate of contact compatible with life within a small group, all excess individuals lose, or never develop, the
capacity for executing behaviors appropriate to survival of the species.

To transform these insights derived from the study of mice to
the human scene requires that we view responsible commitment to values
and causes as the sublimated equivalent of fighting in mice. It says
that the process of identifying with values and goals beyond the bodily
self requires periods of solitude and reflection. In the absence of
this opportunity, the individual matures into a hollow, sterile shell
incapable of commitments whose pursuit can enlarge the welfare of associates as well as the individual's own self. Paucity of involvement in humans becomes the equivalent of unrestricted population
growth in lower mammals. But even the human animal can be caught in
this primitive trap. As Erik Erikson so succinctly points out in his
lectures on insight and responsibility, where the opportunity for involvement in the expression of the generative function through education or creativity is missing, the only recourse to the fulfillment
of this drive lies in duplication of the biological self [21, p.256].

SOCIAL WITHDRAWAL AND SOCIAL VELOCITY

Whenever a group of animals is studied long enough and intensely
enough, it is noted that some individuals will be seen often, while
others rarely appear. We have been studying this phenomenon in great

FIGURE 4

VELOCITY IN A
GROUP OF EIGHT
MICE

Study 103
Universe 13

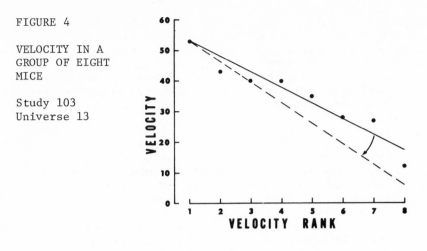

_____ Observed velocity slope shortly after
           colonization
_ _ _ _   Trend slope after final social structuring

detail in the four groups of male mice inhabiting the four-cell universes.* For our present purposes we will examine the results only
from the universe containing eight males (Figure 4).

     From an operational point of view, what we do is give each in-
dividual a velocity score each time it is observed active in a cell
at one of several places where social interactions more frequently
take place. The total score for each individual from 100 or more
such samplings comprises the velocity score. This score reflects
the total time an individual spends moving through that part of the
environment where it is exposed to contact with associates. To
graphically represent the results, the individuals are ranked according to these scores, with Rank 1 assigned to the individual with the
highest score, and then the velocity score is plotted as a function
of the individual's velocity rank.** Even at this early phase of
social structuring of the group, it is apparent that the members of
the group differ markedly on the basis of this measure. After final
structuring of relationships among members of the group, past experience indicates that the velocity scores will approximate a trend

---

* I am indebted to my colleagues, G.A. Bagley, C.L. Bishop, and
G.G. Wheeler for their conduct of this study.

** See Footnote next page.

shown by the lower dashed line. That is to say, time will produce
an even more marked difference in velocity scores. If one knows
only the relative velocity scores of the members of a group, fairly
precise predictions can be made about the characteristics of the behavior of each individual. Since the animals shown here are all
males, it will be more informative if I present the general picture
which has been revealed from our studies of a number of groups of
both mice and rats:

For simplicity's sake let us divide any group into an upper, a
middle and a lower third according to their velocity scores. The
upper third will contain the territorial and other dominant males.
They receive relatively few wounds during fights and exhibit normal
effective sexual behavior. This normal behavior includes avoiding
ingress into abodes where their presence might disturb nursing females. They move with calm assurance through their range. Overall,
they exhibit those behaviors most conducive to the reproductive survival of the species. A similar picture holds for the females among
the upper velocity ranks. They are the most effective mothers; they
construct excellent nests, provide their young with ample opportunity
for nursing and move the entire litter from one place to another as

---

** Eqs. (113) and (126) in J.B. Calhoun, "The Social Use of Space" [9],
provide means of calculating expected velocities. Where the number
of animals, N, in the universe approximates the optimum number, N_0,
for that space and configuration, then the expected velocity, $v^{(exp)}$,
may be calculated either as:

$$\frac{N - R + 1}{N} \left[\frac{2 \sum_1^N v^{(obs)}}{N + 1} \right] \qquad \text{(113 derived)}$$

or

$$\frac{N - R + 1}{N} \left[v_\alpha^{(obs)} \right] \qquad \text{(126 derived)}$$

where R = Rank of velocity

$v^{(obs)}$ = Observed velocity

$v_\alpha^{(obs)}$ = Observed velocity, $R = 1$

Where the $v^{(obs)}$ approximates the $v^{(exp)}$ from (113 derived) then
$N = N_0$ and the social system has obtained equilibrium. From the
fact that the $v^{(exp)}$ so calculated for $R = 1$, and $R = 8$ are respectively 61.8 and 7.7, it is obvious that either N does not equal N_0 or the
social system has not yet obtained equilibrium. Other observational
data suggest that social equilibrium has not yet been attained. With
further withdrawal by lower ranking mice Eq. (126 derived) predicts
the dashed line of Figure 4.

this action may decrease the likelihood of interference from invading disturbed adults. As with the males, they exhibit the whole reper- toire of behavior most conducive to the reproductive survival of the species.

Individuals in the middle velocity ranks exhibit a strikingly different complex of behaviors. Males rarely win aggressive encounters. Despite this failure, they repeatedly place themselves in positions which elicit attacks from more dominant high velocity males. This arises from a propensity for continual involvement in sexual activities. Despite repeatedly being wounded, such males persist in invading areas dominated by high velocity males which estrous females enter to seek respite from the advances of these lower velocity males. It is this proclivity for involvement in sexual activities, of continual probing into the domains of dominant males, that gives them the appearance of being much more active than their velocity scores reveal. Their sex- ual behavior exhibits a wide spectrum from near normalcy to extreme deviation. It includes an often heightened intensity of response ex- pressed as maintaining a mount on the female many times the normal duration, and this often without intromission. Furthermore, such males exhibit a wide range of other reproductively ineffective behav- iors. They will mount other adult males as well as non-receptive fe- males, and in extreme instances will mount immature individuals of either sex.

The deviance of behavior is equally striking among females of the middle velocity ranks. Though they often become pregnant, their maternal behavior becomes so disrupted as to make the chances of their rearing any young very low. They lose the capacity to build nests or to keep their litters intact at any place. Even when they retain the ability to move their young from the place where a disturbance has oc- curred, the several members of the litter are deposited at scattered points and eventually deserted. Such females less often reside in areas where they more regularly receive protection from the dominant males from the excessive advances of their lower velocity male asso- ciates. As a consequence of the stress experienced, their conception rate becomes reduced, and embryos die before term. Some of the low- est velocity females in this middle group exhibit male sexual behav- ior. They mount adult males as well as other adult females.

What is most striking about the members of the lowest velocity ranked group is the extreme lack of involvement in social relation- ships. Part of this lack of involvement may be traced simply to the fact of their rare emergence from those places of retreat utilized mostly by higher velocity individuals only for sleeping. And yet, even when these low velocity individuals do appear, as they must if they are to secure food and water, they neither elicit responses from associates nor actively initiate interactions. They are merely nutri- tional machines, making no contribution to the reproductive survival of the species. Many of these individuals are so isolated from social reality that, despite the proximity of associates, these associates just do not seem to exist for them. They do not experience stress from participation in social life. This is reflected by their small adrenals, kidneys and hearts, as well as their exceptionally large deposits of fat.

I have come to the conclusion that this velocity stratification of a group, with all the attendant alterations in behavior, will develop even under the most optimum environmental circumstances. That is to say, it will develop even where all needed physical resources are ample and easily accessible and where no undue crowding exists. At first sight it may seem strange that evolution has allowed such a consequence of group life to persist. We may justifiably wonder why evolution has not maximized normalcy of behavior in terms of a much larger proportion of a group exhibiting those behaviors which contribute to the reproductive survival of the species. It is true that the individuals with reduced velocity and more abnormal behavior do often become active at times and places which expose them to predators. Although this circumstance may contribute to the survival of the more normal segment of the population and thereby increase the chances of their producing progeny successfully, I suspect that this fact has absolutely no bearing on the inevitability of the origin of abnormal behavior, at least abnormal in the sense of not seemingly contributing directly to reproductive survival. This is a very puzzling question. Why should behaviors persist through the history of a species when no individuals which express them leave any significant number of progeny? The obvious explanation is that heredity has little bearing on their origin. I am not proposing that heredity cannot influence the origin of abnormal behavior. Rather, I am proposing that environmental circumstances associated with group living will result in abnormal behavior despite the most advantageous hereditary constitution.

I will shortly return to an explanation of the inevitability of abnormal behavior. Before doing so, we may inquire if there may be some advantage to the development of reduced velocity despite the accompanying abnormal behavior. I would like to share with you the observation that first gave me an insight into this question. In a study of wild rats in a large enclosure, there came a time when the contained population had divided itself into 13 local colonies, each consisting of about 12 adults. One of these was an all male group whose members were quite socially withdrawn; they had developed low velocity status with many of the accompanying abnormal behaviors, including not only considerable homosexual propensities, but also a reduced ability to maintain their burrow in the earth in good repair. And yet they made a discovery which on the human level would be comparable to developing the wheel. In enlarging the tunnel system of a burrow, the usual procedure followed by rats is to scratch loose dirt and then alternately push and kick the loose dirt until it has been deposited on a mound surrounding an entrance. Very rarely, if

the earth is moist, as it often is, rats will exhibit a more efficient
method of removing dirt from the burrow. They will pack it into small
wads which they will pick up with their teeth and then transport it
out in the same fashion that they do small rocks. It is also fairly
normal for rats to push and roll out larger rocks which they encounter
during their excavations. What these fairly withdrawn, abnormally behaving rats did was to discover how to build an artificial round rock
just smaller than the diameter of the tunnels. What they did involved
taking 40 or 50 wads of dirt and packing them together until they
had a nice round ball; then they would roll it out and deposit it on
the mound. I, of course, cannot rule out the possibility that this
behavior has a strong hereditary component contributing to its origin,
much as is the case of the typical ball formation among dung beetles.
In support of my contention that this was a truly creative act, I can
only say that I have examined thousands of mounds of wild rats not exposed to the extra intense forces producing social withdrawal in my
enclosed population. Never did I observe this ball formation under
these more natural conditions, where low velocity rats are not likely
to survive very long.

        Other instances of developing novel and useful behavior only by
rats with reduced social velocity have been observed. In a search
for the possible reasons for this proclivity by moderately withdrawn
rats, I have screened rats of varying velocity in an apparatus which
records the duration and sequence of a number of behavioral states
such as sleeping, grooming, eating, drinking and locomoting. High
velocity rats tend to have much more order in the sequences. On the
other hand, the lower velocity individuals exhibit greater randomness
of their sequences. For them, one can predict much less well what
the next behavior will be on the basis of the ongoing one. As velocity lowers, the chances increase that there will arise some new ordering of behaviors that might be advantageous. From such observations I have concluded that a flowing back and forth with regard to
degree of social withdrawal or reduction in velocity is conducive to
creativity. The reduction of velocity permits dissolution of former
fixed sequential activities and permits new combinations of behavioral
states. Reduction of the pressures which led to social withdrawal
permits increased velocity and a fixation of the new sequence which
arose during the lowered velocity state.

        To the extent that these insights may have applicability on the
human level, it necessitates placing a new perspective on the general
issue of mental health. Fostering high velocity and heightened involvement in social interactions promotes the acquisition of that
knowledge and those sequences of behavior most conducive to adequate
functioning under the conditions most prevalent in the here and now.
Increased social withdrawal and reduction of velocity promotes dissolution of prior patterns of behaving and thinking and their replacement by different sequences. Then the opportunity to resume social
involvement, to increase velocity, permits fixation of the new patterns

evolved while in the more withdrawn state. Whether these new patterns
of behaving are judged as creative by society depends upon their functional utility under altered circumstances, or whether they may contribute to producing altered conditions deemed desirable by society.
From the point of view of augmenting the prevalence of creativity,
the concept of mental health must incorporate the desirability of
fostering the shifting up and down the scale of velocity, even though
this may involve some expression of behaviors judged undesirable from
other points of view.

THE "MYTHEMATICAL" SOCIAL POOL GAME

Although considerable empirical data buttress the concept of
velocity, we may appreciate its origins and implications better by
examining a diagram of the "mythematical" social pool game, a crude
representation of a more complex mathematical model [9].

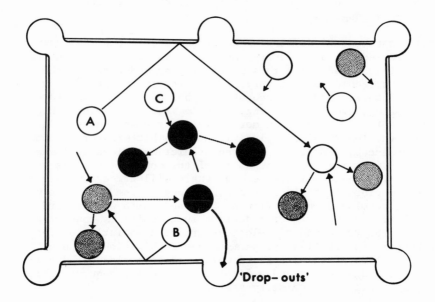

FIGURE 5 - THE "MYTHEMATICAL" SOCIAL POOL GAME

Consider several billiard balls on a table (Figure 5). Each
has certain attributes. Each moves at a constant velocity, as if
propelled by some inner force. The physical diameter of each is
equal to that of every other ball. All move within a fixed space
or area. How often one ball will on the average collide with another
will depend upon these three factors, velocity, diameter and area, in
relationship to the number of balls present in the area. Furthermore,

each ball from time to time develops a need state for contacting some
other ball in an equivalent need state. Ball "A" with a bent arrow
indicating its path of movement represents such a ball in the need
state of encountering another ball in a like state. As shown, it
does encounter such a ball. Each then gains from the encounter; each
enters a state, which may be designated as gratification, that lasts
for some time after the encounter. Residing in this state of gratification is indicated by the balls becoming stippled. After a specified period of time elapses, each of the stippled balls will complete
its stay in the gratification state and return to the state of need-
ing further contact with other balls.

One such ball, "B", by chance encounters a ball which is still
in the gratification state from a prior satisfactory encounter. This
latter ball remains uninfluenced by the encounter with "B"; it remains
stippled. However, its failure to interact appropriately to the needs
of "B" transforms "B" into a state of frustration indicated by the
ball becoming black. In like fashion, when another ball, "C", meets
a ball in the frustration state, it too will be thrown into the state
of frustration, in which it will remain for some period of time before
returning to the original need state for contact. At all times every
ball is in one of three states: in need of contact, gratified from a
satisfactory contact, or frustrated from an unsatisfactory contact.
Purely by chance some balls will be frustrated more often than others.
The more these balls are frustrated, the more they will try to escape
from the field, the area within which meaningful contacts might occur.
They seek the side pockets of their area of habitation. Here they are
not visible to view; their "dropping out" leads to a lowered estimate
of their velocity in terms of the total path traversed in the contact
opportunity area over extended periods of time.

Furthermore, we can assume other attributes of these balls.
Each contact involves a particular repertoire of actions by each con-
tactee toward the other, if the one or both in the need state for contact are to be rewarded, i.e., to be precipitated into the state of
gratification. When any ball in a need state for contact is not responded to appropriately, because the ball it contacts is in a refractory state of gratification or frustration, it will by this inappropriate response not have its own actions rewarded. As a consequence,
its behavior will become somewhat deviant as it emerges again into
the need state for contact. Thus, in proportion to the number of
frustrating experiences to the number of gratifying ones, a ball will
exhibit more deviance of behavior as frustrating experiences increase.
As a consequence, the members of the group will vary with respect to
both velocity and deviance of behavior.

Two other variables are involved, the intensity or strength of
contact and the number of individuals inhabiting the area. Now let
us assume that the balls have acquired the property of replicating
themselves and of possessing a mechanism for passing to succeeding

generations properties which will increase the likelihood of expression of appropriate behavior. The most important of these relates to the intensity of involvement at the time of contact. Depending upon the number of balls in the area, there is a specific intensity of contact which will maximize the amount of time spent in the state of gratification. This arises from the property of duration of remaining in refractory states of gratification or frustration being proportional to the intensity of contact. There is another peculiar consequence of life within such a system of contacts: balls will attempt to maximize the amount of time spent in the state of gratification. This attempt has the consequence of producing an equivalent amount of frustration. Since this is the nature of life, the genetic basis of physiology for its proper functioning comes to demand experiencing of equal amounts of frustration and gratification. Alterations from optimum group size, that is any change in the number of balls on the pool table of customary size, leads to an imbalance in fulfilling these two needs. When too few balls are present, the average ball will experience too little of both gratification and frustration. When the number of balls in the area reaches the square of the optimum number, every individual will essentially be frustrated as a result of every encounter since every other ball is essentially always in a frustrating refractory state. In this situation, every ball will develop maximal withdrawal, maximal reduction of velocity. No ball will have any awareness of any associate, even though they are crowded closely together. So far our experiments have not fully validated this conclusion, but they point in the direction of its correctness.

We call such balls by various names. Some are called mice, some rats, others man. Even fairly casual observation of such balls, each with its species-specific attributes, confirms the general validity of the above formulation. I call such simulations of more complex phenomena "Mythematical Games". This term reflects a core conviction of mine--any particular expression of behavior as a sample of a wide range of possible variation is relatively meaningless, and even unintelligible. True appreciation of individual isolated episodes comes only from viewing them against the backdrop of a conceptual formulation never ever expressed as such. In this sense the concept is a myth which forms the only reality.

In a later section we will need recourse to a simple expression of one aspect of the above mythematical formulation.

Let: A = area inhabited by N individuals

       v = average velocity of an individual through A

       d = target diameter of an individual

Where the individual is considered as a ball the
target diameter is simply the diameter of the ball.
In general, d encompasses any attribute which biases
the probability that an individual will be detected
and contacted by associates.

μ = communication constant reflecting the likelihood
of contact

Then: μ = dv/A

when a species is in evolutionary equilibrium

μ = 1.0

that is to say: A = 1.0 and both d and v have the value, $(A)^{\frac{1}{2}}$. Each
will change over time symmetrically with A. When I say that a species
is in evolutionary equilibrium, I mean that there is an optimum number
of individuals inhabiting each unit of area, A. As a secondary ab-
straction, and a more meaningful one, evolutionary equilibrium con-
notes an appropriate number of contacts per unit time per individual
to maximize gratification, and as a by-product to produce an equivalent amount of frustration.

THE CONCEPT OF THE OPTIMUM (BASIC) GROUP SIZE, N_b

The previous formulations indicate the necessity for a constant
group size inhabiting a particular sized area. When we look across
the many species of mammals surviving today, there is obviously a
wide range of optimum group sizes. Some species customarily lead a
fairly solitary way of life, others live in various intermediate sized
groups, and some form very large aggregates. However, there is one
particularly common optimum sized group which demands our attention.
This is the one consisting of 12 individuals. We have to look far
back into the roots of mammalian evolution for its origin, although
much of the picture I will develop may be seen in contemporary species which reflect earlier evolutionary stages.

In Figure 6 each dot represents the center of the range of an
individual mammal of any species which has the capacity of establishing a single or several closely neighboring homesites. For simplicity's sake, let us think of a single homesite in the exact center of
each individual's range. If we take any typical individual and represent the extent of its range by a circle, it may be seen that the
range of every individual will overlap those of several associates.
The reason for this lies in certain peculiar properties with which
every individual moves through its range and responds to resources
located in it. Many excursions terminate near the central homesite.
Per unit area, fewer and fewer terminate at increasing distances from
the range center. Were individuals maximally antagonistic, to the

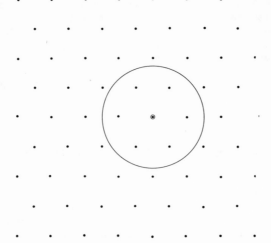

FIGURE 6 - THE IDEAL DISTRIBUTION OF HOME RANGE
CENTERS OF ASOCIAL MAMMALS

The range of each individual about its center has
the extent of the example shown by the circle.

extent of there being no overlap of the ranges of neighbors, the total population would make very ineffective utilization of resources,
since no individual often visits regions in the outer portions of
their respective ranges. Evolution, abhorring such inefficiency, has
permitted the development of mutual tolerance, implemented by appropriate spacing behaviors, to the extent that the degree of overlap of
adjoining ranges will permit an equal utilization of resources over
all space inhabited by a population. There is a specific mathematical equation, that of the bivariate normal distribution function,
which adequately describes the distribution of responses of an individual over its range [9,10]. This equation includes a parameter,
σ, here a measure of distance such that the radius of the home
range equals 3σ. When animals attempt to maximize distance between home range centers, and to achieve the most effective use of
resources, the distance between the home range centers of any two
neighbors will be 2σ.

With this degree of overlap of neighboring ranges, each individual will occasionally encounter neighbors. To the extent that individuals come to know each other, a force of attraction counteract-

ing the more primitive dispersion resulting from antagonisms will
come into play. Animals will begin to clump about those individuals,
any set of them, whose ranges do not overlap. Individuals whose
ranges do not overlap cannot know each other, and therefore cannot
be attracted toward each other. The large circles in Figure 7 represent three such individuals. The homesites of their neighbors are
represented by dots, squares, or triangles. Each of the three particular individuals we are particularly concerned with will attract
to themselves their six nearest neighbors, whose original homesites
are represented by dots. Each of the three individuals shown, about
whom a condensation of social structure is developing, also has 12
next-nearest neighbors whose homesites are represented by squares or
triangles.

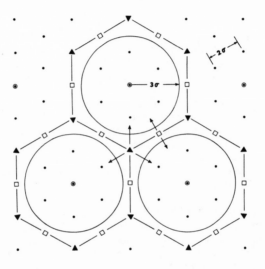

FIGURE 7

CONDENSATION
OF DISPERSED
INDIVIDUALS INTO
SOCIAL GROUPS

◉   = Individuals whose ranges do not overlap and who do not
       share nearest neighbors. These are alpha individuals.

●   = Beta individuals; they form sets of six nearest neighbors
       to alpha individuals.

□   = γ_1, gamma type 1, individuals, who may be attracted to
       either one of two neighboring individuals.

▲   = γ_2, gamma type 2, individuals, who may be attracted to
       either one of three neighboring alpha individuals.

The condensation leads to an average group of 12 individuals
with a range of 7 to 19.

Consider one of these neighbors whose home range center is represented by a square. It lies halfway between two of the individuals
about whom condensation of the social structure is taking place. It,
thus, has the opportunity of becoming attached to either one of them.
Let us designate as alpha individuals the ones to whom associates are
being attracted. Then it may be seen that each alpha individual has
six of these next-nearest neighbors, each of which has a 50-50 chance
of being attracted to him. On the average, each alpha individual will
have three of these next-nearest neighbors attracted to himself. By
like reasoning, each of the next-nearest neighbors, whose homesite
is shown by a triangle, has a one-third chance of being attracted to
each of its three alpha neighbors. Since each of the alpha individuals has six such next-nearest neighbors, he will on the average attract two of them to himself. Thus, by this condensation process,
the average social group will come to be comprised of 1 + 6 + 3 + 2
= 12 individuals.

At first, such groups are hardly recognizable as such. The
alpha individuals's neighbors merely shift their homesites slightly
toward his. Over considerable evolutionary time, the group further
condenses until all members live at the same place or may even move
together through their now common range. Among the many species of
mammals which have developed an optimum or basic group of 12, there
is the Norway rat, several species of primates and man himself. For
the purposes of designating the optimum group size, socially immature
individuals do not count. These immature individuals must mature
within the social context of an approximately optimum sized group,
but for our present purposes they must be considered as comprising
essential background noise.

Maturing individuals will eventually enter the adult ranks.
They will tend to remain as members of the parent group as long as
possible. Some will replace older members which die. But if survival is sufficiently high, the size of the group will gradually increase to more than the optimum number. A particularly critical
point is reached when the number of individuals in the group attains
one less than twice the optimum size. It is at this point that the
members of the group become particularly sensitive to the increased
frustrations of life within the context of a larger than optimum
sized group. The normal response at this point is for the group to
split. One half can remain in the original area, while the other
half must seek a new area for colonizing. In time, all suitable terrain available to the species will be filled up; then disease, predation, and intra- and inter-group strife come into full play to bring
natality and mortality into balance.

In only rare instances has any species other than man been able
to overcome this barrier to further development. Outstanding is the
example of baboons. Through the development of genetically determined
sexual dimorphism, the optimum group size has been able to expand from

12 to 24 adults [19: p.335-367; 20,22]. Presumably this role differentiation, making possible an increased group size, has also been accompanied by the evolution of more effective means of extracting
energy resources. We can see a similar process in operation among
the Hutterites of South Dakota, Montana and Canada. With upwards of
four children per family, the optimum total group including children
appears to be about 75. This is indicated by the fact that when the
total group reaches 150 it divides and one half must seek a communal
farm elsewhere [1: p. 298, 32,33]. This indicates that the optimum
group size has increased to 24. There is little reason to anticipate that this increase has been brought about by genetic changes.
We must, therefore, conclude that role differentiation among the
Hutterites is just sufficient on a cultural basis to make the overall group essentially two groups of 12 sharing the same area through
restricting with whom it is appropriate to interact. Then, in so
far as any individual is concerned, the number of his interactions
per day will remain much as it was within a primitive hunter-gatherer
group of 12 adults. No doubt the Hutterites have been able to approximate the Eden state of incipient agriculture. Archeological
studies of Jarmo in Iraq of nearly 10,000 years ago indicate that
this early agricultural society was able to develop and tolerate a
total group size of 150 individuals [4]. And yet, by this approach
to an Edenic way of life, the Hutterites confirm my suspicion of the
inevitability of the origin of behavioral deviation and mental illness as an unavoidable consequence of group life [2: p.638].

But confirmation of this inevitability is not the reason for my
particular search. Rather, it has been to try and determine if there
may be a logical basis for determining what the optimum upper number
of man on earth may be.

CONDENSATION OF HUMAN SOCIAL GROUPS AND AN EMERGENT CONCEPT OF CULTURE AREA

Man like most creatures is intrinsically conservative. He obeys
what has been called "Romer's Rule".* This law holds that even when
the weaker groups of a species are excluded from former terrain, they
search for a new opportunity for reestablishing the former way of
life; but in so doing they may be forced to adapt genetically or culturally to some unanticipated circumstance. The strong remain where
few crises arise demanding change and adaptation--they remain firmly
traditional. The weak from necessity must become creative to survive.

---

* C.F. Hockett and R. Ascher state Romer's Rule as: "The initial
survival value of a favorable innovation is conservative, in that it
renders possible the maintenance of a traditional way of life in the
face of changed circumstances" and in following discussion they emphasize that weaker or excluded groups, or those less well able to
maintain fully the traditional way of life are more likely to be in-
novative [23: p.72].

Romer's Rule proposes that there is survival of the weak; survival of the meek. This proposal conforms to my formulation that rejection and withdrawal preceding reestablishment of a normal way of life is essential to creativity.

Now let us look back upon primitive hunter-gatherer man, who for countless millenia had followed a very simple and extremely slowly changing way of life. In so long as new terrain remained for groups budded from former ones to enter, there was no impetus for radical change. The old way of life could be reduplicated. However, at some point in time, extensive land masses became filled with these small bands containing an average of 12 adults and 18 children each. Each band roamed over a range 3σ in radius. Although each band might temporarily reside at several sites, the site most frequented lies at the center of the range. The points in Figure 8 represent these most frequented sites, which will simply be referred to as the village site. Just as with the home range centers of small asocial mammals, the village sites must be uniformly distributed with a 2σ interval between them in order to achieve the most efficient utilization of resources by a large population of bands. Once this state of affairs had developed over extensive regions, there existed no further place to go when groups increased to a size dictating that they split and one move away. They then faced a real dilemma. The need to maximize gratification demanded that there be a constant area for each group in order that the appropriate number of contacts per unit time would be realized. Since this need is grounded in physiology determined by heredity, this means that in so long as heredity remains essentially unchanged, there must remain as an invariant a particular sized area per adult individual.

Even though there was no more space to invade, man's ability to maintain natality greater than mortality tended to force the size of groups to increase. The conservative response was to increase mortality by inter-group fratricide or intra-group infanticide. Obviously this is an extreme oversimplification, but it does reflect the character of the conservative traditional response. At some point in time, some downtrodden group or groups discovered a new kind of space, a new kind of area they could move into. I shall call this "conceptual area". For the group to double in numbers while residing in the same physical space, it must acquire a conceptual area equivalent to its physical area. In this sense, conceptual area amounts simply to the acquisition of values and codes which permit role differentiation to the extent that, even in a double-sized group in the original physical area, meaningful social contacts would continue at the rate necessary to maximize gratification. In all probability, the first major role differentiation involved a culturally defined sexual difference in modes of extracting food and related resources. In fact, it was probably the need to discover more efficient means of extracting such resources by a denser population that first precipitated the development of the new roles and the new technologies which comprised the discovered conceptual area for invasion and exploitation.

Discovery of any new parcel of conceptual space requires retreat into another kind of space, the world of fantasy, a creative space. By analogy this creative space is involved in a creative communication constant, μ', where

$$\mu' = d'v'/A'$$

Here A' is the creative fantasy space, where the withdrawn individual generates objects for interaction out of his store of memory traces. These may be fantasied other people, but may just as well be any rearrangement of information which he finds pleasing. v' represents a sort of velocity with which the individual moves among the objects of his intellectual creation. Similarly, d' represents a sort of target diameter of the fantasying self and of the ideational objects created which permit them to contact and interact. The most intimate and intense of these fantasied interactions culminate in an intellectual orgasm, the eureka experience of the truly creative episode. Retreat into fantasy area by some members of the group is a prerequisite to developing the concepts which form the structures which force conceptual area to expand in harmony with population increase. We need feel no pity for individuals who have withdrawn into fantasy area. As many of you know from personal experience, life there can be lush and rewarding. What society has to provide is the means for enticing such individuals to return to the so-called normal reality of social intercourse where created concepts can be subjected to scrutiny and accepted if they prove to be a valuable addition to the existing conceptual area. For these concepts to warrant acceptance they must contribute in some way to role differentiation or to the development of resources or to their more efficient extraction. With this essential aside, let us return to the problem of conceptual area, or we may call it conceptual space to maintain a feeling of consistency with the title of my presentation.

With the first acquisition of a conceptual space equivalent to that of the physical space already occupied, man emerged as truly Homo sapiens. From that point on, man could continue to justify this appellation by making sufficient additions to conceptual area as population increased to maintain constant the total area available to each individual. This is my basic hypothesis: increases in conceptual area must keep approximately abreast with increases in total population.

It is impossible to maintain this process solely within the confines of the local group occupying one of the village sites represented in Figure 8. At some point in time, at some point in the process of increasing conceptual space, there must arise a sociopolitical union of the village sites, each of which then contains

more than two times the original optimum number. By this time the
typical village will already have participated in the emerging Agricultural Revolution. Each site will have become more firmly fixed
in space. Condensation or crystallization of the social structure
by such union must proceed without the shifts of location that characterized the much earlier formation of compact groups from dispersed
individuals. This restriction on shifting requires that the ranges
of influence of village sites, about which this social condensation
develops, must be packed as closely as possible without overlapping,
since such overlapping would produce initial undesirable disharmony.

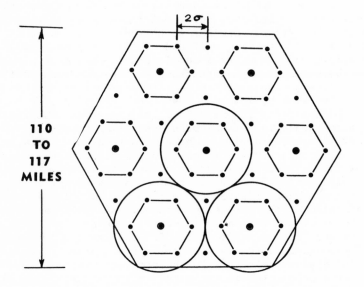

FIGURE 8 – FORMATION OF UNIFORMLY SCATTERED VILLAGE
SITES INTO SEVEN DISTRICTS WHICH LATER
COALESCE INTO A SINGLE "CULTURE AREA"

Village sites are 2σ distance in miles apart.

◉ = Village sites which will become district capitals.

The radius of influence of a district = 3σ , where
σ = 7.5 miles, as in western South America and Meso-
america south of Mexico City the culture area covers
11,840 sq. miles.

The ranges of influence of three such villages are shown as
circles in Figure 8. It will be noted that each such range having
a 3σ radius encompasses the locations of six other village sites.
Together they form a "District". With further increase in total
population over an extensive area, development of messengers and
traders as specialized new roles forming a part of the increased conceptual area permits adjoining districts to be bound together in a
single socio-political union. The topography of the distribution of
districts makes such union most practical and efficient, if one such
district dominates its six nearest neighboring districts. To show
the relative extent of such an assembly of districts, a hexagon may
be circumscribed about the ranges of influence of the peripheral six
districts. This is the outer hexagon shown in Figure 8. It will be
noted that I have included a range of 110 to 117 miles as defining
the distance across this complex, which I define as a "culture area".
Obviously, I have adapted this term "culture area" in the present
specific meaning from its more general usage by Kroeber and others
[25]. What is not apparent is the origin of the distances representing the more common expected diameter of the hexagon enclosing the
culture area.

I can only trace briefly the origin of this estimate of distance.
In 1962 I had the opportunity of spending a year at the Center for
Advanced Study in the Behavioral Sciences at Palo Alto, California.
Although I did complete my major theoretical work on the social use
of space at that time, I decided to spend most of my time searching
the literature relating to population, archeology, anthropology and
history for insights about man's evolving use of space. In this process I scanned a fairly large body of literature and examined several
hundred books and articles in detail. Somewhere along this process,
which has continued to the present, I became impressed with the frequency of encountering significant socio-political unions, the diameter of whose physical domain was slightly over 100 miles. Early
in 1967, while I was immersed in the literature on the Calusa Indians
of Florida, the present formulation of culture area crystallized in
my mind. If there were any merit to this concept, some initial confirmation of its possible validity might be revealed by examining the
distances between district, provincial and national capitals of Central America and northern and western South America. If the theory
is correct, only certain distances would be anticipated, with a specific number of each kind of distance. Furthermore, each distance
could be translated into sigma units of the range of the average village. The analysis of 386 such distances between actual cities gave
an estimate of 7.5 miles for sigma. As indicated in Figure 8, the
distance between the centers of adjoining village sites is 2σ. From
this it may be calculated that the distance across the hexagonal
culture area is 15.59σ. With a σ of 7.5 miles, this distance across
the culture area is 117 miles and includes a total area of 11,840
square miles.

According to the present theory, the culture area forms a mold which will be preserved and reflected in much later spheres of socio-political influence. One such type of sphere of influence is represented by the central place theory of economics which identifies hierarchical overlapping spheres of influence of successively greater scope within which a single city serves as a focus for and encompasses all smaller areas of influence. Woldenberg's recent synthesis is particularly instructive [40]. One of his examples is that of Christaller's study of eight such spheres of influence dominated by Strassburg, Frankfurt, Stuttgart, Zurich, Munich, Nuremberg, Linz, and Pilsen. Each presumably represents the long aftermath of culture areas established several thousand years ago. These eight cities provide 13 inter-city distances with an average of 110.5 miles, which I have rounded off to 110 miles, which gives an estimate of 7.0 miles for the γ range parameter of an original village site according to the present model as shown in Figure 8.

These two examples of estimating the range of a village merely serve to indicate the quite crude methodology for making this intuitive hypothesis of culture area more specific. Other much more general indications of support for the idea are provided by examples which seem to conform to the hypothesis. For example, there are the seven Basque "nations". These "nations" correspond to the districts of the present formulation. Similarly, there are the seven sheikdoms of the Trucial Coast, or we can note that the Romans divided what is modern Portugal into three administrative units, each of an area comparable to a culture area.

All of this focus on the concept of culture area was directed toward establishing a basis for predicting the upper optimum limit of world population. For this effort to be successful, it was necessary to establish how far population growth could continue within a culture area as a consequence of expansion of conceptual space that did not go beyond inclusion of socio-political union that was confined within the culture area itself. One of the initial clues involved the report that Alvarado met a force of nearly 30,000 warriors when he invaded Guatemala. Portions of my earlier theory on the evolution of social groups suggested that 7/12 of the basic social groups represent the more dominant segment. If the maximum fighting force at full development of the culture area as an isolated independent socio-political unit included 7/12 of the adult males, it would take a total population of over 200,000 persons to muster such a force.

Attaining this number involved several doublings of the population within the culture area and consequently several doublings of the conceptual area. Looking back to the time when the culture area was first fully settled within primitive hunter-gatherer groups, the total population included 61 bands, each on the average with 12 adults and 18 children, making a total population of 1,830 individuals.

Seven successive population doublings pass through totals of 3,660;
7,320; 14,640; 29,280; 58,560; 117,120 to 234,240. We may take the
latter as the upper optimum population of a self-contained culture
area. Confirmation that this number does represent the terminal
phase of the isolated culture area is provided by the fact that in
1745, the time of the Battle of Culloden when the Scottish people
were finally and firmly brought within the larger socio-political
union of the English Crown, there were 245,000 persons inhabiting
the seven crofting counties (districts of my terminology) of Highland Scotland. I cannot at this time be exhaustive in this analysis;
at each level of analysis I only continue the search long enough to
feel that I am on the right track.

THE OPTIMUM WORLD POPULATION

In a perfectly uniform terrain, each culture area will be sur-
rounded by six others. Each such set of seven culture areas then
forms the basis for a further socio-political union. Such unions
form as aspect of the increasing conceptual space which will permit
the population within each culture area to double to 468,480. The
union of seven culture areas I will call a "nation" (Figure 9). As

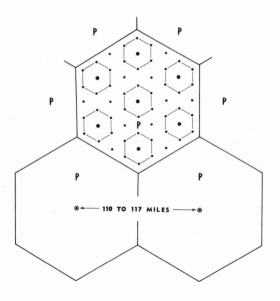

FIGURE 9 - FORMATION OF A "NATION" FROM THE UNION OF SEVEN
"CULTURE AREAS". THE CONTAINED CULTURE AREAS
BECOME "PROVINCES", P, OF THE NATION.

Table 1.

Theoretical population growth associated with doubling of population with each coalescing of seven of the prior levels of socio-political organization and accompanying increase in conceptual space.*

Socio-political Unit	Number of Contained Culture Areas per Unit	Number of Units	Unit Population	World Population	Theoretical Date
"Culture Area" at "City State" Level	1	2401	234,240	562,410,240	1709
"Nation"	7	343	3,279,360	1,124,820,480	1868
"Empire"	49	49	45,911,040	2,249,640,960	1948
"League"	343	7	642,754,560	4,499,281,920	1988
"World Union"	2401	1	8,998,563,840	8,998,563,840	2008

* This formulation assumes complete similarity of phasing of development over all time over all the world. In a more general application to the real world coalescence of "City States" into "Nations" begins with the local development of a technological-scientific revolution paralleled by comparable increases in philosophical conceptual space.

an isolated socio-political unit, it will include a total population of 3,279,360. By a similar process, seven nations can unite to form an "empire". This union will permit the population of each contained nation to double to 6,558,720 and the empire will therefore contain a total population of 45,911,040. By a similar process, seven empires can unite into a "league". This will permit the population of each empire to double to 91,822,080, and thus the league will contain a total population of 642,754,560. Again by a similar process, seven leagues will unite to form a "world union". This will permit the population of each league to double to 1,285,509,120 and the world union to include 8,998,563,840 individuals. This "nine" billion is the optimum upper world population. This process is summarized in Table 1.*

Completion of this process requires 7^4 or 2,401 culture areas. Since the average culture area covers 11,840 square miles, the world union will include a minimum of 28 million square miles. (It is obvious that the above process of socio-political union could not continue for another round since it would require four times the land surface of the earth to satisfy the spatial requirements of the theoretical 126 billion population). With only slightly less than 47 million square miles of land surface not now in deserts or frozen wastes, this leaves less than 19 million square miles which might continue as primarily the domain of other forms of life. And yet the world population will probably overshoot the optimum population of nine billion, since it seems unlikely that population increase can be brought to a halt before it reaches 13.5 billion. This amount of overshoot will place extreme burdens on man to preserve adequate communities of other forms of life, particularly during the period required to decrease again to nine billion. Our sceneria for the future should, at a minimum, extend through the period of overshoot until the optimum upper population is reattained.

TO SUMMARIZE: Man stands unique among animals in learning how to bypass the strictures placed by limitation of physical space on further population growth. He has made this escape by discovering how to create conceptual space, the total information pool generated by man from which rules, codes and theories may be condensed which permit more effective coping with the physical and social environment. In particular, this process of increasing conceptual space as population increases permits each individual on the average to become involved in the same number of social interactions per day as held true in the earlier times, when life was primarily confined to experiences within a hunter-gatherer band of 12 adults and their associated children. To continue enlarging conceptual space requires involving more and

---

* In the present instance, dates are based on a slight modification of the von Foerster equation to one in which each doubling of the population requires half the time as the prior doubling; otherwise, the same data are presented elsewhere [15].

individuals in a common communication network. Socio-political union enhances the enlargement and effectiveness of such networks. Such union will continue until the entire world population becomes incorporated into a single network. This point will arrive when the world population reaches nine billion. For this reason, nine billion is set as the optimum world population in which individual human beings serve as the primary nodes and the primary links in the communication network.

CONCEPTUAL TARGET DIAMETER AND VELOCITY

I have earlier indicated that where life was primarily confined to functioning within physical space, contacts culminating in gratification and frustration are influenced by a communication constant, μ, where $\mu = dv/A$. By analogy contacts relating to life within conceptual space are similarly governed by another communication constant, μ'', where $\mu'' = d''v''/A''$. d'' represents conceptual target diameter, that property or consequence of the store of concepts which the individual has been able to acquire and utilize for both mining resources and control of contacts with associates. Similarly, conceptual velocity, v'', represents a kind of movement through the conceptual space of available information in a manner which permits sufficient acquisition of concepts to maintain the individual's target diameter, or to enlarge it as the population increases or as the number of others met increases. Conceptual velocity represents the cortical processes of scanning or exploring conceptual space, A''.

The evolution of the genus _Homo_ involved a more rapid increase in cortical mass in proportion to body mass than had been true among other mammals. This increase permitted each individual within its own life span and solely by its own experiences to learn more effective ways of coping with the environment. Then, as _Homo sapiens_ emerged within the genus, increase in cortical mass gradually ceased. This cessation was brought about by the gradual acquisition of the capacity for creating conceptual space and the ability to pass most of its structure on to the next generation. At the time when we may say that _Homo sapiens_ had clearly emerged as a cultural species, as distinct from the physical attributes which define him as a biological species, the conceptual space or conceptual area available to each individual became equivalent to the physical space available to him. At this time, $A = A''$. As we will shortly see, this time may be approximated as 38,710 B.C.: a time at which, if the world of man were developing uniformly, there would have been 146,461 primitive bands at the 12-adults-per-band stage. With their children they formed a total population of about 4.4 million. Since man as a truly cultural animal, one with the ability to generate conceptual space, likely emerged first in the more crowded central portions of his range, the actual date of his first cultural emergence must have been somewhat before 40,000 years ago. In any case, at this time of emergence man must have been in equilibrium with his conceptual space.

Therefore,

$$\mu'' = d''v''/A'' = 1.0$$

At this time it may also be considered that $d'' = v''$. It follows that both d'' and $v'' = (A)^{\frac{1}{2}}$.

   At some time in the distant past, man utilized his cortex to the extent of incorporating a unit of conceptual space equivalent to the physical space in which he lived. At this time, we may view the actual diameter of the head as representing the degree of utilization of the cortex and thus equivalent to conceptual target diameter. Later enlargements of conceptual target diameter thus may be depicted as enlargements of the head, while the rest of the body remains constant in size (Figure 12). Where d_μ stands for diameter of a sphere equivalent to that of the utilized cortex* then:

$$d_\mu = 2(A'')^{1/6}$$

Obviously, there will arrive a time at which maximal utilization of cortical mass will be attained. Since population growth, which permits realization of individual potentialities, depends upon continual expansion of conceptual space, it follows that, when maximal utilization of cortical mass is reached, any further increase in numbers will lead to a decline in effective realization of potentialities, since the extra individuals will impede acquisition of relevant information. By some strange coincidence, it looks as though maximum use of the cortex will actually arise at the time

---

* Let r_μ, d_μ and A_μ represent radius, diameter, and volume of a sphere representing utilized cortical mass. And employing " = " in the sense of "proportional to", we have: $A_\mu = r_\mu^3$, $d_\mu = 2r_\mu$; and from the logic in the text $d'' = (A'')^{\frac{1}{2}} = A_\mu$. Therefore: $A_\mu = (d_\mu/2)^3$; $d_\mu = 2(A_\mu)^{1/3}$.

   Substituting $(A'')^{\frac{1}{2}} = A$ in the latter equation, we have $d_\mu = 2[(A'')^{\frac{1}{2}}]^{1/3} = 2(A'')^{1/6}$. d_μ's at times of sequential doublings of A'' were calculated. These, with slight modifications for artistic purposes were utilized in the preparation of Figure 12. It follows that $d_\mu = 2(d'')^{1/3}$ or $d'' = [d_\mu/2]^3$. The original concept of target diameter [9,10], elaborated this contact enhancing factor through a transition from mere body width or diameter to involvement of other attributes, such as plumage or stance, which increased the likelihood of two individuals interacting. Thus, target diameter comes to include any force or condition or process enhancing contact. Ability to acquire and utilize concepts, in the sense of d'' as representing conceptual target diameter, in like fashion influences whether or not two individuals will interact.

of reaching the optimum upper level of population. However, it will
be necessary to develop the formulation a little more before returning to that point.

We also need to inquire further as to the meaning of conceptual
velocity. If the logic being developed here is correct, movement in
physical space and movement in conceptual space should have much the
same properties. You will recall from the earlier discussion of
making empirical operational measures of velocity in mice, that our
procedure was to record how often each individual was noted moving
through its available physical space. All such movement is noted
during episodes of locomotion between which the mouse was asleep or
engaged in some nonlocomoting activity. The final index of velocity
results from the interaction of two variables, how frequently episodes of locomotion begin and how long they last. We shall here
only be concerned with the latter. Each episode of locomotion is a
particular instance of the behavioral state of moving through the
physical environment. When a large sample of such behavioral states
is examined with regard to their duration, it is noted that all last
at least for a length of time, T; and there is some maximum duration
beyond which no instance extends. Then the span of time from the
end of T to the maximum duration may be divided into a number of
class intervals of length, t, and the number, N, of behavioral states,
β, of each class interval of duration tallied. When this is done, as
we have done for many large samples obtained in our studies of rats,
N as a function of T + t forms a negative exponential curve as shown
in Figure 10. This is the most common pattern. Such results mean
that after any β has continued for a duration of time, T, there is
a constant probability, p', that it will terminate in the next unit
of time, t, regardless of how long it has already lasted.

However, if we select a sample of episodes of locomotion in
which each instance was preceded by a relatively long period of other
activities or states than locomotion, a pattern having a much longer
mean duration is revealed. The change in pattern in the shorter durations is that shown by the trend of the open dots in Figure 10.
The interpretation of this change is as follows: Beginning at the
termination of time duration, T, there is a marked inhibition of the
impulse that terminates the behavioral state. The longer the behavioral state continues, the less strong is this inhibitory influence,
until, at a time denoted by the intersection of the two lines of Figure 10, it no longer functions. Beyond this time the constant probability of the behavioral state terminating in the next interval of
time, t, holds as in the first pattern described above. Although
this description is presented here because it describes the behavioral state of locomotion from which estimates of velocity are obtained
in the free-ranging situation of animals as members of social groups,
I wish to point out that this transition from the first to the second pattern adequately describes the whole repertoire of behavioral
states in the rat. It holds for the behavioral states of eating,

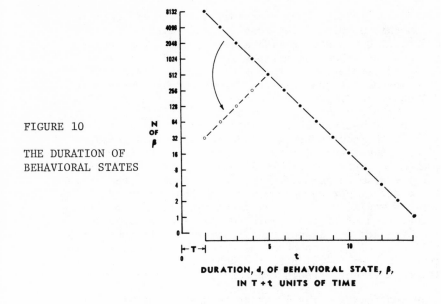

FIGURE 10

THE DURATION OF
BEHAVIORAL STATES

DURATION, d, OF BEHAVIORAL STATE, β,
IN T + t UNITS OF TIME

Pattern One is that of the solid points only.

Pattern Two has a shift of the shorter durations
to that shown by the open dots. Shift from Pattern One to Two produces a doubling of the average
duration.

drinking, self-directed activities we pool under the general designation of "grooming", as well as for three distinct kinds of sleep.
In fact, it appears that we have discovered a basic pattern of
functioning of the central nervous system.*

If this is so, it should apply to behavioral states in man involving the elaboration or entrainment of concepts as a category of
behavioral states. Every written paragraph represents an instance
of such a behavioral state. The duration of paragraphs may be mea-

---

* Our full formulation of the CNS control of occurrence, sequence
and duration of behavioral states based on our studies of rat behavior remains to be published. Essentially, we have been able to calculate the probabilities of functioning of four signals which permit
a fairly comprehensive description of changes in behavior over time.
One governs initiation of behavior; two, its terminations; and the
fourth, the likelihood of entrainment.

sured as the number of letters each contains. Two samples were selected to explore this problem. One consisted of 3,198 paragraphs
selected from about 7,000 pages of literature relating to population and mental health. These paragraphs were judged to include
particularly cogent formulation of theory or insight. This sample
conformed to the second pattern described above and had an average
duration of 826 characters. The second sample consisted of 1,171
paragraphs, nearly the whole book, of Norbert Wiener's "The Tempster".
This book was selected because we have good reason to believe that
Wiener ranked among the top in recent times in being able to elaborate complex conceptual sequences, and yet in this book he was re-
sorting to an age-old device of storytelling. Although N of β as
a function of T + t also conformed to the second pattern, the average number of characters per paragraph was much less, only 396. It
is obvious that storytelling forms a distinct behavioral state from
that of the formulation of concepts into complex insights. But of
much greater importance here is the confirmation that the behavioral
state which reflects velocity in physical space has a similar basis
in central nervous system function as the behavioral state which reflects velocity of movement through conceptual space.

CULTURAL REVOLUTIONS AND THE INCREASE IN NUMBERS OF MAN

Von Foerster and his colleagues have made an analysis of the
numbers of man on earth based on the past 2,000 years [38]. This
analysis is most cogent for the present inquiry. In essence, they
found that each successive doubling of the population required only
half the time necessary for the prior doubling.* Presumably this
characteristic of population increase extended far back through the
history of the species, at least as far back as the time when communication between contiguous bands enhanced the ability of the members of each band to cope with the contingencies of their physical
and social environment. Likewise, this process leading to a continually shorter time between doublings of the population will presumably continue for some time into the future. However, as they
point out, this process cannot continue for very long into the future, because, if it does, each successive doubling will be requiring an extremely short time, nearly infinitely short. This time,
t_o, at which the population becomes unbounded, they term "Doomsday"
and calculate as 2027 A.D.

Doomsday has several closely related implications. It means
that the unique process of population increase, which sets man off

---

* The von Foerster equation [9,10] for calculating the total
population at any time τ, the number of years before 2026 A.D.
(the date at which the population will go to infinity if the pattern of increase over the past 2000 years continues), is
$N = 1.79 \times 10^{11}/\tau^{0.99\pm0.009}$. Since the exponent of τ could be at
least 0.999 we have considered it to be 1.0 in the interest of
symmetry.

as a cultural species as distinct from his existence as a biological one, must soon terminate, unless he is to continue as only a
biological species. It follows that <u>Homo</u> <u>sapiens</u> must cease as a
species set off by a set of characteristics which to date have made
him distinct. Examination of the past historical process is required to gain an insight into what sort of species he must become
if he is to survive. The Von Foerster equation permits calculation
of the dates at which a series of doublings of population, as shown
in Figure 11, leads to the optimum population of nine billion.

FIGURE 11

THE VON FOERSTER CURVE
OF INCREASE IN WORLD
POPULATION OF MAN
DURING THE SAPIENT
DOMAIN OF EVOLUTION

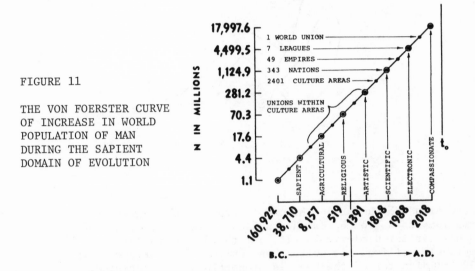

I have already pointed out the reasons for anticipating that, after
the origin of man as a cultural species about 40,000 years ago, each
doubling of population would require a doubling of conceptual space,
A". Conceptual target diameter similarly increases, but more slowly.
With every two successive doublings of population and conceptual
space, there will be a doubling of conceptual target diameter. These
times of simultaneous doublings of population and conceptual target
diameter are shown by the circled dots in Figure 11. These seven
points (all but the earliest) represent particularly pivotal eras
in human history which I will term "conceptual revolutions". Each
involves a complete reorientation in the manner in which life and
the forces of nature are perceived. Each also involves elaboration
of a new strategy for coping with this life and these forces.

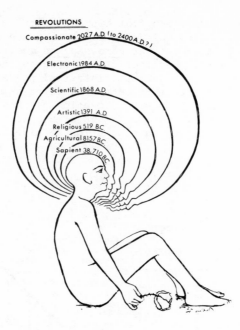

FIGURE 12

THE CONCEPTUAL
HOMUNCULUS

   I have tried to summarize this whole process of progressive
transformations as a "conceptual homunculus". The body of man has
remained his earlier biological self, but the degree to which he
has effectively utilized his cortex has continually increased. In
Figure 12 the diameter of the head is proportional to conceptual
target diameter, d". This figure indicates the degree of enlargement of conceptual target diameter at the time of each of the revolutions. Each revolution is given here a single name. However,
each should be designated by a hyphenated term reflecting the new
"perspective" and the new means of "coping". I will attempt this
here, but will leave to others better grounded than I in history,
philosophy and futuristic scenarios to characterize these revolutions more effectively:

1. The Traditional-Sapient Revolution of about 38,710 B.C.

   Tradition and myth formed the core of the new perspective which
permitted the concept of existence to be extended back into the past
and, to a much lesser extent, to establish the expectations of the
future. Codification of knowledge resulting from experience became
the basis of the new means for coping.

2. <u>The Living-Agricultural Revolution of about 8,157 B.C.</u>

The term, "living" as a new perspective implies an awareness
of life as a continuing process of birth, development and death,
with a dependence of one species upon another. Agriculture, as a
way of coping, represents a conscious, but empirical means to mine
resources more effectively.

3. <u>The Authoritarian-Religious Revolution of about 519 B.C.</u>

The prior perspective of awareness of life culminated in the
conviction that there must be some directed design of the forces
guiding nature and the destiny of man. Revealed formulations of
the design, which demanded conformity of response to them, comprised
the new format for coping.

4. <u>The Holistic-Artistic Revolution of about 1391 A.D.</u>

Further reflection on the question of design produced a per-
vading feeling of wholeness, accompanied by a tendency to withdraw
from the daily routine of life in order to pursue its search. This
lead to an apparent dichotomy of designs for coping. On the one
hand, we find artistic expressions spanning philosophy, poetry,
painting and sculpture, while, on the other hand, this effort culminated in empirical technological procedures and machines--a total
reorientation commonly designated as the Renaissance period.

5. <u>The Scientific-Exploitive Revolution of about 1868 A.D.</u>

The Holistic perspective of life lead to a scrutiny of the processes involved in producing change in some portion of the design of
nature. We speak of the employment of this perspective as the "Scientific Method". Resultant insights are then transformed into technological devices or procedures for exploiting nature for the benefit of man.

6. <u>The Communication-Electronic Revolution of about 1988 A.D.</u>

There gradually arose a time when personal contact among the
members of a much enlarged communication network proved particularly ineffective. Furthermore, the capacity of the cortex to process
information necessary to formulate concepts became surpassed. These
and similar limitations forced upon us the new perspective of life
as an information exchange network and lead to the development of
theories and electronic technologies for the transfer and condensing
of information as the means for enchanced coping. In deference to
Orwell's [31] premonition of a possible course of dystopian derailment of this revolution [39], I have slightly altered the calculated
time of this revolution to 1984 A.D.

7. The Compassionate-Systems Revolution of 2018 A.D.

Use of the term "systems" to designate the new means for coping also reflects the new perspective. As an outgrowth of information theory relating to the transfer of information over networks in conjunction with the related development of the field of cybernetics, there arose a body of concepts designated as "general systems theory" [37]. This theory views all of nature and all of human activity as a hierarchically arranged structure of levels of interlocked subset systems in which the process of any particular subset system affects and is affected by other subset systems at its own level, as well as below or above it. We are now moving into an era when this perspective (involving the related techniques and strategies for designing and guiding interrelationships, and for permitting self-organization of subsystems) has become imperative. Selection of the term "compassionate" to designate the perspective of this revolution requires comment.

Roles requisite to the adequate functioning of subset systems will continue to increase in both kind and number. Fulfilling each role requires maximizing the particular set of values requisite to its expression. And yet no one role can be fulfilled unless all the other roles are being adequately met. This means that the diversity of values guiding action will increase. Furthermore, the present era of radical change will become intensified as the character of roles needed to meet new functions also changes. Thus, in the presence of this increased exposure to value conflict, there will be required an augmented awareness of the necessity for others to maintain value sets differing from one's own. Furthermore, realizing one's own functional role requires expenditure of considerable effort in assisting others to fulfill the objectives of their value sets. It is this awareness of, and participation in, the realization of values held by others which characterizes the compassionate perspective. This perspective also includes an awareness that many individuals will experience extreme difficulty in developing and altering their roles and value sets in accordance with the demands of an overall system which is changing and becoming more complex. Holding to this perspective further requires marked attention to assisting others, whom we ourselves might earlier have been, to recoup from this hopefully temporary derailment. In this recognition and implementation of the rights of others, compassion becomes a sublimated and transformed submission. There are other parameters of perspective and coping involved in the compassionate-systems revolution which I will return to after giving consideration to the implications of attaining an optimum upper world population. It will also be noted that I have listed the date of 2027 A.D., with possible continuance to 2400 A.D., as the time of the compassionate-systems revolution rather than the calculated date of 2018 A.D. This is because of its convergence with "doomsday" and the forthcoming transitional period into a new domain for further evolution.

THE SZILARDIAN DOMAIN OF EVOLUTION

Slowing down the present rate of population increase so that the ultimate maximum world population will not greatly exceed the optimum of nine billion requires continuing attention to the present efforts to reduce birth rates. It is quite likely that the rate of reduction in births will be insufficient to prevent an overshoot in population above the optimum. What this overshoot will be cannot be estimated with any reliability at present. I can only hope that this overshoot can be kept to no more than 13.5 billion as a maximum world population. Were the world population to double from the nine billion optimum to 18 billion, it might prove extremely difficult to curtail this process of continuing population increase. I shall assume that the present apparent rate of curtailment of population increase will continue to become more pronounced, to the extent that this slowing down will not culminate in the maximum world population of 13.5 billion until about 200 years from the present.

Whether or not there is a gradual reduction of the world population to the optimal level, we will be faced with the possibility of a continuing and relatively stable population somewhere between 9.0 and 13.5 billion. This continuance of a stable population for a very long time raises some interesting questions. Foremost among these is the problem of conceptual space. So far the entire course of the evolution of man as a cultural species has involved a dual progression of a doubling of conceptual space keeping pace with a doubling of population. Maintaining this historical relationship implies that when population growth terminates, so also will increase of conceptual space terminate. Likewise, the conceptual target diameter of each individual will stabilize at a magnitude equivalent to the square root of the conceptual space available to him. This means that the total involvement of man in relationships and functions will become constant. He will become part of an unvarying static system. The environment of man will have reached its carrying capacity for concepts. Similarly, the habitats of all other species have a carrying capacity for protoplasm or biomass. For humans there will be a carrying capacity for "ideomass", I, in which I is a product of the number, N, times their average target diameter, d".

$$I = Nd'', \text{ and } I \text{ is a constant}$$

The full meaning of I remaining constant is far from clear. Comparison with the ecological concept of carrying capacity for biomass provides a lead. The energy resources of the environment can support either a large number of small individuals, or a smaller number of larger ones. In a similar fashion, the world as a habitat for man is fast approaching a time where it can support either an increasingly larger number of individuals, each of which has a decreasing conceptual target diameter, or a fewer number with a corresponding enlarged conceptual target diameter. This leads to three options for

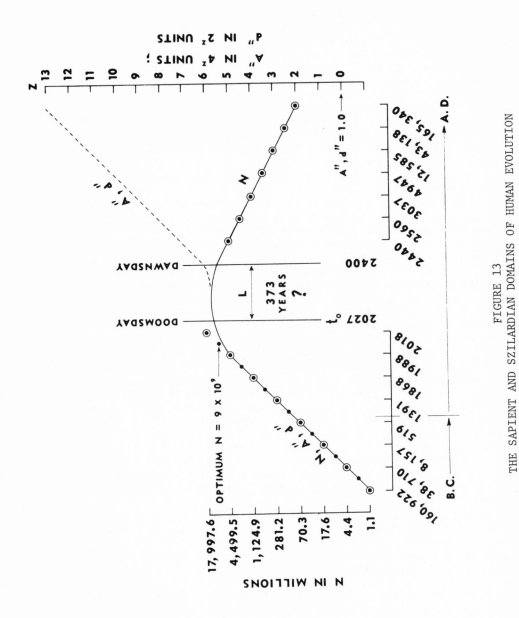

FIGURE 13

THE SAPIENT AND SZILARDIAN DOMAINS OF HUMAN EVOLUTION

for future human evolution which may be summarized as follows:

1. Traditional Encapsulation

This is the case where world population becomes fixed near the upper optimum of about nine billion. There will be no need for conceptual space to increase. Preservation of the past conceptual space and all its informational denizens will assure that each person develops only that conceptual target diameter, that individual conceptual mass, which will permit him to fulfill one of the available static roles. Little occasion will arise for any individual to deviate from the exact pattern harmonizing with a traditional niche he entered early in life. Few will ever encounter challenge or crisis. Man will have achieved the bliss of lungfish. (My verbalized spoonerism at this point was the "blish" of lungfish.) Like these inhabitants of Lake Manyara in Tanzania, we would have discovered how to encapsulate ourselves in a conceptual mudball, avoiding all opportunities and challenges. By this option we would reenter a traditional tribal way of life resembling that at the beginning of the human experience, with the exception that a single tribe would circle the globe.

2. Maximizing Biomass

The whole prior historical record of human progression reveals man's ability to free himself from the stricture of a carrying capacity for his biomass. Now that he is encountering another stricture, that of maintaining ideomass constant, he can still retain his freedom for some time to come from the stricture of maintaining a constant biomass. At least this can be done if there is a slowing down of population growth sufficient to harmonize it with utilizing the developing technologies of food production. With ideomass remaining constant, that is $I = Nd''$, it is apparent that if N increases, d'' must decrease. The conceptual target diameter of the average individual will decrease as population increases. Most individuals through successive generations will progressively be less aware of less and less. I prefer not to be involved in life dictated by either this or the first option. However, once either of these two routes had been followed for several generations, no one would suffer from not having considered the third option. The trajectory of survival would have long since erased the possibility of considering its existence.

3. Maximizing Conceptual Target Diameter

This option is that of enhancing the scope of human potentiality. For this to continue after ideomass remains constant means that as conceptual space, and therefore conceptual diameter, continues to increase, population must likewise continue to decrease. However, there will be a price exacted if this option is selected.

The course of human history has been one of placing increasing emphasis on individual development, despite the necessary focus on the integrity of enlarging groups. We, therefore, need to examine the path of this option and the price it will exact.

The left-hand side of Figure 13 duplicates Figure 11 except that, beginning at about the present, a decrease in population growth will permit avoiding the doomsday effect. Then natality will balance mortality. Included in this portion of the Figure are the conceptual revolutions, indicated by circled dots, as described above. Another, and the initial revolution, which was not discussed above is represented by the attainment (about 160,922 B.C.) of a stage of development of Homo erectus at which there began a very gradual recruitment of conceptual space. This culminated in the transformation of this species into Homo sapiens. Ordinate scales for conceptual space, A", and conceptual target diameter, d", are so constructed that their changes in magnitude over time are also represented by the same left-hand curve as represents increase in population.

Provided that birth control becomes sufficiently effective, a decrease in population can set in which will permit the world population to decline from an overshoot level back to the optimum of nine billion. This number reflects that population at which further socio-political union can no longer contribute to the effectiveness of communication among its members or the increase in their conceptual space. It is appropriate to designate this time as "dawnsday", for it introduces the opportunity of entering a new domain of evolution. I can only guess the duration of this lag-time, L, between doomsday and dawnsday. I have arbitrarily assigned L = 373 years. For this degree of decline to be realized, there must be a period before dawnsday during which there is about one child produced per female.

As population begins to decrease, it will then be possible for conceptual space to again begin increasing and still maintain ideomass constant. The issue then arises as to the nature of the rate of increase in conceptual space, as well as the rate of decrease in population after dawnsday. Dawnsday is approximated as 2400 A.D. After dawnsday, conceptual space will increase in a reciprocal fashion with respect to time as it did before doomsday. This increase in conceptual space permits the population to decrease within 40 years after dawnsday to the same number as about 40 years before doomsday. That is to say, there will be the same population in 2440 A.D. as in 1988 A.D. It may be noted that both population and conceptual space doubled twice in the 120 years up to 1988 A.D. If conceptual space doubles twice in the 120 years after 2440 A.D., population must drop in half. During this 120 years, conceptual target diameter would have doubled and, thus Nd" would maintain ideomass, I, constant. As the population decreases, it will require its members a longer time to create doublings of conceptual space. Every time conceptual target diameter doubles and population halves, we may anticipate a conceptual revolution of perspective and means of coping comparable to those which preceded doomsday. The time intervening between any two successive revolutions will be four times that between the first of these two and the one which preceded it. This is exactly the reciprocal pattern of the time sequence of conceptual revolutions before doomsday.

Continuation of this process would ultimately lead to a time when target diameter approaches infinity and population approaches zero. This is an unreal time, in the sense that it is many billions of years away. However, we need to examine the implications of d" increasing as N decreases. A reason for the electronic revolution is that we have approached a limit of the cortex to process information necessary for its codification into concepts. By the same token, we are in much more difficult straits with regard to the ability of the cortex to integrate and condense concepts to the point that they represent sufficiently significant units of creativity to enlarge conceptual space. This means that we will shortly need electronic prostheses which will function much as does our cortex. We become linked to these to permit further enlargement of our conceptual target diameters beyond the limitations imposed by the cortex.* Such coupling with thinking prostheses represents the character of the evolutionary progression after dawnsday. All further increases in conceptual target diameter after dawnsday will result from elaboration of thinking prostheses to which we may link. Maintaining these linkages is the price we will pay if we elect the third option of further enhancing human potentialities as the desired course of evolution. If the projected process of decrease in population and increase in conceptual target diameter continues for as long after dawnsday as the human experiment continued from the Homo erectus revolution to doomsday, then more than 99% of the conceptual target diameter of the average individual will result from activity within thinking prostheses to which he is linked. This time, which is about 165,340 A.D., I will designate as Szilard time, t_z, in memory of

---

* Our laboratory has been working for some time on the development of a model of the relationship between generic concepts, which if further substantiated would have some bearing on the design of thinking prostheses. By "generic concept" we mean broad concepts such as indicated by such words as change, misery, design, health, or adaptation. Where every such concept is represented by a ball and equal-length rods (representing linking concept descriptors) connect balls; then a network is formed in which the balls connected to any particular ball form the corners of a icosahedron. The centermost concept is apparently either "design" or insight" and the opposite poles of one major axis through the center are the concepts "balance" and "loss".

Leo Szilard who visualized its arrival. Szilard in his short story.
"Calling All Stars", projects to a time on a planet he calls "Cyber-
netica", when the population of thinking organisms had already gone
to zero and all that remained was 100 minds, 100 thinking prostheses,
then subservient to beings living on the North Star [35, p.122]. I
find it difficult to believe that Szilard was just spinning a yarn,
but rather that from the depths of his insights into nuclear physics,
coupled with his deep concern for human survival, there was a premonition of the possibility of the course of the third option I have
been outlining.

For this reason, I wish to designate the domain of evolution
from dawnsday to t_z as the "Szilardian Domain of Evolution". At
its inception it will no longer be appropriate to designate man as
Homo sapiens. He, rather, must be given a specific name reflecting
the developing linkage with thinking prostheses. At that time it
may be appropriate to designate man as Homo leo for a dual reason.
This specific name reflects Leo Szilard's vision. It also reflects
the propensity of man to develop commensal relationships. I have
in mind here a commensal bond between earlier forms of man and the
lion, Felis leo, which permitted them both to evolve. This hypothesis of mine of this earlier commensal relationship must remain in
its present form as a mere assertion until I have completed further
documentation.

CONCLUDING REMARKS

One normally thinks of space in one of two general ways. During the past few years the attention given to launching man into explorations of interplanetary space has focused so much on this view
of space that we have tended to ignore ways of viewing space here on
earth. Perhaps the present efforts to explore extra-terrestrial
space will have a bearing on the inception of a domain of evolution
involving communication between planets which will follow the Szilardian domain of evolution. With regard to space on earth, we view it
from its dimensional properties, from its structural content, and
from the activities which take place within it.

My whole career has been dominated by a concern with physical
space as it relates to the welfare of members of contained individuals and the growth of populations. In 1955 Leonard J. Duhl and
I organized a committee for considering "The Influence of Physical
Environmental Variables on Mental Health".* Under Duhl's leader-

---

* Beside the organizers, the initial members who remained as core
participants throughout the several years of meetings were: Cathe-
rine Bauer and/or Melvin Weber (city planning), Edward S. Deevey, Jr.
(ecologist), A.B. Hollingshead (sociologist), Erich Lindemann (preventive psychiatry), Richard Meier (social planner, chemist), Richard Poston (community planner, journalist), Nicholas Rashevsky (mathe-

ship, this group continued to meet for two three-day sessions each
year for 12 years. After two years, the designation of the group
was changed to a committee to consider "Physical and Social Environmental Variables as Determinants of Mental Health". Because of the
cumbersomeness of this designation, we soon acquired the appellation,
"The Space Cadets", in recognition of the interdependence of social
processes to the properties of the physical space within which they
transpire. My association with the many leading minds which flowed
through this committee strongly influenced my continuing search for
the meaning of space for the life and survival of man. Were it not
for this association with this wide scope of ideas in ferment, I
would have been unable to follow the relationship between physical
and conceptual space and envision the impact that the emerging electronic and compassionate revolutions will have on society.

Every conceptual revolution brings with it new demands on communication, including adaptation of old forms to new circumstances
and development of new forms. The present time is particularly
acute and unique in this connection. We are simultaneously involved
in four revolutions, because of the extreme foreshortening of the
time intervals between conceptual revolutions. This situation is
aggravated by the fact that those parts of the world which were delayed in attaining earlier revolutions are now caught up in a process of telescoping a formerly slower change. This produces a nearly
simultaneous embarking upon several revolutions. Even the nations
at the forefront are still tying up the loose ends of the scientific-
exploitive revolution while they are preparing to usher in the communication-electronic revolution. And, as is true with the emergence
of all conceptual revolutions, a minority segment of the population
is involved in grappling with the issues which will later dominate
the scene. This concerned minority, now directing its attention toward the compassionate-systems revolution, is rapidly swelling its
ranks. On it falls the additional burden of plotting the path
through the transition of cessation of population increase into a
new and challenging domain of evolution. No one can escape participation in these present times of crisis; literally everyone must become involved in developing the opportunities these crises present.
A small collection of functions and attitudes stand out as meriting
our attention:

1. The Alerting Function [11, p.7]

The just terminating scientific-exploitive revolution, in its
focus on mining resources, has evolved extremely efficient administrative capacities for directing motor functions of institutions.
Execution of administrative functions subsumes established goals.
On the sensory side, institutions remain relatively blind. Few in-

---

matical biology), John Q. Stewart (astro-physicist, social physics),
John R. Seeley (sociologist), Thomas Gladwin (anthropologist).

corporate adequate means for assembling and integrating knowledge relevant to how the actions of other institutions, or other sub-systems, affect their own performance and how their own function has effects permeating beyond the restricted conception of their mission. In particular, most institutions lack accessibility to information prerequisite to the evaluation and reorientation of their missions. Fulfilling the alerting function requires that the institution devote as much effort to this sensory function as to the more customary administrative motor functions. It is imperative that these two functions be kept distinct, though tightly linked. They must be performed by different individuals and different groups.

2. The Appreciative Function*

Given that an adequate functioning of the alerting system makes all necessary information available, there still remains the problem of its utility in reevaluating former goals or in producing new directions for the institution. Effecting this function requires a special group of individuals who serve as a linkage between the appreciative system and the administrative system. Members of this linking group within the institution also have the responsibility for developing directions and formulating evaluations. These evaluations relate both to impacts on the institution from outside of it and to impacts generated within it. Final decisions based on this information, which will govern the later activities of the institution, remain as an integral responsibility and prerogative of the administrative function. The number and complexity of concepts, as well as the volume of simpler forms of information required to develop these evaluations and directions, place excessive demands on cortical function. There already exists a need for techniques and technologies which simulate brain function to meet the demands which should be placed on appreciative systems.

3. The Dialogue Function**

Dialogue is the muted confrontation among parties seeking fuller awareness of common problems, resolution of value conflict or agreement upon principles and theory. I am reminded of the wild stray tomcat that adopted our house as his home. For some months he would accept handouts only after we had retired from where they were left. Perhaps he also sensed that I had not held cats in particular high regard. At first my slightest touching him elicited a swatting scratch or an attempted bite. Now, a year later, when I tease or

---

* Original formulation of "appreciative system" by G. Vickers, [36], related treatment of development of new images by K.E. Boulding [3, p.199] and J.B. Calhoun [12, p.9].

** J.B. Calhoun proposed this in the introductory remarks to the symposium, "The Dialogue of Change: Systems in Interaction" [13, p.9]. Since this symposium was held, the public information media in particular have focused on the subject of dialogue with increasing frequency.

stroke him too vigorously, he slaps his paw with claws retracted against my hand, or holds on to my fingers with his teeth without breaking the skin. How well we have resolved our differences, I am not sure. I can only say that I now find it difficult to sit down in my favorite chair to read without a furry ball of fat landing in my lap.

Provocation of crises through violent confrontation may at times be necessary to precipitate a more meaningful exchange between individuals or institutions. Social tradition and lack of designed relations have sufficiently separated them that they no longer can communicate about common interests. The need is to develop the muted confrontation of dialogue as soon as possible. However, present values and institutional arrangements are inadequate to make dialogue effective. Without more effective dialogue, we will encounter extreme difficulty in arriving at the compassionate-systems revolution and passing through the transition to the next domain of evolution.

4. Commitment

Moving down into the more individual level of function, commitment to goals beyond ourselves brings us to the full implication of the superposition of conceptual space upon physical space. We need to develop more effective means of becoming committed to involvement in furthering the realization of values and goals contributing to survival of society and expansion of individual potentialities. Commitment requires a preceding identification with values and goals, an increase in personal conceptual space. Actions implementing commitment involve defense of conceptual space. They replace the primitive "territorial imperative", and imply effective involvement in dialogue to permit shifts in commitment harmonizing with the evolving design for the survival and evolution of man and nature.

5. Compassion

I have already remarked in some detail about the perspective of compassion. Simultaneous expression of compassion and commitment becomes somewhat difficult and conflicting. This arises from compassion representing a transformation of subordination and submission, which takes place in conjunction with territoriality and the social hierarchies of physical space. Decreased status in physical space leads to acceptance and acknowledgement of the rights of others. By implication, acquiring the capacity for compassion requires periodic attainment and acceptance of the role of the "suffering servant".*

---

* Isaiah 52:13 to 53:12. For the initial formulation of "the Compassionate Revolution" see J.B. Calhoun, "A Glance Into the Garden" [14].

6. Creativity

I have already commented on the apparent dependence of creativity on an oscillation between periods of withdrawal from social pressures and the stresses of life and periods of reinvolvement with reality. This of course presupposes prior acquisition of a sufficient variety of knowledge and behaviors from which some meaningful reassembly may arise. Through such reorganizations having value for society, enlargements of conceptual space emerge. Beyond this, creativity serves the dual function of being a sublimation or replacement for both aggression and the need to express biological generativity. Lorenz points out that the threat behavior of territorial defense in primates is accompanied by pilo-erection and rearing to full height with elbows outward and chin up [27, ch. 13]. This stance in turn is accompanied by a feeling of exhilaration, of a shiver running down the back and arms. This exhilaration becomes compounded into what Lorenz terms "militant enthusiasm", when many individuals simultaneously engage in action providing this satisfaction to the aggressive drive. By implication, the releasor for militant enthusiasm becomes any threat, any set of strange objects, altered circumstances, or a divergent set of values. Lorenz further notes that the presence of an opposing camp provides the most essential circumstance permitting satisfaction through release of militant enthusiasm. So we must identify an "opposing camp" toward which there may be a legitimate expression of militant enthusiasm. This camp is recognized as any conceptualization suspected of inadequately enhancing experience or survival. This experience of exhilaration during aggressive defense of territory is essentially identical with the eureka experience of exultation classically described as accompanying creative associations. Thus, militant enthusiasm can find expression in creative effort.

As already mentioned, Erikson holds that curtailment of procreation can arise only when the generative need can be fulfilled by either involvement in the generative function of transferring one's values to others, or by engagement in the highest level of generativity creating new values or insights [21]. These three functions of creativity give a high priority to increasing the number of persons capable of creative acts.

7. The Psychedelic Trap

Since man emerged, increases in population have often swept far ahead of increases in conceptual space. These were times of crowding when no unsettled physical space remained and the needed conceptual space remained to be discovered. Peoples of all times and all places discovered the means of "turning on" and turning inward to a seeming replacement for the needed conceptual space. From Caapi in Brazil, to Karavi in Bombay, to Catha in Kenya [5,30], similar "mind-expanding" drugs from plants have been discovered. Each in its own way leads to a transient feeling of having conquered the deficit of conceptual space, with hardly ever any meaningful creative association as an accompaniment. I use the word "meaningful" here to imply "relevance for survival". Because of the nearness of Kenya to the original Eden of man, I would like to adapt the word "Catha" to represent the state of exhilaration resulting from the use of mind-expanding drugs. Spelling Catha as "katha" incorporates the sense of the Egyptian word "ka" for spirit. Thus, katha is the exhilaration of the transient impression of having enlarged conceptual space. In contrast, eureka, though a transient exhilaration also, accompanies the creative act of contributing a unit of conceptual space to the evolving needs of man. Knowing katha is as easy as swallowing a cube of sugar. Knowing eureka often requires a difficult, frustrating, lonely, and usually time-consuming journey. Which route one selects depends upon how concerned one is for man's future.

PROMOTION [16]

Once man mastered the problem of sheer physical survival, he turned his attention to developing therapies for correcting the ills which beset his body, mind and society. Focus on correction led to awareness of the origins of pathology. This enlargement of conceptual space resulted in new roles devoted to prevention. Implementation of this new perspective reduced the effort devoted to therapy. Preventive activities extended to elimination or reduction of circumstances producing environmental pollution. The concept of conservation arose as a companion to prevention. It included corrective actions to recuperate from pathologies induced by the encroachment of technological society on nature. Conservation also amounts to prevention in that actions stemming from this concept intervene to ward off additional encroachments.

The new roles and new concepts that are developing as we begin to enter the compassionate-systems revolution now permit institutionalization of an approach having more immediate positive consequences than either therapy or prevention. This approach may be called "promotion". Promotion involves a design of efforts to enhance the development of potentialities, as well as assuring a continuance of the opportunity for their expression. Concern here is for both individuals and institutions. For promotion to become effective, the alerting, appreciative, and dialogue functions must be highly developed. The goal of the compassionate-systems revolution is promotion. It includes active participation in guiding evolution, evolution of all other forms of life as well as that of man.

REFERENCES

1. Bennett, J.W.: Hutterian Brethren. Stanford University Press, California, 1967.
2. Berelson, B. and Steiner, G.A.: Human Behavior. Harcourt, Brace and World, New York, 1967.

3. Boulding, K.E.: The Meaning of the Twentieth Century. Harper
        & Row, New York, 1964.
4. Braidwood, R.J. and Reed, C.A.: The achievement and early con-
        sequences of food production. Symp. Quant. Biol.,
        22:12, 1957.
5. Caldwell, A.E.: History of psychopharmacology. In Clark, W.G.
        and Del-Giudice, J., eds., Principles of Psychopharma-
        cology. Academic Press, New York, 1970.
6. Calhoun, J.B.: A comparative study of the social behavior of
        two inbred strains of house mice. Ecol. Monogr.,
        26:81, 1956.
7. _____: Population density and social pathology.
        Sci. Amer., 206:139-148, 1962.
8. _____: The Ecology and Sociology of the Norway Rat.
        Public Health Service Publication No. 1008, p. 288.
        U.S. Government Printing Office, Washington, D.C.,
        1968.
9. _____: The social use of space. In Mayer, W. and Van
        Gelder, R., eds., Physiological Mammalogy, Vol. 1.
        Academic Press, New York, 1964.
10. _____ and Casby, J.V.: Calculation of Home Range and
        Density of Small Mammals. Public Health Monograph No.
        55. U.S. Government Printing Office, Washington, D.C.,
        1958.
11. _____: Recommendations for the Establishing of an Alert-
        ing Unit Within the National Institute of Mental Health.
        URBS Document 105:7, 1966.
12. _____: Behavioral states and developed images. Annual
        Meeting of the AAAS, Berkeley, California, 1965.
13. _____: Dialogue, the new force. Introductory remarks
        to the symposium: The Dialogue of Change: Systems in
        Interaction. Annual Meeting of the AAAS, Washington,
        D.C., 1966.
14. _____: A glance into the garden. In Three Papers on
        Human Ecology. Mills College Assembly Series, Mills
        College, Oakland, 1966.
15. _____: Population. In Allison, A., ed., Population
        Control. Penguin Books, Middlesex, 1970.
16. _____: Promotion of Man. Presented at the symposium:
        Global Systems Dynamics. University of Virginia,
        Charlotteville, Virginia, June, 1969.
17. Coit, M.L.: John C. Calhoun: American Portrait. Houghton-
        Mifflin, Boston, 1950.
18. Darling, F.F.: West Highland Survey, An Essay in Human Ecology.
        Oxford University Press, Oxford, 1956.
19. De Vore, I. and Washburn, S.L.: Baboon ecology and human evolu-
        tion. In Clark, F.H. and Bourliere, F., eds., African
        Ecology and Human Evolution. Aldine Publishing Company,
        Chicago, 1963.
20. _____ and Hall, K.R.L.: Baboon Ecology. Draft manuscript,
        1962.

21. Erikson, E.H.: Insight and Responsibility. W.W. Norton, New
        York, 1964.
22. Hall, K.R.L.: Numerical data, maintenance activities and loco-
        motion of the wild chacma baboon (Papio ursinus).
        Proc. Zool. Soc., 139:181, 1962.
23. Hockett, C.F. and Ascher, R.: The human revolution. Amer. Sci.,
        52:70-92, 1964.
24. Kessler, A.: Interplay Between Social Ecology and Physiology,
        Genetics and Population Dynamics of Mice. Rockefeller
        University, New York, Thesis, 1966.
25. Kroeber, A.L., Lowie, R.H. and Olson, R.L.: Cultural and nat-
        ural areas of native North America. Archeology, Uni-
        versity of California Press, Los Angeles, 1939.
26. Kuhn, T.: The Structure of Scientific Revolutions. University
        of Chicago Press, Chicago, 1962.
27. Lorenz, K.: On Aggression. Harcourt, Brace & World, New York,
        1966.
28. McPherson, L.D.: Calhoun, Hamilton, Baskin and Related Families.
        Tampa, 1957.
29. Moncreiffe, I.: The Highland Clans. Barrier and Rockliff,
        London, 1967.
30. Opler, M.K.: Cross-cultural uses of psychoactive drugs. In
        Clark, W.G. and Del-Giudice, J., eds., Principles of
        Psychopharmacology. Academic Press, New York, 1970.
31. Orwell, G.: 1984. Harcourt, Brace and World, New York, 1949.
32. Pratt, W.F.: The Anabaptist explosion. Natur. Hist., February,
        1969.
33. Rountzounif, J.: Pockets of high fertility in the United States.
        Population Bull., 24:2, 1968
34. Scott, W.: Rob Roy. Dutton, New York, 1963.
35. Szilard, L.: The Voice of the Dolphin and Other Stories. Simon
        and Schuster, New York, 1961.
36. Vickers, G.: The psychology of policy making and social change.
        Brit. J. Psychiat., 110:465-477, 1964.
37. Von Bertalanffy, L. and Rapoport, A.: General Systems, Vol. XIII.
        Yearbook of the Society for General Systems Research,
        1968 and preceding volumes.
38. Von Foerster, H., Mora, P.M. and Amiot, L.W.: Doomsday: Friday,
        13 November, A.D. 2026. Science, 132:1291-1295, 1960.
39. Walsh, C.: From Utopia to Nightmare. Harper and Row, New York,
        1962.
40. Woldenberg, M.J.: Energy Flow and Spatial Order, with Reference
        to Mixed Hexagonal Central Place Hierarchies. Office
        of Naval Research Contract No. 00014-67A-0298-0004,
        Harvard University, Cambridge, 1958.

ANIMAL INDEX

GEOGRAPHICAL INDEX

NAME INDEX